Industrialization in Canada

Industrialization
in Canada

Joseph Smucker

Department of Sociology and Anthropology
Concordia University

Prentice-Hall of Canada, Ltd. Scarborough, Ontario

To members of my extended family, who know something about the Ultimate Dialectic.

Canadian Cataloguing in Publication Data

Smucker, Joseph, 1934-
  Industrialization in Canada

Bibliography: p.
ISBN 0-13-464198-1

1. Canada — Industries. 2. Industrialization.
3. Labor and laboring classes — Canada. 1. Title.

HC113.S68   338'.0971   C79-094790-0

©1980 by Prentice-Hall of Canada, Ltd.
All rights reserved. No part of this book may be
reproduced in any form without permission in writing
from the publishers.

Prentice-Hall, Inc., Englewood Cliffs, New Jersey
Prentice-Hall International Inc., London
Prentice-Hall of Australia, Pty., Ltd., Sydney
Prentice-Hall of India Pvt., Ltd., New Delhi
Prentice-Hall of Japan, Inc., Tokyo
Prentice-Hall of Southeast Asia (Pte.) Ltd., Singapore

ISBN 0-13-464198-1

Production Editors: Luba Zisser, Joerg Klauck
Designer: Gail Ferreira
Composition: J & E Graphics Ltd.

1 2 3 4 5 WC 84 83 82 81 80

Manufactured in Canada by Webcom Limited

Contents

Preface

In this book I attempt to examine some of the major social processes of industrialization in Canada. I view these processes as unique parts of the larger experience of the western world. In reviewing the material on this ongoing phenomenon, I have been struck by the intricate and shifting interplay between the forms of social organization and the interpretive values which have been attached to them. The tensions which have resulted have, I believe, provided the motive force for the industrialization process itself.

I have drawn upon the analytic works of Karl Marx and Max Weber in order to provide a classical theoretical underpinning to my own interpretation. The interpretation itself is restricted to the argument that there has been a continual strain between the values of freedom and equality, each of which is in conflict with the other, and the authority systems of typical industrial enterprises.

During the decline of the Feudal Era in Western Europe these values of freedom and equality were most exuberantly expressed by an emerging moneyed, though landless, group of individuals. Theirs was an expression of freedom from the social bonds of feudalism and of hope for equality with the landed aristocracy. But these expressions also came to mean freedom from assuming responsibilities for the social welfare of a dependent labor force, and equality, not among individuals, but among opportunities which themselves became defined according to unique sets of production-related, rational criteria. Such restricted definitions have created tensions not only between labor and management but also within the personal lives of individuals. They reveal themselves in a variety of contradictions among the roles individuals are expected to play. For example, while occupying unequal positions in rational production enterprises, individuals are expected to exercise equal rights as citizens; while restricted to repetitive work routines, individuals are expected to exercise their freedom of choice as consumers.

One can also note that these tensions exist at the international level. As a producer and exporter of primarily raw materials and semi-finished products, Canada often finds herself relegated to a role which is subservient to other economies. In a world-spanning system of production, Canadians have been dependent on decisions made elsewhere for other purposes. Meanwhile, they are given to believe that they exercise freedom of choice in consuming imported goods.

In this book, I examine the derivation and consequences of these tensions as they are expressed within the production enterprise, within the Canadian labor movement, and, finally, within the experience of individuals in their work roles. I conclude my analysis by raising some questions about the continuing impact of contemporary authority systems on the enactment of the values of freedom and equality. My intention is to provide an analytic survey by which materials related to the Canadian experience of industrialization can be integrated. In attempting a project of this nature, I have had to make decisions about the inclusion of materials, the degree of importance to place upon them, and the degree of abstractness of interpretation. There are undoubtedly serious omissions but I hope that the overall outcome will prove to be useful and provocative for the reader.

The book itself is intended to serve as a text for courses dealing with issues in industrialization. I am well aware that there is a great variety in the ways in which these courses are taught. Not everyone will agree on the sequence in which I have presented the material; nor will every instructor wish to use all the chapters. Accordingly, the sections and chapters are relatively self-contained, which should permit a considerable amount of freedom in the use of the book.

I should point out that this is not intended to be another exercise in condemning the social ills of industrialization. (Very few of us would want to return to a pre-industrial state of life.) Nor is it a Doomsday Book giving an account of the uncontrollable forces that "govern" our lives. It is rather an account of the social consequences of decisions made by individuals, some having more influence than others. By drawing attention to these consequences I hope to heighten the reader's sensitivity to paradox and irony. Actions taken with the best of intentions can have disastrous results and the intentions themselves may merely serve the interests of some already privileged individuals to the detriment of others less privileged. We continue to have the opportunities to reap the benefits of industrialization while correcting its social ills. I hope that in some small way this book will stimulate clearer visions of these opportunities.

There are a host of people who have contributed to the creation of this book. Certainly William Faunce, William Form, James McKee, and Don Summers provided early stimuli for my interest in the general phenomenon of industrialization. Discussions with Anton Zijderveld showed me the analytic utility of a wider historical vision of sociology. Fred Bird, through the example of his encyclopedic reading and analytic perceptions, prodded me on to discover insights in Marx that would otherwise have eluded me. His general support was most valuable. I learned much from Alexander Stewart, Anthony Giddens, Kenneth Prandy, and Robert Blackburn at Cambridge University. I only regret that I could not include more of the fruits of my sojourn there. Hubert Guindon and John Jackson read parts of earlier versions of the manuscript and stimulated my interest in the intricacies of Canadian history. Other colleagues who contributed in different ways to the completion of the manuscript include Michael Rosenberg, Norman Klein, Vivienne Walters, Francis Westley, William Reimer, Peter Illich, and Brian Milton.

I also wish to thank Muni Frumhartz who made facilities available to me at Carleton University in 1973 when I first began to gather materials for this book during my leave from Concordia University. While there, I was fortunate to have financial aid from the Canada Council and to benefit from the major research contributions of Bobbi Siu, Rosemary Warskett, and Marie-Josée Dancoste.

I am indebted to Wallace Clement who critically reviewed the entire manuscript. While we may disagree on a variety ofissues, I wish to thank him especially for the thoroughness with which he went about his task. Similarly, I am indebted to Terrence White and James Rinehart for their reviews. While they too may retain their reservations, their comments were most useful to me.

Elva Jackson, Judy Emond, Gisela Preusser, and Linda Dubeau did the major part of the typing on various versions of the manuscript. I am grateful for their contributions. I especially wish to thank Linda Dubeau who, through her generosity and competence, kept the distractions of administering a department to an enjoyable minimum. Finally, I wish to acknowledge Luba Zisser of Prentice-Hall who served as an excellent editor.

Grateful acknowledgment is made to the following for permission to reprint; From *Karl Marx: Selected Writings in Sociology and Social Philosophy* translated by T. B. Bottomore. Copywright© 1964 by T. B. Bottomore. Used with permission of McGraw-Hill Book Company; From Max Weber, *The Methodology of the Social Sciences* translated and edited by Edward Shils and Henry A. Finch. Copyright© 1949 by The Free Press. Used with permission of Macmillan Publishing Company Inc., New York; From Max Weber, *The Protestant Ethic and the Spirit of Capitalism* translated by Talcott Parsons. Copyright© 1958 by Charles Scribner's Sons. Used with permission of Charles Scribner's Sons Publishers, New York; from "Global Companies: Too Big to Handle?" Copyright 1972 by Newsweek, Inc. All rights reserved. Reprinted by permission; From "The Rewarding Strategies of Multinationalism." Reprinted by permission of Fortune Magazine,© 1968 Time Inc.; From Frederick W. Taylor *The Principles of Scientific Management*. Copyright 1911 by Frederick W. Taylor, renewed 1939 by Louise M. S. Taylor. By permission of Harper & Row, Publishers, Inc.; From H. A. Logan *Trade Unions in Canada: Their Development and Functioning*. Copyright 1948. Reprinted by permission of the Macmillan Company of Canada Limited; From Michael Mann *Consciousness and Action Among the Western Working Class*. Copyright 1973. Reprinted by permission of Macmillan Administration (Basingstoke) Ltd.

There are many other persons whom I "exploited" in one way or another. To acknowledge them all would require a chapter in itself. I hope they will not be offended if I thank them *en masse*. Obviously, while all those mentioned have influenced the final outcome of this project, they cannot be held responsible for its contents. The responsibility is mine alone.

J.S.

Introduction

The term *industrialization* basically refers to the replacement of human skills in the production of goods and services with machines and the replacement of human or animal energy with inanimate sources of power. In the course of their development and use, machines and inanimate sources of power together have brought about social innovations that have had a continuing multiplicative effect. The use of inanimate sources of power required that individuals be brought together to one place in order to work in concert with machines. This further involved a division of work roles and necessitated the creation of structures to coordinate and control those work roles. As a result of these developments, elaborate social organizations designed specifically for production have emerged. The alteration of community and family patterns is an additional consequence of these changes: urban centers have expanded, while the influence of rural areas has steadily declined.

These changes did not result from abstract forces, nor did they flow from cooperative consensus. Rather they involved conflicts among individuals who attempted to protect and further their own interests, whether they were the interests of landed aristocrats, travelling merchants, guild craftsmen, or early manufacturers, peasants, clerks, journeymen, or unskilled factory workers. Ultimately, ownership and control of manufacturing organizations and financial houses became the new bases for power. This in turn created new class structures resting in large part upon the relationship of individuals to these organizations—a relationship that has been continually shifting as new occupations and new organizations have emerged, contributing to, but also influencing the course of industrialization itself.

These processes have had their impact on Canadian society and, along with their derivatives, continue to do so. Yet one must also point out that the course of industrialization has been different in Canada than in Great Britain or Germany, Japan or the United States. In fact, the history of industrialization varies considerably according to the region, area, or society that undergoes the experience. One concern of this book will be to point out the major variations unique to Canada.

It must be remembered that the impact of industrialization is not the same now as it was 75 years ago or 100 or 150 years ago. The continuing ramifications of industrialization—the expansion of science and technology, the development of comprehensive public education systems, the changing

1

roles played by the state, the power of multi-national corporations—each exerts its own contrasting influences upon individuals, catching them in a milieu which offers enrichment to some, debilitating stress to others.

Industrialization and its accompanying changes have had both their supporters and critics. On the one hand, they have raised the economic standard of living for most people experiencing their effects. They have improved health standards, they have freed the vast majority of people from devoting most of their waking hours to meeting subsistence needs, and they have imbued individuals with a hope of attaining ever-improving levels of wealth and achievement. They have, in effect, made individuals masters, rather than servants, of their natural environment.

On the other hand, critics have pointed out that industrialization and its associated processes have exacted their own high costs upon individuals. They have replaced dependency upon the vicissitudes of nature with dependency upon the fluctuations of prices, wages, and employment opportunities. They have tended to reduce people to functional appendages of the production process. While they have enabled individuals to meet their subsistence needs in a relatively effortless manner, they have also created additional needs leading to ever higher levels of consumption. Indeed, many would argue that the traditional relationship between production and consumption has been reversed: individuals are encouraged to consume in order to maintain production rather than to produce in order to meet their needs.

Few persons would want to return to a pre-industrialized mode of existence. However, what is now being questioned is whether or not a continuation of these processes will ultimately become a force of destruction. The history of industrialization has been one of periodic crises. But whereas crises in the past were seen primarily as economic problems requiring largely technical solutions, analysts are increasingly reinterpreting these crises as having wider implications—implications requiring a reevaluation of fundamental values that are as important for their social implications as they are for economic ones. The shift from the optimistic themes represented by the rags to riches stories of Horatio Alger, Jr. in the late nineteenth century to the theme of disillusionment in Arthur Miller's *Death of a Salesman* written in 1949 illustrates a loss of faith in the assumptions which have propelled western societies into industrialized states.[1] Ever more people dependent on wage or salaried employment for gaining a livelihood are raising questions about social welfare and equitable economic distribution. Further, in a kind of poetic justice, the processes of industrialization have drawn such a high toll upon the natural environment that individuals are required to confront the basic problems of their very physical survival once again. What have been identified as social problems of continued economic development have finally become problems confronting the limits of the natural environment.

Written from a sociological perspective, this book presents a way to think about some selected processes of industrialization and the crises which they foment, to raise questions about their benefits and costs, and to sensitize the reader to the occasions of paradox. Such a perspective brings together the age-old disputes regarding prior realities: experience alone of events or the meanings brought to the experience. The meanings are what constitute the socially constructed world by which all of us order and interpret our experiences. It is the *manner* in which these social constructions emerge and are altered which is of special interest in the chapters to follow. For example, why has Canada's manufacturing sector not been more fully developed? What conditions gave rise to the predominance and power of large foreign corporate structures? What is the significance of the shift of an increasing proportion of the labor force to the "service" sector? Why is the labor movement in Canada characterized by such complexity? What conditions account for the variations in the interpretations placed upon the role of working? I cannot presume to provide definitive answers to these and other questions, but I do hope to present to the reader some of the answers that have been attempted. But more importantly, I wish to suggest a perspective that will lead the reader to analyze these and related questions more fully.

Conceptual Distinctions

Most social analysts would agree that the different sets of meanings by which individuals order their lives are fundamental to the social constructions which we call "society." They are expectations which individuals come to hold about others' actions and their own as well. When called upon to justify their behavior, individuals appeal to *values*, or assumptions about what are desirable or undesirable actions. The assumption that working to produce commodities is the mark of a worthy person is one such value. The manner in which production is organized as a consequence of this value constitutes, in turn, intricate systems of meanings in the sense of expectations about behavior. People tend to expect that they will be employed in a job most of their lives, that they will be subject to different hierarchies of authority, and that they will be rewarded with wages or salaries if they perform their jobs adequately.

Working, as a value, provides interpretations, reasons, and justifications for action. The systems of meanings which support this value provide the defining elements of actual behavior. Both *values* and *systems of meanings* are within the realm of ideas that people hold about the social world, but they must be *acted* upon in a physical sense for these to be of social consequence.

The *consequences* of actions are continual tests for the appropriateness of the definitions. However, there is more involved than this. The *experience* of acting itself is also a referent for interpretations. It is one thing to read about a strike, another to observe it, and still another to participate in it. In each instance, the event of the strike is transformed into something meaningful; as a result of the transformation, it is possible that individuals may not experience another strike in the same way. Reading about a strike may prompt individuals to participate in a future one and the experience of the participation may provoke greater commitment to the cause of the strike and hence bring about further social changes.

It would be enormously difficult to unravel all the complexities involved in connecting individual actions to social structures and relating this to social change. But if one can assume that values and meanings are key components of social action, one can also presume that individuals, in the course of acting upon these interpretations, bring about their transformations and consequent social change. One can note, for example, that the values that served to stimulate and justify the development of industrial capitalism in eighteenth century England contributed ultimately to their own transformation, so that by now they are highly modified, if not obsolete. The question for the analyst to ask of any value is what would be the consequences if the value were to be followed to its most logically extreme expression? What, for example, would be the consequences if gaining ever-increasing profits were the sole motivating force of industrial corporations?

The distinction between values and systems of meaning is dependent upon what are to be taken as justifications and what are to be taken as a set of expectations, or meanings, about behavior. With the development of a complex division of labor, the relationship between values which justify and meanings which order expectations can become highly attenuated. As such, they can be analyzed in their own terms as well as in relation to each other as individuals act upon them. Further, while individuals order their actions on the basis of sets of meanings and justify them with values, they can also modify both in the process of acting upon them.

Individuals, then, constantly create and recreate their social constructions, and validate them through their actions. Indeed this is what distinguishes human beings from instinct-driven animals. If these social constructions are not taken seriously in their own terms, in the analysis of both social institutions and individual actions, that is, if they are viewed merely as "passive reflections of material circumstances," then individuals themselves are reduced to being passive agents and do not play an active, creative role in the world.[2] One aim of this book is to maintain the image of individuals as creators or "producers" of these social realities.

The distinction between values and systems of meaning may appear to be the same as the traditional distinction between *culture* and *social structure*. However, the problem with these traditional terms is that it is never clear to what they refer. "Social structure" may be defined in behavioral terms or in terms of *expectations* about behavior. It may be defined by the actor or the observer. "Culture" is viewed most frequently as a set of beliefs about the world. This often makes it a very sloppy concept which is often used to sop up the remains of those social attributes not explained by "social structure."[3]

It is for these reasons that I prefer to concentrate upon the distinction between values and systems of meanings, viewing them as continually supported and/or modified by the *actions* of individuals. The distinction may be unclear in many instances, but without some notion of the commitments of individuals and the assumptions they have about their worlds, we cannot make sense of the changes which have occurred in the past, nor predict possible developments in the future. It is the sociologist's task to dissect the social constructions, to examine how they influence and are influenced by the actions of individuals.

In summary, the approach this book adopts is derived from the argument that through the actions of individuals, values and meaning systems become elaborated, each in their own terms, with the result that they can become incongruent with each other. At some point correctives must be made either, or both, at the level of values or the level of meanings.

Two values which early capitalists used to justify their actions were *freedom* and *equality*. They are, of course, highly abstract and thus amenable to a variety of interpretations and changes. But because of their very abstractness, they have been employed in many ways throughout the process of industrialization: they have been used as a rallying cry for social change; they have been used as a justification for opposing social change and they have been used to justify the actions of different groups with vested interests. For example, from the point of view of owners of an industrial enterprise, freedom can justify the ease with which they are able to lay off workers; on the other hand, the same value can be used by workers to justify their right to strike.

Equality can also be employed in diverse ways and with diverse meanings, and can also be in conflict with the justifying value of freedom. What makes it even more amenable to diverse definitions is that it may be employed to mean "egalitarianism" by which each actor is to receive equal portions of rewards—social, economic, and political—or it may mean that opportunities to achieve some end are equally available to everyone. This latter interpretation means that individuals are to be assured an equal opportunity to compete for *unequal* rewards. The competition, however, must be carried out within some set of criteria of merit. These values have often played an insidious role in the history of industrialization, for while they may serve to justify individual achievement, they can also, if taken seriously, force responsibility for failure upon individuals rather than upon those social conditions which themselves foster "failure."

The transformation of these values throughout the history of industrialization must be seen within the context of the transformation of systems of meanings. In this book I am most concerned with those meanings which structure *authority* within organizations. This book postulates that as the structures of authority in production enterprises have become more "rationalized," as they have incorporated more segmented and routinized roles, as these roles have become more rigidly defined and hence behavior within them more controlled, the application of the values of freedom and equality as justifications have become more questionable. At the same time, these values have served as major premises in challenging the authority structures themselves.

During the process of industrialization, these two values, while once justifying the actions of an emerging capitalist class in conflict with a landed aristocracy, have had to be extended to justify the increasing importance of industrialization itself. This includes the role of the marketplace, the justification of competition, the justification of rationalized authority structures, and the treatment of individuals on a formal contractual basis. But their extension has led to crises stemming from the lack of "fit" between their justifying rationale and the demands of changing authority structures as experienced by individuals within them. The result has been continual revisions of the interpretations of these values. The revisions in turn have been dependent upon who has been justifying what actions, whether these are managers justifying their actions, labor unions justifying theirs, consumer groups justifying their actions, or individual workers seeking justifications for their life experiences.

Within this context, I aim to give an account of three interrelated developments in Canada: (1) the transformation in the organization of production, (2) the evolution of the trade union movement, and (3) the interpretations of the importance of work within industrial organizations. While the focus is on Canada, the approach is comparative, incorporating data and interpretations from other industrialized societies. To provide a coherent framework for the understanding of these processes, I draw upon the analyses of both Marx and Weber: Marx, because I believe that he captured most completely the basic logic, if not the substance, of the contradiction inherent in industrial capitalism; and Weber, because of his insistence to keep these processes open-ended and contingent upon the interplay of a myriad of social attributes influencing the decisions of individuals. (Of course, Marx and Weber were not the only social theorists concerned with the effects of industrial capitalism upon the social order. But their works represent analytic statements which continue to have a direct influence upon contemporary analysts of industrial societies.)

The Plan of the Book

This book is divided into four separate parts. Part One, Chapters 1, 2, and 3, introduces the reader to two major variations in the analysis of industrialization: those of Marx and Weber. These are then brought together in Chapter 3 in order to present a broad perspective by which the events of Canada's experience of industrialization can be understood.

Part Two of the book deals with selected issues in the history of industrialization in Canada. In theoretical terms, the emphasis is upon the development of "rational" authority structures within a rationalized market economy. The intent here is to weave together the processes that have accounted for the lagging development of Canada's manufacturing sector, her dependence upon foreign ownership of major industrial sectors, the emergence and continuing development of forms of corporate structures, the consequences of these developments, and the symbolic means which those in power have employed to justify these processes. Chapter 4 is a historic survey of economic development in Canada while Chapters 5 and 6 are devoted to an analysis of the typical industrial corporate structures. Chapter 7 examines methods by which authorities within corporate structures justify their power. This chapter focuses on the way in which ideological statements are used to overcome the contradictions between the justifying values of freedom and equality and the demands of rational authority structures.

Part Three looks at labor movements in Canada and the contemporary structure of labor unions. In Chapters 8, 9, and 10, I attempt to describe the process by which labor movements became transformed from social protest movements into institutionalized components of Canadian society. This process can be seen as a series of conflicts stemming from the efforts of skilled labor seeking to preserve its status and expertise, as well as from the efforts of unskilled workers struggling to achieve the basic requirements of physical survival. The appeals to the two values of freedom and equality have been the means by which labor organizations have developed their momentum and gained their legitimacy. (It is well to note here that whereas those controlling the modes of production tend to emphasize equal opportunity, labor has tended to emphasize equal rewards.) The degree to which these processes have been translated into "class consciousness" is the subject of Chapter 11.

Part Four, encompassing the final two chapters, deals specifically with the work experiences of individual workers. It is within the work organization that individuals experience most directly and poignantly the discrepancy between the image of a free society with equal opportunity extended to all and the demands placed upon them in their work. Here the paradox is most supremely felt. At the very time in which freedom of choice and equal opportunity—if not equal rewards—are most strongly emphasized by apologists for industrialization, the trends of rationalization of authority systems make the actual enactment of these values more difficult. Chapter 12 describes how individuals cope with this dilemma, while Chapter 13 examines how these contradictions have resulted in privatizing experiences to the detriment of the public good.

Notes

1. Jerome S. Bruner, *On Knowing: Essays for the Left Hand* (New York: Atheneum, 1973).
2. Anthony Giddens, *Capitalism and Modern Social Theory* (Cambridge: Cambridge University Press, 1971), p. 211.
3. It is interesting to note that Anglophone analysts seem to be more ready to use cultural explanations to account for the minority power position of Francophones in Quebec, thus minimizing the impact of "social structure." On the other hand, Francophone analysts have tended to employ almost exclusively a social structural approach in which values or "culture" has played a secondary role.

Part One

Theoretical Issues

chapter one

The Analytic Legacy of Marx

Introduction

One of the consequences of the social turmoils of nineteenth century Europe was a search for their explanation. The Age of Enlightenment of the eighteenth century had given individuals a new sense of power as they sought to control rather than be controlled by their environment. But these hopes, built upon an image of rational and reasonable man, had been brought into question by the violent aftermath of the French Revolution and the social disruptions accompanying the process of industrialization, first in Britain, and then in Western Europe.

Karl Marx (1818-1883) attempted to take a new look at the causes of these social phenomena and to locate the role of the individual in relation to them. He and Engels came to identify modes of production in general and the newly formed bourgeoisie or capitalist class in particular as the basic driving forces behind these changes. The capitalists had taken advantage of the voyages of discovery to expand local commerce into world trade. They were responsible for developing a manufacturing system and the modern industrial enterprise, and had been instrumental in establishing representative governments, in which they tended to exert a dominant influence. Not content with their past accomplishments, they continued to change and improve productive relations in order to enhance their profits. As a consequence, "The bourgeoisie, during its rule of scarce one hundred years, has created more massive and more colossal productive forces than all the preceding generations put together."[1]

These changes had also created disturbing social problems. The factory system created a breakdown in traditional family patterns as the workplace became separated from the household. The creation of wage labor resulted in migrations as people became subject to shifting employment demands and wage levels. The suffering of this transient population became extraordinary as capitalists sought to maximize their profits by making huge work demands on these people. The capitalists paid them barely subsistence wages and required them to work in abhorrent conditions.

In this chapter I want to examine the major themes in Marx's analysis of industrialization, as well as how Marx arrived at his conclusions. I will pay special attention to his logic and methodology. Along with the relevant interpretations of Max Weber, this analysis of Marx will provide a basis for a more general perspective from which one can interpret the major processes of industrialization in Canada.

Intellectual Influences

Marx was deeply influenced by various philosophical schools that were products of the Enlightenment: the utilitarians, the utopian socialists, the materialists, and the idealists. But Marx argued that each of these philosophies apprehended only selected aspects of the social changes that were being experienced. Furthermore, he believed that each reflected the narrow class interests of the bourgeoisie. Thus, he believed that an entirely new conception of the individual and his role in society and history was required.

The utilitarians, such as Adam Smith, Jeremy Bentham, James Ricardo, and John Stuart Mill, viewed the individual as a creature with material needs, egoistic drives, and lively passions. Yet they also sought to discover what they believed to be the natural laws underlying social and economic relations. They argued that the ultimate source of economic value was human labor and undertook to analyze the implications of the changes in the division of labor upon society.

Marx admired the empirical perspective of the utilitarians, as well as their concept of the individual. He borrowed from them many fundamental concepts of his economics. Like them, he attempted to combine the fields of moral and social philosophy with political economy. Yet he sharply criticized them because they assumed an ahistorical and overly individualistic interpretation of social existence. In taking such an atomistic view of society, they failed to recognize the influence of those social conditions that allowed them to adopt such a perspective in the first place. Theirs was a capitalist view which interpreted the misery of the working classes as merely a temporary expedient.

The utopian socialists, such as Saint-Simon, provided a framework for an ideal state, but Marx criticized them because they did not provide realistic alternatives for the basic and immediate problems caused by industrialization in Europe. Further, they tended to thwart rather than augment and humanize the productive forces of society.

The materialists, such as Hobbes, Locke, and Feuerbach, played an important role for Marx insofar as they undermined traditional metaphysics and exposed the human origins and bases of religion and morality. But Marx argued that the problem with materialism, especially the materialism of Ludwig Feuerbach, was that it did not really examine the historical changing economic bases of human relations nor the capacity of individuals to influence the development of the social world.

While Marx was most partial to the utilitarians and the materialists, the overall scheme of his historical and social analysis owes much to the idealism of Hegel.

The Imprint of Hegel[2]

Hegel (1770–1831) posited a theory of progressive evolution of civilizations. His theistic approach was based upon a belief in a God who is the creative source of individuals and the world, transcending them, but also immanent among them. Hegel argued that this progress was directed toward a fusion of individuals with God, which would come about through the attainment of Absolute Knowledge. Not only would individuals have knowledge of the world, but they would also know how they came to have such knowledge. Events would be seen not only in their objective appearance, but also in terms of their role in the larger course of history. They would be seen not only as events in themselves, but also as events having causes and consequences which in turn serve as necessary components in the larger scheme of the evolutionary stages toward an utopian existence.

The relationship between individuals and God is, in Hegelian terms, one in which there is continuing attempt at fusion from both parties. The image is one of God working with imperfect instruments—individuals—in order to create a perfect state of being. Hegel sees the process of history as one in which individuals create social forms not only in order to survive within the world but also to understand it. True understanding occurs when individuals are aware of the relationship between themselves as creators and what they have created. This requires that what is created first be seen as external to individuals themselves. Ideally, this preserves a sense of self in relation to what has been created, and the true relationship between the two is perceived and maintained. However, what has happened in the past is either that there has been an over-identification with the social forms, so that the sense of self is lost, or the sense of self has become too strong, resulting in destructive power relationships among individuals and thus tearing apart the social order. In such states, individuals are alienated; that is, the correct relationship between the individual and the social forms designed for the social collectivity is lost.

Either the ultimate values are centered upon the organization of society or they are placed upon the self, with no account being taken of the relationship between the two.

In Hegel's view, Greek forms of democracy were at a higher level than "Oriental despotism," since in the latter case individuals were completely subsumed in their loyalty to a single ruler, while in the former case loyalty was directed toward the collectivity in the form of representative government. Yet in both cases there was nearly a complete denial of the sense of self in relation to these forms. In Roman civilization, the Greek forms of government were preserved, but they merely became the means by which individuals sought power and influence for themselves. Little cognizance was taken of the value of contributing to the welfare of the collectivity as a whole. Rather, the Roman civilization became entirely self-centered.

It was through the intervention of Christianity, especially following the Protestant Reformation, Hegel argued, that a proper balance began to be struck in the relationship of the individual to society. This took its ideal form in the Germanic or non-Roman civilizations that included representative forms of government. What remained in this schema was a further developmental stage in which individuals would achieve an awareness of the external reality of social forms, an awareness of self, and an awareness of the relationship between the two. As a consequence of such a state of being, coercive institutions would no longer be required. Basic wants would be met and the search for more desirable conditions for one's self would also mean more desirable states for others. This, as applied to the whole of man's understanding, would constitute a utopian existence of Absolute Truth—a fusion with God.

Hegel did not see these stages as merely automatic developments. Rather, they evolved out of a greater awareness among individuals at each stage. Individuals may view the initial forms of society as ideal but eventually they come to see them as having limitations. Thus, social movements emerge to bring about their end. A *thesis* about the world and man's place in it is eventually challenged by an *antithesis*. The resolution of these contradictions brings about a new *synthesis*, only to be challenged by a new antithesis once its weaknesses become apparent. And so the process continues. Meanwhile, during these cycles, individuals are acting in response to their social forms, but with each act, they add to further social structural development, which eventually also brings about an awareness of the shortcomings of these forms. The acts of specific individuals may appear to have little relevance, but viewed in the historical long run, along with other acts, they have consequences for significant change in the structure of societies. The key term that captures this drive toward self-perfection is *alienation*. Individuals seek to overcome alienation, whether it stems from an over-identification with the social order or from an over-identification with the self alone.

Marx's Analysis

As a student, Marx seized upon Hegel's conceptualization. He eventually reinterpreted it as calling for the development of God-like qualities in Man, not because of the pull from a God, but because man, as a social being dependent upon his created social forms for his survival, inherently had it within his power to construct a social order that would transcend any needs for dominance or social inequity among individuals. Meanwhile, Feuerbach the materialist, a contemporary of Marx, argued in his *Essence of Christianity* that it was not a matter of God acting through individuals that was the ultimate force behind the progress of history. Rather, it was man's actions that brought these changes about, and more than that, "God" was merely a construct of individuals and represented their ultimate projection of themselves as infinite all-knowing persons. The theistic properties of Hegel's system came to be deistic in Feuerbach's approach. Feuerbach had simply inverted Hegel's logic and centered it on Man rather than on God. In these terms, once the aspirations of individuals are ultimately met, religion as such disappears. Individuals become perfected through complete knowledge.

Marx's analyses further pursue the problem posed by Hegel and Feuerbach: How does one account for the processes of history? (A teleological bias underlies the question, in which it is presumed that societal changes lead to higher forms of social order, although in Hegel's scheme the higher forms did not occur within the same society.) Taking his cue from Feuerbach, Marx moved an additional step away from Hegel. He posed the question not within the realm of thought and spirit, but in the physical experience of individuals. Marx's image of individuals is of physically acting beings rather than of contemplative beings. Experience comes before contemplation in the pursuit of understanding. Indeed, for Marx, when individuals are in a social context in which they are in perfect harmony with themselves, there is no need for contemplative thought or philosophy since experience becomes the very essence of understanding; they are simultaneous. This is the meaning of his term "praxis."

With this transition accomplished, Marx, in his later writing, focused on the dynamics of change in general and a critical analysis of capitalism in particular. In this endeavor, he combined the formal perspective of Hegel with a radical claim to the priority of the experiencing individual. This meant that the approach of empirical science could be incorporated into Marx's perspective. The manner by which this was accomplished was through the "science" of political economics.

Marx's theory of political economics was premised on the assumption that the value of a commodity is proportional to the value of the labor required to produce it. Further, since the supply of labor is dependent upon a class of persons willing or required to sell it to those controlling the means of production, Marx was able to combine the empirical realities of production with an analysis of the social forms of capitalism. Central to his approach was the idea of social class, defined by the social influence, or power, of individuals, which in turn is reflected in their degree of control over the production of goods and services.

The Development of Capitalism and its Consequences

In Marx's view, individuals have devised arrangements to meet the basic needs of physical survival. It follows that the most important of these is the organization for the production of goods such as food, clothing, and shelter. These forms of social organization, however, become environmental elements which individuals must confront as surely as they must confront the natural environment itself. That is, if roles contributing to production are allocated to individuals, the resulting system of roles takes on a reality of its own and influences behavior beyond that of merely producing goods. Thus, Marx is able to make the statement that the forms or "modes" of production will influence the characteristics of the larger society:

> "In acquiring new forces of production, men change their mode of production, their way of earning their living; they change all their social relations. The hand mill will give you a society with a feudal lord, the steam mill a society with the industrial capitalists."[3]

With the imposition of the social reality of the organization of production upon individuals, original causes can become lost and the immediate experience within the social roles becomes the dominant influence upon their lives. This means that positions of coordination might become positions of power. Once this occurs, individuals in these positions can construct ideologies which serve to justify their exercise of power and thus bridge the gap between earlier value assumptions and present social realities. For example, a textile mill may be constructed to meet the need for cloth. Some individuals may assume positions of coordination in order to ensure the efficiency of the total work enterprise. But eventually, they, or others in these roles, may define these positions as a consequence of "natural selection," arguing that coordinating tasks are more important than other work roles and that they require extraordinary people to carry them out, hence they should be accorded social deference.

These beliefs further influence the interpretation of events, and subsequently individuals' behavior, so that, as Marx puts it, "The 'idea', the 'conception' of these conditioned men about their real practice is transformed into sole determining, active force, which controls and determines their practice."[4] But of course the process doesn't stop there, for as individuals continue to act upon these perceptions and, in effect, reproduce these forms, they contribute to further changes.

The organization for production—"modes of production"—is the most important element in the formation of societies in Marx's view. The continued elaboration of these forms, and the varying consequences of them for the larger society, result in societal changes. However, identifiable stages in the progression of societies do not occur until previous ones have reached their peak of development. Development, in this sense, means the achievement of their full productive capacities given their modes of production. Directly related to this is the nature of societal organization as a whole.

During the initial stages of any one society, a slave-master relationship, for example, the economic and social interests of both groups may be met, even though there once was a forcible take-over of one group by another. Masters assume responsibility and slaves gain security. However, masters may tend to consolidate their interests and to monopolize the exercise of power while reneging on their responsibilities. Ideologies may soon come into play which explain the division of society in terms that are beyond the control of individuals; genetic endowment, for example. In a sense, this may be viewed as a social expression of Hegel's "wish for infinitude." The class of masters becomes concerned primarily with entrenching its own interests, rather than permitting further change. As Bendix and Lipset put it in their interpretation of Marx, "upon its emergence as a ruling class, it turns from a champion of progress into a champion of reaction."[5] This occurs not so much from a conscious drive to power as a consequence of one class legitimizing its power over another. The need to legitimize increases as the original socioeconomic supports for the division become less important. This further contributes to states of alienation as individuals assign responsibility for their own actions to their social creations in such a way that they deny the possibility for themselves to bring about change.

In the process of rationalizing its own superordinate position, the ruling class (the masters in my example) becomes ever more oppressive to the subordinate class of individuals. There thus evolves a discrepancy between the value premises of the social order and the realities experienced by individuals within it. The process begins first with a discrepancy between the organizations for production and the social organization of larger society (e.g., modes of production versus class relations) and then a questioning of basic values. In the case of feudal society and its transformations, Marx made the observation that, "the feudal relations of property become no longer compatible with the already developed productive forces."[6] The process is spelled out in the following quotation from Marx:

> "The mode of production of material life conditions the general process of social, political and intellectual life. It is not the consciousness of men that determines their existence, but their social existence that determines their consciousness. At a certain stage of development, the material productive forces of society come in-

to conflict with the existing relations of production or—this merely expresses the same thing in legal terms—with the property relations within the framework of which they have operated hitherto. From forms of development of the productive forces these relations turn into their fetters. Then begins an era of social revolution. The changes in the economic foundation lead sooner or later to the transformation of the whole immense superstructure. In studying such transformations it is always necessary to distinguish between the material transformation of the economic conditions of production, which can be determined with the precision of natural science, and the legal, political, religious, artistic, or philosophic—in short, ideological forms in which men become conscious of this conflict and fight it out."[7]

Marx briefly wrote about what he considered to be stages in societal development: primitive communism, slavery, feudalism, capitalism, socialism, and an advanced state of communism. The ruling class will cling more tenaciously to an ideology which has little grounding in the realities of an evolving production system, while the lower class, most directly influenced by these realities, will just as tenaciously oppose the ruling class. These two classes are concrete embodiments of Hegel's thesis and antithesis.

The exploited class will eventually win in the confrontation since it is most closely allied with the realities of existence. Having won, the formerly subordinate class emerges in a ruling position. It has happened in the past that the formerly revolutionary class eventually became an exploiting class and the process has been repeated, culminating in a state of capitalism. The processes continue as long as the modes of production generate social divisions, which, in turn, curtail the ability of individuals to control and improve their own destinies, both individually and collectively. With communism, however, utilizing the superior technology of production created by capitalists, the division of labor based upon power and control is no longer necessary. Further, there is no justification for social classes. Societal forms and the organization for production become compatible and the fusion between philosophy and practice, between value premises and material existence becomes complete. Social constructions resulting in states of alienation no longer exist.

Within this general schema, Marx carried out an analysis of the dynamics of capitalism. This occupied most of his later productive life and focused on the fundamental economic premises of capitalism and their social consequences. An overview of his approach follows.

The Capitalist Economy and the Role of Industry

According to Marxian interpretation, the increasing prevalence of trade during early capitalism fostered the emergence of a set of premises, which shifted from the use to which a product could be employed to the value a commodity could command as an item of exchange for other commodities. One can trade cloth for cattle if one has more need for beef than for clothing. This would be an exchange based upon use. However, if one desires to trade cloth for cattle in order to eventually obtain sheep, then some unit of equivalence must be derived for these goods other than merely their use.

For Marx, and the political economists preceding him, the unit of equivalence is the amount of labor required to produce any given commodity. A new logic thus emerges. If the efficiency of labor can be increased so that the same amount of labor time can be expended to produce more cloth, then the same number of cattle, and subsequently sheep, can be acquired at less labor expenditure or "cost." In this case, "profit" would be represented by the time saved through increased efficiency. When profit rather than use is the objective of trade, then goods became evaluated on the basis of their "exchange" value rather than "use" value.

If a capitalist has hired workers to produce cloth, the profit which he makes is dependent not only upon the efficiency of the workers but also upon the amount of wages which he must pay his employees. Obviously, the minimum wage which he must pay is one that meets the subsistence needs of the workers. Computed in terms of hours of work, this may require the wage equivalent of only four hours a day to pay for these needs (e.g., the needs of food, shelter, and clothing). Any additional hours he can get his employees to work beyond the absolute sum of the wages for four hours contributes to both his own subsistence and his profits.

In Marx's theory of the dynamics of capitalism, presented in its simplest form in Volume 1 of *Capital* and in its more elaborated version in Volume III, maximizing profits is the basis of competition among capitalists. An individual capitalist will normally reinvest a major share of his profits in order to expand his operations and thus protect himself from his competitors. His competitors, of course, are acting from the same motives. If we assume that all capitalists are employing the same level of technology in their productive enterprises, then one way in which any given competitor can increase his profits is to demand increased efficiency from his workers and require them to work longer hours. But there is a limit to these demands. Hence, the capitalist may seek to add more individuals to his labor force and thus increase his volume of production—provided that the market can absorb this increase. Two things happen, however, when he takes this course of action: (1) His competitors will likely be embarking upon the same course of action, thus causing scarcities in the supply in labor and thus raising the wage level which workers can command. (2) With each additional worker, the added increment of production will decline through increased costs in administrative overhead and additional equipment. Thus, the costs of additional labor tend to increase to that point where overall production costs meet selling costs of the commodities plus a profit margin that is roughly the same for all capitalists. Any additional profit, at given levels of technology, must be derived from increased efficiency obtained from the work routine of the labor force.

However, labor alone is not the only factor in production, nor the only source of profits. It is labor in relation to the means of production, the tools and equipment, land, and money. All of these taken together constitute what Marx called the "organic composition of capital." Marx placed primary emphasis upon labor and "fixed capital" or machinery since these were of principal importance in industrial capitalism.

Given this state of equilibrium, it may occur to one capitalist that an improvement in technology can improve production efficiency with the same work force. In the short run, he will maximize his profits relative to other capitalists, but eventually his competitors will also utilize technological innovations in order to remain competitive. When this occurs, the trend is toward a new level of equilibrium, but one at which technology plays a proportionately larger role in the production process. All capitalists can produce more commodities more cheaply—assuming that the returns derived from expenditures on technological improvements are greater than that derived from additional workers. But despite the fact that the first capitalist may have earned windfall profits, by the time all his competitors catch up with him, the rate of profits averaged out among all of them becomes less than it was before. Earnings may be higher in absolute terms but profits have declined per commodity unit sold.

For Marx, the decline in the profit rate occurs because of the lesser role labor plays in the production process relative to machinery. Since profits are based upon "surplus labor"—that labor which is beyond the pay-time required for workers' subsistence—the lower the proportion of labor incorporated in the production process, the lower will be the rate of profit for each commodity unit produced.[8]

Marx singled out the labor component of production as the principal factor which produces profit because it is the only one that can be employed in a variety of ways. Machinery, once purchased, is fixed in what it can perform. Labor is still required to operate it. Workers may be enticed, or forced, to work longer hours than is required to pay for their subsistence needs at the same rate of pay. Or, failing that, their rates of production can be manipulated by organizing them in different ways. Thus, they become the only "factor" which, when related to machinery, can create varying degrees of profit. Variability is further insured by the manner of paying for costs. Most workers are paid on the basis of their completed work. Machinery must be paid for, whether it is in operation or idle.[9]

Given the competitive forces of the market, individual capitalists are essentially driven to employ higher levels of technology (a "higher order of organic composition of capital") than their competitors. But when their competitors follow suit, the proportion of labor expended in the production process for the entire industry is reduced, while the prices of the commodities are reduced and their volume increases. However, the average rate of return to the capitalists, their profits, declines. The capitalists cannot simply hire more labor since it would be impossible, given the more advanced levels of technology, to produce the same volume of goods at equivalent costs. Thus the overall trend is to adopt improved technology while maximizing labor efficiency.

Once capitalists have obtained their machinery, they must operate it and thus continue to produce in order to pay for their costs and remain competitive. Since the labor component becomes increasingly reduced, individual capitalists have less flexibility in dealing with fluctuations in shares of the market (fluctuations in demand). Every time a competitor increases his share of the market, others lose, creating economic crises. In addition, costs increase for technological improvements as losses are suffered from depreciation of older machinery.[10]

With each crisis, more affluent capitalists are able to buy out less successful ones. Hence, capitalists become fewer in number and larger in size of operations. Meanwhile, with each cycle produced by the continuing competition, the labor component becomes smaller: there is less need for skills and those workers who are employed are driven to achieve higher rates of efficiency. If markets cannot be expanded, then unemployment increases. (Given the declining proportion of labor in the production process, in absolute terms, employment levels can be maintained only if markets expand at a greater rate than technological improvements in production.) This is the basis for the impoverishment and "immiserization" or hardship of workers. Not only is there greater unemployment but those who are employed lose control over greater proportions of the work process due to the elimination of skills by technological improvements.

Figure 1 presents a simple version of the interaction of these forces of production.

FIGURE 1 **The Interaction of the Drive for Profit with the "Organic Composition of Capital."**

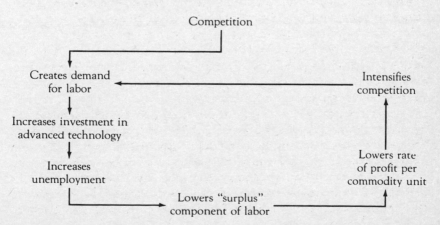

The computation of the rate of profit, in Marxian terms, can be illustrated in the following manner: if *c* equals investment in fixed capital (land, machinery), *v* equals labour and *s* equals surplus labor, or labor which is employed beyond that required to meet workers' subsistence needs, then the exchange value of each commodity is the sum of each of these. The surplus value of any one capitalist is held in check by the price of his commodities relative to his costs of production. If company A is labor intensive, its proportion of production factors might be 10 parts *c* and 90 parts *v*. While a capital intensive company, B, might have the proportions 90 parts *c* and 10 parts *v*. Suppose the surplus labor in each company is equal to the cost of labor at subsistence level. (Workers will work twice as long as the period required to pay for their subsistence.) Then the exchange value of a commodity for company A will be 10 *c* plus 90 *v* plus 90 *s* or 190. The exchange value of a commodity for company B will be 90 *c* plus 10 *v* plus 10 *s* or 110. The cost of the commodity may be less for company B, but its profit on each commodity is also less since there is less labor and hence less surplus value. Absolute levels of profit may increase, because of larger sales, but profits per commodity unit become less.

While in the long run the tendency inherent in capitalism is for the rate of profit to fall with a decline in the proportion of labor in the production process, Marx pointed to other factors at work that slow down or reverse this process during short periods. These include the development of foreign trade in which investment in economies with higher labor content will bring higher proportionate returns, the shift of some workers made unemployed by technology to the manufacture of labor intensive luxury items, the advantages gained from shorter time periods elapsing in the conversion of raw materials to finished commodities, and the likely lowered costs of natural resources as means of transportation are extended and technologies for acquiring them improve.[11] Despite these mitigating factors, the basic process leading toward a lowering of the rate of average profit will continue. Put in more basic terms, in capitalism, the productive capacity of the economy tends to outrun the capacity of the market to absorb its products. What creates this contradiction is the competitive nature of capitalism expressed in terms of maximizing or protecting rates of profit.

The social expression of this contradiction is carried out in class terms: a growing body of workers, both employed and unemployed, confronting a smaller body of powerful capitalists. Eventually, workers will break the power of the capitalists since the experience of work in the production enterprise has taught the workers the collective discipline necessary for such an undertaking. Further, there are simply more of them than capitalists. The value premises which once provided legitimation for the capitalist system and the ideologies constructed by capitalists are no longer compatible with the experiences of the workers in advanced capitalist societies. This "integument" is at last broken with the success of the proletariat. Marx expresses the process in the following manner:

> Along with the constantly diminishing number of the magnates of capital who usurp and monopolise all advantages of this process of transformation, grows the mass of misery, oppression, slavery, degradation, exploitation; but with this too grows the revolt of the working class, a class always increasing in numbers and discipline, united and organized by the very mechanism of the process of capitalist production itself . . . centralization of the means of production and socialization of labour at last reach a point where they become incompatible with their capitalist integument. The knell of capitalist private property sounds. The expropriators are expropriated.[12]

An Evaluation

Although most social analysts after Marx had to come to terms with his perspective and his polemics, the influence of Marx himself in North America was all but dead during the 1950s and early 1960s. The revival and reconsideration of Marxian analysis can probably be attributed to both the rejection of Western economic models by developing countries and the failure of orthodox sociologists, in their use of equilibrium models, to adequately analyze and predict the social unrest within their own societies. More importantly, however, it is likely that a post-World War II faith in the benefits of technological advances diverted attention away from their potential social costs.

Marx's theory of capitalism is a theory of production. In contrast, classical economic theories based upon utility are theories of consumption. Factors of production from the perspective of these latter views are ultimately a function of consumer demand for commodities. The responsibility for production rests with the consumer. The "unseen hand" of the marketplace is a composite result of wants for commodities in relation to their prices. This presupposes a model of man with insatiable wants.

Marx attempts to demystify this process and to place the dynamics of capitalism squarely with calculating capitalists who attempt to safeguard their interests against the encroachment of their competitors. Bottomore and Rubel paraphrase Marx's concern in the following manner:

> How does it happen that human beings project upon outside objects, upon rarefied abstractions those powers which are truly their own—that, for example, they consider the state as a power which organizes society, when it is in fact the structure of society which gives rise to the state, or that they regard wealth in the form of capital, which is a creation of social labour . . . as an independent active force which "employs" human beings?[13]

Marx's question attempts to apply a general principle which entails positing an independent influence—means of production—upon the manner in which individuals can order their social world. What needs to be exposed, he argues, is the contradiction between the social forms—institutions—as they exist and the means of production. This contradiction offers alternative possibilities for social institutions. Marx, in effect, demystifies not only the role of religious beliefs, already begun by the eighteenth century Enlightenment philosophers, but also what had been taken to be the "natural" laws of the marketplace. He does this by attributing ultimate causes to individuals themselves as they are confronted with the problem of physical survival.

The labor theory of value in the Marxian perspective links the modes of production, social classes, and finally social analyses that go beyond the "laws" of capitalist economics. Without this linkage, Marx's analysis in *Capital* would have been disembodied from his larger concern—to arrive at a theory which would predict and explain what he believed to be progressive stages in history. The economic analysis provided the empirical materialist basis for what remains essentially a Hegelian logic—that there is some ultimate end in history to higher states of being where social classes and hence social inequities no longer exist; where, in Hegel's terms, perfect knowledge is attainable.

For ease in exposition, I will deal with Marx's formulations in terms of his assumptions, the resulting logic of analysis and finally an assessment of the utility of his perspective. Marx's assumptions appear to be the following: that man alone is the creator and reproducer of social institutions, that the historical process of production and reproduction of these social forms follows identifiable law-like regularities which ultimately lead to more desirable societies, and that the basis of these regularities is to be found in the manner in which the production of material products is organized. The ultimate expression of the organization for production is social class.

Taken alone, the first of these assumptions can provoke little controversy. However, there are problems when one considers the remaining two assumptions. If in fact there are basic historical regularities of change which lead progressively to a more favorable final state, then the role of creative man becomes questionable, except as a first cause. Marx, however, wanted to say more than this. In his analysis of the French Revolution in 1848, he takes his stand against a "Great Man" theory of history—that single individuals can dictate the course of historical events. But he is also opposed to historical determinism which views the course of history as a process disembodied from acting individuals. For example, Marx wished to show how the class struggle in France created the conditions that permitted Louis Bonaparte, hardly a great leader, to take over the government. "Men," wrote Marx, "make their own history, but they do not make it just as they please; they do not make it under circumstances chosen by themselves, but under circumstances directly encountered, given and transmitted from the past."[14] Yet the making of history follows a law-like path which Engels called "the great law of motion of history." Men may be acting on their past history and subsequently invoke new social forms, but if this process is ultimately a deterministic one then Marx's assertion can be little more than a mere platitude.

Marx's analysis of the 1848 Revolution in France is an attempt to explain why the proletariat could not gain predominance. In effect, conditions were not right; hence it could only be a revolution of change from a "bourgeois monarchy" to a "bourgeois republic." Marx insists however that eventually there will be a successful revolution of the proletariat against that ruling bourgeoisie class. In the long run, this makes his theory deterministic and provides a means of pointing to a utopian society. But one can ask, in what sense are individuals capable of controlling their own destiny if they merely act in accordance with what is already going on? Marx seems to imply that the role of individual actors is restricted to hastening the process of history and that during periods of social disorganization there is some latitude for individuals to influence the course of events.

The third assumption, that the basis for the law-like regularities in history is to be found in the social organization for the production of material goods is also questionable. This assertion initially appears plausible, but its validity is best established in societies where the logic of the marketplace, especially in industrial capitalism, already exists. It requires some rather tortuous logic to assign to a particular production system the primary cause of, for example, a society dominated by religion. It suggests that all actions are ultimately economically motivated. But motivations can take on many forms. One may seek social recognition through economic means or through political or religious means. There may be economic consequences for political or religious recognition, but that is not to say that these forms of recognition are economically motivated.

But having said this as a criticism, it is not clear to what degree Marx emphasized the economic dimension as a methodological device for analysis while recognizing the importance of other dimensions or whether he viewed it as the tenet of reality. Engels, Marx's collaborator, tended to support the latter interpretation. In his preface to the third edition to Marx's *The Eighteenth Brumaire of Louis Bonaparte,* Engels wrote that Marx's "great law of motion of history" whether expressed by struggles in the "political, religious, philosophical or some other ideological domain," are in fact struggles between social classes. Social classes are, in turn conditioned by "the degree of development of their economic position, by the mode of their production and their exchange determined by it."[15]

If Marx had meant that individuals produce their own social institutions, some of which are economic, it would not have been difficult for him to expand his perspective to posit that different institutional sectors become predominant over different historical periods in any given society; that the status concerns within legalistically defined feudal society, for example, contributed to bringing about the market conditions of capitalism. The problem here is what Marx took to be valid "scientific" data. This required a unit of analysis that could be objectified and measured in a way in which values or legal systems never could be. In fact, Marx relegated these factors to the domain of epiphenomena; hence, within his theory, economic factors had to be basic.

Turning next to the logic of Marx's analysis, it is important to remember that theories are systems of logically interrelated propositions about observable phenomenon. What matters about a theory is whether it explains and hopefully predicts in a parsimonious manner. The logic of Marx's theory rests on dialectical reasoning. The question to raise with respect to Marx's use of such reasoning is whether or not it is the most parsimonious expression of change, whether it is applicable to change in general and, if not, what restrictions are to be put to its use.

Marx attempted to demonstrate that given forms of social organization themselves created the necessary conditions for their own change and finally, their demise; that in this sense there was no need to posit forces external to the capitalist system to account for its decline. Rather, its end would be a result of those very elements that developed capitalism to its most advanced state. What mediates between acting men and these social processes of change is the individual state of "alienation".

Further attached to these processes is a three-part movement of unity (thesis), opposition (antithesis), and a higher form of social unity (synthesis). Conflict and destruction are inherent in this interpretation. Social classes evolving into mutual antagonism with each other are fundamental to Marx's schema. Now if it is true that Marx's assumptions make his a deterministic theory of social change, then his logic of analysis can permit no exceptions. To do so would deny the validity of the theory. As a result of this dilemma there have been questionable practices in the application of Marxian theory. Interpretations of history tend to be selective so that events are made to fit the overall schema, with social history being reduced to a history of production systems and economic exchange. In addition, with no time limits placed upon stages of development, or clear indications of the role of all of the variables affecting development, there is no possibility to validate the theory. One can hold to the thesis of the ultimate collapse of capitalism indefinitely. Since Marx, the tendency to introduce contingent conditions and mitigating factors into the overall theory of social change and the analysis of capitalism in particular has continued. I have noted a few of these which Marx himself had expressed. In addition, one can point to revisions which include the arguments that the force for change will come from the white-collar proletariat rather than blue-collar workers; that class conflict should be expanded and reinterpreted to refer to the exploitative relations which the wealthy nations have with the poor; and that capitalist control of information media prevents workers from organizing themselves into a viable and politically conscious social class.

These contingent explanations tend to turn Marxism into more of a faith than an analytic theory. As such it is self-sustaining. Marxists in capitalist societies can welcome both conservative militancy, because this is interpreted as the beginnings of class polarization, and leftist radicalism, because this is taken as a sign of an emerging class consciousness among the working class. It is even conceivable to argue that one should encourage the capitalists rather than the workers, since this would hasten the polarization process.

In terms of an overall schema of historical change, it should now be apparent that Marx's theory has severe limitations. The utility of his thesis, however, is most apparent in the analysis of industrialized capitalist societies alone. Still, it is not at all obvious that in capitalist societies there must be violent conflict in order to bring about new social forms and class realignments. One can discover enormous social changes that have come about without violence. Further, violent revolutions have frequently failed to bring about those societal changes that their advocates had proposed.

It is ironic that while Marx insisted upon the fundamental reality of modes of production as the ultimate cause of societal transformations and argued that there could be no transformation of capitalism until it had reached its highest state of development, his theory as an *ideology* has become the driving force for change in every society where socialist forms currently exist. In no case have these societies gone through what could be identified as the final stages of capitalism. It will be recalled that the final stage requires that there must be increasing and unbearable hardship for workers. To date, in industrial societies, this has not occurred in economic terms (a psychological interpretation may be another matter, however). Over the long term, there has been an increase of participants in the labor market and overall purchasing power has increased at a greater rate than inflation. Further, the proportion of earnings of industrial enterprises going to the labor component has not fallen but has remained constant.

On the other hand, what remains unanswered is whether or not these conditions can continue should markets not be able to continue to expand. Recent events contributing to high unemployment and high inflation rates suggest that Marx's analysis of industrial capitalism, if not of historical change in general, must be taken seriously.

The Merits of Marx's Analysis

Having the advantage of hindsight, the products of Marxist scholars, and the perspective of a doubting age, one can become too glib in criticizing the original thesis of Marx. In fact, if one transforms the determinism and teleological thesis of Marx into one which demonstrates how the apparently autonomous forces of the market are really consequences of the social organization of society, the Marxist perspective becomes a powerful tool of analysis.

Focusing specifically on Marx's analysis of capitalism, Robinson has noted three basic processes which remain dominant within contemporary capitalism. These are as follows: (1) the theory of the reserve army of unemployed labor, which shows how unemployment tends to fluctuate with the relationship between the stock of capital offering employment to labor and the supply of labor to be employed; (2) the theory of the falling rate of profit which shows how the capitalists' greed for accumulation stultifies itself by reducing the average rate of return of capital; (3) the theory of relationship of capital good to consumption good industries which shows the evergrowing productive power of society knocking against the limitation upon the power to consume which is set by the poverty of the workers. As Robinson puts it, together these themes produce an image of capitalism that is "racked by its own inherent contradictions generating conditions for its own disintegration."[16]

The main argument economists have had with Marx does not concern these themes, but rather the technical aspects of his thesis, e.g., his labor theory of value, which becomes far too unwieldy and has been supplanted by the marginal utility theory of value, and his conception of profits, which does not exclude the cost of rent and interest.

No less an economist than Keynes had to recognize the merits of Marx's prognosis of capitalism. The correctives Keynes introduced did not refute Marx as much as they took his logic into account in order to preserve the system of capitalism. In this regard, Heilbroner has noted that "the attitudes of business have proved to be as capable of enlightenment as the attitudes of any other class, including . . . the working class."[17] The effect of Keynes's remedial strategy during the Great Depression of the 1930s was to induce governments to play a more direct role in dampening the fluctuations in economic cycles and ameliorating the severity of differences in economic classes. (Whether this tactic transforms governments into tools of the capitalist class or represents a means by which socialism can emerge rather than by revolution remains a matter of continuing debate.)

I will make reference to specific observations and analyses of Marx in later chapters as these become appropriate. What is important for the moment, however, is to have a sense of Marx's approach and to keep in mind the fundamental elements of his perspective: individuals are producers of their own social structures, and the impact of these structures influence the course of future creations. If one removes Marx's deterministic bias while retaining the dynamic tension between acting individuals and their creations, one has the beginnings of a perspective that will guide him through the processes in-volved in industrial capitalism. The analyst steeped in Marxist traditions becomes sensitized to paradoxes and contradictions as the key processes of social change in general, and industrialization in particular. However, a sociological corrective to the deterministic influences of Marx's formulations requires a review of Max Weber's analysis of the emergence of industrial capitalism and its transformations.

Notes

1. Robert C. Tucker, ed., *The Marx-Engels Reader* (New York: Norton, 1972), p. 339. I am indebted to Fred Bird for his insights and contributions to the development of this chapter.
2. This brief description relies heavily upon Shlomo Avineri, *Hegel's Theory of the Modern State* (Cambridge: Cambridge University Press, 1972).
3. Karl Marx, *The Poverty of Philosophy* (New York: International Publishers, 1963), p. 109. In this quotation "forces of production" refers to technology, while "modes of production" refers to the entire organization of production. While Marx appears as a technological determinist in this passage, this in fact is not the case. But throughout his writings, the relationships among technology, the organization for production, and the characteristics of the larger society are not at all clear.
4. Karl Marx and Frederick Engels, *The German Ideology*, Parts I and III (New York: International Publishers, 1967), p. 30.
5. Reinhard Bendix and Seymour M. Lipset, "Karl Marx Theory of Social Classes," in *Class Status and Power*, ed. Reinhard Bendix and Seymour M. Lipset (Glencoe, Ill.: The Free Press, 1953), p. 26.
6. Ibid., p. 27.
7. Karl Marx, *A Contribution to the Critique of Political Economy* (Moscow: Progress Publishers, 1970), pp. 20–21.
8. A contemporary expression of this decline of profits is indicated in a report in the Montreal *Star*, January 4, 1978, of the research of Sidney Schaeffler, head of the Strategic Planning Institute of Cambridge, Massachusetts. An analysis of 200 companies revealed that profits declined as businesses become more capital intensive. The *Star* quotes Schaeffler in stating that competition becomes "a much rougher and meaner game" as corporate managers attempt to maintain volume of production in order to keep their machines occupied.
9. If workers become salaried and tenured, as has been suggested in the American steel industry, or as exists for tenured faculty members in universities, then their costs become more fixed like machinery. In this case degrees of variability as factors of production become reduced.
10. For a more detailed account, see Alexander Balinky, *Marx's Economics: Origins and Development* (Lexington, Mass.: D.C. Heath, 1970).
11. Ibid., pp. 131–133.
12. Karl Marx, *Capital: A Critical Analysis of Capitalist Production*, Vol. I, trans. Samuel Moore and Edward Aveling (Moscow: Progress Publishers, n.d.), p. 715.
13. Karl Marx, *Selected Writings in Sociology and Social Philosophy*, ed. T.B. Bottomore and M. Rubel (New York: McGraw-Hill, 1964), p. 5.
14. Karl Marx, *The Eighteenth Brumaire of Louis Bonaparte* (New York: International Publishers, 1963), p. 15.
15. Ibid., p. 14.
16. Joan Robinson, *An Essay on Marxian Economics*, 2nd ed. (London: Macmillan, 1966), p. 4.
17. Robert Heilbroner, *The Worldly Philosophers*, 3rd ed. (New York: Simon and Schuster, 1967), p. 152.

chapter two

Weber's Response

This chapter deals with the response of Max Weber to the Marxian analysis of the rise of Western capitalism and the consequences of industrialization. The emphasis of analysis shifts for Weber to the role of men's beliefs in effecting societal change. I first compare Weber's assumptions and methodology to those of Marx. Then I present Weber's own analysis of the emergence of Western capitalism and resulting industrialization. The key theme that should be emphasized in this chapter is Weber's interpretation of a particular form of *rationality*. This provided, for Weber, the core of meanings which justified behavior that was once held in low regard.

The Assumptions and Methodology of Weber

While Marx viewed individual men, especially in his earlier writings, as active agents participating in historical events, his main concerns were with the general laws of history, and specifically, with the dynamics of capitalism. His analysis rested upon the processes of economic production. Further, these were processes which, once initiated, could not be altered.

Now, Marx's position in this regard rests on the assumption that events can be known in and of themselves—if one just looks. Thus, thought, philosophical systems, and especially ideologies, can lead to illusions at worst and distortions at best. It is the task of the empirical analyst to uncover the reality behind men's ideas about the empirical world. That reality for Marx can be found by examining the most basic human problem—physical survival. Everything else is a derivation of that problem. It is not that thought does not influence human behavior. But if one goes back an additional step in the causal chain, the behavior can be traced to the physical experiences of men which, in turn, are determined by the roles they play in the system of production. Thought, beliefs, values, and ideology are merely variables that intervene between the modes of production and the actions of men.

Weber finds the intervening variables to be problematic. While granting that economic concerns are important in the structure of societies, he views values that men hold as crucial sources of data. They are important if one wants to understand the variations in the characteristics of societies in general and the rise of industrial capitalism in particular.

It is at this point that one must have an understanding of Weber's methodological assumptions. Weber believed that it is impossible for men to know things in and of themselves. Knowing is derived from the manner in which men conceptualize their experienced world. If the social scientist seeks to understand human behavior, then he must analyze the manner in which these concepts are derived and the consequences of these concepts. On the surface, the resulting form of investigation appears to differ very little from Marx. Actually, the logic of investigation is quite different and the consequences differ more than might be supposed.

One can continue to assert naturalistic causes for human behavior, but one cannot escape the fact that this in itself is a form of conceptualizing about the world. It is the forms of conceptualization of men in everyday life that Weber is interested in, their origins and their consequences. A crude illustration may not be out of order here. One can say that the essence of all buildings is the material in their construction. But one cannot say much about the form of a building knowing only the properties of a brick. A blueprint derived from the architect's conceptualizations gives us a much better grasp of the likely form a building will take. Weber is interested in the conceptualization. He believed Marx, to continue the analogy, was primarily interested in the "brick." Marx, and more especially, "Marxists," he believed, were oversimplifying cultural phenomena by reducing causes to a materialistic base:

> The so-called "materialistic conception of history" with the crude elements of genius of the early form which appeared, for instance, in the Communist Manifesto still prevails only in the minds of lay-men and dilettantes. In these circles one still finds the peculiar condition that their need for causal explanation of an historical event is never satisfied until somewhere or somehow economic causes are shown (or seem to be operative).[1]

Weber grants Marx every right to analyze capitalism in terms of the evolution of productive systems. He objects, however, to the assertion that this is to be taken as a scientific law. Marx, of course, was free to do this since he started with the assumption that events can be known in and of themselves which, in turn, means that the apparent orderliness of the universe can be *discovered*. The Marxian analysis is, for Weber, only one aspect of a configuration of events that resulted in industrial capitalism and its transformations. The explanation itself can be viewed as a product of the very ethos Marx analyzed. The analytic problem now is to characterize this ethos and to thereby explain the societal changes in terms of it. Marx could point to the economic variables that contributed to the emergence of industrial capitalism and to their influence in the processes of capitalist society. But *why* that particular form of capitalism emerged in western Europe was a question that his model could not adequately treat. It is this question that Weber made his own.[2] And for this he turned to an analysis of what men took to be reality in their time, in effect, a historical cultural analysis.

To carry out his investigation, Weber employed the methodological device of the *ideal-type*, a device he thought to be peculiarly suitable for historical and cultural analyses of change. The ideal-type is a consciously derived mental construction of reality as experienced by men. It attempts to bring into clear focus the predominant characteristics of an historical event or of a cultural phenomenon. It is a means by which the researcher focuses upon what he has determined to be the essential facets of a phenomenon. It is, thereupon, employed for comparative purposes to ascertain the degree to which observable phenomena adhere to the derived characteristics.

The ideal-type asks questions about "cultural" events.[3] In natural science, there are well-defined limits as to what qualifies as proper events for inquiry. But science *itself* is a cultural event. Thus, in an inquiry about culture the range of possible constructions to explain these are infinite since even the limits of natural science are lacking. Further, a cultural event such as industrial capitalism is significant in its individuality, rather than as an instance of a uniformity. Thus, a causal analysis cannot be derived from any law in the sense as an observable event in natural science. From this perspective, then, Weber incorporates the ideal-type as simply a device by which the analyst makes clear how he is conceptualizing the infinitely complex cultural phenomenon in his analysis. Weber's analytic statements are of a functional rather than deterministic nature.

The Imprint of Values: *The Protestant Ethic and the Spirit of Capitalism*

In characterizing what he believed to be the core elements of the "spirit of capitalism," Weber cites a series of aphorisms written by Benjamin Franklin. One example is the exhortation that "time is money."

> He that can earn 10 shillings a day by his labour and goes abroad, or sits idle one half of that day, though he spends but 6 pence during his diversion or idleness ought not to reckon that the only expense; he has really spent, or thrown away 5 shillings besides.[4]

Weber is concerned with the *ethos* of capitalism—those values, petty or otherwise, which ordered men's lives—that provided a rationale for capitalists' actions.

Now, Weber notes that "the impulse to acquisition, pursuit of gain, of money, of the greatest possible amount of money, has in itself nothing to do with capitalism."[5] Capitalism, as Weber views it, is economic action "which rests on the expectation of profit by the utilization of or opportunities for exchange, that is, on (formally) peaceful chances of profit."[6] Even this, however, does not characterize the *western* style of capitalism that Weber had in mind. He notes that capitalism as just defined has existed "in all civilized countries of the earth so far as economic documents permit us to judge."[7] Contemporary western capitalism included these features, but in *addition*, it included the "rational capitalistic organization of (formally) free labour."[8] This phrase is loaded with additional nuances and implications that need further examination. Let us first determine what Weber means by "rational" and then note the further implications of his phrase.

In the context of capitalism, Weber has a restricted definition of "rational." He defines it as the logic which governs action in terms of the characteristics of the goal desired by an actor. It is the type of logic which determines the most efficient and effective means to attain the goal. This contrasts with a set of values that overrides any unique expediency in governing behavior. To use an example from Aron, a captain who feels duty bound to go down with his sinking ship regardless of the circumstances is a person whose action is governed by a set of values which transcend any particular context.[9] This differs from the situation-defined logic of Weber's self-serving, rational man. Further, the pragmatic characteristics of Weber's definition differ from a logic which rests upon states of emotion such as spontaneous acts which have no cause other than an emotional or effective one. Lastly, the type of rationality Weber has in mind differs from traditional justifications for behavior—that men act in a manner that is congruent with past traditions. If there is any commitment to values or traditions for the rational man in Weber's view of Western capitalism, it is toward rationality itself which, in turn, is defined by the nature of the intended ends.

In addition to this form of rationality, Weber was concerned with the apparent irrational commitment of men to its pragmatic logic. The commitment of Benjamin Franklin toward efficiency as a good in and of itself expresses this historically strange phenomenon. It is this that Weber took to be the key distinguishing element in western capitalism. Consequently, work became an end in itself; wealth was not to be enjoyed, but was to be employed in further pursuits; science was to be put to technological use; and bureaucracies became a standard form of work organization. Such an orientation served to undermine the feudal social order based on the traditional social ties existing between the landed aristocracy and serfs, ties that the members of the rising capitalist class saw as inefficient and ineffective in serving their own ends.

Weber set out to discover the key element that would explain not only the unique characteristics of western capitalism, but also its continued dynamics. The clue seemed to lie with the doctrinal characteristics of

Protestantism. Bendix notes that it had been a rather common observation in Europe that Protestants seemed to have more of an affinity for commercial enterprises than other religious groups.[10]

One explanation for the correlation between Protestantism and commerce was that people in wealthy regions had turned to Protestantism if it aided them in their pursuit for economic gain. But this presented a paradox for Weber since the Protestants—especially those of Calvinist and Baptist lineages—appeared to be far more committed to their beliefs than other religious groups. How was it possible that persons obsessed with religious concerns should be in the vanguard of the then most secular of activities?

A second argument was that the outcasts of society or minorities were more likely to engage in commercial activities. It was their minority group status rather than their religious beliefs that explained the commercial propensities of the Protestants. To this, Weber pointed out that the Catholic minority which had suffered from social exclusion in Germany since 1870 and the Catholic minorities of Holland and England did not exhibit attributes similar to the Protestant minorities. The Huguenots in France and the Nonconformists in England, however, were deeply involved in commercial activities. Further, while the Jews as a minority group were also likely to be involved in trade and commerce, their orientation towards their endeavors was distinctly different from that of the Protestants. The Protestants were unique in the emphasis they placed upon hard work, seriousness, frugality, thrift, and the refusal to enjoy the profits of their labors.

Given this initial evidence, Weber wished to demonstrate that there was a very definite thread of continuity between the beliefs of Protestants emerging in the sixteenth century and capitalists' endeavors practised in Weber's time, the early twentieth century. Weber's analysis focused on the reasons for the transformation of *speculative* capitalism into a capitalism of careful, long-term, rational planning. The answer seemed to lie in the content of religious beliefs.

The Emergence of Calvinism

Before the Reformation, the Catholic church had been undergoing serious strains. The practice of indulgences had become corrupt and, generally, the church seemed to be more an instrument of man than of God. More attention appeared to be paid to church form and structure than to faith. While other voices had called for reform, Luther's was the more radical.[11]

Luther believed, among other things, that priests had no special standing before God. All men, Luther maintained, are "called" by God to their appropriate "stations" in life, which included, in our terms, their occupations. In effect, for Luther, every man was his own priest in the sense that God calls him to his occupation and man in turn is expected to carry out the duties of his occupation with an ascetic commitment of the same order as a priest.

Luther believed that grace is achieved not merely through ascetic contemplation. Rather, since all "proper" occupations are sanctified, it is attained through diligent commitment to one's occupation. Luther's doctrine gave a sacred character to the work role, but only insofar as it was an expression of obedience to God's ordinances. It was not an expression of man's control over nature. That was to come later.

It was not until the doctrines of Calvin became widespread that the additional link between religious beliefs and the later characteristics of western capitalism was established. Weber had noted that while Lutherans had become diligent workers, they were not as likely to have the same sort of zealous commitment to expansion, improvement, and development in their work ethic as the Calvinist and Baptist sects.

The Consequences of Calvinist Beliefs

The doctrines of Calvin were considerably more terrifying than those of Luther. Calvin taught that God was omniscient and omnipotent. Thus, there was nothing men could do to ensure God's grace, since the fate of each individual was predestined. After all, men existed for the sake of God, not God for the sake of men.

In such a deterministic world-view, one might expect that men would be content to live what Calvin would call a slothful life. After all, if the fate of men is predetermined what is the value of good works? Why not eat, drink, and be merry? These rhetorical questions seem logical enough, but fail to address the *psychological consequences* of such a belief system. This has to be seen in the context of what Weber believed to be an extraordinary concern which individuals at that time had with life after death—how they would spend eternity. Eternal hell is a fearsome thing and it would be a great consolation if men knew whether or not they were saved from it. The problem, however, was that the Calvinist doctrine had discredited the Church as a source for ascertaining one's state of grace. Obviously, the priests were of no help since "the elect," whoever they were, could understand the work of God only in their own hearts. Nor did the sacraments ensure a state of grace. Even God was of no help since Christ died for the elect, not for the doomed.[12]

Solace for the individual was to be found purely through faith. One must believe that he is among the elect in order to find peace in this world. This further meant that one must act as a steward of God doing his duty. Self-doubt was a ploy used by the forces of evil; lack of self-confidence was an indication of lack of faith. To ward off self-doubt, the believer was to work ever more diligently and thereby keep his mind occupied and sustained against his doubts. Thus, according to Weber, Calvinists sought to maintain the faith that they were saved by looking for tangible evidence that they were in a state of grace.

Other Protestant groups whose beliefs seemed to Weber to contribute to the emergence of the spirit of capitalism were the Pietists, the Methodists, and the Baptist sects. The Pietists derived their beliefs from Calvinism, but they placed primary emphasis almost solely on worldly asceticism. As Weber states, they wished partly to make visible the invisible church of the elect, and this could only be done through their works.[13] Methodists differed from Calvinists primarily in their emphasis upon fervent emotional expressions of certainty.

The Baptist sects (which include Quakers and Mennonites), however, were doctrinally independent of the Calvinists. Essentially, their beliefs stressed that the Church could only be comprised of believers, and that an individual could take spiritual possesion of God's gift of salvation. But Weber points out, "this occurred through individual revelation by the working of the Divine spirit in the individual and only in that way."[14] It was incumbent upon the individual to welcome the coming of the spirit by resisting a sinful attachment to the world, which could be achieved only by maintaining social seclusion from the world. Thus, the stress upon maintaining the collective purity of believers resulted in the exercise of extreme social pressure upon individual members to maintain their ascetic way of life.

All these strains of Protestantism converge, Weber points out, in the belief that the state of religious grace "could not be guaranteed by any magical sacraments, by relief in the confession, nor by individual good works. That was only possible by proof in a specific type of conduct unmistakably different from the way of life of the natural man."[15] Weber continues, noting the consequences of this belief for individual behavior:

> From that followed for the individual an incentive methodically to supervise his own state of grace in his own conduct, and thus, to penetrate it with asceticism. But, as we have seen, this ascetic conduct meant a rational planning of the whole of one's life in accordance with God's will. And this asceticism was no longer an *opus supererogationis*, but something which could be required of everyone who could be certain of salvation. The religious life of the saints, as distinguished from the natural life, was—the most important point—no longer lived outside the world in monastic communities, but within the world and its institutions. This rationalization of conduct within this world, but for the sake of the world beyond, was the consequence of the concept of calling of ascetic Protestantism.[16]

Asceticism, formerly confined to the monastery, now ruled the lives of all men. As Weber picturesquely describes the process, "Now it rode into the market place of life, slammed the door of the monastery behind it, and undertook to penetrate just that daily routine of life with its methodicalness, to fashion it into a life in the world, but neither of nor for this world."[17]

A set of ethics emerged out of the religious doctrines emphasizing the aloneness of man before God and the concern for a state of grace within the ascetic nature of the work role. Weber, drawing from what he considers to be representative of ascetic Protestantism, posits these ethics as the essential link between the religious beliefs and the "spirit of capitalism." The common themes running through the exhortations are as follows: (1) the virtues of hard work; (2) an emphasis upon personal responsibility "to do the works of Him who sent him as long as it is yet day"; (3) the necessity to be efficient and thrifty in the use of time and money; and (4) the cautions against self-indulgence, especially in the enjoyment of wealth.

The ethics of this religion which represent a transition from belief to practice eventually pass over into "sober economic virtue." The religious underpinnings are lost in the memories of men, giving way to "utilitarian worldliness." As Weber further notes, "what the great religious epoch of the seventeenth century bequeathed to its utilitarian successor was, however, above all an amazingly good, we may even say pharisaically good, conscience in the acquisition of money, so long as it took place legally."[18]

Accordingly, the "bourgeois" businessman could follow his pecuniary interests wherever they led so long as they remained within the "bounds of formal correctness."[19] In addition, moral sanctification of economic behavior legitimized the existence of unequal distribution of goods. It was taken as a special dispensation of Divine Providence, according to Weber. Its effect was to legitimate not the moral correctness of social classes as such, but to account for their existence. While Luther might have regarded social classes as part of God's master plan requiring man's total commitment to his "station" in life, the Calvinists regarded Man as a steward of God. Hence, the station in which he found himself was the result of his own responsibility in carrying out his stewardship: were he a better steward, he would find himself in a better economic position.

With the emphasis placed upon the *ethic* rather than the *doctrine* of Protestantism, and with hard work, thrift, frugality, and business acumen all regarded as virtues in themselves, the "spirit of capitalism" emerges in its secular form. At this point, Weber reintroduces Benjamin Franklin as a spokesman of the secular utilitarian orientation of western capitalism. The common thread accounting for the transformation from commitment to religious other-worldliness to a rational control of the world is complete. The effects of this transformation are noted by Weber:

> The Puritan wanted to work in a calling; we are forced to do so. For when asceticism was carried out of monastic cells into everyday life, and began to dominate wordly morality, it did its part in building the tremendous cosmos of the modern economic order. This order is now bound to the technical and economic conditions of machine production which today determine the lives of all the individuals who are born into this mechanism, not only those directly concerned with economic acquisition, with irresistible force. Perhaps it will so determine them until the last ton of fossilized coal is burnt. In Baxter's (a Puritan writer) view the care for external goods should only lie on the shoulders of the "saint like a light cloak, which can be thrown aside at any moment." But faith decreed that the cloak should become an iron cage.[20]

Thus, regardless of religious beliefs, all men are finally forced to come to terms with the effects of western capitalism and especially its product—industrialization.

Weber noted that the "mechanical foundations" of capitalism rather than any transcendental belief system now propel western capitalism. In this sense, it is utilitarian rationality which legitimizes the actions of men. Viewing the Enlightenment as another offshoot of wordly asceticism (its "laughing heir," as he calls it), Weber notes that it too seems to be fading and "the idea of duty in one's calling prowls about in our lives like the ghosts of dead religious beliefs."[21] Weber permits a brief glimpse of his own pessimistic evaluations:

> Where the fulfillment of the calling cannot directly be related to the highest spiritual and cultural values, or when, on the other hand, it need not be felt simply as economic compulsion, the individual generally abandons the attempt to justify at all. In the field of its highest development, in the United States, the pursuit of wealth, stripped of its religious and ethical meaning, tends to become associated with purely mundane passions, which often actually give it the character of sport.
>
> No one knows who will live in this cage in the future, or whether at the end of this tremendous development entirely new prophets will arise, or there will be a great rebirth of old ideas and ideals, or, if neither, mechanized petrification, embellished with a sort of convulsive self-importance. For at the last stage of this cultural development, it might well be truly said: "Specialists without spirit, sensualists without heart; this nullity imagines that it has attained a level of civilization never before achieved."[22]

It is clear that Weber is highly skeptical of the effects of the utilitarian rationality which paradoxically emerged out of the worldly asceticism of the early Calvinist and Baptist sects.

An Evaluation

Weber's intellectual interests were deceptively modest: "To ascertain whether and to what extent religious forces have taken part in the qualitative formation and quantitative expansion of that spirit (the spirit of capitalism) over the world."[23] He pursued variations of this problem for nearly all of his intellectual life. Further, these investigations were always conducted in the context of economic change. Weber could state that economic institutions were predominant in western capitalism, but he was unwilling to view economic institutions as the major cause of the characteristics of all societies. As Fischoff has pointed out, for Weber, western capitalism did not dominate the minds of men until an apparent historical accident resulted in the fusion of two disparate elements: the commercial activities of early capitalism and the secular implications of the Protestant Ethic. Acts will not become routinized until a set of beliefs give them authenticity; thus, Calvinism and later the Protestant Ethic provided the set of beliefs which gave incipient forms of western capitalism its authenticity and finally perpetuated the process of western industrial capitalism itself. It was not the logic of Calvin's doctrines themselves which provided the authenticity, but the set of ethics which developed from them.[24]

One writer has termed the thesis of The Protestant Ethic and the Spirit of Capitalism a test of the Marxist interpretation that the Protestant Reformation was a byproduct of the rise of capitalism.[25] The Protestant Ethic in Weber's interpretation could not have been merely a byproduct, since the Puritans themselves were directed far more toward non-worldly concerns and their ethics were far more restrictive than those of the Catholics, Anglicans, and Lutherans. Western capitalism, with its accompanying ethical system, had to be seen as an outgrowth, unintended of course, of these beliefs. The mediating link between religious beliefs and western capitalism was a psychological reaction of anxiety on the part of the believers. Weber notes that it was not simply wealth that defined western capitalism, but the sense of commitment to the enterprise of work: the rewards of work were to be seen as rewards of the good steward in God's "vineyard." Weber notes that the inhabitants of Florence, the money capital of the world during the fourteenth and fifteenth centuries, would have viewed the attitudes which characterized backwoodsmen of eighteenth-century Pennsylvania with disdain and intolerance. It was the woodsman who characterized the western capitalism that Weber had in mind: he was the individual who viewed work and economic gain as the essential virtues in life.[26]

Weber did not dismiss the importance of economic factors, but as Gerth and Mills point out, Marx failed to distinguish among what is strictly economic, what is economically determined, and what is merely economically relevant. They note, for example, that feudal pilgrimages to Rome had consequences for money markets, but that does not make the pilgrimages economic enterprises. The influence of religious or political ideas on economic institutions does not transform these ideas into economic factors.[27]

Further, it is worth repeating that Weber's denial of a "realist" interpretation of the world was an underlying reason for his disagreement with the thesis of Marx. The law-like formulations of Marx were unacceptable to Weber since reality was not self-apparent, but was subject to the conceptualizations of men. Explanations had to lie with the interactional effects between the experienced world and man's interpretation of it.

Although in his analysis of The Protestant Ethic and the Spirit of Capitalism, Weber focused on the economic effects of a religious belief system, his overall approach to social science was based on a model of continued interaction. At the close of his work he notes,

> Here we have only attempted to trace the fact in the direction of its [Protestantism] influence to their motives in one, though a very important point. But it will also further be necessary to investigate how Protestant Asceticism was in turn influenced in its development and its character by the totality of social conditions, especially economic.[28]

He further adds:

> ... it is, of course, not my aim to substitute for a one-sided materialistic an equally one-sided spiritualistic causal interpretation of culture and history. Each is equally possible, but each, if it does not serve as the preparation, but as a conclusion of an investigation, accomplishes equally little in the interest of historical truth.[29]

Critics of Weber's approach have questioned its methodology and the resulting interpretation of historical events. As we have noted elsewhere, Weber employed not only the use of ideal-types, but also a technique of artificially reconstructing history by asking what would have happened had antecedent events been different or not occurred. This approach was consistent with his belief that, as Aron stated,

> a causal relation is never a relation established between a totality of a movement T and the totality of a previous movement T-S; a causal relation is always a partial and artificial relation between certain elements of historically particular and certain antecedent facts.[30]

Since this approach rests upon mental constructions against which inferences are made about the occurrence of historical events, how does one minimize the arbitrary nature of analyses? For example, how does one put meaningful, and ultimately empirical, constraints upon these mental constructions? How does one determine the degree to which the events under study come under the purview of the mental construct? How does one avoid the danger of explaining the complex by over-simplified themes?

One can argue that the use of mental imagery has difficulties no different in kind from the more general question of conceptualizing phenomena. How do we ascertain whether our concepts actually carry the meanings of the events they stand for? We can never be certain, Weber would say. But we can obtain greater precision by constantly refining and using validity checks, available through an interactional approach, by first holding one element constant, then another, in the process of analysis. What Weber did was simply to make explicit the assumptions that historians and social scientists tend to leave implicit. For example, Weber attempted to demonstrate that the social and economic conditions were adequate for the rise of western style capitalism in China, but the ethical (value) system of Confucianism was not. In India, the caste system was not really a deterrent to capitalist development, but the belief in the transmigration of souls was hostile to it.[31] Thus, while appropriate economic conditions may exist, the motivation for western style capitalism requires a special belief system.

Weber's approach likely lends itself to criticism precisely because Weber tried to make the derivation of his conceptual tools of analysis as explicit as possible. The refusal to rest his case on a model of universal causality required him to do so.

Conclusions

The importance of beliefs in legitimizing behavior has been a pervasive theme in the literature of social analysts and social commentators. Their importance has been even more strongly emphasized in the analysis of processes of social change. This theme can be found in the writings of economic historians, development theorists, and political scientists.

Following Weber, one can argue that the ideology of the West—Western Europe and North America—now rests upon a secularized version of the Protestant Ethic. Stripped of its religiously based ethics which stressed the importance of means in the pursuit of ends, it emphasizes only the pursuit of self-oriented ends. This may maximize the individual's own private welfare but it is doubtful whether such an orientation alone is sufficient to improve or even maintain the welfare of society as a whole.

Marxism, as an ideology stresses the unity of individuals with historical processes. Collective endeavor is thus the route to salvation in a secular, political sense. The individual acts out of a sense of moral commitment to the collectivity. It is for these reasons that Marxism has a special appeal for many individuals who speak in behalf of the working class or in behalf of developing countries.

The stress upon individual salvation and its economic consequences has, to date, been unique in human history. Weber doubted that the secular version of this orientation could survive. He believed that with the loss of belief in transcedent values, the stress upon utilitarian rationality would eventually be insufficient to maintain the integrity of society. Nationalism or the political connotations of "class consciousness" appear to provide these transcendent values. Yet Weber believed that these too would eventually lose their transcendent content. They would become increasingly rationalized in a utilitarian manner as societies became industrialized.

Some would interpret the consequences of utilitarian rationality as the ultimate in freedom for the individual. Others would agree with Weber that without transcendent content, Man, individually and collectively, loses sight of his role in society and in history. The theme of Man the creator versus his created societal forms, the basic issue raised by both Marx and Weber, provides the central perspective for examining the trends and consequences of industrialization in Canada.

Notes

1. Max Weber, *The Methodology of the Social Sciences*, trans. and ed. Edward Shils and Henry A. Finch (New York: The Free Press, 1949), p. 68.
2. There is some question here about whether or not this is a "constructed" problem. If Marx meant to point out merely the *limits* to the variety of social forms that the

production system causes, then Weber's response shrinks in importance. But this interpretation would be inconsistent with the underlying deterministic character of Marx's concept of historical materialism. Thus, Weber's response seems to be well founded.

3. Wrote Weber: "The type of social science in which we are interested is an *empirical science* of concrete reality *(Wirklichkeitswissenschaft)*. Our aim is the understanding of the characteristic uniqueness of the reality in which we move. We wish to understand on one hand the relationships and the cultural significance of individual events in their contemporary manifestations and on the other the causes of their being historically *so* and not *otherwise.*" (Weber, *The Methodology of the Social Sciences*, p. 72).

4. Max Weber, *The Protestant Ethic and Spirit of Capitalism*, trans. Talcott Parsons (New York: Scribners, 1958), p. 48.

5. Ibid., p. 17.

6. Ibid.

7. Ibid., p. 19.

8. Ibid., p. 21.

9. Raymond Aron, *Main Currents in Sociological Thought*, Vol. II (New York: Basic Books, 1967).

10. Reinhard Bendix, *Max Weber: An Intellectual Portrait* (Garden City, N.Y.: Doubleday, 1962), p. 55.

11. Erasmus, a contemporary of Luther, stressed the need for practical piety in opposition to the legalism and superstition that were rife in the church. But in a letter to Luther, he stated, "I will put up with this Church until I shall see a better." "I always freely submit my judgment to the decisions of the church, whether I grasp or not the reason which she prescribes."

12. Bendix, op. cit., pp. 58–60.

13. Weber, *The Protestant Ethic and the Spirit of Capitalism*, op. cit., pp. 129–130.

14. Ibid., p. 145.

15. Ibid., p. 153.

16. Ibid., pp. 153–154.

17. Ibid., p. 154.

18. Ibid., p. 176.

19. Ibid., p. 177.

20. Ibid., p. 181.

21. Ibid., p. 182.

22. Ibid.

23. Ibid., p. 91.

24. Ephraim Fischoff, "The Protestant Ethic and The Spirit of Capitalism: The History of a Controversy," in *The Protestant Ethic And Modernization: A Comparative View*, ed. S.N. Eisenstadt (New York: Basic Books, 1968), pp. 67–86.

25. Nicholas Timasheff, *Sociological Theory: Its Nature and Growth*, 3rd ed. (New York: Random House, 1967), p. 172.

26. Weber, op. cit., p. 75.

27. H.H. Gerth and C. Wright Mills, eds. from *Max Weber: Essays in Sociology* (New York: Oxford University Press, 1958), pp. 47–48.
28. Weber, *The Protestant Ethic and The Spirit of Capitalism*, op. cit., p. 182.
29. Ibid.
30. Aron, op. cit., p. 194.
31. Timasheff, op. cit., p. 174.

chapter three

An Analytic Perspective

Marx and Weber both directed their analyses to the general issue of social change and, more specifically, to changes represented by the Industrial Revolution. In my treatment of the two theorists I have emphasized two principal themes in their analyses: (1) the interaction between acting individuals and their social constructions, and (2) the inter-relationship among the social constructions.

In this chapter, common themes in the approaches of the two theorists will be brought together, and then used as a basis for formulating an analytic perspective which can account for ongoing processes of change within contemporary industrialized societies in general, and Canada in particular. I shall present the perspective in very broad terms. It remains for future chapters to address specific issues pertaining to the experience of industrialization in Canada.

A Selective Review of Marx and Weber

Both Marx and Weber viewed society as composed of the ongoing constructions of acting individuals.[1] For Marx, the key components which determine the characteristics of society are the social relations required for production. For Weber, values and beliefs are fundamental elements in any system of relations among individuals; they have the same potential to influence the actions of individuals, and consequently their social constructions, as do the means of production. Weber viewed the relative importance of these factors as continually open to empirical inquiry.

Both analysts had fundamentally different interpretations of historical processes of change. Marx held to a premise of historical materialism which, when tied ultimately to the evolving forces of production, makes his a deterministic model of explanation. Individuals may have created their social environments, but they were restricted and hence determined by the manner in which they produced for their material or physical needs. Capitalism and the industrialization process were to be seen in the context of these broader principles. The connecting link between the means of production, acting individuals, and the consequent characteristics of society was furnished by the concept of *alienation*. At first glance, this concept contains a sense of continuing futility; that once social structures have been created, they then control the course of individuals' lives. However, individuals can gain control after the macroprocesses have worked themselves out to such a degree that there is finally the possibility of a perfect match between the desires and decisions of individuals and the requirements for collective living. Incorporated into the image of futility for the individual is, ironically, hope for the eventual end of such a state.

The approach articulated by Marx contains an unresolved paradox. If the course of societal development is indeed determined, then there is in fact no place for decision-making individuals, except as mere elements in the predetermined course of social change. Further, if the conditions of alienation are to be resolved only by individuals' control of their own fates, this resolution can hardly be compatible with ongoing secular laws of social development.

Weber's approach avoided this dilemma because it was not based upon a deterministic model. For him societal development remained open-ended, although he could see no way out of the trend toward greater rationalization. For Weber, the processes of social change were enormously complex and did not depend upon one single evolutionary cause. Values and beliefs, such as those embodied in religions, may have more influence on the actions of individuals than does the organization for production. Relative strengths of influence of these and other factors (such as political organizations) can change. This means that Weber's analytic approach rests upon probabilistic and contingent statements rather than determinant ones. There is no ultimate determinism involved in Weber's approach, although he did express fears of the continuing influence of formal rationality.

Despite these differences, both theorists were loyal to a view of social change in which social structures are both delimiting and enabling influences upon the actions of individuals. As individuals act upon the premises of these social constructions, the structures themselves are subject to variation and change. Here the attempt is being made to combine the image of decision-making individuals with the social influences affecting those decisions. It is clear that both analysts sought to demystify the process of social change in general, and the evolvement of capitalist societies in particular. Marx attacked the smug idealism of the rising bourgeoisie, while Weber attacked the one-sided approach of economic determinists. Both theorists, however, had similar conceptions of industrial capitalism. Further, both treated industrialization as one of the consequences of capitalism.

As for the analysis of industrialization itself, the combined views of Marx and Weber provide a powerful perspective for understanding both historical and contemporary processes. I use the term "perspective" with some care to distinguish it from "theory." A perspective may be viewed as a general orientation embodying certain key assumptions about events. A theory, on the other hand, is a far more precise body of logically inter-related propositions about events. Theories are derived from or related to general perspectives, and, to continue the formal, deductive route of scientific inquiry, empirically testable hypotheses are derived from theories. What I aim to present in the balance of this chapter is a perspective which will provide an organizing theme throughout this book.

A Derived Perspective

The analytic approaches of Marx and Weber have been of fundamental importance to sociologists. They represent classic statements of a basic epistemological stance, namely, that while individuals create (and hence can destroy) social structures, whatever their basis, these structures in turn influence individual actions.[2] Sociological analyses have tended to focus on the impact of social structures and less on how they have been created. For example, there is a wealth of information on the influence of class, occupation, organizational position, ethnic group status, and sex status on individual actions. What is less understood is how changes come about in the structures themselves.[3] This question forms the basis of the debates between Marxists and Weberians. I wish to argue that the concept "structure" should be seen not only as a social phenomenon, but also as a dynamic process that is endemic to personal existence itself; that "structure" is required for the individual to understand his experiences; and finally, that in the act of structuring, different aspects of *social* structures become modified.[4]

The idea of structure is more than merely an artificial assumption or conceptual tool. Piaget's experiments on the learning behavior of children suggest that even acts of creativity are carried out in a systematic and orderly fashion. Each new experience is incorporated into some meaningful framework.[5] Learning is, for Piaget, a process of relating the unknown to existing structures of knowledge.[6] Indeed, he argues that all forms of life are constantly involved in assimilation, in "continual relating, setting up correspondences, establishing of functional connections and so on. ..."[7] Man is constantly involved in the act of "self-construction" and he does this by incorporating his experiences into meaningful structures.[8] But these structures are not "eternally predestined either from within or from without" man, the actor.[9] They are determined by individual actors. In each act of understanding, "some degree of invention is involved . . ."[10] and this is done in relation to previously constructed structures.

But individuals do not carry on this process in any manner they choose. They are also subject to the organized interpretations of others that constitute *social* structures. They both enable and constrain individuals to act in a meaningful way. This further means that such structures have a historical continuity in that the structures themselves provide the rules for behavior and a common frame of reference for interpreting experience. Yet the actions of individuals remain creative within this framework. One can note, by analogy, that individuals learn rules of using language, yet in the act of putting these into use, the rules themselves become elements for creating new and novel forms of meaning. Similarly, most music in Western societies is based upon a scale consisting of five whole tones and two half tones, which is standard regardless of the key in which the scale is heard. Yet, despite this fixed format, there are almost endless musical variations possible.

This conceptualization of the linkage between individual actors and social structures incorporates a view of the individual as an agent of "reproduction." That is, to use this Marxian term, individuals continually reproduce their social structures, but they do so in the context of their own experiential world. This means that, from a sociological point of view, the characteristics of social organization and social institutions, and their continued existence depend on the meanings that individuals attribute to them and their subsequent actions. Further, in the very act of "reproduction" individuals will bring about changes in these *social* structures as they simultaneously structure their own individual experiences in meaningful ways. Variations in actions and changes in the characteristics of social structures thus become inherent consequences of reproduction just as language-in-use becomes a creative enterprise while at the same time being "governed" by rules of grammar.[11]

On Social Change

A considerable body of research and commentary supports the idea that social change occurs even while individuals act within existing social structures. Certainly this is a basic theme for both Marx and Weber. More recent examples include Buckley's "open systems" approach to the analysis of "social systems." He refers to the process of elaboration and change as "morphogenesis," a process by which actors make decisions on the basis of previous experience, but by enacting their decisions also introduce new elements into the system. The effects of each actor's decisions provide the basis for, as well as the limits to, future decisions.[12] In his "value-added" thesis, Smelser points out the ongoing cumulative effects of actions upon subsequent acts.[13] Landes has drawn out these effects in his analysis of the development of machine technology.[14]

Yet these changes do not necessarily occur without conflict. In analyzing patterns of economic development among former colonies, Smelser observes that beliefs which stress national identity and future utopian-like states of existence are necessary to get people mobilized in order to support a new socioeconomic system. But when this mobilization reaches a point where technical skills are required, these beliefs may impede rather than further the process of development. This happens because a more restricted and utilitarian rationality is needed to foster specific skills, rather than a commitment to merely broad political programs for social change.[15] At this point there is almost invariably conflict between factions which hold these opposing views.

Kuhn has made a similar point in a different context. He has argued that scientists pursue their research activities within the conceptual limitations of particular paradigms. In the course of performing "normal science" within these conceptual systems, the systems are continually refined to account for an increased range of events. Adherents to the paradigm may initially view events which do not support the paradigm as merely anomalies. But for some, the existence of anomalies calls the adequacy of the entire paradigm into question. The problem emerges whether to further modify the paradigm to account for these events or whether to create a new paradigm altogether.[16] The resolution may entail full-scale debates, if not conflict, between proponents of each view.

From these observations it becomes apparent that individuals' experiences are structured in such a way as to make them meaningful; that social structures involving patterns of interaction rest upon shared meanings; and that processes of change—excluding the impact of external events— are processes of elaboration of different aspects of "social structures." But if one were to stop at this point, social change and history itself would be merely automatic processes.

The fact that conflict may be involved in the two examples just given—from the analyses of Smelser and Kuhn—suggests that this is hardly the case. What must be added is the element of *reflection*—the possibility that individuals understand their own and others' experiences in relation to some meaningful criteria. "Without this possibility we are dealing not with meaningful behavior but with something which is either mere response to stimuli or the manifestation of a habit which is really blind."[17] Of course, these criteria do not remain fixed since they arise from experience itself. But at the same time, the experience can only be interpreted by these criteria. Another way of putting this is to say that one of the components of a "social structure" is a set of abstract meanings which guide behavior "in principle." But this set may be reinterpreted and reformed for the specific experience. This process involves the ability to reflect, to entertain other possibilities.

Reflection is the key link that explains the dynamics of social change and locates it with individual actors. The act of reflection involves not only the issue of *understanding* via a set of meanings, but also of *evaluating*. Thus *values* are also involved and this implies an awareness of a moral order. If those revolutionaries who seek to continue with policies of destruction of an old regime come into conflict with their colleagues who attempt to end that stage in an effort to build a viable society, the conflict is fought on moral grounds, that is, over differences regarding appropriate actions to take in order to create a better society. (For a related example, consider the factional disputes in China that followed the death of Mao.)

The conflicts concern the degree to which systems of meaning which *structure actions* are consistent with a set of *values*; when they are not consistent, a state of crisis, or at least confusion, is created. The possibility of a discrepancy between structured "meaningful" activity and a set of values derives from the process of elaboration at both levels. The former has to do with simply understanding behavior, the latter with evaluating it. When there is an inconsistency, its resolution depends on the degree to which the activity is made consistent with a set of values or to which the values are altered in their interpretation so that the activity is made acceptable.

It is the principal thesis of this book that the course of industrialization represents a process of elaboration among those systems of meaning that structure the organization of production, which may be viewed as *systems of authority*, and that this in turn has taken place within the context of a set of *values*. The crises that have emerged have resulted when the structure of organization—of authority—has not been consistent with ongoing values. Or, to put this another way, critical questioning, by way of reflection, occurs whenever the processes of elaboration, of values on one hand, and of the authority systems, on the other, are not mutually supportive. In industrialized societies, the crucial arena where these discrepancies have been most directly experienced has been in the world of work.

To provide a historical perspective, the next chapter will examine how the values and authority systems that once supported commercial ventures ultimately contributed to the emergence of industrial capitalism. This was not a necessary outcome but rather represents one consequence of the conflict between groups who adhered to opposing solutions to emerging discrepancies. (It is conceivable that the rising industrial capitalists could have been prevented from gaining ascendency by a feudalistic aristocracy, or that another outcome could have occurred, as Weber has implied, or finally, that a modification of the process was possible. In fact, it will be argued that the Canadian experience represents a unique modification.)

The values that I believe have been of primary importance in justifying the process of industrial capitalism are *freedom* and *equality*. In effect, these are secular expressions of Weber's portrayal of the Calvinist: free from the social dictates of estate and Church, equal before his fellow men, if not before God. What has marked the changes in these values is their elaboration and subsequently the way in which they have been expressed. For example, "freedom" may be interpreted to mean freedom from social obligations, freedom from want, freedom to choose any occupation, or freedom to choose among autocratic employers. "Equality" may mean equal value as a person, but unequal in possessing qualifications for a given job; equal in participating in decision-making but unequal in influence.

Concurrently, the structure of meanings which have shaped authority in production systems has, in its own autonomous development, continually threatened to undercut the values of freedom and equality. These values may be required to *recruit* individuals into production enterprises, but the continued elaboration of rational forms of organization through the use of machine technology and the segmentation and routinization of work roles has meant that these values are not sustained by individuals' experiences. These discrepancies lie behind the conflicts between workers and employers. The push for wage increases is a push for greater economic equality. The grievances against management controls are grievances in support of the freedom for workers to govern their own work-related activities. Indeed, underlying Marx's concept of alienation is the assumption that individuals should have equal rights while remaining free to control their own activities. (Of course more than this is implied, for Marx would equate the control of one's own activities with a contribution to the general welfare of society and this, as we have seen, requires different societal structures than what we have experienced to date.)

Both Marx and Weber saw the work role as the most important context of experience in industrial capitalism. Weber restricts its importance to the post-Calvinist era, but Marx views the world of work as fundamental to the experience of mankind regardless of the nature of society. While discrepancies between a set of values, or their interpretation, and systems of authority may be experienced in other contexts—in organized religion, in education, in the polity, for example—the experiences in the work role have remained central to the inquiries into industrialization processes. It has been the principal reference point by which individuals assess others and themselves. Social analysts are currently debating the following questions, among others: Will the work role continue to be a crucial arena of experience? Would stripping it of its value promote a general state of alienation? Can other contexts of experience replace the work role in importance and thus limit the negative effects of the restrictions imposed upon it?

I have argued so far that the concepts of social structure and social change are linked by the actions of reflective individuals. Further, the two major components of social structures are values and those meanings attributed to experience which do not imply evaluative content; each component undergoes separate processes of change as a result of the actions of individuals, processes that are not necessarily coordinated.[18] I then argued that the values of freedom and equality were predominant in industrialized societies facilitating those systems of authority required for the production of goods by machine technology. I then viewed the systems of authority as relatively value-free, constituting one type of meaning system. (This is drawn from Weber's concept of "formal rationality," which I shall discuss in chapter seven.) Finally, I argued that crises occur when the elaboration of these two components are not coordinated. The general theme can be diagrammed as follows:

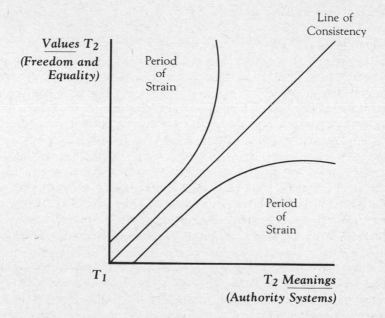

I wish to point out in this diagram that social change may be relatively unnoticed as long as changes in meaning structures are consistent with predominant values or interpretations of them. Periods of strain, or crisis, occur when, across the dimensions of time (indicated by the axes, $Time_1$ to $Time_2$), changes in the two components are inconsistent. It is more often the case that changes in systems of meaning precede changes in values, although there are frequently attempts to accomplish the latter. (Some religious and political movements are examples of this.) Perceived coordination of the two components is most likely when values are expressed in relatively abstract terms.

It follows that the processes of elaboration and change, and hence the incidence and severity of stress, are further reinforced and accelerated as societies become more complex and differentiated. Under these conditions, individuals can transfer meanings gained from experiences in one context to other contexts. Leaders of labor unions, for example, may employ the techniques of management that have been developed in business organizations. But in so doing, they may bring about conditions in their own organizations that they originally opposed. Church leaders may employ secular fund-raising agencies to gain increasing financial support and inadvertently make their organizations subject to secularization. Metaphors employing models of understanding in other contexts are frequently used to make linkages between authority systems and values. Spokesmen for employers once converted the biological model of Darwin into "social darwinism" in order to justify social inequities and employers' authority.

Elites, Power, and Conflict Resolution

Not every individual or group of individuals has equal influence in altering or maintaining social structures. No society has lacked leaders or elites, whose actions, by definition, will have greater consequences upon social structures than those of other individuals. The basis of the criticisms levelled against elites are twofold: are elites acting in the best interests of all societal members and is entrance into elite status determined by criteria which have consensual support? The two concerns are inter-related. Most analyses in North America have focused on the social origins of elites, assuming that if their social backgrounds are similar, the elites are acting on behalf of their own interests, rather than those of the general population, and that entrance to the status of elites is controlled by those who are already members.[19]

Elites direct the exercise of authority. Authority, in turn, rests upon meanings which define the exercise of power as legitimate. I have viewed authority systems within industrial capitalist societies in a Weberian sense as relatively value-free because they are based upon "formal rationality." This assumes that individuals "contract" to participate in organizations in order to achieve their own objectives, which may not be the same as those intended by elites. It is the *structure* of authority in its formal sense that remains at the level of meanings without evaluation. It is when the individual is *forced* to submit to the authority system that his freedom of choice is denied. It is at this point that the authority structure and the exercise of authority may be questioned within the context of the values of freedom and equality.

When considering the structure of authority, one must also deal with the issue of power, for behind these meanings there is always the possibility of physical coercion. Conflict has to do with the degree of agreement on the exercise of authority and ultimately with the justification of the authority system itself. The exercise of physical coercion is a final response by elites, if there remains no justification from the point of view of participants within the system. However, overt conflict and coercion are costly endeavors for both parties in conflict; there are a variety of strategies which elites can employ in order to maintain their authority. One strategy is to incorporate the symbols of dissident groups into the statements which elites use to justify their power. Marcuse, for example, has noted the ability of ruling elites in liberal capitalist societies to absorb the dissent within the rhetoric of liberalism and thereby blunt the thrust of opposition groups.[20] Gramsci argued that the pervasiveness of elite-serving symbols of meaning prevents the development of a class consciousness necessary for marshalling a social movement of dissent against the authority system of society. This is what he means by his term "hegemony of Western Culture."[21]

Ruling elites may also alter slightly the structure of authority by *co-opting*-members of their opposition into decision-making bodies. While representatives of a dissident group may participate in these bodies, they have relatively little impact on the actual exercise of authority. Alternatively, a third strategy is to define an opposition group as having legitimate grounds for existence. Agreements can then be made on the terms in which conflict is to be expressed. This, in effect, *institutionalizes* conflict, that is, relegates it to specific issues; its form of resolution or attempts at resolution follow well-defined patterns. This approach has evolved in much of the labor-management relations and is formalized in collective bargaining.

On the other hand, opposition groups may simply *withdraw* and set up their own social structures. Attempts by workers to establish their own cooperative enterprises is one example of this response. However, when there is a complete denial by each of the parties in conflict of the other's existence, *repression*, or *revolution*, or both may follow.

Finally, there is always the possibility that the structure of authority will be radically modified to include a greater degree of participation among all parties in decision-making bodies. This, of course, requires a release by elites of their monopoly over power. It is a response not likely to occur without the mobilization of sufficient power by an opposition group or groups.

The Role of Ideology

In arguing that changes are not necessarily smooth, I have perhaps over-dramatized the role of overt conflict. Individuals may also compartmentalize discrepancies, or work out new systems of interpretation designed to maintain some semblance of consistency. For example, the emphasis upon the value of freedom may exacerbate an individual's feelings of failure when he realizes that he may not fulfill the aspirations he once had. Rather than seek rectification by mobilizing support for social change, he may resolve the issue by raising in importance those activities in which he does feel more competent, or he may view himself as virtuous for being a "responsible" person, and identify his rewards as a trouble-free life or eternal life after death.

As for social institutions, individuals may simply redefine them when they are no longer compatible with a changed set of values. One example is the anomaly of a monarchy existing within those countries where the values of freedom and equality are held to be dominant. In Great Britain, for example, there seems to be little reason for the existence of the Royal Family, at least in terms of an earlier day. Viewed historically, the justification for its existence has evolved from outright power to one of authority, then to a symbol of national strength and unity, and finally to its current significance as a symbol of tradition and continuity. It now serves much the same function as a national flag.

In instances of crisis or perceptions of disjunctions between values and authority systems, ideologies may emerge to bridge the gaps. Ideologies can be viewed as those beliefs which provide explanations for the causes of a crisis while offering programs for correction. They are belief systems which attempt to mobilize individuals to attain particular ends. They may be aimed at justifying existing authority systems or they may offer arguments in support of change in these systems. A dramatic instance of the emergence of ideologies, both "reactionary" and "progressive," occurred following the French Revolution. Geertz argues that the reason was "not that either personal insecurity or social disequilibrium were deeper and more pervasive than at many earlier periods—though they were deep and pervasive enough—but because the central organizing principle of political life, the divine right of kings, was destroyed."[22] These ideologies represented attempts to establish another organizing principle and hence to mobilize people to bring about some consistency between values and meanings in structuring their lives. (Of course, it should be recognized that while principles may be articulated in order to mobilize, their continued existence also depends on the success of the mobilization itself.)

The construction and use of ideologies is a common device employed by individuals in positions of authority to justify their right to control or the manner in which they exercise their control. Marx noted that recourse to ideology was a typical, initial response of ruling elites to threats to their authority.

Ideologies are apparent in the efforts made by employers to maintain their own authority within production enterprises. They are also used by leaders of labor movements to bring about change. To be successful in mobilizing individuals, ideologies must incorporate elements of the dominant values and demonstrate how they can be better implemented or at least how they have been violated. The ideology of employers tends to emphasize freedom of individual behavior and to lay stress upon equality of opportunity rather than equality of individuals. Labor leaders who argue for a more radical restructuring of the authority systems emphasize equality of individuals and an ethic of social obligation in carrying out the value of freedom.

Conclusions

This perspective is based on the analyses of Marx and Weber. It also incorporates standard sociological forms of conceptualization, although these have been presented in a different way. I have not made the typical distinction between "culture" and "social structure" because I believe that it has become imprecise and misleading. "Social structure" is usually identified as the relatively stable relationships which exist among the roles that people play. "Culture" tends to be relegated to the position of an ethereal presence of beliefs and values. It is frequently treated as a residual category for explaining the existence and characteristics of social institutions and also behavior. When all else fails, or when there remains more to be accounted for, one can always refer to "the culture." Finally, since interaction itself depends on interpretations and expectations, it is often not clear just what constitutes "culture" and what is to be identified as "structure." Such an approach lacks an account of the structural characteristics of culture itself. Not only is behavior structured in a meaningful way, but so are the evaluations attached to it. It would seem that the term "social structure" is sufficient as a general concept and that the conceptual division of values from meanings and more specifically systems of authority is useful for analytic purposes.

I do not mean to assume an idealistic stance in this perspective, but it must be recognized that values and meanings are the essence of social interaction. Experience is the confirming element in this scheme, but even it must be interpreted. In fact, there is a basic tension in everyday life between the relative importance of "experience" on one hand and its interpretation on the other.

The main point of this chapter is the assertion that transformations of social structures occur in the process of individuals acting out of commitment to, and on the basis of, systems of meanings and values. I then restricted the application of the term "meanings" to authority structures, especially those which Weber defined as "rational." I argued that periods of strain or crisis occur for both individuals and groups when actors become aware of the discrepancies between these structural components. Attempts at resolution may implicate the distribution of *power*. Initial steps in confronting the effects of unequal distribution of power involve a conscious manipulation of beliefs— the use of ideology—to mobilize support for specific programs designed to resolve the crises.

I have dealt primarily with the endogenous nature of change—that processes of change may be found within social structures themselves when these are viewed in relation to acting individuals. I have only alluded to change resulting from the incursion of events from outside specific social structures. When such change occurs, adjustments similar to those I have described are also made.

Notes

1. For other comparisons of Marx and Weber, see Norman Birnbaum, "Conflicting Interpretations of the Rise of Capitalism: Marx and Weber," *British Journal of Sociology*, IV (1953), pp. 125–141; and Anthony Giddens, *Capitalism and Modern Social Theory* (Cambridge: University of Cambridge Press, 1971).

2. For a more complete description of this process, see Peter Berger and Thomas Luckmann, *The Social Construction of Reality* (Garden City, N.Y.: Doubleday, 1966).

3. For a discussion of causes of change see M. Ginsberg, "Social Change," in *Readings in Social Evolution and Development*, ed. S.N. Eisenstadt (London: Pergamon Press, 1970), pp. 37–69. Gunnar Myrdal has chided social scientists for relying too heavily upon static models of social structure and seeking "basic factors" external to these systems in accounting for change. He asks for a more common-sense view of reality, one based upon "dynamic social causation" which is a part of the structure itself. Gunnar Myrdal, "A Methodological Note on the Principle of Cumulation," in *An American Dilemma* (New York: Harper and Row, 1944), pp. 1065–1070.

4. The idea of structure as a construction for the interpretation of events is central in the approach of Schutz. He, in turn, notes the role this plays in the views of Whitehead, William James, Dewey, Bergson, and Husserl. See Alfred Schutz, *The Problem of Social Reality*, in *Collected Papers*, Vol. I, ed. Maurice Natanson (The Hague: Martinus Nijhoff, 1967), pp. 3–7. For a classic statement on "structure" within the discpline of sociology, see S.F. Nadel, *The Theory of Social Structure* (New York: Free Press, 1957).

5. See Jean Piaget, *The Construction of Reality in the Child*, trans. Margaret Cook (New York: Basic Books, 1954). Piaget stresses the active role of the child as he transforms "chaos into cosmos." (p. xiii.) In their commentary on Piaget, Gruber and Vonèche note that intelligence for Piaget begins with the knowledge of the *interaction* between the self and things. This means that each child must invent his own structure by which he relates himself to the world. See Howard E. Gruber and J. Jacques Vonèche, eds., *The Essential Piaget* (London: Routledge and Kegan Paul, 1977), p. xxxiii.

6. This is not to suggest some Platonistic idealism. The existing structures are also of the child's own making—of elements which he recreates for himself.

7. Jean Piaget, *Structuralism*, trans. and ed. Chaninah Maschler (New York: Basic Books, 1970), p. 71.

8. Gruber and Vonèche, op. cit., p. xxviii.

9. Piaget, *Structuralism*, op. cit., p. 119.

10. Jean Piaget, *Genetic Epistemology*, trans. Eleanor Duckworth (New York: Columbia University Press, 1970), p. 77.

11. For an excellent statement of the dilemmas involved in conceptualizing these processes, see Anthony Giddens, *New Rules of Sociological Method* (London: Hutchinson, 1976). Giddens uses the concept of "structuration" to attempt to deal with one aspect of these processes. The role of holistic structures is central to the perspectives of Lévi-Strauss and also of Louis Althusser. For an informative analysis of the two, see Miriam Glucksmann, *Structuralist Analysis in Contemporary Social Thought: A Comparison of the Theories of Claude Lévi-Strauss and Louis Althusser* (London: Routledge and Kegan Paul, 1974).

   Runciman argues in favor of Piaget's approach since, in contrast to Lévi-Strauss, Piaget has an epistemology outside the "system" itself which in turn is isomorphic to the system. The approach of Lévi-Strauss objectifies the structural nature of experience and its interpretation, while neglecting the manner in which the actor incorporates and reproduces the structure within his own experience. See W.G. Runciman, "What is Structuralism?" *British Journal of Sociology,* XX (1969), pp. 253–265.

12. Walter Buckley, *Sociology and Modern Systems Theory* (Englewood Cliffs, N.J.: Prentice-Hall, 1967), pp. 58–62. Etzioni refers to a similar process which he calls "epigenesis." But both his and Buckley's term refer to the generation of new behavior patterns. What I mean to convey is the idea that not only can actors generate new patterns of behavior, but that they also generate revisions and modifications of the meanings assigned to the same behavior. See Amitai Etzioni, *Studies in Social Change* (New York: Holt, Rinehart and Winston, 1966), pp. 2–3, 50–57.

13. Neil Smelser, *Essays in Sociological Explanation* (Englewood Cliffs, N.J.: Prentice-Hall, 1968), pp. 210–211.

14. David S. Landes, *The Unbound Prometheus* (Cambridge: Cambridge University Press, 1969).

15. Neil Smelser, "Toward a Theory of Modernization," in *Social Change: Sources, Patterns and Consequences,* ed. Amitai Etzioni and Eva Etzioni (New York: Basic Books, 1964), pp. 264–265.

16. T.S. Kuhn, *The Structure of Science Revolutions* (Chicago: University of Chicago Press, 1968).

17. Peter Winch, *The Idea of a Social Science* (London: Routledge and Kegan Paul, 1958), p. 63.

18. There is another variation to this assertion. Durkheim once noted that, "a (social) fact can exist without being at all useful either because it has never been adjusted to any vital end or because after having been useful it has lost all utility while continuing to exist by the inertia of habit alone." Emile Durkheim, *The Rules of Sociological Method,* trans. Sara Solovay and John Mueller, and ed. George Catlin (New York: The Free Press, 1964), p. 91. For a somewhat similar formulation of the perspective presented here, see Chalmers Johnson, *Revolutionary Change* (Boston: Little, Brown, 1966).

19. Several ambiguities remain in these analyses, however. First, it is not clear just what constitutes an authentic constituency of the "larger society." Second, it is not clear just what is expected of elites. Third, it is not clear what constitutes a legitimate set of criteria for assessing candidates to elite positions. For classic studies of Canadian elites see John Porter, *The Vertical Mosaic: An Analysis of Social Class and Power in Canada* (Toronto: University of Toronto Press, 1965); Wallace Clement, *The Canadian Corporate Elite: An Analysis of Economic Power* (Toronto: McClelland and Stewart, Carleton Library, 1975); Wallace Clement, *Continental Corporate Power: Economic Linkages between Canada and the United States* (Toronto: McClelland and Stewart, 1977).

20. Herbert Marcuse, "Repressive Tolerance," in *A Critique of Pure Tolerance,* ed. Robert Wolff, Barrington Moor, Jr., and Herbert Marcuse (Boston: Beacon Press, 1968), pp. 81–123.

21. Quintin Hoare and Geoffrey N. Smith, eds. and trans., *Selections from the Prison Notebooks of Antonio Gramsci* (London: Lawrence and Wishart, 1971), pp. 416–418.

22. Clifford Geertz, "Ideology as a Cultural System," in Geertz, *The Interpretation of Cultures* (New York: Basic Books, 1973), pp. 219–220.

Part Two

Changing Industrial Structures in Canada

chapter four

Patterns of Change in the Economic Development of Canada

Introduction

In dealing with the economic development in Canada, it is first necessary to take into account Canada's initial status as a colony and then to trace her emergence as an autonomous political entity. The thesis of this chapter is that these processes rest upon the responses of leaders, or power elites, to paradoxes and crises.[1] These, in turn, are the consequences of the cumulative effects of actions as they are carried out in a socially structured manner through systems of authority. Stated more concretely, this chapter is concerned with selected aspects of the industrialization of Canada. It argues that the unique attributes of this development can be assigned to two interrelated processes: (1) the relatively enduring influence of Canada's colonial status and the mercantilist orientation of its elites, and (2) the resulting responses of the power elites to economic and political crises.

The emphasis here is on very broad processes, especially as these influenced the development of different production sectors in Canada's economy. It is designed to provide an historical background for the analyses of more specific concerns to be treated in the chapters to follow.

The Influence of Mercantilism

Industrial capitalism did not arrive on the social scene in a clearly formulated manner. Historical antecedents always influence present realities and this has been the case with the various patterns of industrialization. Canada's status as a colony, first of France, then of England, has had a strong effect on the course of her economic development. Her role as a colony can best be seen within the context of those economic politics frequently grouped together under the term "mercantilism." The term is often used to describe the dynamics of the economies in Western Europe during the period from the early sixteenth century to about the middle or late eighteenth century. During this period, relatively strong, autonomous nation-states emerged, long-distance trade increased, as did the use of money for exchange, overseas colonies were acquired, and the economic wealth of the nation-states increased.

Mercantilism was a loosely organized set of ideas that fused images of political power with economic wealth. Although the policies of gaining wealth differed greatly among countries like Spain and Portugal, Holland, and France and England, there was one guiding motive for all of them—the building and strengthening of the nation-state. Yet this nation-building did not emanate from popular movements, but rather served the interests of ruling, feuding elites, whether these were royalty or commercial entrepreneurs.[3]

Mercantilism was a form of what is now termed "political economy" which employed economic practices as a means to pursue political power. It provided a relatively clear definition of power, as long as wealth remained seen as a fixed commodity to be controlled rather than created. Power was based upon the control of wealth—preferably the control of gold because of its potential to buy off enemies and to mount armies. Spain and Portugal gained their power by seizing gold from South America. Failing the outright control of gold, France and England attempted to acquire wealth by the sale of other desirable commodities. In this competition for power, it was to the advantage of the elites of a nation-state to maintain as huge a surplus of exports over imports as possible and to minimize the costs of imports.[4]

While the idea remained that wealth was finite, the attempt to increase the control of wealth stimulated commercial activities designed to ultimately trade commodities for gold. Such an orientation stimulated the growth of colonial empires, since colonies furnished cheap resources and assured the mother country of the monopolistic control of the resources' sale and conversion into marketable commodities[6]. Controlling elites encouraged settlement in the colonies only if it contributed to the flow of these resources to the "mother-country." England and France both exploited the fishing areas off the coast of Newfoundland in the mid-seventeenth century, and both countries discouraged settlement on the island. On the continent, France developed the fur trade, which was later taken over by the British following their conquest in 1759.

England pursued a policy that eventually broke the monopolistic hold of Holland over shipping and commerce and resulted in the production of commodities which could be exchanged for gold or the promise of gold—money. Initially, the emphasis was on producing commodities which required a minimum amount of investment in the translation from resource to finished product. Canada as a colony of England was an important source of fish, furs, and later, timber and agricultural products. It served this function until well after England had passed from Mercantilism to Industrial Capitalism.

What is important about Canada's role as a colony is that its economic infrastructure was geared toward furnishing raw materials and staple products to the "home countries" of France, and then of England. This retarded the development of a manufacturing sector and cast Canada's history of industrialization into a unique mold. In contrast, the commitment of England to mercantilist policies acted ultimately as a *stimulant* for the development of a firm industrial base, because processing for further sale of commodities was done there. Canada's economy was geared toward the sale of resources; England's evolved into an economy of manufacturing and commerce.

Behind its political-economic aims, mercantilism rested upon a moral order that stressed the value of social distinctions and the unquestioned legitimacy of ruling elites. In contrast, the process of industrialization destroyed the supports for this value as skills and expertise came to be valued regardless of the social origins of those who possessed them. Since within this context wealth is seen as something to create rather than merely to control, the moral basis of industrialization came to stress the values of freedom and equality rather than obedience and security.

In Canada, the economic infrastructure inherent in her status as a colony continued until well after Great Britain severed its protective ties. This served to sustain a mercantilist oriented elite who, in turn, made decisions that influenced the course of Canada's industrialization. This influence requires further examination.

Mercantilism and the Export of Staples

A major consequence of Canada's role as a colony was the development of an economy heavily dependent on the sale of "staples." Staples are commodities which are largely resource-based, requiring little labor in their preparation for sale. Their development does not depend upon the more complicated organizational and technological needs of manufacturing. Thus, they are attractive areas for investment since they can net relatively quick returns. Earnings are derived principally from transportation and servicing charges, rather than from the preparation of the products themselves.

Colonial Canada enjoyed secure trade arrangements with England through trade of these commodities. When Balkan timber supplies for Britain were threatened during the Napoleonic Wars, timber became a dominant income-earning staple. Later, agricultural products, especially wheat, became of principal importance. Those who gained economic dominance within Canada as a result of this trade were the English-speaking merchants in Montreal who made up the "Chateau Clique" and those merchants who made up the "Family Compact" in Upper Canada. These metropolitan elites controlled the production and sale of staples from the hinterland of Canada to Great Britain.

The trade in partially finished goods has continued.[5] The role which staples have played in the economic development of Canada has been an issue of considerable academic debate, centering on the degree to which this trade stimulates demand for commodities requiring the development of manufacturing sectors. The "staples thesis" of economic development argues that manufacturing sectors will be stimulated as staples production generates an increase in the labor force, thus stimulating consumer needs, and, as more technical means are employed in extracting staples, requiring the manufacture of machinery. But the more important issue is where these developments will take place: whether the manufactured goods will be produced within the same country producing the staples or whether the staples will be exchanged for foreign-made machinery.[6] In Canada, the latter pattern has been more predominant owing to her former status as a colony, then to her response to the demands for her resources from the manufacturing sectors in Great Britain and then in the United States. Throughout her history, natural resources and partially fabricated goods have accounted for a higher proportion of Canada's exports than has been the case for most other industrialized countries.[7]

A Challenge to the Canadian Mercantile Elites

Under the mercantilistic policies of Great Britain, the Canadian colonies enjoyed a thriving trade within the confines of preferential trade agreements with Britain. Not only had the colonies experienced considerable economic growth, but they had also absorbed some 800 000 immigrants from the British Isles between 1815 and 1850. However, during this period of time, the government of the United Province of Canada, a union of Lower Canada (Quebec) and Upper Canada (Ontario), grew increasingly apprehensive over the intentions of the United States. Government and economic elites were further concerned with the growing political restiveness of farmers and small businessmen, of some professionals, and of French Canadians throughout the occupational spectrum. All these groups sought to break the tight political control of the merchant elites.

More importantly, a fundamental split was developing between the elites and the small producers and farmers. The elites sought to maintain their positions of power by both political and economic means. However, the economic structure was changing from one based on the export of low investment staples, such as timber, to one requiring higher capital investment, such as wheat farming. As cash crop producers, wheat farmers resented the control of the Montreal elite. One illustration of this control was the fact that Montreal merchants levied high duties on imports, only one fifth of which was regained by the population in Upper Canada. The strains inherent in the movement toward higher investment staples contributed to the violent revolts in 1837 in both Lower and Upper Canada. A rising class of small producers was confronting an elite who had gained and maintained their power by monopolistic control over trade; producers were contesting the power of brokers.

The precipitating causes of the rebellions of 1837 were as follows: (a) land grant policies which were blatantly designed to maintain the power of the elites; (b) demands to eliminate political privileges based upon economic position; (c) demands to end the control of the executive power in governance by the merchant elites; (d) a protest against collusions between state and church; and finally, (e) opposition to restrictions by powerful banking interests of credit facilities for small businessmen. Mackenzie in Upper Canada argued for a political solution based upon the American model of Republicanism. Papineau in Lower Canada sought to break the alliance between the Catholic clergy and French-Canadian public officials with the English-dominated Château Clique. The final catalyst which led to the revolts was the international depression of 1837, which saw economic collapse in the United States, curtailment of trade with England, and crop failures in Canada.[8]

The rebellions failed in part because of their lack of organization, but also because of the nature of choices projected to the larger populace by the elites. They were images of the extremes of a secular republicanism of Andrew Jackson to the south, versus the "stable" policies of the mercantilist elites in the provinces of Canada. An elite-dominated conservatism may delimit freedoms, but it does provide security and orderliness which were not at all apparent in the experience of the United States.[9]

The rebellions are significant in that they represent the first dramatic threat to the power of the elites. The elites gave little thought to the significance of the development of productive enterprises and markets for manufactured goods within Canada until relatively late. They apparently saw the implications of the growing development of industrialization in Great Britain, and later in the United States, only in terms of providing markets for low-cost staples. Such an assumption was reinforced by the easy access to natural resources and the easy access to British and American markets. The chief concerns were not with manufacturing goods, but with devising better means for obtaining and transporting goods requiring little processing.

Great Britain's Withdrawal from Preferential Trade Agreements

England had long been committed to expanding her trade, first as a means to dislodge Holland from her pre-eminent position in the seventeenth century, then, with Holland's defeat, as a means to maintain her power. The key agents in this process were the merchants, whose commitment to trade and commerce paradoxically resulted in the growth and development of industrialization. Paul Mantoux has explained this process as follows:

> Those capitalists who gained so much from the gradual concentration of the means of production were hardly industrialists. They gladly left to the small producer, gradually bereft of his independence, all the care of manufacture. They did not undertake either to improve or to direct it. They were solely merchants, and industry for them was only a form of trade. They cared for one thing only, commercial profit; the gain which resulted from the difference between the buying and selling prices. And it was only in order to increase this difference, to economize on the buying price, that they became owners first of the material, then of the implements, then of the workplaces. And it was as merchants that they were finally brought to take entire charge of production.[10]

By the early nineteenth century, the protective laws governing mercantilistic trade proved to be counterproductive to the expansion of industries. The issue was no longer protecting sources of supply for resale, but finding markets wherever they existed for commodities manufactured within England. The creation of wealth by manufacture can be seen as an evolving consequence of the commitment to mercantilistic trade. But its effects represent a significant departure from the idea of discovering and controlling the world's store of wealth.

Viewed in terms of the analytic perspective of Chapter 3, this shift represents an undermining of the values associated with mercantilism even as its aims were being sought. England did not have easy access to natural resources. Her power could be sustained only by the use of cheap labor in transforming natural resources from the colonies into manufactured goods. But political agreements with the colonies could be relatively costly if resources could be more cheaply obtained from other areas.

During this period, English classical economists rejected mercantilism on economic grounds. They argued that wealth created through manufacture has little to do with the governments of nation-states per se. They further argued that production, stimulated by individual initiative, creates greater benefits for the state while increasing the wealth of its citizens. They maintained that the allocation of resources in accordance with comparative costs would maximize aggregate output, and that individuals acting in a free and open competitive market would automatically conform to this principle of efficient resource allocation. Far from requiring the protection of governments, manufacture, if it were to be sustained, needed the continual goad of competition to generate wealth for the nation. It is no mere accident that the values of freedom and equality were being advanced at the same time.

This doctrine, whose most articulate spokesman was Adam Smith, made considerable sense in a world where England was the dominant and unchallenged manufacturing country, where labor was seen as a valuable resource in the manufacture of goods, and where manufacturers sought additional markets for their products.

The effects of this new definition of wealth caused Britain to vacillate for several years in her trade policies with Canada. Then, in 1846 she revoked her protective trade agreements with her colonies and Canada lost her preferential status. Britain, as the dominant manufacturing country, now sought markets and trade regardless of her political ties. In Donald Creighton's view, "the (British) interests of industrial specialization at home and world trade abroad, had sacrificed both the agriculture of Great Britain and the commerce of British North America."[11] Britain recalled nearly all her troops from Canada, withdrew her colonial preferences in trade, and abandoned her colonial obligations. In effect, she shifted away from her past political ties to her colonies as she redefined their political role.[12]

The consequence of this shift in policy was of profound importance for both Lower and Upper Canada. An entire economic structure had been built along an east-west axis along the St. Lawrence Valley. The competition between Montreal and the American port cities had been intense. Montreal merchants had invested heavily in a canal system to offset the American Erie canal as a major trade route. Yet as they finished the St. Lawrence and Welland canals, the United States was already shifting to faster railroads.[13]

Further, Montreal was handicapped by higher costs in insurance and pilotage rates, and by a limited shipping season in comparison to ports farther south. New York was gaining ground as a major terminus for trade, for its merchants could offer easier terms of credit as markets grew within the country. Ships arriving in New York could carry pay loads of cargo, while ships arriving in Montreal carried mainly ballast, since interior markets for finished products were not sufficiently developed for trade inland.[14] When the preferential trade agreements with Great Britain that provided an advantage for the British colonies were revoked, the foundation for the economic policy of Upper and Lower Canada had been lost.

In addition to this setback, the United States enacted legislation that permitted grain from Upper Canada to be shipped in bond across American transportation routes without requiring Canadian shippers to pay American import duty. This further increased the flow of goods southward. The Montreal merchants were now in danger of losing their control of trade in staples coming from the hinterland of Upper Canada. Further, the farmers in Upper Canada had excellent wheat harvests in 1847, 1848, and 1849. The northern United States had grown sufficiently industrialized to provide markets for these products. Eastern farmers had similarly found United States markets for oats, barley, poultry, eggs, and butter. This meant that exports were no longer directed only to Great Britain through the United States, but were also consumed in the United States.

As the east-west axis of trade started changing to a north-south direction, the English merchants of Montreal saw their entire economic program fall into disarray: prices fell, credit became tighter, and bankruptcies occurred. The merchants also feared becoming isolated within a predominantly French-Canadian community. As Easterbrook and Aitken pointed out, the merchants saw themselves as abandoned after Britain had "knocked out the keystone of the imperial trading system."[15]

Many of these merchants who had competed so vigorously against American interests sought annexation with the United States in 1849. It was an act obviously prompted by self-interest and self-preservation. However, this movement was relatively short-lived, in part because of a fear of the excesses of American republicanism. There was also a growing belief that if an internal market could be developed, Canada would not remain so dependent on foreign markets. In the meantime, Canadian merchants sought to develop greater access to American markets.

Uncertain Dependence on American Markets

Having lost their trade advantages with Great Britain, Canadian merchants turned to developing favorable trade relations with the United States. The earlier isolation of the United States (first caused by the American Revolution, then continued by the War with Britain in 1812) increased the impetus toward the development of its manufacturing sector. This meant that for Canada, there was a ready market for its natural resources and semi-finished goods.

In 1854 a ten-year treaty of trade reciprocity was signed. As a result of this agreement, coastal fisheries were opened up to both countries, American import duties were abolished on a large number of natural products coming in from Canada, American vessels were permitted on the St. Lawrence River and on Canadian canals under the same terms as British and colonial vessels, and Canadian vessels had equal rights with American vessels on Lake Michigan.

During the period of these agreements, Canadian commercial interests and the government of the United Provinces were rushing to complete the railroad line linking Sarnia with Montreal. Because there were severe problems in financing the railroad, the government raised its tariffs on imported American manufactured goods by 15 percent in 1856 and by another 20 percent in 1859. Technically, this did not violate the previous trade agreement, but it severely displeased the Americans. The tariffs were initially designed to provide added revenue for the costs of the railroad expansion, since outright taxation would have been politically unwise. While these tariffs may have also encouraged the expansion of Canadian manufacturing interests, this was not of primary concern at that time.

The new tariffs, as well as the anti-British sentiment in the Northern United States during the Civil War, and the apprehension of American business groups in New York, Philadelphia and Buffalo toward the growing traffic down the St. Lawrence valley, led the United States Government to declare in 1865 that the Reciprocity Treaty would be terminated in the following year. Again, the economic viability of the settlements in Canada was in question. The United States, emerging from its Civil War as a nation committed to industrialization and expansion, became not only an economic but also a political threat to their survival. The United States seemed bent upon controlling not only manufacturing but also the supply of natural resources.

In an effort to stem these threats, the Province of Canada, New Brunswick and Nova Scotia formed a confederation under the British North America Act in 1867. A parliamentary system of government was designed which preserved French representation. The union itself was fully supported by Great Britain who was eager to avoid the costs of administering colonies and whose investors were eager to bring about a more secure political climate.

Manitoba entered Confederation in 1870 with guarantees of equality of French and English as official languages and the provision for both Protestant and Roman Catholic schools. Ungranted lands were to be administered by the federal government. In 1871 British Columbia was induced to join the union with the promise that the federal government would assume its debts and that it would be linked to the east by a transcontinental railway.

The uncertain trade arrangements with the United States and growing apprehensions over its expansionist designs in the west prompted both government and economic elites to support a transcontinental railway. By 1878, however, there had been five years of economic slowdown and any hopes for free trade agreements with the United States had been blocked by the United States Senate in 1874. Farmers and dealers in staples were especially hard hit by these developments. The economic depression had also resulted in idle factories within the small manufacturing sector that had evolved in Canada.

Small manufacturers supported a renewed tariff structure as a protective wall behind which unused manufacturing capacity could be employed and which would encourage the expansion of the sector. Bankers, dealers in the staples trade, and investors came to support a tariff structure because it was a means to generate revenue for the transcontinental railroad. The railroad, they hoped, would facilitate shipments of wheat from the prairie provinces, create expanded internal markets, and thereby serve as a primary source of revenue from haulage rates.

Transportation links with the West represented a continuation of investment policies whose pattern was first set by mercantile elites. For example, R. T. Naylor argues that banking interests preferred to invest in short-term, three-month loans to agricultural interests in the western provinces rather than longer term, more uncertain investments in fledgling industrial enterprises. There is some evidence to support the view that this pattern of priorities played a dominant role in draining capital from the once-prosperous Maritimes and depriving it of what otherwise may have been a firm manufacturing base.[16]

What apparently was not fully understood at this time was the long-range importance of developing an indigenous manufacturing sector free from foreign control. Rather, the early policy decisions reduced manufacturing to secondary importance—important only insofar as it supported the expansion of trade in natural resources and staples. Meanwhile governments, both at the federal and provincial levels, collaborated with these interests in order to encourage economic growth and to derive political security from American expansion.

Problems of Political and Economic Viability

As part of its platform in the election of 1878, the Conservative Party included a "national policy" designed to appeal to the diverse interests within Canada. It included selected increases in tariffs, completion of the transcontinental railway, and encouragement of western settlement. After MacDonald was returned to office, the policy was put into effect in 1879: the government embarked upon a program of granting land to railway construction companies and to immigrant settlers, and also encouraged capital investment in manufacturing enterprises. Grain farmers never fully supported the tariffs since they served to raise the cost of transport and jeopardized direct access to American markets.

The logic of the National Policy was that tariffs were necessary to raise revenue for the railroads and to stimulate industrialization. Manufacturing enterprises had been developing slowly until the beginning of the depression in 1873, which was to last until 1895. Supporters of the tariffs hoped that Canadian manufacturing would be protected from the competitive threats of more advanced industrial interests in both the United States and Great Britain. It was further hoped that by increasing demands for an industrial labor force, the flow of emigrants to the south would be reduced.

Proponents of the policy also argued that western settlement was necessary in order to create an internal market for manufactures and to provide for further expansion in the export of wheat and flour coming out of the West. Finally, nationalist supporters saw the railway as a political necessity—a means to unify the country and to assure political autonomy by increasing economic self-sufficiency.

The economic significance of the National Policy has been a source of continuing debate. Except for the development of steel production, stimulated primarily by railroad requirements, and the manufacture of farm implements, the overall benefits of the tariffs remain questionable. It was not until 1896 that significant advances were made in the manufacturing sectors of capital equipment, consumer goods, and the processing of natural products.[17] It may well be that the effects of the tariffs upon the manufacturing sectors were both mild and delayed primarily because the financial interests failed to shift the pattern of their investments from staples and resource related industries to the higher risk enterprises in manufacturing.

The transcontinental Canadian Pacific Railroad was completed in 1885. But the period of large scale immigration did not occur for another sixteen years. It appears that land settlements were not due to the railroad as such, but rather to an acceleration of industrialization in Europe, which in turn created increased demands for foodstuffs from North America, the decline of farm land available in western United States, and the development of a hardier, high-yield wheat strain. Government subsidies of transportation rates provided an additional incentive. The railroad itself facilitated settlement, but it was not a major cause. During the period from 1901 to 1911, the population of the prairie provinces increased from 420 000 to 1 300 000. Improved acreage quadrupled from 5 600 000 to 23 000 000 acres.[18]

Critics have pointed out that the tariffs contributed to regional inequities in economic growth and merely supported too many inefficient enterprises within a limited market.[19] They have also noted that while the gross national product rose, the per capita standard of living actually fell because of higher costs of domestic production.[20] Finally, all analysts agree that the tariffs set the stage for a "branch plant" economy, as foreign producers set up their own plants in Canada in order to escape the marketing costs imposed by the tariffs.[21] There was little attempt to control the ownership of these enterprises. The only concern seemed to be the unification of the Canadian economy in the interests of elites who were following a course of "finance" capitalism rather than "industrial" capitalism. In any event, it is likely that the general upswing in the world economy at the turn of the century and the later demands of the First World War played a more important role in Canada's economic growth and in the expansion of manufacturing enterprises.[22]

The use of tariffs to foster industrialization has not been unique to Canada. Both the United States and Germany had used them to compete with the industrial might of Great Britain. But Canada differed in the greater degree to which her governments—local, provincial and federal—permitted and actively encouraged foreign control of her fledgling industrial enterprises.[23] Canadian financial institutions continued to show relatively little interest in investing in the manufacturing sectors. Foreign money, first British, then American, was more likely to finance these enterprises.

Patterns of Economic Development

The sequence of decisions made by Canadian economic and political elites set the stage for further developments following the end of the nineteenth century. The influence of mercantilism, the easy access to natural resources, and the relatively easy access to markets provided the power base for these elites. The shift to manufacturing was only reluctantly supported, the implications of foreign ownership only dimly perceived. But the effects of these factors upon Canada's economic development and pattern of industrialization were profound.

Of course, by the mid-nineteenth century, one could not speak of the practice of mercantilism in the same terms as in the mid-eighteenth century. What remained dominant in the actions of the economic elites in Canada, whether they were the middle-men in the sale of staples or the merchants of resources for manufacturing, was their orientation toward economic activity. They sold their goods wherever there were markets and these markets were to be found in those countries which already had highly developed manufacturing sectors. As manufacturing increased in importance in the world economy, the role and nature of the Canadian economy also shifted. (These shifts are most apparent in Canada's sectoral developments, in its organization for production, in its regional variations and in government participation.)

In tracing the patterns of development of Canada's economy, a distinction should be made between "economic growth" and "economic development." Economic growth, in the most general sense, simply means the increase of total production over time. It says nothing about the pattern of growth or the economic standard of living. For example, a particular country may become extremely wealthy merely on the basis of exports of natural resources. The economic standard of living may remain low if that income is monopolized by a few individuals. Kuwait may have the highest per capita income in the world, but its wealth is far from being equally shared among its population.

Economic development has to do with the pattern of industrialization. This, in turn, suggests structural transformations within a given society. More concretely, it suggests processes leading to the development of a viable and self-perpetuating manufacturing sector and a further development of a service sector supporting and being supported by manufacturing. The term "economic development" has some difficulties because it implies an evolutionary scheme leading to a final stage of an "industrialized society."[24] It remains unclear just precisely what attributes define an "industrialized society." My concern is to trace the change in the *structure* of the Canadian economy without implying a universally standardized model of development.

In order to provide a context for interpretation, I shall first describe Canada's population growth patterns, then describe her economic growth, followed by an analysis of sectoral shifts, size of production units, concentration, regional variations, and government involvement.

TABLE 1 Canadian Population Growth, 1851–1976

Years	Natural Increase		Net Migration		Population at end of period x 1000	Total Increase	
	Number x 1000	Percent[a] per annum	Number x 1000	Percent[a] per annum		Number x 1000	Percent[a] per annum
1851–1861	611	2.16	182	0.64	3 230	794	2.82
1861–1871	610	1.76	−150	−0.43	3 689	459	1.33
1871–1881	690	1.72	− 54	−0.13	4 325	636	1.59
1881–1891	654	1.43	−146	−0.32	4 833	508	1.11
1891–1901	668	1.31	−130	−0.25	5 371	538	1.05
1901–1911	1 025	1.63	810	1.29	7 207	1 836	2.92
1911–1921	1 270	1.59	311	0.39	8 788	1 581	1.98
1921–1931	1 360	1.42	230	0.24	10 377	1 589	1.66
1931–1941	1 222	1.12	− 92	−0.08	11 507	1 130	1.03
1941–1951[b]	1 992	1.56	166	0.13	13 648	2 503	1.96
1951–1961	3 148	1.95	1 080	0.67	18 238	4 229	2.62
1961–1971	2 608	1.31	772	0.39	21 568	3 330	2.12
1971–1976	933	−.70	492	0.37	22 993	1 425	1.07

[a] Percentages based on average of population at beginning and end of periods.
[b] Includes Newfoundland in 1951 but not in 1941.

Sources: *Canada Year Book, 1975* (Ottawa: Statistics Canada, 1976) Tables 4.1, 4.2, *Canadian Statistical Review, September 1977* (Ottawa: Statistics Canada, 1977), Section 2, Tables 2, 5, 6.

Population Growth Patterns

Table 1 indicates the patterns of growth in the population of Canada from 1851 to 1976. The total rate of increase for each of the decades ranges from 10.3 percent to 29.2 percent. Most of these increases were due to natural factors—greater birth rates in comparison to death rates.

Immigration rates have varied considerably and have often been offset by relatively high rates of emigration. Thus, the next immigration figures have varied from losses during the period 1861 to 1901 and 1931 to 1941 to relatively high gains during the period 1901 to 1911. In general, emigration rates have tended to increase when immigration rates increased. Except for the economic expansionary period from 1901 to 1911, immigration has contributed very little to the population increase. During the period from 1851 to 1950, there was a total immigration of 7 790 000 persons. Yet, 7 260 000 persons emigrated out of the country.[25]

It is likely that the factors accounting for the high emigration rates were the severe geographic and climatic conditions of Canada, the relatively cheap western land in the United States which was available until the end of the last century, the attraction to urban centers in the United States in which per capita income was considerably higher than in Canada, and also the more favorable employment opportunities for skilled and semi-skilled persons in the United States' urban areas.[26]

Patterns of Economic Growth

While the Canadian population has doubled approximately every forty years since Confederation, production has, in approximate terms, quadrupled. (The average rate of increase of the Gross National Product has been a little over 3 percent per year since 1867.)[27] There has been an increase of approximately 1.65 percent per year of actual goods and services that are available to each person. Or, stated in a different way, per capita availability of goods and services has doubled approximately every forty years.[28]

The pattern of growth has not been a steady, continual year-by-year increase. Rather, there have been periods of expansion and contraction. A period of slow growth occurred from the time of Confederation to 1896. Between 1896 to 1913 there was a pronounced expansion. Growth continued less spectacularly until 1921 and became virtually non-existent during the Depression in the 1930s. The Second World War brought an upsurge in the economy which then declined after the war. Then, in 1950 to 1956, the economy again expanded, only to be followed by five years of stagnation until the recovery in 1962 which continued, with the exception of a drop in 1970, until about 1974. Currently, the economy is relatively stagnant.

During the period from 1896 to the First World War, growth in the Canadian economy was mainly due to the development of internal markets. The First World War stimulated the development of the manufacturing sector, but after the war foreign demands for natural resources and energy and semi-finished products altered the course of growth.

During the First World War, the steel industry grew to such an extent that little change in capacity occurred until the outbreak of the Second World War.[29] It was also during the First World War that refining capacities were developed for copper, zinc, and magnesium. Shipbuilding also expanded during this time and an aircraft industry was started. Meanwhile, the pulp and paper industry grew to become a dominant sector after supplies in the United States became depleted as early as 1910. Up to the 1930s transportation services expanded, mineral products were further developed, and chemical and allied products took on major importance in the economy.

The Depression in the 1930s dramatically retarded the growth rates in the manufacturing sector, but with the Second World War and the conversion to war production, this sector and allied industries again increased in relative importance. Between 1939 and 1943, the output of steel increased by 120 percent and the production of aluminium increased by 500 percent.[30]

Since the 1950s there has been a demand in the foreign market for Canada's energy resources, especially oil and natural gas. In addition, there have been increased demands for iron ore and non-ferrous metals. These developments have stimulated the manufacture of extracting, refining, and transport equipment, but the main effect has been an unusually strong dependence on the export of raw materials and semi-finished products in exchange for finished products.

A major factor accounting for this development has been Canada's heavy reliance on trade with the United States. While Great Britain declined in importance as a major trading partner after Confederation, the United States increased in importance. As early as the 1890s it took over Great Britain's dominant position. In 1974 the United States was responsible for roughly 68 percent of Canada's imports and 65 percent of Canada's exports.

In 1976 Canada had a $11 billion trade deficit in end products. Imports accounted for 40 percent of the domestic market for high technology industries. Imports of machinery alone accounted for 71 percent of the domestic market, while domestic production of machinery accounted for 51 percent of the total production of machinery (this includes production for export). Imports of "low technology" industries (these include industries such as food and beverages, textiles, furniture and fixtures, and paper and allied products) accounted for only 17.4 percent of the Canadian market in 1976. Clearly, Canada has remained heavily dependent on imports of more complex manufactured products, while its wealth has been earned primarily from the sale of natural resources and semi-finished goods.

These data suggest that the manufacturing sector in Canada has not developed a strong enough base that would permit manufacturing enterprises to play a more significant role in both internal and global markets. Were it to do so, it would be less dependent on the vagaries of American and world demands for materials and semi-finished products. This, as well as the high degree of foreign control of crucial resource and production industries, makes Canada unusually vulnerable to the dictates of relatively few foreign interests.

In 1977 the Science Council Committee on Industrial Policies expressed its concern over the implications of the relatively underdeveloped manufacturing sector. Its report points out that during the 1960s, a period of economic expansion, "few countries (except in the Third World) did as badly as Canada in raising the proportion of finished manufactures in their exports."[32] Natural resources, partially finished goods, and products requiring a low level of technology constituted the major share of earnings. The report, basing its measure of industrialization upon a previous study in which the "value of manufactures per capita" is employed along with the "value of finished manufactures," finds Canada barely able to qualify among the group of industrialized countries. If automobile exports were removed, it would remain with Australia and New Zealand as "prosperous, primary producing" countries.[33] But it would not be included among the group of major industrialized countries such as Japan, France, West Germany, or the United States. Even when the auto industry is included, the manufacturing sector still accounts for one of the smallest proportions of total exports in comparison to most West European countries and Japan.[34]

Foreign trade plays a significant role in the economies of most countries. In 1975 exports contributed 20.8 percent to the Gross Domestic Product of Canada. In comparison, exports contributed 19.2 percent to the Gross Domestic Product of Great Britain, 21.3 percent to West Germany, 16.0 percent to France and 11.4 percent to Japan. For the United States, exports accounted for only 7.2 percent of its Gross Domestic Product.[35] A relatively large domestic market for a diverse range of goods and a highly developed manufacturing sector tend to reduce the role which exports play in the overall output of domestic economies.

Throughout the history of Canada's economic development the question has continually been raised: Why couldn't the entire process of natural resource extraction and high technology manufacture have been developed more fully within Canada? It would appear that the influence of mercantilism provided the dominant framework for crucial decisions which directed the course of development. Given the faster returns on investments in primary rather than in high technology industries, as well as the immense resource requirements of already industrialized societies, especially the United States, it was financially more attractive to export these commodities rather than incur the costs and reduced rates of immediate return which would result from developing Canada's own manufacturing sector.

Shifts Among Production Sectors

Viewed in aggregate terms, Canada has followed the shifts in sectoral development characteristic of other industrialized societies, but the development within each sector has remained unique. Further, the shifts, both in terms of proportion of labor employed and in value of production, are also due to characteristics unique to Canada. Typically, the economies of industrialized societies have been divided into three major sectors: "primary," which includes agriculture, fishing and mining; "secondary," involving manufacturing and construction; and "tertiary," which represents a wide range of industries including public utilities, government services, and such industries as financial institutions, tourism, retail outlets, counseling services, advertising agencies, and all other activities which produce services rather than goods.[36] In the process of industrialization the secondary and tertiary sectors expand at the expense of the primary sector.

In Canada, the primary sector has played a dominant role somewhat longer than has been the case in other industrialized societies. In England, the proportion of the labor force engaged in agriculture, forestry, and fishing declined to less than 50 percent by 1841. Conversely, the proportion in manufacturing and especially service or tertiary industries increased. This shift occurred in France by 1866, in Germany by 1870, and in the United States by 1880.[37] In Canada, this change did not occur until after 1891. However, goods-producing industries have never claimed more than a third of the labor force, one of the lowest proportions among the industrialized countries. Further, Canada's manufacturing output per capita has been only about two thirds the output in the United States in recent years.[38] The major growth sector has been in the tertiary or service sector. This is illustrated in Table 2.

For those who hold to a uniform pattern of economic development involving sequential stages, the expansion of the service sector represents a continuing process leading to a new, qualitatively different type of society, a "post-industrial society." This means that there is a steady progression from primarily agricultural employment to a higher proportion of workers employed in the manufacturing sector, to finally, a greater proportion employed in the service sector. This latter stage is said to involve the increased requirements for the manipulation of symbols and for a greater use of highly specialized skills. Given these changes, the basis of power is shifted from the outright control of production to the control of knowledge and expertise, which both includes and transcends the production of goods. Such an assertion implies that the dynamics of a society are qualitatively changed.[39] One consequence of this thesis is that traditional Marxist class analyses no longer apply or must be drastically revised. Power and conflict become situated not in terms of ownership of the means of production; rather they are defined by the control of knowledge, skills, and expertise.

There are several reasons why this thesis must be considered with caution in general, and especially in the instance of Canada. First, the service sector incorporates a huge range of industries. Some of them are required for the *development* of manufacturing, like transportation and utilities, financial services, and communications. Other services are made possible as a *result* of a higher level of affluence, such as recreation-linked industries including travel bureaus, hotels, and cinemas. Still other services have been generated to

TABLE 2 Percentage Distribution of Persons Working, by Industry, Canada, Selected Years, 1871–1976

Year	Agri-culture	Other Primary Industries	Total	Manu-factu-ring	Con-struc-tion	Total	Transpor-tation, Public Utilities	Other[a] Service Indus-tries	Total	Total
1871	50.0	0.0	....	13.1	....	....	....	....	17.0	100.0[b]
1881	48.0	3.2	51.2	13.8	15.6	29.4	....	....	19.4	100.0
1891	45.8	3.7	49.5	16.2	10.1	26.3	....	....	24.2	100.0
1901	40.2	4.1	44.3	17.3	10.6	27.9	....	....	27.8	100.0
1911	34.3	5.2	39.5	19.9	7.2	27.1	....	....	33.4	100.0
1921	32.8	3.8	36.6	17.5	9.0	26.5	....	....	36.9	100.0
1931	28.8	3.8	32.6	11.3	5.2	16.5	....	....	50.9	100.0
1941[c]	25.8	4.8	30.6	16.8	4.8	27.9	6.4	34.8	41.2	100.0
1951	19.2	4.1	23.3	26.3	6.9	33.2	8.5	35.0	43.5	100.0
1961	11.1	3.0	14.1	25.0	6.7	31.7	8.4	45.8	54.1	100.0
1971	6.3	2.8	9.1	22.2	6.1	28.3	8.7	54.0	62.7	100.0
1976	4.9	2.5	7.4	20.3	6.7	27.1	8.7	56.8	65.5	100.0

a Includes trade, finance, insurance and real estate, public administration, and other services.

b The percentages entered for 1871 total only 80.1 percent. The distribution of the remaining workers is not known.

c The census for 1941 reported a separate category of "labourers" who were not included in the total of manufacturing and construction. The total number of all persons includes 0.3 percent who were not elsewhere classified.

Source: Data from 1871 to 1931 inclusive and for 1951 are from 0. J. Firestone, *Canada's Economic Development: 1867–1953* (London: Bowes & Bowes, 1958), Table 66, p. 185. Firestone's information "covers gainfully-occupied (as) reported in the census for 1871–1941 inclusive, and persons with jobs reported in the labour force surveys for 1945–53 (with military personnel excluded)." For 1871 through 1901 his data "relate to the beginning of April." For the remaining reported years the data are as of the beginning of June.

Data for 1941 are from the *Census of Canada*, 1941, Vol. VII, Table 4, pp. 26–34. Data for 1961 are from the *Canada Year Book, 1965*, Table, 4, p. 724. For 1971 the data are from the *Canada Year Book, 1975*, Table 8.4, p. 322. Data for 1976 are from the *Canada Year Book, 1978–79*, Table 8.4, p. 362.

facilitate the increased complexities of industrial organizations. In Canada, these services are linked not only to manufacturing enterprises within the country, but also to companies engaged in importing goods from other countries. As enterprises and establishments grow in size and complexity, increased services are required to meet financial needs, solve distribution problems, and plan marketing strategies. In one study in Great Britain, it was estimated that 60 percent of the persons employed in the service sector made direct contributions to the production of goods.[40]

Government services have also increased over the years. These serve welfare functions and monitor and protect manufacturing and other business interests. Finally, as rates of participation in the labor force have increased, an increased number of formerly unpaid household services such as cooking, laundry, cleaning, child care, and care for the handicapped and aged have been taken over by commercial interests.

Occupational shifts have also been cited as evidence for the emerging "post industrial" society. Here the evidence is said to be in the proportional increase in white-collar occupations. In Canada in 1901 these accounted for approximately 15 percent of the labor force. In 1976 these occupations accounted for over 40 percent. But the most dramatic increases occurred among clerical occupations: over 95 percent of the workers in these occupations are women engaged in secretarial jobs, key-punching, record keeping, and similar tasks. The increased participation rates of women in the labor force are shown in Table 3.

As Table 3 illustrates, male participation rates have declined from 84 percent to 78 percent during the years from 1951 to 1976. During this same period there was a dramatic increase in women participants—from 24 percent to 45 percent. The greatest number of women were between 35 and 64 years of age.

Table 4 reveals in what occupations these shifts have been most pronounced. In agriculture, male employment has dropped from 39 percent in 1911 to 7 percent in 1971. Female employment in these occupations has always been low—4.4 percent in 1911 and 2 percent in 1971. The percentage of males in manual occupations has actually increased slightly over the years, from 41.6 percent in 1911 to 46 percent in 1971. Meanwhile, for females, the percentage has declined from 27 percent to 14 percent. For males, these shifts involve an increased percentage in manufacturing and mechanical occupations and a decreased percentage of "laborers." The participation rates of females have declined in the manufacturing and mechanical occupations.

As Table 4 shows, the highest participation rates for women have been in white-collar and personal service occupations. The female participation rates for the latter have declined while the former have increased. A higher proportion of women than men have typically gone into professions (note the women-dominated professions such as nursing and teaching.) But most dramatic is the increase in participation rates among women in clerical occupations, from 9 percent to 32 percent. For men the increase has been in the professional and the proprietary and managerial occupations. The increases in these two occupation categories seem to carry the weight of evidence of those who argue that a "post-industrial" society is about to descend upon North America, and Canada in particular.

Given the nature of these distributions, especially the fact that in 1971 46 percent of the male employees remained in manual or blue-collar occupations and that most of the women were in routine clerical occupations, the data seem more supportive of a trend toward more rational authority structures still tied to and serving the production of goods.

It is doubtful, then, that these changes provide the underpinnings for a post-industrial society. Meanwhile, some additional cautionary points need to be made. First, it is obvious that the service sector has grown over the years at the expense of the primary sector, not the secondary sector. The proportionate share of employment in manufacturing enterprises has not diminished significantly. Second, one should examine the nature of the occupation roles which are classified in the service sector and which comprise "white-collar" occupations. The occupations categorized in the service sector are extremely diverse. Third, if one considers just the occupations themselves, then, while white-collar occupations as a single category incorporate the highest percentage of workers in comparison to other occupational categories—blue-collar, transport and communications, service and recreation occupations and primary occupations such as farming and fishing—for most people these jobs are similar to blue-collar work in terms of their routine nature and the degree of authority their holders are permitted to exercise. Even for those occupations that require high levels of preparation and training, the nature of the work is frequently not only specialized but also highly routine. Continued rationalization of organizations fosters this process of routinization.

Finally, it should be pointed out that the tertiary sector has claimed a relatively large proportion of the labor force throughout the history of most industrialized societies. In the United States, it accounted for a higher proportion of the gainfully employed than the manufacturing sector from 1870 to 1910, and since then its proportion has never dropped below approximately 25 percent of the labor force. In Canada, the primary sector was dominant for a longer period of time. The tertiary sector claimed a smaller proportion of the labor force than the secondary sector from 1871 to 1901, but thereafter its rate of growth overtook the secondary sector, so that by 1945 it became the dominant employment sector. The period of greatest expansion occurred during the Depression in the 1930s, when government services were greatly enlarged.

Growth in Size of Establishments

Along with the shifts among the economic sectors, there have also been structural changes in the nature of production units. These changes will have increasing significance in later chapters, where it will be argued that they

TABLE 3 Labor Force Participation Rates, by Age and Sex, 1901–78

Year	Both Sexes 14 years of age and over	All ages 14 and over	14–19	20–24	25–34	35–64	65 and over
				Men			
	%	%	%	%	%	%	%
1901	53.0	87.8	....	....	....	....	....
1911	57.4	90.6	....	....	....	....	....
1921	56.2	89.8	68.4	94.3	98.0	96.9	59.6
1931	55.9	87.2	57.4	93.9	98.6	96.7	56.5
1941	55.2	85.6	54.6	92.6	98.7	96.1	47.9
1951a	54.5	84.4	53.7	94.2	98.2	95.0	39.5
1961a	55.3	81.1	40.6	94.4	98.4	95.3	30.6
1951b	54.3	84.1	53.5	94.0	98.1	94.8	39.1
1961b	55.1	80.8	40.5	94.2	98.0	95.0	30.4
1971c	58.0	76.4	46.6	86.5	92.6	88.6	23.6
1978c	62.6	77.9	54.8	85.8		81.0	
				Women			
	%	%	%	%	%	%	%
1901	53.0	16.1	....	....	....	....	....
1911	57.4	18.6	....	....	....	....	....
1921	56.2	19.9	29.6	39.8	19.5	12.0	6.6
1931	55.9	21.8	26.5	47.4	24.4	13.2	6.2
1941	55.2	22.9	26.8	46.9	27.9	15.2	5.8
1951a	54.5	24.4	33.7	48.8	25.4	19.8	4.5
1961a	55.3	29.3	31.7	50.7	29.2	29.9	6.1
1951b	54.3	24.2	33.4	48.5	25.1	19.6	4.4
1961b	55.1	29.1	31.7	50.4	28.9	29.5	6.0
1971c	58.0	39.9	37.0	62.8	44.5	41.5	8.3
1978c	62.6	47.8	48.0	70.3		44.0	

a Excludes Newfoundland.
b Includes Newfoundland.
c Includes only persons 15 years of age and over.

Sources: For 1901 inclusive, Frank T. Denton, The Growth of Manpower in Canada (Ottawa: Dominion Bureau of Statistics, 1970), Table 7, p. 44. For 1971, Historical Labour Force Statistics — Actual Data, Seasonal Factors, Seasonally Adjusted Data (Ottawa: Statistics Canada, 1975), pp. 274-313. For 1978, Ibid., 1979, pp. 112–113, 115–116, 118–119. The data for 1971 and 1978 are based upon average monthly non-seasonally adjusted figures.

represent changes in authority systems that call into question the predominant values that have influenced the course of industrialization. What is of

TABLE 4 Percentage Distribution of the Labor Force, 15 Years and Over, by Occupation and Sex, for Canada, 1911–1971

Occupation	1911		1921		1931		1941		1951		1961		1971	
	Male	Female	Male	Female	Male	Female	Male	Female	Male	Female	Male	Female	Male	Female
White Collar	**15.0**	**30.5**	**21.1**	**48.2**	**20.2**	**45.5**	**21.4**	**44.8**	**25.3**	**55.4**	**30.6**	**57.2**	**40.0**	**63.0**
Proprietary and Managerial	5.2	1.6	8.2	2.0	6.4	1.6	6.2	2.0	8.7	3.0	9.6	2.9	13.	4.0
Professional	2.4	.7	3.0	.1	3.7	.8	4.5	.7	5.3	14.4	7.7	15.5	13.	18.
Commercial and Financial	4.4	6.8	5.2	8.4	5.7	8.4	5.2	8.8	5.4	10.5	6.6	10.2	7.[11]	9,[11]
Clerical	3.0	9.4	4.7[3]	18.7	4.4	17.7	4.5	18.3	5.9	27.5	6.7	28.6	7.	32.0
Service	**3.1**	**37.2**	**3.5**	**26.8**	**4.2**	**33.9**	**4.6**	**34.3**	**6.6**	**21.2**	**8.5**	**22.6**	**7.[13]**	**22.[13]**
Personal	2.8	37.1	2.2	25.8	3.3	33.8	3.2	34.2	3.3	21.0	4.2	22.1		
Manual	**41.6**	**27.9**	**36.2**	**20.9**	**40.2**	**16.9**	**41.6**	**18.5**	**46.3**	**19.4**	**45.3**	**13.4**	**46.0**	**14.0**
Manufacturing and Mechanical[8]	11.7	26.3	10.3	17.8	11.3	12.7	16.2	15.4	17.9	14.6	18.4	9.9	31.	11.
Construction	5.5	–[6]	5.5	[6]	5.6	5.8	–[6]	7.1	.1	7.1	.1	[12]	[12]	
Transportation and Communication[9]	6.3	1.5	5.9	3.0	7.0	2.4	7.5	1.7	9.2	2.9	9.8	2.2	7.	2.
Mining, Quarrying	2.6[7]	[6]	1.7	[6]	1.8	[6]	2.1	[6]	1.6	[6]	1.4	[6]	1.	[6]

Logging	1.8(5)	(6)	(6)	(6)	2.4	(6)	2.5	(6)	1.7	(6)	1.	(6)	
Laborers(10)	13.7	.1	13.2	3.6	7.6	1.4	8.0	1.8	6.9	1.2	6.	1.	
Primary	**40.5**	**3.7**	**35.2**	**3.6**	**33.0**	**2.3**	**20.6**	**2.8**	**13.2**	**4.3**	**7.3**	**2.0**	
Agricultural	39.0	3.7	33.7	3.6	31.5	2.3	19.3	2.8	12.2	4.3	7.	2.	
Fishing, Hunting, Trapping	1.5	1.1(4)	1.5		1.5		1.3(4)		1.0		.3		
Not Stated	—	.2	.3	—	.3	—	.2	.1	**1.1**/2.7	**1.1**/2.5	**.3**		
Total Percentage	**100.2**	100.1	99.9	99.8	99.9	99.9	**100.1**	99.9	99.9	100.3	100.0	100.3	101.0
Total Labor Force (x 1 000)	2 341.4	357.0	2 658.5	485.1	3 244.7	663.3	3 352.4	831.1	4 114.4	1 162.2	4 694.3	1 763.9	5 353.0 2 782.0

(1) Excludes Yukon and Northwest Territories; includes Newfoundland in 1951 and 1961.
(2) Excludes persons on Active Service on June 2, 1941.
(3) Includes proofreaders, shippers, weighmen, and postmen classified elsewhere in other years.
(4) Excludes Indians living on reserves.
(5) Includes pulp mill employees.
(6) Less than .05 percent.
(7) Includes almost all mine and smelter employees, except clerical workers.
(8) Includes stationary enginemen and occupations associated with electric power production.
(9) Includes "Communications."
(10) Laborers in all industries except those engaged in agricultural, fishing, logging or mining operations are included in this division.
(11) Includes only those classified as "Sales."
(12) No Separate category for "Construction."
(13) "Service & Recreational."

Note: The "Gainfully occupied" rather than the "Labor force" concept was used prior to 1951 for determining labor force status. The labor force figures exclude a few persons seeking work who have never been employed. Occupations for 1911, 1921, 1931, 1941 and 1971 were rearranged on the basis of the 1951 Classification though some adjustment of the 1951 grouping was necessary.

Sources: 1961 Census, Labour Force Historical Tables (Ottawa: Ministry of Trade and Commerce, 1962); The Labour Force (Ottawa: Statistics Canada, 1972).

immediate relevance is that plants and factories have grown in size, as have the enterprises controlling them.

The historical data dealing with these changes are of uneven quality and have some problems of comparability. But viewed in terms of overall developments they show a trend within the manufacturing sector toward fewer plants and factories relative to the gross value of products produced. This pattern is indicated in Table 5.

Data in the table from 1880 to 1910 are not strictly comparable to the remaining years, since they include industries not a part of the later definition of "manufacturing." In addition, the data for 1900 and 1910 deal only with establishments with five or more employees. Still, there remains a consistent trend. After 1890, the average gross value of production increased more rapidly throughout the years than the increase in the number of establishments. Only during the years from 1880 to 1890 were the number of establishments (plants and factories) increasing at a faster rate than the average gross value of production.

Another way of interpreting these developments is to note the variations in size of establishments in relation to their share of the total value of production. This is shown in Table 6 for the years 1949, 1961, 1971, and 1974. Of special significance in this table is that for the time period illustrated, there has been an increased proportion in the total value produced by establishments manufacturing goods worth 5 million dollars or more. The shift has been from 49 percent in 1949 to nearly 77 percent in 1974. However, even though the trend toward larger size is apparent in the table, the data must be interpreted with caution since the amounts are given in current dollars and do not take into account the effects of the decline in the value of the dollar. The trend toward larger size of plants and factories is due to what is often taken to be "economies of scale." This refers to the reduction of the cost of production of each unit through large volume production.

Growth in Size of Enterprises

Not only has there been an increase in the size of establishments, but enterprises which control them have also expanded. The factors which have stimulated this pattern have to do more with protecting earning capacity than with production efficiencies as such. Historically, the increase in size of enterprises relative to particular industrial sectors has occurred through mergers (including take-overs) of enterprises and through expansion of single enterprises by successful competition.

TABLE 5 **Number of Manufacturing Establishments and Value of Production**

Year	Number of establishments[c] (x 1000)	Gross value of production[a] ($ Million)		Average value per establishment
		Current dollars	Constant dollars[1] 1935-39	$ Million
1870[b]	41.3	222	278	6.73
1880	49.7	310	432	8.69
1890[c]	14.1	369	549	38.94
1900[c]	14.1	481	771	54.68
1910[c]	19.2	1 166	1 485	77.34
1920	23.4	3 772	1 856	79.32
1930	22.6	3 280	2 905	128.54
1940	25.5	4 529	4 194	164.47
1950	36.5	13 818	6 543	179.26
1960	32.2	23 280	10 130	314.60
1970	31.9	46 381	16 194	507.65
1974	31.5	82 455	17 909	568.54

[a] Manufacturing as defined in the decennial censuses includes construction, hand trades, custom work, repair, and central electric stations up to and including 1910. The data for years 1970 and 1974 is value of shipment of own manufacture.

[b] Covers four provinces only.

[c] Covers only establishments with five or more employees in 1890 to 1910.

Sources: Index — Price Index from 1870-1950 from *Prices and Price Index, 1949-52,* Dominion Bureau of Statistics; Ottawa, 1954. Price Index from 1960-1974 from Canadian Statistical Review, Vol. 37, July - December 1972, July - December 1975.

Data relating to establishments/enterprises 1870-1920, *Manufacturing Industries of Canada 1924*; Ottawa, 1927; 1930-1940, same 1949; Ottawa, 1951. 1950-1960, same 1961, Ottawa, 1964; 1970-1974, same 1974; Ottawa, 1976.

[1] The constant dollars for the gross value of production was calculated from the wholesale price index (1935 - 39 = 100), and the current dollar values for each year given.

i.e., $\dfrac{\text{current dollar value} \times 100}{\text{wholesale price index}}$ = constant dollar

where the wholesale price index is defined in the following manner:
"Base period weights of the 1935-39 base indexes represent full value of marketings at successive levels of processing from crude materials to end products."

Index for $r_t = \dfrac{\Sigma q_0 p_1}{\Sigma q_0 p_0} \times 100$

q_0 Weights for items in the base period
p_0 price averages for these items in the base period
p_1 the prices in the period r_t

Computations by Peter Illich.

The dominant form of merger activity has traditionally been "horizontal." That is, enterprises have taken over other enterprises in the same industrial category in which the activities of the companies are duplicated. (One should exercise some caution in interpreting this, however, since the identification of industrial categories may be somewhat arbitrary.) Yet although this form of merger has been predominant, other types of take-over have been pronounced at different historical periods. At the turn of the century, second in importance to horizontal acquisitions were mergers that included both "backward" and "forward" vertical integration. The former refers to acquisitions in which enterprises gain control over the supply of natural resources and operations which are required prior to the manufacture of the finished product. Forward vertical integration refers to those processes in which enterprises gain control of operations leading to manufacturing and perhaps ultimately to marketing. A more recent form of merger which has been especially prevalent during the 1960s and 1970s has been the formation of "conglomerates." This form of merger is often prompted by directors who seek to invest surplus liquid capital or gain the assets of a "target" company. In the 1970s it has often been cheaper for directors of companies to buy existing facilities rather than develop their own. Lecraw and Thompson report that during the middle 1970s, in which there was a depressed securities market, many enterprises were valued at only 50 percent to 70 percent of the cost of actually replacing their capital assets.[41]

The periods in which mergers of various kinds have been most pronounced are indicated in Table 7. Because of various omissions, the number of mergers are actually under-reported. Nevertheless, the relative numbers provide an indication of especially active periods. These periods are 1909 to 1913, 1925 to 1930, 1943 to 1946, the mid-1950s, the early 1960s and finally 1968 to 1973.

Typical of the large corporations which were formed during the period from 1909 to 1913 were Canada Cement, Amalgamated Asbestos, Canada Car and Foundry, Dominion Steel Corporation and Steel Company of Canada.[42] In addition to these companies, consolidations also occurred within the industries of textiles, tobacco, brewing, milling and paper-making.

A second period of merger activity occurred during the period from 1925 to 1930. A primary reason for these moves was to control price competition. Existing facilities were being expanded at the same time that administrations of different companies were being merged. The specific industries in which most of these movements took place were pulp and paper, milling, baking, brewing and distilling, meat packing, canning, and chemical and dairy products.

American-owned corporations also contributed to these shifts. By 1940, the following American-owned corporations were dominant in their Canadian industrial sectors: Imperial Oil, Imperial Tobacco, Canadian Celanese, Canadian Westinghouse, Canadian General Electric, Aluminium Limited, International Harvester, Ford, General Motors, Chrysler, and the largest tire

TABLE 6 Establishments by Value of Shipments of Goods of Own Manufacture per Establishment, 1949, 1961, 1971, and 1974.

Size group	1949			1961			1971			1974		
	Establishments	Value of shipments of own manufacture	Proportion of total shipments	Establishments	Value of shipments of goods of own manufacture	Proportion of total shipments	Establishments	Value of shipments of own manufacture	Proportion of total shipments	Establishments	Value of shipments of goods of own manufacture	Proportion of total shipments
	Number	(x 1 000)	%	Number	(x 1 000)	%	Number	(x 1 000)	%	Number	(x 1 000)	%
$	16 176	145 908	1.2	4 230	22 733	0.1	1 443	8 257	—	715	4 204	—
10 000–				5 015	84 047	0.4	2 795	48 381	0.1	1 804	32 007	—
25 000–	4 884	174 899	1.4	4 677	168 079	0.7	3 784	138 028	0.3	3 033	112 690	0.1
50 000–	4 487	320 878	2.6	4 562	328 307	1.4	4 223	304 161	0.6	3 915	286 467	0.3
100 000–	3 630	514 922	4.1	4 260	610 675	2.6	4 219	607 535	1.2	4 029	587 546	0.7
200 000–	3 195	1 000 486	8.0	4 555	1 462 027	6.2	5 370	1 728 645	3.4	5 270	1 720 675	2.1
500 000–	1 494	1 041 236	8.3	2 400	1 689 457	7.2	3 372	2 393 689	4.8	3 790	2 719 231	3.3
1 000 000–	1 505	3 164 936	25.4	2 875	6 123 965	26.1	4 853	10 813 881	21.5	5 965	13 573 590	16.5
5 000 000–	421	6 116 329	49.0	783	12 949 667	55.3	1 849	34 233 339	68.1	2 964	63 418 699	76.9
Total	35 792	12 479 594	100.0	33 357	23 438 957	100.0	31 908	50 275 916	100.0	31 535	82 455 109	100.0

Source: Manufacturing Industries of Canada: Type of Organization and Size of Establishment, 1970 (Ottawa: Statistics Canada, May 1974), Table 10, p. 63; ibid., 1974 (Ottawa: Statistics Canada, 1977), Table 10, p. 65.

TABLE 7 **Number of Consolidations and Number of Enterprises Absorbed, 1900–1948; Total Number of Acquisitions Recorded, 1949–1976.**

Year	Consoli-dations	Enterprises Absorbed	Year	Consoli-dations	Enterprises Absorbed
1900	3	5	1925	31	79
1901	3	10	1926	33	69
1902	2	45	1927	46	86
1903	1	4	1928	87	179
1904	3	3	1929	74	148
1905	7	27	1930	44	74
1906	10	21	1931	26	37
1907	5	10	1932	16	16
1908	3	7	1933	18	21
1909	10	40	1934	14	19
1910	25	73	1935	16	22
1911	28	46	1936	12	16
1912	22	37	1937	9	11
1913	12	25	1938	13	16
1914	2	7	1939	10	13
1915	7	8	1940	7	8
1916	9	9	1941	6	6
1917	9	11	1942	12	12
1918	4	5	1943	18	21
1919	13	21	1944	25	29
1920	15	16	1945	30	56
1921	5	7	1946	32	49
1922	9	9	1947	16	20
1923	18	52	1948	18	20
1924	9	9			

	Total Number of Acquisitions Recorded, 1949–1976					
Year	Foreign[a]	Domestic[b]	Total	Year	Foreign[a]	Domestic[b]	Total
1949	11	27	38	1960	93	110	203
1950	9	36	45	1961	86	152	238
1951	19	61	80	1962	79	106	185
1952	17	59	76	1963	41	88	129
1953	25	68	93	1964	80	124	204
1954	43	61	104	1965	78	157	235
1955	56	78	134	1966	80	123	203
1956	54	81	135	1967	85	143	228
1957	35	68	103	1968	163	239	402
1958	60	80	140	1969	168	336	504
1959	66	120	186	1970	162	265	427

Year	Total Number of Acquisitions Recorded, 1949–1976			Year	Foreign[a]	Domestic[b]	Total
	Foreign[a]	Domestic[b]	Total				
1971	143	245	388				
1972	127	302	429				
1973	100	252	352				
1974	78	218	296				
1975	109	155	264				
1976	124	189	313				

[a] Foreign–owned or foreign–controlled acquiring company.

[b] Acquiring company not known to be foreign–owned or foreign–controlled.

Source: 1900–1948: J.C. Weldon, "Consolidations in Canadian Industry, 1900–1948" in L.A. Skeoch, ed., *Restrictive Trade Practices in Canada* (Toronto: McClelland-Stewart, 1966), p. 233. These figures are not directly comparable to the data given for years since 1948. They leave out enterprises in the financial sector, gold mining and petroleum and those mergers which do not affect at least two enterprises with assets in Canada and those which pass into government ownership.
1949–1959: Steven Globerman, *Mergers and Acquisitions in Canada: A Background Report*, Royal Commission on Corporate Concentration, Study No. 34 (Ottawa: Supply and Services Canada, 1977), p. 55.
1960–1979: *Annual Report, Director of Investigation and Research, Combines Investigation Act*, (Ottawa: Consumer and Corporate Affairs, 1978), p. 58. The table entries for 1949 through 1976 are based upon published sources of Canada, the United States and Britain. Excluded are Crown Corporations, cooperatives and personal corporations.

producers. Reynolds at that time commented, "While the parent concerns were being prosecuted and dissolved under the Sherman Act (in the United States), their Canadian offspring led an untroubled life and still dominate their respective industries."[43]

Up until about 1940 between 85 percent to 90 percent of the mergers were horizontal. But since then vertical and especially conglomerate mergers have become increasingly more prevalent. This is indicated in Table 8.

The corporate interlock of Gelco, Power Corporation and Warnock-Hersey is an example of the conglomerate style of merger. This interlock has controlling interests in a variety of industries, including glass production, steamship lines, real estate, insurance, mining companies, and furniture companies. In 1965, the four largest manufacturing enterprises together controlled plants and factories in twenty-nine different industries.[44] Of special sociological interest in the conglomerate style of merger is the suggestion that enterprises are becoming more removed from the objectives of manufacturing products. They are becoming like financial organizations concerned more with cash flow regardless of the nature of the production activity.

In addition to these merger activities, enterprises have continued to grow relative to their particular industrial sectors in which they invest most of their activity. With increasing growth, the issue of "concentration" emerges.

TABLE 8   **Percentages of Mergers By Type, 1900-1975**

Period	Horizontal	Vertical	Conglomerate	Total
1900–1909	90	4	6	100
1910–1919	85	10	5	100
1920–1929	85	11	4	100
1930–1939	88	7	5	100
1940–1948	73	19	8	100
1945–1961	63.9	23	13.1	100
1960–1968	63	19	18	100
1968–1973	56	18	25	99

Source: Donald J. Lecraw and Donald N. Thompson, *Conglomerate Mergers in Canada*, Royal Commission on Corporate Concentration, Study No. 32 (Ottawa: Supply and Services Canada, 1978), p. 64. The authors gathered their data from a variety of sources at different intervals. The comparisons are approximate only.

This is the degree to which a relatively few enterprises control the major share of production and the market within particular industrial sectors. The effect can be "oligopolistic" control and the prevention of additional entries into the field of competition. Obviously, complete control by a single enterprise constitutes a monopoly.

Actual measures of concentration are crude and imprecise. Industrial sector classifications do not always give a clear picture of the nature of the competitive market (plastics products may be in competition with those made from metal). Further, measures of concentration themselves vary. These typically include the proportion of manufacturing assets, or the proportion of value added by processing, or the proportion of the labor force, all accounted for by a given number of enterprises. Industrial sectors in which four enterprises have accounted for 80 percent or more of these indices in Canada have included, since 1948, cotton textiles, motor vehicles, petroleum refineries, tobacco, breweries, distilleries, rubber tires, and aircraft and parts manufacture.[45] Raynauld, basing his calculations on 1961 data from Statistics Canada, ordered the forty leading manufacturing industrial sectors by the number of establishments required to include 80 percent of the employees (excluding office employees). The ten most concentrated industries at that time, listed in order from most to least concentrated were motor vehicles, rubber tires and tubes, iron and steel mills, tobacco products, smelting and refining, railroad rolling stock, aircraft and parts, flour, cotton yarn and cloth, and synthetic textiles.[46]

It should be kept in mind that mergers do not necessarily increase concentration within industrial sectors. The shift toward a greater proportion of conglomerate style of mergers during the period 1960 to 1973 has been accompanied by a slight decline in concentration in those sectors not already highly controlled by a few enterprises.[47] Thus, concentration indices are not necessarily reliable in determining the degree of economic power of particular enterprises.

In comparing Canada with other industrialized countries, it appears that the periods of unusual merger activities and the patterns of growth in concentration levels are roughly the same throughout the industrialized world. The industrial sectors within Canada, however, tend to be more highly concentrated. While the smaller scale economy contributes to these high levels, additional reasons include the very weak Canadian legislation aimed at preventing monopolistic control and the continuing expansion of large foreign corporations. Meanwhile, the two dominant Canadian conglomerates, Power Corporation and Argus Corporation, have also continued to expand their holdings in different sectors.

Enormous economic power is also concentrated within financial institutions, such as banks and insurance companies, and within the natural resource and energy sectors. In all sectors, small producing units continue to exist. However, the huge corporations set the pattern of policies to which smaller companies are subject.[48]

Regional Variations

While regional variations in the industrial structure would exist even if Canada's economy were self-contained, heavy reliance upon trade with the United States has undoubtedly reinforced these differences. The center of manufacturing activity is in Ontario and, to a lesser extent, in Quebec. In the period from 1961 to 1975 there has been some shifting, with relative gains in proportional distribution going principally to Alberta and losses sustained by both Quebec and Ontario. Quebec has suffered the larger proportional loss. These shifts are illustrated in Table 9.

One can also indicate the regional variations by citing the proportion that each province's population forms of the total Canadian population and relating this to the proportion of manufacturing sales. This is indicated in Table 10.

The Atlantic provinces, Newfoundland, Prince Edward Island, and especially Nova Scotia and New Brunswick, were once the center for fishing and transoceanic trade of timber and other inland products, as well as a developing manufacturing sector. Currently, primary sector industries account for roughly one third of the area's production. This formerly wealthy area is now the poorest in Canada. The estimated value of production per capita is a little more than one half of the national average. In 1975 the area accounted for only about 5 percent of the national production of goods as measured by the value created by the manufacturing process. Food and beverages accounted for roughly 37 percent of output within the manufacturing sector. Paper and allied products manufacture, located principally in New

Brunswick and Nova Scotia, accounted for another 28 percent of manufacturing output. Remaining industries included metal and fabricating, wood, transportation equipment, petroleum and coal production, printing and publishing, and non-metallic minerals production.

Both Quebec and Ontario have evolved from primarily staple producing areas—furs, then agricultural products—to the manufacturing centers of Canada. Manufacturing now accounts for approximately two thirds of the production in this region. The two provinces account for about three fourths of the total manufacturing in Canada.

In 1975 in Quebec within the manufacturing sector, food and beverage products accounted for nearly 13 percent of the province's production as measured by value of shipments. Following closely behind were paper and allied industries, metal fabrication, the clothing industry, primary metals industries, chemicals and chemical products, and electrical products.

In Ontario, transportation equipment accounted for 12 percent, while food and beverage production accounted for 11 percent of the province's manufacturing production. These were followed by metal fabrication industries, primary metals industries, electrical products, and chemicals and chemical products industries.

Taken together, agricultural production is the primary form of economic output in the three Prairie provinces of Manitoba, Saskatchewan, and Alberta. These provinces accounted for nearly 10 percent of the manufacturing output in Canada, with Alberta alone accounting for slightly over 5 percent. Within the manufacturing sector, food and beverage products accounted for 21 percent of Manitoba's production, 28 percent of Saskatchewan's, and 24 percent of Alberta's.

The remaining manufacturing sectors of major importance in Manitoba, listed in order of proportion of production by value added, were metal fabrication, machinery, transportation equipment, and printing and publication. In Saskatchewan manufacturing sectors of considerably less importance than food production were petroleum and coal products, machinery, printing and publishing, and non-metallic mineral products.

In Alberta in 1975 major manufacturing sectors which ranked behind food and beverage production were metal fabrication, non-metallic mineral products, chemicals and chemical products, and primary metals. But apart from the manufacturing sector, it should be remembered that oil production has become the major source of earned income in Alberta.

In British Columbia, the manufacturing sector is heavily dominated by wood industries and paper and allied products. These accounted for about 47 percent of manufacturing output. Food and beverage products accounted for about 13 percent of manufacturing products, with primary metals and metal fabrication the lesser of these sectors accounting for at least 5 percent of the manufactured products, as measured by value added.[49]

The regional variations, like the sectoral shifts and the concentration patterns, have been influenced by many factors, but three which seem to be most important are the influence of early mercantilism, political concerns, and the continued attractions of foreign markets for Canada's staples, raw materials, and partially processed goods.

TABLE 9   **Value of Shipments of Goods of Own Manufacture**

	Value of Shipments x 100 (Total in Canada)		Magnitude of Increase (+) or Decrease (–)
	1961	1975	1975–1961
Newfoundland	.61	.73	+0.12
Prince Edward Island	.14	.12	– 0.02
Nova Scotia	1.70	2.06	+0.36
New Brunswick	1.74	1.89	+0.15
Quebec	31.28	27.10	– 4.18
Ontario	51.51	50.22	– 1.29
Manitoba	3.19	2.92	– 0.27
Saskatchewan	1.48	1.33	– 0.15
Alberta	4.17	5.34	+1.17
British Columbia	8.58	8.28	–0.3
Yukon and Northwest Territories	.015	.015	0

Source: "Preliminary Bulletin. 1975," *Annual Census of Manufactures* (Ottawa: Statistics Canada, 1977), p. 1.

TABLE 10   **Regional Distribution of Employment and Sales in Manufacturing, 1976**

	Proportion of Canada's population	Proportion of provincial work force in manufacturing	Proportion of manufacturing sales
Newfoundland	2.4	12.0	0.6
New Brunswick	3.0	15.0	1.9
Nova Scotia	3.6	15.0	2.0
Prince Edward Island	0.5	9.0	0.1
Quebec	27.1	24.0	26.2
Ontario	36.0	25.0	51.0
Manitoba	4.4	14.0	2.8
Saskatchewan	4.0	6.0	1.2
Alberta	8.0	9.0	5.3
British Columbia	10.7	16.0	8.9

Source: "The Canadian Manufacturing Sector," *Financial Post*, December 17, 1977.

Government Interventions

Throughout the history of Canada, municipal, provincial, and federal governments have played an active role in the process of economic development,
much more so than the governments in the United States. It is probably not
too far off the mark to suggest that governments in the United States played
more of an arbitrating role in the process of economic development, enacting
legislation in response to economic demands and crises. In contrast, Canadian
governments have always been active in encouraging, promoting, and influencing the course of economic growth and development.

The close interplay between government and business interests is
illustrated by McNaught who writes:

> If Ottawa endorsed the policies and raised most of the required revenues to sub-
> sidize the gigantic expansion, the real policy originators and controllers were to
> be found in the financial houses, and the railway and industrial head-offices of
> Toronto and the English-speaking community of Montreal.[50]

In 1902 these business interests had persuaded the federal government
to subsidize two transcontinental railroads in addition to the Canadian
Pacific. But by 1916 it was obviously apparent that Canada could ill afford
such extravagance. One additional transcontinental line had been completed,
but poor management and continued losses prompted the Conservative
government under Borden in 1919 to bring all the major railways, with the
exception of the Canadian Pacific, under public ownership. This now constitutes the Canadian National Railway system. Since that time, the federal
government has continued to subsidize freight rates.

Prior to the First World War, government involvement in economic
growth and development was especially intense. In an effort to strengthen the
east-west domestic trade, both the federal and provincial governments
employed their powers of regulation and control. They provided property in
the form of land and mineral rights, and they invoked their fiscal powers to
tax, borrow, and spend. These powers were most dramatically employed in
developing the railroad networks and, to a lesser extent, in settling the prairie
provinces.

After the First World War, governments focused their attention upon
stabilizing the economy and providing needed social services. The Combine
Investigation Act of 1910 was strengthened in 1919. A board was created to
investigate and restrain combinations, monopolies, trusts and mergers, and to
control price-fixing among companies. Provincial governments took the lead
in providing social services until the Depression years of the 1930s when the
federal government assumed major responsibilities.

The policies of Canadian governments since the Second World War
have included continued involvement in social welfare, as well as in promo-
tional activities in economic growth and development. The pattern of involvement, however, has been complicated by the erosion of federal powers in relation to provincial governments. To adequately treat the different forms of

government participation requires much more space than is available here. Nevertheless governments at all levels have been active participants in the marketplace rather than merely regulatory bodies. Such involvement can be illustrated by citing the role of the federal government through the "crown corporations." In general, these are designed to fulfill a public need, "having commercial characteristics which private enterprise is unwilling to fill, should not be expected to fill or is unsuitable to fill. . . . "[51] These government-related organizations are intended to stimulate continued economic expansion by assuming the economic risks of private economic interests. (However, many of these are in direct competition with private enterprises.)

Apart from those crown corporations which provide regulatory functions or those which serve specific needs of the government, there are also "proprietary" crown corporations, which pursue objectives similar to private enterprises, but which are subject to review by the federal government. In addition to the take-over of the railroads in 1919, the federal government in 1932 instituted crown corporations for the operation of network broadcasting (the Canadian Broadcasting Corporation) and for developing transcontinental air lines in 1937 (the Trans-Canada Air Lines, later to become Air Canada). During the Second World War, proprietary crown corporations were formed to manufacture synthetic rubber (the Polymer Corporation, formed in 1942), to provide insurance for exporters (the Export Credits and Insurance Corporation, established in 1944), to control the production of uranium (the Eldorado Mining and Refining Corporation, 1944), and to handle farm mortgage credits (the Farm Credit Corporation, 1944). In 1945 the Central Mortgage and Housing Corporation was established; in 1949 the Canadian Overseas Telecommunications Corporation took over the services of the Canadian Marconi Company and the Canadian assets of Cable and Wireless Limited. And, in 1954 the St. Lawrence Seaway Authority was created.

In an effort to exercise more Canadian control over foreign industries, the federal government created the Canada Development Corporation in June 1971. The company is designed to "help develop and maintain strong Canadian controlled and managed corporations in the private sector of the economy (that) will give Canadians greater opportunities to invest and participate in the economic development of Canada."[52] While formed by the government, it is officially not a crown corporation, but acts as a private investment corporation. One of its first most dramatic acts was to acquire controlling interest in Texasgulf Incorporated, an American company holding extensive mining operations in Canada.

In 1977 the Canada Development Corporation had three subsidiaries: CDC Nederland B.V., CDC Oil and Gas Ltd., and Connlab Holdings Ltd. Connlab Holdings, in turn, had 26 sub-subsidiary corporations. In addition, CDC owned a part of 42 other associated corporations, including Cross Canada Flights Ltd. and PoP Shoppes of Canada. In total, the federal government at this time owned "all or part of the shares in 366 corporations."[53]

Governments of Canada continue to play active roles as participants in the economy. They have been increasingly concerned with the development of the manufacturing sector and with restricting the foreign control of enterprises.

Conclusions

The processes of economic development in Canada are extraordinarily complex. But we can gain some insights by viewing them as the consequences of the actions of influential individuals responding to opportunities which served their own interests but which may have had other than the intended consequences. Viewed in more concrete terms, the decisions of Canada's early economic and political elites formed the nature and range of options for their successors. Their influence can subsequently be seen in the sectoral developments and regional variations in Canada's development. It is no accident that primary resources have played such a dominant role, nor that the regional variations reflect the market patterns of the United States.

Notes

1. For more detailed treatment of early Canadian elites, see Wallace Clement, *The Canadian Corporate Elite: An Analysis of Economic Power* (Toronto: McClelland and Stewart, Carleton Library, 1975); Donald Creighton, *Towards the Discovery of Canada* (Toronto: Macmillan, 1972), pp. 84–121; David S. Macmillan, "The 'New Men' in Action: Scottish Mercantile and Shipping Operations in the North American Colonies, 1760–1825," *Canadian Business History*, ed. David S. Macmillan (Toronto: McClelland and Stewart, 1972), pp. 44–104; Gustavus Myers, *A History of Canadian Wealth* (Toronto: James Lewis and Samuel, 1972), pp. 63–89; R. T. Naylor, "The Rise and Fall of the Third Commercial Empire of the St. Lawrence," *Capitalism and the National Question in Canada*, ed. Gary Teeple, (Toronto: University of Toronto Press, 1972), pp. 1–42; Gary Teeple, "Land, Labour and Capital in Pre-Confederation Canada," ibid., pp. 43–67; Gerald Tulchinsky, "The Montreal Business Community 1837–1853," Macmillan, op. cit., pp. 125–143; Stanley B. Ryerson, *Unequal Union* (Toronto: Progress Books, 1973), pp. 29–41.
2. Shepard B. Clough, *European Economic History: The Economic Development of Western Civilization* (New York: McGraw-Hill, 1968), p. 218.
3. Ibid., pp. 218–219.
4. .Joseph Vinter, "Mercantilism," *International Encyclopedia of the Social Sciences*, ed. D. Sills (New York: Macmillan and the Free Press, 1968), pp. 435–443.
5. For a concise review and commentary on the staples thesis, see Richard Caves and Richard Holton, *The Canadian Economy: Prospect and Retrospect* (Cambridge: Harvard University Press, 1961,) pp. 31–47 and pp. 141–144.
6. The "staples thesis" has been the subject of considerable debate among economic

historians. See Harold A. Innis, *The Cod Fisheries: The History of an International Economy* (Toronto: Ryerson Press, 1946). See also Innis, *The Fur Trade in Canada* (Toronto: University of Toronto Press, 1970). Innis has argued that a staples-based economy may in fact never stimulate an indigenous manufacturing sector. For earlier discussions, see the articles by W.A. Mackintosh, "Economic Factors in Canadian History," *Canadian Historical Review* (March, 1923), pp. 12–25, and "Some Aspects of a Pioneer Economy," *Canadian Journal of Economic and Political Science* (November, 1936), pp. 457–463. Mackintosh had argued that the transition to manufacturing would be nearly automatic.

Critical articles include the following: Kenneth Buckley, "The Role of Staple Industries in Canada's Economic Development," *Journal of Economic History*, XVIII (December, 1958), pp. 439–450; G. W. Bertram, "Economic Growth in Canadian Industry, 1870–1915: The Staple Model and the Take-off Hypothesis," *Canadian Journal of Economic and Political Science*, XXIX, No. 2 (May, 1963), pp. 162–184; M. H. Watkins, "A Staple Theory of Economic Growth," *Canadian Journal of Economics and Political Science*, XXIX, No. 2 (May, 1963), pp. 141–158.

7. André Raynauld, *The Canadian Economy* (Toronto: Macmillan, 1967), pp. 362–364; Caves and Holton, op. cit., pp. 386–402; O. J. Firestone, *Canada's Economic Development: 1867–1953* (London: Bowes and Bowes, 1958), pp. 155–170.

8. Kenneth McNaught, *The Pelican History of Canada* (Harmondsworth: Penguin Books, 1969), pp. 84–89.

9. Erwin C. Hargrove, "On Canadian and American Political Culture," *The Canadian Journal of Economics and Political Science*, XXXIII, No. 1 (February, 1967), pp. 107–111.

10. Paul Mantoux, *The Industrial Revolution in the Eighteenth Century* (New York: Harper Torchbooks, 1961), p. 90.

11. Donald Creighton, *Towards the Discovery of Canada* (Toronto: Macmillan, 1972), p. 124.

12. Ibid., p. 125.

13. W. T. Easterbrooke and Hugh C. J. Aitken, *Canadian Economic History* (Toronto: Macmillan, 1956), p. 295.

14. Ibid., p. 352.

15. Ibid., p. 354.

16. R. T. Naylor, "Finance and Politics in Canada in the Nineteenth Century: The Case of the Canadian Banking System" (paper delivered at the McGill Colloquium, "Canadian Society in the Nineteenth Century," Montreal, Quebec, January 17, 1975). For one of the most comprehensive accounts of the interplay between economic and political interests in the development of Canada, see Tom Naylor, *The History of Canadian Business: 1867–1914*, 2 vols. (Toronto: James Lorimer, 1975).

17. O. J. Firestone, *Industry and Education: A Century of Canadian Development* (Ottawa: University of Ottawa Press, 1969), p. 25.

18. Caves and Holton, op. cit., p. 198.

19. Ian Drummond, *The Canadian Economy: Structure and Development*, rev. ed. (Georgetown, Ontario: Irwin-Dorsey, 1972), pp. 35, 155–156.

20. Drummond, ibid., pp. 154–155; Harry Johnson, *The Canadian Quandary: Economic Problems and Policies* (Toronto: McGraw-Hill, 1963), pp. 109–110, 122; John Dales, "Some Historical and Theoretical Comment on Canada's National Policy," *Queen's Quarterly* (Autumn, 1964), pp. 297–316.

21. Drummond, op. cit., pp. 155, 186–187.

22. Caves and Holton, op. cit., pp. 236–238; Dales, op. cit., p. 305; Firestone, op. cit., pp. 206–208, 219–220.

23. Stephen Scheinberg, "Invitation to Empire: Tariffs and American Economic Expansion in Canada," in *Enterprise and National Development*, ed. Glenn Porter and Robert Cuff (Toronto: A. M. Hakkert, 1973), pp. 80–100.

24. The classic statement of "stages" of growth is in W. W. Rostow, *The Stages of Economic Growth: A Non-Communist Manifesto* (Cambridge: Cambridge University Press, 1960). For exceptions to this deterministic approach see, Simon Kuznets, *Modern Economic Growth* (New Haven: Yale University Press, 1966), pp. 86–159; Alexander Gerschenkron, *Economic Backwardness in Historical Perspective: A Book of Essays* (Cambridge: Belknap-Harvard, 1962); Maurice Dobbs, *Capitalism, Development and Planning* (New York: New World, 1970).

25. Caves and Holton, op. cit., p. 52.

26. Ibid., pp. 54–56.

27. Raynauld, op. cit., p. 50.

28. Ibid.

29. Caves and Holton, op. cit., pp. 70–71.

30. Firestone, op. cit., p. 211.

31. *Financial Post*, December, 17, 1977.

32. Science Council Committee on Industrial Policies, *Uncertain Prospects: Canadian Manufacturing Industry, 1971-1977* (Ottawa: Minister of Supply and Services, 1977), p. 17.

33. The reason for removing the automobile industry from consideration is that through the provisions of the "Auto Pact" in 1965, the industry was rationalized for the entire North American market. The flows of automobiles and parts between the United States and Canada are primarily within enterprise channels and thus obscure trade 0atterns.

34. *Uncertain Prospects*, op. cit., p. 18.

35. *OECD Economic Surveys, Canada*, July, 1977.

36. While this has been the traditional division, it is of considerably more utility to further differentiate the service sector into divisions such as utilities (including transportation, storage, communications, public utilities), wholesale trade, retail trade, finance, and government services.

37. Reinhard Bendix, *Work and Authority in Industry* (New York: Harper Torchbooks, 1956), p. 254.

38. H. E. English, "Growth of Manufacturing in Canada," *Canadian Economic Issues*, ed. I. D. Pal (Toronto: Macmillan, 1971), p. 325.

39. Daniel Bell, *The Coming of the Post Industrial Society* (New York: Basic Books, 1973).

40. J. I. Gershuny, "Post-Industrial Society, The Myth of the Service Economy," *Futures*, Vol. 9 (April, 1977), pp. 1–3, 114. Cited in Science Council Committee on Industrial Policies, op. cit., pp. 20–21.

41. Donald J. Lecraw and Donald N. Thompson, *Conglomerate Mergers in Canada*, Royal Commission on Corporate Concentration, Study No. 32 (Ottawa: Supply and Services Canada, 1978), p. 17.

42. Lloyd G. Reynolds, *The Control of Competition in Canada* (Cambridge: Harvard University Press, 1940), p. 6.

43. Ibid.

44. *Concentration in the Manufacturing Industries of Canada* (Ottawa: Department of Consumer and Corporate Affairs, 1971), p. 15.

45. See *Canada Year Book, 1978-1979* (Ottawa: Supply and Services Canada, 1978); *Concentration in the Manufacturing Industries of Canada,* op. cit.; and Gideon Rosenbluth, *Concentration in Canadian Manufacturing Industries* (Princeton: Princeton University Press, 1957).

46. Raynauld, op. cit., pp. 144-45.

47. Steven Globerman, *Mergers and Acquisitions in Canada: A Background Report,* Royal Commission on Corporate Concentration, Study No. 34 (Ottawa: Supply and Services Canada, 1977), p. 29. See also Christian Marfels, *Concentration Levels and Trends in the Canadian Economy, 1965-1973: A Technical Report,* Royal Commission on Corporate Concentration, Study No. 31 (Ottawa: Supply and Services Canada, 1977). For issues regarding concepts and measurements, see Betty Bock, *Dialogue on Concentration, Oligopoly, and Profit: Concepts vs. Data, A Research Report from The Conference Board,* 1972.

48. For an account of the consequences of the conservative policies of Canadian financial institutions, see Robert L. Perry, *Galt, U.S.A.* (Toronto: Maclean-Hunter, 1971).

49. Source of data for "regional variations": "Preliminary Bulletin," *1975 Annual Census of Manufactures* (Ottawa: Statistics Canada, 1977).

50. McNaught, op. cit., p. 197.

51. Crown corporations are classified into proprietary, departmental, agency, and "unclassified." A proprietary corporation is one which conducts its operations without parliamentary appropriations. It is responsible for financial operations or for managing those operations requiring the production of, or dealing with, goods and services to the public. Departmental corporations hold no assets of their own. They provide "administrative, supervisory or regulatory services of a governmental nature." Agency corporations are responsible for managing trading or service operations on a quasi-commercial basis or for procurement, construction, or disposal activities on behalf of the government. These corporations include Atomic Energy of Canada Limited, Canadian Arsenals Limited, National Harbours Board, and others.

    The "unclassified" crown corporations are diverse in nature. They include the Bank of Canada, the Canadian Wheat Board, the Canada Council, the National Productivity Council, and others. See C. A. Ashley and R. G. H. Smails, *Canadian Crown Corporations* (Toronto: Macmillan, 1965).

52. *Canada Development Corporation Act,* Statutes of Canada, 1970-71-72, c. 49.

53. *Financial Post,* May 14, 1977.

chapter five

The Industrial Enterprise

Introduction

Andrew Hacker once wrote of a mythical American firm of the future that owned all its own shares and that was fully automated. In the course of an inquiry by a group of senators regarding the company's support of a tariff bill, the witness testifying for the company asserted that the actions taken in support of the bill were not in behalf of the stockholders, since there were none; nor were they in behalf of the employees, since the factory was automated. The witness further stated that eight of the ten directors did not personally favor the protective legislation. They supported it solely for "the good of the company." Indeed, the witness claimed the directors looked upon themselves merely as civil servants, "doing the job for which we were hired—to look after the company's interests."[1]

The image that Hacker paints of a large corporation with a life of its own, forcing minion-like men to render service to its demands, is one that is consistent not only with popular imagery, but also with the consequences of a social construction that has become reified. It never occurs to Hacker's witness, for example, to question the proper objectives of the company. Its existence is taken for granted, its protection is held as a sacred trust.

Many social scientists have also tended to view formal organizations in a reified manner, referring to an organization's functions, its requirements, and its goals.[2] This may be quite appropriate for certain types of analyses where it can be demonstrated that actors themselves perceive the organizations in which they participate in this manner. But the danger of this type of analytic conceptualization is that it loses sight of the active, decision-making men who, in turn, influence the characteristics of organizations including their *raison d'être*. Indeed, for the social scientist to treat the large-scale organization as an indestructible reality is to reinforce the alienating consequences of reified social constructions. It is this image that lies at the heart of

Marx's criticism of capitalist societies.

Thus, there are normative consequences for this type of approach. It tends to argue—at least implicitly—for the continued necessity of existing organizational forms and, as a consequence, closes off possibilities for entertaining alternative forms of collective endeavor.

The important sociological questions to ask of any social organization or industrial enterprise are the following:

1. How did the characteristics of the organization emerge?
2. What factors account for its continued existence?
3. What factors account for variations in the composition of different organizations?
4. What influence has the organization for the larger social environment?

We may view the industrial enterprise as an authority system that brings together the necessary elements to produce goods or services. It is the product of entrepreneurs who organize the necessary factors of production, including access to natural resources, investment capital, a reliable labor force, a consumer market, technological expertise, and a system of beliefs that initiates and justifies the behavior required for production. Participants within the organization submit themselves to the authority systems in the hope of attaining their own privatized objectives.

Historically, there have been two major developments that have contributed to the rise and ubiquity of the industrial enterprise and the large-scale organization: (1) the continued development of technologies of production which foster the large-scale mobilization of individuals to carry out narrowly defined tasks; and (2) an interpretation of the values of freedom and equality which stresses freedom from social ties while emphasizing an equality of opportunity to compete for material wealth. The incentives to produce goods are attached to personal gain, eventually expressed in terms of unlimited wealth.

In this chapter, I present an overview of the historical evolution of industrial firms in Western Europe and North America. It is important to be familiar with these processes because they have provided the historical antecedents for the forms of production organizations in Canada, whether these have been designed for resource extraction or manufacturing. It is important, in this regard, to recall Weber's emphasis upon the rational organization of formally free labor as the final defining element of western capitalism, whether this occurred in government bureaucracies, armies or organizations designed for the production of goods. Or put in other terms, these represent expressi;ns of rational authority systems. Also, these processes are not to be viewed as deterministic. Rather, they represent the accumulation of decisions made by individual actors in relation to the options available to them in given historical periods.

The Evolution of Production Systems

If we separate commercial activities from those tied to landed estates, then we may point to merchants as constituting the dominant *economic* class throughout most of the history of Western Europe. The life of the aristocrat centered around the country estate. The merchant, however, was a townsman, trading his goods in local market settlements. By the eleventh century, merchants completely dominated the life of the towns. Acting in their own interests, merchants sought to establish steady supplies of goods for their trade which in turn contributed to their own economic gain. They sought to control prices and to ensure stable relations with, and among, producers of commercial goods.

Guilds

It is likely that the development of craft guilds as early production units was a result of an agreement between merchants—the dominant class in the towns—and producers. The merchants who were in control of the towns granted to different craftsmen exclusive rights to manufacture goods in the city. In return, they demanded "that artisans submit to the Church's principle of a just price (*justum pretrium*), which meant . . . a fair and usual market price, and to a variety of regulations which would guarantee a high standard of product."[3]

In exchange for a steady supply of goods, artisans were assured of a continuous market and security in their trades. By the end of the eleventh century, artisans throughout Europe were forming fraternities along lines determined by the goods which they produced for retail sale. It is likely that their models of organization were the merchant guilds and religious societies, each of which was formed for mutual protection of its members.

Individual guilds were organized on a town-wide basis as associations. They were in a sense monopolies, exercising control over the number, quality, and price of the goods being produced by individual units. The structure of the individual units was simple: it consisted of a master craftsman, his journeyman whom he hired as wage labor, and apprentices who received no wages, but for whom the master craftsman furnished room, meals, and necessary clothing. The structure of the production units was tied to elaborate procedures for training labor and for controlling the supply of skilled labor. Apprentices were usually required to serve for seven years before they were eligible to become journeymen. Journeymen, in order to become master craftsmen, had to prove not only their skill, but also had to demonstrate that they had enough capital to set up their own shops and that they were able to pay their membership and other guild fees. They also had to be members in good standing within the local community and had to agree to abide by guild regulations.

In most instances, there were detailed rules governing production methods and selling procedures. While these rules were ostensibly designed to assure the quality of the products, they were actually intended to maintain economic equality among the masters. Members were required to use the same techniques and were forbidden to introduce new methods unless approved by the local guild.[4]

Pirenne states that the period of greatest expansion of craft guilds was after 1250. Often, there were associations among different guilds. In Florence, for example, painters were linked with surgeon apothecaries.[5] The craft guilds acquired such power and influence that in many towns the merchant class was severely threatened, if not displaced. Yet, the growing strength of craft guilds was eventually their own undoing. Inequalities began to appear among individual guild units, as some guild masters became more wealthy and enlarged their enterprises. In addition, they hired more apprentices and journeymen and increased their control over production by preventing the emergence of new masters. Family monopolies further added to their power. In some cases, craftsmen contracted their work out to other producers and to relatively unskilled workers. Some wealthy textile producers in Florence used expensive, but primitive, machinery to maximize their production and their profits.[6]

Meanwhile, by the fourteenth century, wage-earners within the guild systems—of which there were an increasing number—formed their own protective associations. These were designed to find work for their fellow members and to defend their interests in their relations with masters. Conflicts between journeymen and masters were often violent. Clough reports uprisings in Florence led by clothworkers during the years 1378–1382. He reports additional uprisings in Rhenish, Flemish, English, and French towns during approximately the same period. The English Statute of Labourers of 1350 and the French Royal Ordinance of 1351 were both aimed at controlling the workers by setting maximum wage standards and forbidding any collective attempts to alter working conditions. Powerful craftsmen and merchants remained relatively well protected by the law until the end of the eighteenth century.

Several processes, each with its own chronology, led to the eventual decline and final demise of the guild system. Town governments moved to restrict the growing political power of the guilds. Internal competition among masters weakened their monopolistic hold. Finally, the growing antagonism of the wage journeymen further added to the internal divisions within the organization.

In addition, expansion of trade reduced the power of monopolistic control within individual towns. The construction of canals and improved water transport meant that goods could be transported more cheaply as demand for military equipment and consumer goods increased. It was the merchants, rather than the producing guilds, who had the necessary capital to invest in these long-term enterprises. To meet the growing demand for goods, merchants and craftsmen-turned-merchants circumvented the guild system, devising simpler means for constructing and fabricating materials and employing relatively unskilled labor to carry out specific tasks. These new work roles could be carried out within households. They constitute what we now call the domestic system.

Textile manufacturing was especially amenable to this practice. Spinning and weaving were simple and light enough tasks to be carried out by nearly anyone—children included. Textile merchants capitalized on this ready-made labor force in the countryside and took the necessary raw materials to peasant families, and often furnished them with looms and spinning wheels.[7] The merchants would collect the finished products, pay the workers on a piece-rate basis, and market the finished goods.

Growing markets, merchants attempting to maximize profits, and payment by piece-rate gave further incentives to develop new techniques for production. In addition, many merchants formed trading companies and associations which challenged the structure of the guild system. By the end of the eighteenth century, France had passed a formal decree abolishing guilds. Similar decrees were later passed during the first half of the nineteenth century in England, Spain, Austria, Prussia, and the states of Italy.

The Domestic System

The domestic or "putting out" system of production was very simple in its social organization. But two types of innovations influenced its eventual dominance over the craft guild system:

(a) the development and increasing use of investment and credit systems;
(b) technological inventions which permitted goods to be produced by relatively unskilled labor carrying out more narrowly defined tasks.

The domestic system of production was most prevalent from the mid-fifteenth to the mid-eighteenth century. Merchants provided the capital for investment in both production and shipment. Their profits were made through trade rather than through production.

The formal organization of this type of production system was relatively simple. The merchant-capitalist held title to the materials and a contractual relationship existed between him and the rural families who carried out the required tasks. Oftentimes, the merchants, in order to ensure the loyalty and productivity of the peasants, kept them firmly bound in debt or prevented the peasants from owning the tools of production. Nevertheless, from the point of view of contemporary industrial standards, this type of production was grossly inefficient. Merchants lost much time in simply transporting semi-finished goods and it was extremely difficult to maintain even standards of quality. Further, there was considerable wastage of materials and the peasant workers often engaged in petty embezzlement.

Yet, the demand for goods increased as population increased, especially during the eighteenth century, and as military needs and colonization movements continued. These incentives stimulated continual technological improvements in production. Utilization of natural sources of power stimulated a movement away from the domestic system to centralized workplaces. These represented the early beginnings of the factory system. It meant that the owners of the means of production or their appointees had a better opportunity to oversee the actual process of production.

The Factory System

The factory system, an outgrowth of continuing economic pressures to maximize production, introduced new forms of work organization. The formal relations within this system were contractual ones, based upon a growing pool of "free" labor. That is, labor became free in the sense that traditional bonds of fealty to landlords no longer tied peasants to their estate. This in fact meant, however, that the worker was free only to sell his labor to the highest bidder.

The shift to the factory system of production resulted in a new social role of considerable influence—the role of the entrepreneur. The orientation and activities of the entrepreneur were quite different from those of the guild master or the merchant-capitalist. He was primarily oriented toward production: his profits were to be gained, not solely from trade, but from the sale of the commodities which he was able to produce. He invested capital in land, labor, and machinery, and sought to maximize profits by efficiency in investment and production. Monies earned by trade and haulage were not his principal sources of income, but rather the production and sale of goods and services. The vision of the entrepreneur was being directed towards *creating* wealth rather than seizing a portion of fixed wealth. This was to be achieved through the application of new technologies and new inventions to the manufacture of goods. It is with this in mind that Schumpeter characterized the function of the entrepreneurs as reforming or revolutionizing the pattern of production:

> ... by exploiting an invention or more generally an untried technological possibility for producing a new commodity or producing an old one in a new way, by opening up a new source of supply of materials or a new outlet for products, by reorganizing an industry and so on.[8]

Perhaps some of the most important institutions that contributed to the rise of the entrepreneur and the continued expansion of the factory system of production were those that controlled the accumulation and flow of money. Capitalism itself is a system based upon relatively large amounts of money which are easily transferred and readily available at moderate interest rates to persons who are good credit risks. Money supplied under these conditions permitted the entrepreneur to hire labor and to embark upon production ventures requiring relatively large amounts of capital. The resources of banks, pooled from collective reserves of individual savings, issues of promissory notes, and lending instruments, greatly extended the ability of entrepreneurs to expand their enterprises and to take risks with an eye toward future returns.

While these social mechanisms existed before the development of the factory system, the demands for huge outlays of capital for machinery and labor contributed to their growth and refinement. Savings, investments, the extension of credit, and expanding markets laid the economic foundation for the developments of large and complex social organizations designed for large-scale production of goods. These were organizations characterized by specialization of tasks, each of which was dependent and coordinated with one another and organized within an authority system. Individuals who carried out these tasks were bound by contractual agreements. The continued development and expansion of these organizations is the hall-mark of contemporary industrialized society.

The transitions from guilds to the domestic system and then to the factory system represent not only changes in forms of production, but also shifts in the social relationships between those in authority and those who labor for them. These forms have to do with the process of production of commodities and they also reflect changes in the demand for labor.

Canada did not undergo the same sequence of production-related organizational forms which England and Western Europe experienced since her development came at a later stage. But Canada did experience the shift in labor relations from what might be termed a feudal model, in which the employer's responsibilities extended to the care of the worker outside the work context, to the capitalist model, in which responsibility was restricted to only the workplace. Pentland argues that feudal labor relations were dominant in Canada until 1850, especially within the context of agricultural production.[9] An uncertain supply of labor prompted employers to take on the obligations of their workers' welfare in order to maintain a permanent and reliable labor force.

A capitalist labor market—one in which contractual relations between employer and employees are restricted to the workplace—emerged in Canada when there was a surplus of labor. This meant that to the degree that skills could be easily replaced, there were no compelling economic reasons for employers to assume responsibility for workers' welfare outside the work area. The old European guild system assumed a shortage of skills; but the factory system assumed easy duplication within a context of surplus labor. As the availability of labor increased in Canada in concert with the use of machine technology, so could the shift be made toward a capitalist labor market as the demand for skills declined. As we shall see, the ability to replace skills by technology became a major stimulant for the development of labor unions in Canada.

Contemporary Forms of Industrial Organizations

The need for large amounts of capital and the use of contractual relations in carrying out collective endeavors has resulted in the growth in importance of legal definitions of collective enterprises. While there are many forms of organizations designed for production, the *corporation* is perhaps the most powerful. It is a legalized entity whose directors are authorized to sell stock to the public. This, of course, puts the organization in a strong financial position both in terms of assets and in terms of credit standing. While the corporation as a legal entity is liable to claims upon it, each shareholder has a limited liability—only to the extent of his holdings in that corporation. This is quite different from a *proprietorship*, in which the entrepreneur is subject to unlimited liability should there be financial claims laid against him. That is, not only are his business assets subject to claims by his creditors, but his personal possessions as well.

The corporation also differs from the *partnership*, which is made up of two or more individuals jointly controlling an enterprise. This form provides a greater base of assets, providing the enterprise with a more favorable position for ventures and for instruments of credit. However, liability is again without limits. Each partner is initially liable to his percentage of ownership, but if the partners cannot pay their share should claims be made against them, then all can be liable to the full extent of their personal fortunes for debts incurred by the partnership.

While proprietorships and partnerships represent the largest number of enterprises over all sectors, they have relatively little impact upon the current market. Further, their average life span in Canada is relatively short, averaging around three years. The corporation has become increasingly dominant. In the manufacturing sector in 1946, individual ownerships accounted for an estimated 47.3 percent of the manufacturing establishments, partnerships accounted for 16 percent, cooperatives accounted for 3.3 percent and incorporated companies accounted for 33.4 percent. In 1970 the percentages were 23.2 percent for individual ownerships, 5.7 percent for partnership, 1.6 percent for cooperatives and 69.5 percent for incorporated companies.[10]

In contemporary industrialized society, it is the large corporation that sets the patterns of market behavior. It offers an efficient form of organization while minimizing risks for any one person. Should claims be brought against it or should it suffer losses, bondholders of the corporation receive first priority in protecting their assets (bonds are a security, promising to pay a certain number of dollars every so often until they mature, at which time the borrowing corporation promises to pay off the principal of the bond at face value). Persons holding preferred stock are next in line in protection of their investments. (Preferred stockholders have no right to vote on company policies. They receive a stated dividend of the face value of the share.) Common stockholders who can vote on company policies are most subject to losses, but they also stand to gain in earnings during periods of increased profits. Indeed, the voting privileges and the increased earnings during periods of increased profits are the attractive features of common shares.

Since the Industrial Revolution, price competition and continued increases in costs of production factors have given added impetus to the use of machine technology. Legal entities, such as the corporation, enabled entrepreneurs to amass huge sums of capital for investment in their industrial enterprises. Once in use, machine production required a continuous rate of sufficiently large volume of production in order to amortize its costs. This served as a further impetus for entrepreneurs to increase consumer demand. In the second half of the nineteenth century, market expansion for industrialized European countries, especially England, occurred through the acquisition of overseas colonies. But by the end of that century, colonies receded in economic importance in the face of increased purchasing power by growing indigenous populations in industrialized European countries.[11]

Economies from machine technology can be gained only through a large volume of production. Under such conditions, it is to the entrepreneur's advantage to be assured of stable stocks of supplies and stable markets. Hence, by the 1890s in the United States, and in the period from 1909–1912 in Canada, huge industrial enterprises were fashioned not only by expansion of single corporations, but also and more importantly, by take-overs of other enterprises. Commercial enterprises devoted primarily to marketing goods were especially subject to this process. In the United States before 1870, nearly all the American industrial enterprises concentrated solely upon the manufacture of goods. By the end of the century, the great enterprises not only manufactured goods, but they also sold them directly to retailers and in some cases to the ultimate consumer. They also were likely to produce their own raw materials or to control other companies who produced them.[12] Where there once had been separate organizations for the sale of raw materials for manufacture, for wholesaling, and for retailing, they now became incorporated into one organization. The same process also occurred in Canada.

Typical Structures of Large-Scale Corporations

In Chapter 4, I noted the high degree of concentration which existed within major Canadian industrial sectors. While this is partly a function of the relatively small scale of the Canadian economy, it also indicates the existence of huge organizations designed to administer the production process, whether for the extraction of resources, for the manufacture of goods, or for servicing capital.

Typically, in a very small firm, a single person can coordinate tasks and allocate individuals to fill them. This is the classic role of the capitalist entrepreneur. But with increased size, the entrepreneur must delegate the responsibility for many supervisory functions to other individuals, since there are limits to the number of workers and the diversity of tasks over which any one person can exercise control. Such delegated authority tends to be allocated along specialized functions within any one enterprise. For example, when a manufacturing enterprise employs more than about 100 workers, separate departments of accounting, purchasing, and engineering begin to emerge. As the enterprise increases in size beyond 500 employees, production control, industrial engineering, personnel, and inspection divisions tend to be formed.[13]

These or similar divisions represent not only separate departments, but they also produce management roles which are hierarchically ordered. Chandler and Redlich have pointed out that generally, there are roughly three levels of management: those managers at the lowest level who deal with day-to-day operations within the objectives set for their departments; the middle-level managers who typically represent field offices and are expected to coordinate the operations of the specific divisions; and the top-level managers who set company goals and policies for the entire corporation.[14] They establish objectives regarding growth, sales and profit margins; decide on mergers, take-overs and liquidations; and approve marketing strategies and product designs.

In enterprises with many plants (or "establishments") these three levels also imply geographical differentiation as well. Thus, head offices tend to be located in major financial centers. (In Canada, Toronto has supplanted Montreal as the dominant center.) This is because corporate planning invariably involves the accumulation and investment of capital. The presence of head offices in turn attracts more and larger financial organizations. Field or district offices are dispersed throughout the market area of a particular economy. (In Canada, other cities such as Vancouver, Edmonton, Calgary, Winnipeg, Saskatoon, Quebec City, Halifax, and St. John's are the locations for these offices.) Managers of particular establishments or divisions may be even more dispersed throughout the country. Such divisions can create geographical specializations within a single economy. A consequence of this is centralized control from a metropolitan center extending out to the "hinterland." Obviously, this has implications for the division of power and the degree of regional autonomy. A commodity that might sell well in Quebec, for example, may not be produced for the market if it does not serve the larger interests of a corporation. Those interests, in turn, may be shaped by executives whose perspectives are influenced by the head office environment.

As enterprises grow in size, proportional shifts in types of job specialties continue. The proportion of administrative personnel increases, first at a faster rate than the actual growth of the enterprise, then there is a proportional decline, while technicians and specialized staff personnel increase at a faster rate than the rate of growth in overall size. As might be expected, the more highly mechanized the enterprise, the higher the proportion of technical experts and administrative employees.[15] Technical experts typically serve in "staff" positions. They are not included in the direct line of command but rather make recommendations to those in authority. Personnel involved in research and development are typically viewed as filling staff functions. Those in positions which provide the primary chain of authority occupy "line" positions. (Supervisors, or foremen, represent the final link relating workers to management. As such, they occupy one of the most conflict-ridden roles in the organization. They must mediate between managers who tend to view workers as merely cost factors, and workers who obviously have a different orientation.)

One should also mention clerical workers, who represent the fastest-growing segment in the occupational structure. The majority are women who process records and communications. In the past, their status within the organization was identified with their immediate supervisors—executive secretaries might receive gestures of deference similar to those given to their boss. However, to the extent that the office becomes mechanized and skills become diluted, these groups of workers will likely lose their standing and consequently become amenable to union representation.[16]

Finally, above the authority structure itself is the board of directors. This body may include major shareholders, representatives of suppliers of capital, members of the founding family of the enterprise, or senior executives from within the firm. While this body is potentially powerful, Dill states that most of the relevant research concludes that it seldom exercises its power in fact. He cites Gordon and Chamberlain, who claim that in most cases the board appears to depend on the expertise of management. In actual fact, the authors note, the board provides three functions:

1. It periodically forces discussion of important problems at the top management level;
2. It can bring useful knowledge, experience, and contacts to the organization which it serves;
3. By holding power to appoint the top executive of the corporation, the board puts some limits on the range of things executives will venture if there is a potential risk to their job tenure.[17]

There is a wealth of evidence showing the homogeneous origins of the relatively few individuals who sit on boards of different corporations.[18] These are persons who are likely themselves to be chief executives of other corporations, who are likely to have come from similar socioeconomic backgrounds, who have attended the same schools and who belong to the same social clubs.

Such homogeneity and interlocking directorates are not surprising if one recalls that a considerable amount of trust must exist among executives within a single organization. Hence, the more similar the background training and experience, the more alike individuals will be chosen for these positions.[19]

The principle involved here is that trust and reliablility in the decisions of management and supervisory personnel can be more readily assumed if managers and supervisors display similar orientations to those already in power. In the context of capitalist liberal societies, the critical question hinges on the degree to which such selection can be justified by the basic values of freedom and equality. These values may not in fact be acted upon in selecting individuals to occupy the most powerful positions. Both Porter and Clement argue that in Canada there tends to be a self-perpetuating and closed elite who control the major corporations.[20] As a result the values are appealed to more as ideological justifications than as operating premises.

The Multi-National Corporation

Incentives to Expand

It is no happenstance that the largest corporations dominating particular industrial sectors in a domestic economy are the first ones to extend their operations to foreign economies. (Massey-Ferguson and Alcan are two examples of Canadian corporations with foreign branches.) If profit-making is the dominant objective of corporations, then to ensure their maintenance, if not their increase, in the face of possible foreign competition, large rational production organizations must expand. (However, in the general case, profits alone do not explain why there is an expansion of production organizations. Within any rational organization, success tends to be measured in terms of quantifiable units, which in turn result in an emphasis upon growth in size and functions.)

Profits can be maintained or increased in two ways: by increasing the size of markets of particular products and by continually modifying commodities for particular markets of consumers.[21] Once a consumer market is created, it is easier for industrial corporations to continually modify products for receptive consumers than to create new markets for consumer goods. (One reason is that a supportive infrastructure must be created. Toasters are hard to sell to people who lack cheap and reliable sources of electricity.) Thus, the pattern of growth has stressed product innovation for receptive consumers first, with secondary emphasis on expanding markets.

Product innovation requires relatively huge outlays of money for capital equipment. Competitiveness in the marketplace, while stimulating innovation, also creates uncertainty about the successful sale of any commodity. Production organizations have sought different means to control this uncertainty, and thereby protect their capital investments, even though they may make their investments in order to utilize surplus profits. Before and after the First World War, there were agreements among large corporations throughout the industrial world on the allocation of shares of markets, pricing policies, volume of production, and geographical areas of marketing. Such arrangements, known as "cartels," provided a more rationalized and predictable environment within which production and sales could be more easily controlled and hence profits assured. But as Tugendhat has pointed out, these agreements were never very stable, since executives' interests in the welfare of their own corporations invariably took precedence over collective agreements.[22] Further, anti-monopolistic laws initiated in the United States, largely as a result of pressure from small business interests, outlawed such agreements. This prevented American corporations with export operations in foreign markets from making agreements with other corporations which further undercut international agreements. Consequently, while cartel-like arrangements have continued to exist, the dominant form of expanding the scope of operations and hence protecting profits has been to establish foreign-based operations either through a corporation attaining direct control of existing foreign enterprises or by establishing a new subsidiary enterprise. The result has been the multi-national corporation, that is, a corporation which directly controls both the preparation and sale of goods and services in two or more countries.

Defined in more technical terms, a multi-national corporation is one which engages in foreign *direct investment*. Direct investment is capital investment in an enterprise where the investor has the possibility of voting control of the concern. Control is assured when the investor has more than 50 percent of the voting stock. However, in most cases, effective control may be accomplished by far fewer holdings. Twenty-five percent or even 10 percent control of the voting stock may be sufficient to exercise effective control over the policies of the corporation. This can be done by influencing proxy votes of shareholders: that is, shareholders can sign over their votes to others. Of course, a corporation may have total control over its foreign-based branches. In Canada, these branches can then be defined as privately owned and thus, are not required to make public their financial statements.

Investments do not necessarily imply control. *Portfolio investments*, in contrast to *direct investments*, involve no legal claims to control. They are investments—such as preferred stock or bonds—that lay claim only to remittances of interest. These two types of investments contribute to a further distinction: foreign ownership versus foreign control. The former refers to the ownership of equity shares and debt capital owned by non-residents. The latter refers to the control of voting stock. Foreign ownership may mean that profit remittances may be flowing out of the country, while foreign control means that in addition, decisions regarding the operations of the company may be dictated by foreign interests. These may run counter to the overall economic objectives of the "host" country.

While a dominant reason for establishing foreign subsidiaries is to safeguard profits, this safeguarding is manifested in many ways. Foreign holdings may be acquired in order to ensure a reliable source of natural resources at prices that can be controlled. For example, some American newspapers control their own supplies of pulp and paper through their Canadian subsidiaries in that sector. Ownership of subsidiaries may also serve to minimize unit selling costs in both a foreign and world-wide market. Tariffs, quotas, taxes, capital repatriation requirements, and high transportation and procurement costs may all contribute to the costs of a product if it were exported to a foreign market. Establishing a plant circumvents these costs.[23] Further, factor costs in the preparation of goods and services may be lower in the foreign market. This includes land, labor, and capital service costs.

Finally, it should be pointed out that before foreign direct investments are made in a particular country, political stability must be assured. Corporations are less concerned about the political persuasion of a country than they are about its stability and assurances that gains can be made. They are as likely to invest in China as they are in Brazil if conditions conducive to their interests exist. Obviously, their aims may not be the same as the political and economic objectives of the particular country, but what is more relevant is the fact that their own aims can be realized. In the final analysis this attitude has to do with the role the subsidiary plays in maintaining profit objectives. This, as well as development of easy currency conversion, is a major reason why there was such a dramatic expansion of American penetration into the European market after the Second World War. Aiding this development was the policy of the American government to extend financial aid primarily through private corporations rather than directly from government sources. Finally, it should be pointed out that the expansion into the European and other foreign markets would not have been as extensive without rapid and efficient forms of communications and transportation.[24]

Host countries in which subsidiaries are established may see this foreign penetration as an attractive means to develop their own economies. The investment of foreign capital can stimulate economic activity in many industrial sectors. It can also contribute to building necessary infrastructures, such as transportation and utilities, and it can further stimulate local markets for capital and consumer goods. The problem, of course, is the degree to which host countries can control these investments and derive adequate tax revenue to support additional services.

Once having established a subsidiary, a foreign corporation may gain additional advantages by founding or controlling subsidiaries in still other countries. Additional foreign subsidiaries can increase the flexibility of the controlling corporation by insuring steady, if not increased, returns. This can be accomplished by balancing temporary losses in one country with increased earnings in another. Indeed, taken individually, one foreign subsidiary may be only minimally profitable, but it may contribute more to overall profits of the corporation than if it did not exist. Should there be more restrictive government policies or new entrants into its field in one country, losses can be recovered by more profitable operations elsewhere. According to Litvak and Maule, the shift toward intricate global strategies usually occurs when more than 25 percent of the total output of a corporation is produced in a foreign country.[25]

The increased involvement in global networks means that a multinational corporation has increased flexibility in dealing with unique exigencies of particular markets at its disposal. For example, should labor strikes cripple a subsidiary in one country, management may respond by increasing production in another subsidiary, or it may resort to increasing its exports from its home-based plants. It has been alleged that United Aircraft employed this latter tactic during the long strike at its Montreal plant some years ago. Another tactic is to produce components in foreign subsidiaries and import them into the "home" country, particularly if higher local labor costs cut too deeply into profit margins. American automobile manufacturers frequently employ this strategy. Finally, a corporation may simply transfer the bulk of its operations to low factor-cost areas. Leica, for example, moved its main base of operations from Germany to Singapore.

A multi-national corporation is also in an advantageous position in circumventing many government policies, especially those dealing with taxation and capital repatriation laws. (These are laws governing the flows of earned income back to the host or home countries.) It may seek to establish subsidiaries in those countries which have no or relatively minor repatriation laws or low taxes, or it may circumvent these by transfer pricing in inter-company trade. That is, the parent company may mark up the price of component parts that it exports to its subsidiary, thus reducing the reported earnings of the subsidiary, and thereby avoiding high tax payments, or as in the case of the natural resource industries, parent corporations may mark down the price of exports out of Canada which serve their own industries and accomplish the same ends.[26]

Canada's long status as a colony under the benign political umbrella of Great Britain and the long control by mercantile-oriented elites have undoubtedly contributed to more openness to foreign investments and control. Initially, foreign investments in Canada were primarily portfolio investments—investments which did not mean outright control of locally based companies. This followed the typical pattern of British investments, which remained the dominant source of foreign capital until the First World War.

Since then, investments from the United States have increased and have become primarily direct investments. Even in the late nineteenth century, American companies had compelling reasons for establishing subsidiaries in Canada. Given the Canadian tariff structure, Americans found that establishing branch plants in Canada enabled them to market their commodities at less cost than if they were exporting them. Further, through Canada, they gained access to the Commonwealth preferential trade system. Local communities frequently offered favorable conditions for taxation and the purchase of land. The Canadian patent law (Acts of 1872 and 1903) also encouraged American penetration into Canadian markets. It required the establishment of a local plant within two years if the invention continued to be imported and twelve months after the patent was granted. Failing this, a Canadian manufacturer had to be licensed.[27] During the period from 1870 to 1890, the dominant American-controlled subsidiaries included Imperial Oil, the American Tobacco Company of Canada, Singer Sewing Machine, Bell Telephone, American Screw, and Houston Electric, forerunner of General Electric.

The current concern over foreign—primarily American-controlled—enterprises in Canada stems from the relatively huge influx of American direct investment following the Second World War. After the war, American corporations found themselves with a surplus of liquid capital and declining natural resources.[28] Canada, with huge stocks of natural resources, a growing population which had doubled since the late 1920s, a Gross National Product that had tripled over the same period, and a stable political environment, provided ideal conditions for American investment.

As her resource sector became further developed, Canada became an increasingly inviting market for industrial equipment and consumer durable goods. It was from the end of the Second World War to about 1958 that the pattern of American control became established. Since 1958 the proportion of total American investments claimed by Canada has not changed significantly, although it has played a larger role in Canada's own economy. American investments from this period began flowing to Europe, attracted by increased political stability and by the formation of the European Common Market and the European Free Trade Association. Investment monies also shifted to other parts of the developing world where the political climate was relatively stable.

Nevertheless, in 1978 the *Financial Post* listing of the dominant corporations by 1977 year-end sales in Canada revealed the following facts: (1) Among the top 200 industrials (those companies for which at least 50 percent of sales or revenues come from manufacturing, utilities, or transport operations), 118 had 50 percent or more of their shares owned by foreign interests. Eighty-eight of these major shareholders were from the United States, with the remaining 30 from other countries. Of this group of 118, 71 were wholly owned by foreign interests. Of these, 59 were wholly owned by Americans. Finally, another 27 of the dominant corporations had less than 50 percent foreign ownership, but in most cases this still meant effective foreign control. (2) Among the top 20 petroleum and mining corporations, only 4 were wholly owned by Canadians, the top 3 were wholly owned by Americans, and another 9 were 50 percent or more, but less than 100 percent, owned by Americans. Canadians held majority interest in another two corporations and shareholders from foreign countries other than the United States held 50 percent or more of the shares in the 2 remaining corporations. (3) Among the top 30 merchandising corporations, 20 were wholly Canadian-owned and 7 were wholly American-owned. Three other corporations had 30 percent or more of their shares held by foreign interests. (4) Among the top 40 financial corporations, United States interests of 20 percent or more were involved in 8 corporations. The remainder including the top 15 were wholly Canadian-owned.[29]

A listing of the top 400 industrial, retailing, and financial corporations by *Canadian Business*, also based upon 1977 year-end sales, revealed that for 208 of these, the largest single shareholder came from a foreign country. Of these, 154 were from the United States.[30]

Merely plotting the flow of foreign investments provides neither an adequate index of foreign control nor the full implications of a decline of investments in particular areas. Investments from foreign sources tend to remain high only during initial stages of establishing branch plants or taking over control of indigenous enterprises. Once these become ongoing concerns, they generate additional capital for the parent corporation and capital flows back to the home office. During the period 1960-67, American-based corporations invested 9.6 billion dollars in Europe while receiving only 7.3 billion dollars in remittances. But in Canada, which has had a longer period of direct foreign investment, capital inflows from the United States amounted to 4.1 billion dollars while 5.9 billion dollars left the country in remittances. About eighty-five percent of the capital controlled by American interests and invested in Canada is generated by subsidiaries within Canada.

Latin American countries lost even more. During the same period, American corporations invested 1.7 billion dollars, but cash outflows amounted to 8.8 billion dollars. And 11.3 billion dollars in profits were taken from the Middle East, Africa, Asia, and the Far East, while only 3.9 billion dollars was invested in these areas.[31]

The "home countries" of these global corporations have not necessarily continued to be net gainers. Increasingly, multi-national corporations, most of which are based in the United States, are becoming a world force acting independently of either the home or host countries. As noted before, funds and even plant operations can be shifted among different countries for the maximum benefit of the corporations alone. Thus, cash flows in and out of particular countries do not necessarily indicate the earning capabilities of a multi-national corporation. Rather, capital can be generated within a given country, contributing to the overall profits of the corporation that has subsidiaries in a large number of countries. Profits do not necessarily flow back to the home country of the parent corporation; they become, in effect, "foreign reserves" to be reinvested.[32]

American-based companies may open a new foreign branch, claim it as an initial loss for United States' tax purposes, and later designate it as a foreign-based subsidiary whose profits may be taxed at a lower rate than the maximum established in the United States. According to a *Newsweek* article,

> By adroit bookkeeping and pricing of transactions among subsidiaries across national boundaries profits may be concentrated in the countries where taxes are lowest. Perhaps worse, there have been suggestions that at least a few multinationals have smuggled hard cash into the United States to avoid taxes and to make political payoffs.[33]

Strategies in the operations of multi-national corporations in the international markets require considerable expertise. Sanford Rose related the following with respect to investments and gains to be won from currency exchanges:

> A Ford economist regularly scans the international financial statistics to determine which countries have the highest rates of inflation; these are obviously prime candidates for devaluation. He then examines patterns of trade. If a country is running more of an inflation than its chief trading partners and competitors and its reserves are limited, it is more than a candidate; it is a shoo-in. His most difficult problem is to determine exactly when the devaluation will take place. Economics determines whether and how much, but politicians control the timing. So the analyst maintains a complete library of information on leading national officials. He tries to get "into the skin of the man" who is going to make the decision. The economist's forecasts have been correct in sixty-nine of the last seventy-five crisis situations.
>
> Dupont is one company that is making a stab in the direction of formally measuring environmental uncertainty, basically as a tool for capital budgeting decisions. The project is still in the research stage, but essentially the idea is to try to derive estimates of the potential of a foreign market, which is, of course, affected by economic conditions. The state of the economy in turn is partly a function of the fiscal and monetary policies the foreign government adopts. Policy decisions depend on real economic forces, on the attitudes of various interest groups in the country, and on the degree to which the government listens to these groups.
>
> In the fiscal and monetary part of their broad economic model, the Dupont researchers have identified fifteen to twenty interest groups per country, from small land-owners to private bankers. Each interest group has a "latent influence," which depends on its size and educational level and the group's power to make its feelings felt. This influence, subjectively measured, is multiplied by an estimate of "group cohesiveness," i.e., how likely the group is to mobilize its full resources on any particular issue. The product is a measure of "potential influence." This in turn must be multiplied by a factor representing the government's receptivity to each influence group.[34]

Compounding the problem of cash flows is the fact that the larger resources of multi-national corporations and the relatively stable returns provide an added incentive for investments from host country sources. Canadian investment groups such as mutual funds and trust companies, trusteed pension funds, life insurance funds, and fire and casualty insurance funds tend to invest in multi-national corporations rather than in smaller, less stable Canadian corporations.[35] In 1965, 10 percent of Canada's gross national product was invested in the United States.[36]

Canada's trade deficits with the United States have usually been offset by earnings from other markets. But this is no longer true. Since about 1963 the degree of American control of vital sectors in Canada's economy has been of growing concern among journalists, economists, and, increasingly, government officials. American-controlled corporations are dominant in natural resources, chemicals, and selected manufacturing sectors. They control over 50 percent of the mining and smelter industries, petroleum and natural gas, over 65 percent of the electrical apparatus and aircraft industries, more than 75 percent of the chemical industry, over 80 percent of the rubber industry, and over 90 percent of the automobile industry.

Consequences of Foreign Control in Canada

The draining of capital from the economy is only one consequence of foreign-controlled operations in Canada. There are other effects as well. These include (a) the degree to which Canadian managerial skills remain undeveloped as a result of foreign control; (b) the degree of autonomy the Canadian subsidiaries are permitted to exercise; (c) the export and import performance of subsidiaries; (d) the effects of foreign subsidiaries upon Canadian research and development activities; and (e) the relative efficiencies of foreign-controlled companies.[37] In addition, there are consequences for political autonomy and what has been termed "cultural" autonomy. We can briefly consider each of these issues in turn.

Managerial Skills

Companies with more than 50 percent control by a foreign interest tend to have foreign-born chief executives. These managers may be unable or unwilling to develop policies that are compatible with the unique needs and requirements of the Canadian economic and political context. The long period of time in which General Motors was unwilling to make French the working language in its Ste. Thérèse, Quebec, plant is only one example of such intransigence.

The pressure of foreign-owned companies raises the question of the degree to which Canadians can gain managerial skills and expertise. Frequently, this can be accomplished only if they join a management group in the United States. Additionally, it may well be the case that those Canadians who do move into managerial positions of foreign-controlled corporations are oriented more to the interests of the multi-national firm than to the continued development of the Canadian economy.[38] On the other hand, some Canadian companies welcome the expertise which foreigners, particularly Americans, bring to bear upon their enterprise. One Canadian corporate board chairman wrote in 1978 that, "Since most Canadian business practices, production, and marketing techniques were developed in the U.S., I see no reason why outside directors who have experience in that country should not be included on Canadian boards."[39]

Autonomy of Canadian Subsidiaries

This raises the question regarding the degree of autonomy managers of Canadian based subsidiaries are able to exercise. Obviously, foreign control implies that the parent corporation is the key point of reference for decisions. As the overall operations of the multi-national corporation grow, there tends to be greater decentralization of its operations. This means that managers of subsidiaries of giant world corporations tend to have greater autonomy than those who manage a single subsidiary of a foreign-based corporation. However, the nature of autonomy differs according to the structural relationships between subsidiaries and parent corporations. Subsidiaries which replicate the complete structure of their parents may have more autonomy than those which serve more specialized functions. In the former case, managers may exercise a considerable amount of discretion in the design and marketing of their products. In the latter case, managers may simply carry out "branch plant" roles, following the dictates of their parent corporation in its overall global designs.[40] Examples of this are foreign-owned plants, such as Asbestos Corporation, which export partially manufactured goods to the United States, or other subsidiaries which manufacture component parts.

In the past, American-owned corporations have tended to exercise more constraints upon their Canadian subsidiaries than has been the case with other foreign-owned companies. One reason for this is the relatively long history of economic linkages between the two countries. American executives tend to treat their Canadian subsidiaries in the same way in which they deal with branches within the United States.

Export and Import Performance

Foreign-controlled corporations tend to export a higher volume of goods than Canadian corporations export. But since much of this is derived from American-controlled natural resource industries, and since these products contribute a major share to all of Canada's exports, it is not surprising that the export records of foreign-owned companies are higher. Further, a relatively high proportion of manufactured component parts are shipped to parent companies in the United States for further fabrication. While these exports may be underpriced to the advantage of the parent corporation, they still account for a relatively high proportion of the overall value of exports.

The presence of foreign-owned subsidiaries distorts import patterns as well. Subsidiary enterprises tend to import a greater volume of goods than Canadian companies. However, this pattern is similar to exports. Imports tend to follow lines of ownership. Thus, subsidiaries serve their parents not only in supplying natural resources and partially finished goods; they also serve as outlets for goods from the parent company. According to Levitt, in 1963, 70 percent of the goods imported by subsidiaries were from their parent companies, while 50 percent of export sales of subsidiaries were sales to their parent companies. What has been created is a built-in demand system, relatively free of open market constraints.[41]

Effects on Research and Development

An additional economic issue is the effect of foreign subsidiaries on research and development. These activities are considered important because they are a constant stimulant to economic growth and development. According to a special study done for the Science Council of Canada in 1972, the innovative performance of Canada in comparison to nine other industrialized countries is extremely low, ranking at, or near the bottom on (1) location of the most significant innovations since World War II; (2) "monetary receipts for patents, licences and know-how" (in the period 1963–64); (3) number of patents taken out in foreign countries (1963); (4) export performance in research-intensive industries (1963–65), and (5) export performance in research-intensive product groups (1963–65).[42]

This poor performance is, in part, a result of the major role played by resource-related industries in the Canadian economy. But the presence of subsidiaries of foreign corporations continues to hinder developments in this area, because research activities tend to be carried out by the parent company at its home offices. There is a circular effect at work: because this has been the pattern in the past, the necessary research-related services have not been adequately developed in Canada. The lack of development, in turn, has caused additional research to be carried out in the home country of the parent company. It is, in fact, cheaper for the subsidiary to utilize the innovations developed by the parent company than to develop its own.[43]

The federal government has stepped in with its own funded research and development department, which accounts for 50 percent of the total expenditures for these activities. But these efforts have been relatively ineffective because there has been too little attention directed toward applied technology.[44].

Production Efficiencies

A final economic consequence of foreign-owned corporations in Canada is their tendency to decrease efficiencies of production. Comparing unit production costs of subsidiaries with their parent firms, the 1967 "Watkins Report," officially known as the *Report of the Task Force on Foreign Ownership and the Structure of Canadian Industry*, found that the costs of the former tended to be higher than the latter.[45] The large resources of foreign-owned corporations permit their subsidiaries to introduce excessively diversified products and undersized production runs, which from the perspective of the subsidiaries' operations alone prohibit economies of scale. (This, however, may not be the case for the overall operations of the multi-national corporation.) Further, as we have seen, one factor influencing the presence of foreign-owned corporations has been the tariff structure in Canada. Once in place, tariffs can also serve to protect inefficient industries—foreign-owned subsidiaries and Canadian-owned corporations alike. Since subsidiaries are subject to the overall corporate accounting policies which may include artificial expenses, it is never clear just what constitutes "real" costs.

Political Autonomy

While the earlier decisions of the elites of Canadian governments and industry helped to create an environment conducive to foreign investment and foreign-controlled subsidiaries, the presence of these foreign interests has tended to erode the political autonomy of Canada. In the past, the fact that the options for Canada's economic development are hampered by foreign—mostly American—laws applicable to Canadian subsidiaries has been a matter of concern, as has been the fact that Canada is being drawn into a continental economy controlled largely by the United States.

The past efforts by the United States to prevent Canadian subsidiaries from selling trucks to China and locomotives to Cuba exemplify this concern. The *Gray Report* cited further examples of interference by the United States in Canada's trade with the Soviet Union, Roumania, and Czechoslovakia.[46] The proposed products for export were manufactured by American-controlled subsidiaries in Canada. Their sale was either blocked or severely restricted because the head offices were subject to American laws restricting trade with "enemies" of the United States.

Foreign governments may also step in to protect their own economies at the expense of Canada. When the United States became alarmed about the state of its economy in 1968, Canada felt the effects of decreased capital inflows. The economic guidelines for the United States at that time provided that capital transfers from the United States to "developed" countries could not exceed 65 percent of the 1965–66 base.

More recently, alarm has been expressed about the erosion of political autonomy for both "home" and "host" countries. From a strictly economical perspective, many economists have argued that the integration of Canada's economy with the United States results in multiple advantages from economies of a large market. But to the degree that functions become specialized within a large multi-national corporation and these in turn become geographically defined, this may merely mean that Canada's income is derived from the preparation and sale of natural resources and semi-finished goods to be further processed in the United States. To the degree that economic decisions have political implications, Canada's structural dependence—in economic terms—reduces its freedom of political choice. Canada is limited in a way that is similar to the branch manager in the hinterland who is limited in his decisions by his company's head office. (This perspective is analogous to the arguments employed by recent Quebec governments in relation to the Anglophone dominance of the Quebec economy.)

Cultural Hegemony

Those who have argued against the large-scale presence of American-dominated corporations for "cultural" reasons do so on the premise that it tends to diminish any distinctiveness in the expression of social values that Canada may have in relation to the United States. According to one spokesman, the techniques of rational economic production as developed by Americans tend to dominate the Canadian outlook on the social world.[47] This is reflected in the determination of life styles by mass marketing criteria, the demeaning effects of the ethnocentrism of American managers, and the perpetuation of a "free enterprise" mythology, which may only serve to maintain the vulnerability of Canada to foreign exploitation.[48]

If, in fact, Canada continues to remain a producer of resources and semi-finished products, according to the needs defined by head offices located elsewhere, it follows that the enactment of the values of "freedom" and "equality" that have served as justifications for the industrialization process itself become highly restrictive. Their terms are set by those who make the decisions and this reinforces a mentality of caution and inferiority among those subject to these decisions. If the expressions of "culture" are tied to economic activity, then the role of Canada within the multi-national structures will be reflected in these social definitions. Bearing this relationship in mind, this helps explain why graduate degrees earned in the United States are often more highly prized than those in Canada; why business experience in the United States is also often valued as part of the training of Canadian executives; and why figures in the art and literary world must often gain recognition in the United States before being accepted by Canadians.

Conclusions

In this chapter, I have described the changes in the organization for the production of goods from the guild system to the domestic system, to the factory system, and finally to the evolution of the large-scale industrial corporation. Canada did not experience the full sequential stages of these production systems, since her economy was based initially upon her colonial status as a staples producing area, and then as a producer of resources for foreign manufacturing interests. The changes that Canada experienced were those which accompanied the transitions from the relatively broad social obligations of a feudal type of labor relations in which labor was relatively scarce, to the restricted contractual relationships of the capitalist in which urban labor was relatively abundant.

The growth of the factory system and production systems feeding into it had marked implications for the authority systems which control personnel and capital. The corporation has come to be the prototype of this development. Corporate structures existed, of course, before the Industrial Revolution. The Hudson's Bay Company and the Northwest Trading Company are both examples. They were both formed to spread the costs and share the losses of trading ventures. The industrial corporation serves similar functions, but it requires large amounts of capital in order to finance sophisticated technology. Sophisticated technology is in turn required for gaining the advantages of economies of scale. Further, in order to reduce the effects upon themselves of uncertainties in the market, large-scale corporations have diversified into different sectors and different countries. Perhaps the most important feature of acquisitions and consolidations in the 1970s was that they were undertaken for primarily protective financial reasons, rather than for reasons of production. As a consequence of these developments, organizations have emerged which wield enormous power with international consequences. This suggests a transition to something approximating Hacker's mythical organization, in which the preservation of the organizaiton becomes an end in itself. Further, the awesome economic impact of large-scale corporations on the economy has transformed their relationship with consumers, who are now admonished to consume in order for organizations to produce. Thus production is not encouraged in order to meet needs, but rather consumption is encouraged in order to maintain the organizations and hence the economy and finally social structures in general.

Notes

1. Andrew Hacker, "Introduction: Corporate America," *The Corporation Take-Over*, ed. A. Hacker (New York: Harper and Row, 1964), pp. 3–5.
2. See for example, Richard Cyert and James March, "A Behavioral Theory of Organizational Objectives," *Organizations: Structure and Behavior*, Vol. II, ed. J. Litterer (New York: Wiley, 1969), pp. 349–357.

3. Shepard B. Clough, *European Economic History: The Economic Development of Western Civilization* (Toronto: McGraw-Hill, 1968), pp. 102–103.

4. Ibid., pp. 104–105.

5. Henry Pirenne, "European Guilds," *Encyclopaedia of the Social Sciences*, eds. Edward A. Seligman and Alvin Johnson (New York: Macmillan, 1953), pp. 208–214.

6. Clough, op. cit., pp. 105–106.

7. Ibid., p. 277.

8. Joseph A. Schumpeter, *Capitalism, Socialism and Democracy*, 3rd ed. (New York: Harper Torchbooks, 1962), p. 132.

9. H.C. Pentland, "The Development of a Capitalist Labour Market in Canada," *Canadian Journal of Economics and Political Science*, Vol. XXV (1959).

10. *Manufacturing Industries of Canada: Type of Organization and Size of Establishment* (Ottawa: Statistics Canada, May, 1970), p. 3.

11. Paul Landes, *The Unbound Prometheus* (Cambridge: Cambridge University Press, 1969), pp. 238–241.

12. Alfred D. Chandler, Jr., *Strategy and Structure: Chapters in the History of the Industrial Enterprise* (Cambridge, Mass.: The MIT Press, 1962), pp. 30–31.

13. Cited in William R. Dill, "Business Organizations," *Handbook of Organizations*, ed. James G. March (Chicago: Rand McNally, 1965), pp. 1071–1114.

14. Alfred D. Chandler and Fritz Redlich, "Recent Developments in American Business Administration and Their Conceptualization," *Business History Review* (Spring, 1961), pp. 103–128. Cited in Stephen Hymer, "The Multi-national Corporation and The Law of Uneven Development," *Economics and World Order: From 1970's–1990's*, ed. J. N. Bhagwati (New York: Macmillan, 1972), pp. 113–140.

15. Reinhard Bendix, *Work and Authority in Industry* (New York: Harper and Row, 1956), p. 223.

16. Dill, op. cit., p. 1082ff. For a classic analysis of the origins of modern industrial corporate structures see Alfred D. Chandler, Jr., *Strategy and Structure* (Cambridge: MIT Press, 1962). See also William Serrin, *The Company and the Union* (New York: Alfred Knopf, 1973), p. 96.

17. Dill, op. cit., p. 1082.

18. The most thorough analyses in Canada are John Porter, *The Vertical Mosaic: An Analysis of Social Class and Power in Canada* (Toronto: University of Toronto Press, 1965); Wallace Clement, *The Canadian Corporate Elite: An Analysis of Economic Power* (Toronto: McClelland and Stewart, Carleton Library, 1975); and Wallace Clement, *Continental Corporate Power: Economic Linkages Between Canada and the United States* (Toronto: McClelland and Stewart, 1977).

19. Rosabeth M. Kanter, *Men and Women of the Corporation* (New York: Basic Books, 1977), pp. 52–59.

20. See Porter, op. cit., and Clement, op. cit.

21. Hymer, op. cit., p. 119. Hymer argues that a choice was made to concentrate on "continuous innovation for a small number of people." But this does not explain the continual expansion of consumer markets to include greater numbers of people. The evidence points to an initial emphasis upon limited consumers primed to accept continual innovations followed by gradual expansion of these markets.

22. Christopher Tugendhat, *The Multinationals* (Middlesex, Eng.: Penguin Books, 1973), pp. 40–44, 53–54.

23. I. A. Litvak and C. J. Maule, "The Multinational Corporation: Some Economic and Political-Legal Implications," *Journal of World Trade Law*, Vol. V, No. 6 (November–December, 1971), p. 633.

24. Tugendhat, op. cit., pp. 33, 46.

25. Litvak and Maule, op. cit., p. 633.

26. Ibid., p. 634.

27. Stephen Scheinberg, "Invitation to Empire: Tariffs and American Economic Expansion in Canada," *Enterprise and National Development*, ed. Glenn Porter and Robert D. Cuff (Toronto: Hakkert, 1973, pp. 80-100.

28. H. E. English, "Foreign Ownership Reviewed," *Canadian Economic Issues*, ed. I. D. Pal (Toronto: Macmillan of Canada, 1971), p. 549.

29. *The Financial Post 300*, Summer, 1978, pp. 7-22.

30. "The Top 400," in *Canadian Business*, July, 1978, pp. 60-96.

31. Kari Levitt, *Silent Surrender: The Multinational Corporation in Canada* (Toronto: Macmillan of Canada, 1970), p. 94.

32. *Foreign Owned Subsidiaries in Canada: A Report on Operations and Financing by the Larger Subsidiary Companies for the Period 1964-67* (Ottawa: Queen's Printer, 1970). Internal generation of funds from these subsidiaries amounted to 62 percent of requirements in 1965, 64 percent in 1966, and 71 percent in 1967.

33. "Global Companies: Too Big to Handle?" *Newsweek*, November 20, 1972, p. 97.

34. Sanford Rose, "The Rewarding Strategies of Multinationalism," *Fortune*, September 15, 1968, p. 105.

35. *The Financial Post*, December 4, 1971.

36. *Economic Almanac, 1967* (Ottawa: Queen's Printer, 1969).

37. English, op. cit., pp. 551-553.

38. Wallace Clement calls these individuals "compradors." See *The Canadian Corporate Elite* (Toronto: McClelland and Stewart, 1975), p. 36.

39. Henry R. Jackman, "How to find the Perfect Director," *The Financial Post*, July 1, 1978, p. 12.

40. Arthur J. Cordell, *The Multinational Firm, Foreign Direct Investment, and Canadian Science Policy* (Ottawa: Information Canada, 1971), p. 36.

41. Levitt, op. cit., p. 124.

42. Pierre L. Bourgault, *Innovation and the Structure of Canadian Industry*, Background Study for the Science Council of Canada (Ottawa: Information Canada, 1972). The countries were the following: United States, France, Germany, Italy, Japan, Sweden, Switzerland, the United Kingdom, Netherlands and Canada (p. 38).

43. Ibid., p. 82.

44. Ibid., p. 56.

45. Task Force on the Structure of Canadian Industry, *Report: Foreign Ownership and the Structure of Canadian Industry* (Ottawa: Queen's Printer, 1968).

46. *A Citizen's Guide to the Gray Report* (Toronto: Canada Forum, 1971), p. 77.

47. George Grant, *Technology and Empire* (Toronto: Anansi, 1969).

48. *A Citizen's Guide to the Gray Report*, op. cit., pp. 87-92.

chapter six

Managing the Large Corporation: Theoretical Perspectives

Introduction

As production organizations have grown larger and more complex, problems of coordination and efficiency have become predominant. Added to these structural problems has been the continued restiveness of labor. These factors have resulted in the development of a variety of theories of management, all of which attempt to preserve the rationality of organizations while gaining the allegiance of their personnel. These theories imply that management has become an area of expertise quite independent of the objectives of formal organizations.

This chapter analyzes those major theories of management which have had an impact upon the exercise of authority in formal organizations throughout the western world. Their content is familiar to any student of business administration whether he is Canadian, German, British, or American. From the analytic perspective of this book, this chapter deals with formal expressions of systems of meaning that are designed to enact authority in the most efficient manner possible. Following the analysis in this chapter, Chapter 7 will deal with the attempts of managers to *justify* their authority. These justifications will be treated as *ideologies* because they represent attempts to resolve fundamental conflicts between the exercise of rational authority and the more general values of freedom and equality.

Early Images of the Formal Organization

The reference point of early influential theorists of formal organizations was not the industrial work organization, but the administrative structure of the early German state. Before Marx, Hegel had viewed the emerging state "bureaus" as a link between rulers and populace. The impartiality of the structure was ensured, Hegel had argued, by the use of uniform examinations for recruiting personnel, payment of standardized salaries, and, most important, the commitment of personnel to an impersonal moral code of duty. As a consequence, citizens could be served in a fair and predictable manner. Hegel had further argued that, once in place, such a structure prevented rulers from acting in an arbitrary and capricious manner since they would be constrained by functionaries whose primary allegiance was to the impersonal requirements of the bureaucracy.

Hegel's image of the bureaucracy provided the beginning point for Marx. In a critique written at the age of twenty-four, Marx points out that far from being a check upon the possible excesses of rulers, the administrative bureaucracy becomes a formalized version of the state. It both serves and influences the conduct of rulers of the state:

> The aims of the state are transformed into aims of bureaus or the aims of bureaus into the aims of the state. The bureaucracy is a circle from which no one can escape. Its hierarchy is a hierarchy of knowledge. The highest point entrusts the understanding of particulars to the lower echelons, whereas these, on the other hand, credit the highest with an understanding in regard to the universal; and thus they deceive one another.[1]

Even examinations for positions within the bureaucracy become perverted in their intent. They are nothing, Marx wrote, "but the bureaucratic baptism of knowledge, the official recognition of the transubstantiation of profane into holy knowledge." He adds caustically, "No one ever heard of the Greek or Roman statesman taking an examination. But then what is a Roman statesman even as against a Prussian official!"[2]

Marx goes on to point out that, ultimately, existence of the state bureaucracy serves the interests of the dominant classes in society. Rather than being a mediating link between individuals and the collective requirements of society, the state bureaucracy tends to concentrate power and to separate it from the control of the larger population. This conceptualization re-occurs in Marx's later writings when he is dealing with the economy of capitalist societies. Noting the emergence and growth of joint stock companies, in *Capital* Marx denounced the view that they provided structures that were more responsive to public interests. Rather, he argued, they reproduce a new "financial aristocracy" who are like "parasites" living off capitalist modes of production as promoters, speculators, and nominal directors. They encourage a "whole system of swindling and cheating by means of corporation promotion, stock issuance and stock speculation." The joint stock company was, in Marx's view "private production without the control of private property."[3]

Marx's image of the joint-stock company is an economic version of his perceptions about the Prussian government bureaucracy. Within the context of his view of historical change, it represents the most extreme form of exploitation; even the use of capital is divorced from its owners. Yet at the same time, because it does represent an extreme form, it provides the structural underpinnings in the transition to a "new mode of production."[4]

For Marx, the emergence of large-scale economic corporations is a consequence of capitalist modes of production. But he says nothing about the characteristics of organizations for either production or governance in postcapitalist societies. This void has been a continual source of debate among Marx's intellectual heirs, because it raises the question whether it is possible to meet the organizational needs for production and civil administration without creating a new basis for social inequality and class relations. Lenin argued, for example, that formal organizations are necessary, but not the esteem and special privileges that have traditionally been bestowed upon administrators. Others have taken the position that it is difficult to prevent this from occurring as long as formal organizations exist.

Bureaucracy as an Authority System

It is at this point that Weber's analysis, with its focus upon paradox, becomes relevant. Weber begins his analysis with his concept of "domination." By this he means the probability that a given set of commands will be obeyed by a given group of individuals.[5] The term is used to denote a special instance of power or influence; that is, it presumes a willingness of a group of people to comply with the wishes of another group. The motives for compliance may be highly diverse, ranging from simply habit to the most rational calculation of the benefits to be derived.

When large numbers of people are involved, dominance usually requires a staff—a special group who can be trusted to carry out both the general policies and the specific commands of their superiors. Members of the staff also have their own motives for obedience to their superiors: these can be based on custom, affection, commitment to a set of ideals, or purely material interests. On this last point, Weber argues that purely material interests and calculations of personal advantages are insufficient grounds for promoting stable relations between staff members and their superior officers. "Normally" other non-economic factors are involved as well. Yet even these are, in the long run, insufficient to ensure the stability of a formal organization. The final element required is a belief in the *legitimacy* of the domination of one group

over another—whether it is superiors over staff, or organizational functionaries over members of the larger populace. For example, even if everyone in a
profit-making organization were highly committed to the objective of maximizing profits, relationships would remain highly unstable unless those having a personal interest in the organization agreed among themselves as to who
would make the different types of decisions.

Given these assertions, Weber goes on to argue that individuals in
leadership roles almost invariably attempt to develop and reinforce the
legitimacy of their positions in relation to lower functionaries and to the rest
of society. In this respect, Weber sounds very much like Marx. Weber differs,
however, in his assertion that the basis upon which legitimacy is claimed—its
content—can be highly varied. It cannot be explained merely in economic
terms. For example, the continued loyalty of the staff to executive officers of
one firm may be based upon a tradition of esteem which a family in control
has established. In another firm such allegiance may be ensured by a belief in
the legitimacy of the rules and regulations per se rather than by loyalty to
specific individuals.

While there are undoubtedly many grounds for establishing legitimacy
of a relationship involving dominance, Weber sees most of these as involving
three fundamental types: (a) those resting on a belief in "the exceptional sanctity, heroism or exemplary character of an individual person, and of the normative patterns or order revealed or ordained by him"; (b) those resting on a
belief in the "sanctity of immemorial traditions and the legitimacy of those
exercising authority under them"; and (c) those resting on a belief in the
"legality of enacted rules and the right of those elevated to authority under
such rules to issue commands." The first type defines allegiance that is based
on "charismatic" grounds, the second on "traditional" grounds and the third
type is based on "legal-rational" grounds.[6] According to the kind of legitimacy
claimed, the type of obedience, the type of administrative staff developed to
ensure it, the style by which authority is carried out, and the consequences,
will all differ.[7]

In industrial capitalist societies, the characteristic basis for legitimacy of
authority within industrial organizations is the "legal-rational." Traditional
grounds of legitimacy can provide the basis for some forms of capitalism, but
not for the long-term planning and the organization of labor into highly complex roles. These of course are essential features of an industrial capitalist
society. Further, the more directly the organization is involved in the
dynamics of the marketplace, the more emphasis directors are likely to place
upon the necessity for "rational" forms of organization. This is the most consistent approach, given a belief in the impersonal principles of competition
within the marketplace.

It is within this context that Weber further analyzes the characteristics
of authority based upon legal-rational grounds. He describes the role of functionaries in the following manner:

(1) They are personally free and subject to authority only with respect to their impersonal official obligations.
(2) They are organized in a clearly defined hierarchy of offices.
(3) Each office has a clearly defined sphere of competence in the legal sense.
(4) The office is filled by a free contractual relationship. Thus, in principle, there is free selection.
(5) Candidates are selected on the basis of technical qualifications. . . . They are *appointed*, not elected.
(6) They are remunerated by fixed salaries in money, for the most part with a right to pensions.
(7) The office is treated as the sole, or at least the primary, occupation of the incumbent.
(8) It constitutes a career. There is a system of 'promotion' according to seniority or to achievement, or both. Promotion is dependent on the judgement of superiors.
(9) The official works entirely separated from ownership of the means of administration and without appropriation of his position.
(10) He is subject to strict and systematic discipline and control in the conduct of the office.[8]

Having described the unique qualities of the legal-rational authority system, Weber's enumeration of the qualities of the bureaucracy as an ideal type of the formal organization appears somewhat redundant. They represent, however, the consequences, in behavioral terms, of the authority system. They are the following:

(1) "the principle of official *jurisdictional areas*, which are generally ordered by rules, that is, by laws or administrative regulations."
(2) "the principles of *office hierarchy* and channels of appeal stipulate a clearly established system of super- and supordination in which there is a supervision of the lower offices by the higher ones."
(3) "management of the modern office is based upon written documents (the 'files') which are preserved in their original or draft form and upon a staff of subaltern officials and scribes of all sorts." Weber goes on to note that the office or "bureau" is kept separate from the private domicile of the official.
(4) "Office management . . . presupposes thorough training in a field of specialization."
(5) "official activity demands the *full working capacity* of the official . . ."
(6) "The management of the office follows *general rules* which are more or less stable, more or less exhaustive, and which can be learned."[9]

These attributes describe typical government organizations in advanced societies and the "enterprises" in their economic sectors. The commitment of abstract rules of authority are, he argues, most developed in the modern state and "in the private economy, only in the most advanced institutions of capitalism."[10]

Weber creates an image of an organization in which all the actors within it are totally committed to carrying out the specifications of their jobs or "offices." The result is a far more efficient method of allocating authority than any other type of organization, especially those in which functionaries may be committed to the vagaries of particular individuals (a charismatic structure) or to the ritualism of tradition. For Weber, the fully developed bureaucratic structure "compares with other organizations exactly as does the machine with the non-mechanical modes of production."

> Precision, speed, unambiguity, knowledge of the files, continuity, discretion, unity, strict subordination, reduction of friction and of material and personal costs—these are raised to the optimum point in the strictly bureaucratic administration, and especially in its nomocratic form.[11]

Weber believed that the capitalist market economy demanded that the official business of public administration be discharged with as much speed and precision as possible, and this was more obviously true with respect to business management.[12]

Weber's model of bureaucracy has provided the major point of reference for subsequent formulations on formal organizations. Yet what is often ignored is the fact that Weber emphasized the efficiency in *allocating authority* rather than achieving organizational objectives per se. The distinction is important, for it is conceivable that a perfectly rational model of administration does not ensure the most efficient means of achieving desired ends. For example, lines of authority between a salesperson and his superiors may be clearly defined and efficiently constructed, but they may in fact hinder expansion of sales if the salesperson is not permitted to make decisions which are unique to individual situations. Weber himself does not always make this distinction clear, but his awareness of the distinction is indicated in a parenthetical note in which he points out that the "bureaucratic apparatus" can and often does create impediments for conducting business "in a manner best adapted to the individuality of each case. . . . "[13]

Failure to take this paradox into account has meant that many commentators have attacked Weber's formulation for ignoring the rigidities of bureaucratic structures. Yet this is to misinterpret the context in which Weber discusses these structures. If there is no explicit commentary about the "dysfunctions" of bureaucratic-like structures, it is because Weber saw them as merely one manifestation of the larger consequences of formal rationality which permeated the entire industrial capitalist society. If bureaucracies were rigid in their demands and modes of operations, so were other institutions of such societies. Weber, like Marx, was impressed by the efficiencies organizations were able to exact in industrial capitalist societies. But both he and Marx were appalled by their effects upon individuals.

If the legal-rational, bureaucratic-like organization was the epitome of industrial capitalist societies, it also had its paradoxes. The fundamental paradox involved the stress placed on equality within such societies, while inequities of authority were retained within the formal organization. It seemed to be the case for Weber, that the greater the stress upon equality, the greater the need for rational forms of organization.

Since equality is stressed even more fully in socialist societies, rules and regulations of the formal organization would become even more pronounced. There would be no other organizing principle, such as those linked with class or community mores. (These might include, for example, a sense of social responsibility which would require no explicit formalized codes of behavior.) The state would have to take on more administrative tasks, assuming that the same degree of technical efficiency in production and governance were to be maintained that exists in industrial capitalist societies.

However, as Weber pointed out, with the state dominating such administration, the formal rules and regulations would eventually be put in the service of the "substantive" dictates of those in political control.[14] The effects would be far more pervasive than those which exist where formal organizations compete within a market economy. These effects would curtail the expression of freedom and, Weber added, individual motivation. In capitalist societies with a democratic base, the existence of the economic marketplace gives at least an illusion of freedom (hence the term "demand economies") as long as it remains separate from the state. The only "content" of the rules of these economic organizations is that of economic rationality. Yet, where freedom for the individual may continue to be assured, equality remains a problem. In socialist societies, attempts are made to preserve equality, while individual freedoms remain a problem. Additional specters remain for both capitalists and socialists: for the former it is the possibility of an increasing loss of freedoms because of organizational constraints; for the latter, the organizations themselves may become the structures for a power elite.

While Weber analyzed the conditions giving rise to the bureaucratic-like organization and its consequences, others have raised questions about the internal dynamics of such organizations. Merton points out that the emphasis on adherence to rules and regulations can conflict with the overall objectives of the organization. He notes that an effective bureaucracy requires reliability of response and commitment to regulations. But such commitment results in rules being transformed into absolutes. This interferes with the ability to adapt to special conditions not clearly anticipated by those who drew up the rules. Thus, the elements which result in efficiency in administration in the general case, result in inefficiency in specific instances.[15]

Actually, it does not appear to be the case that individuals within organizations blindly follow the regulations of formal organizations in this manner. The fact that organizational regulations cannot cover every aspect of behavior for every expediency permits individuals to manipulate the rules for their own ends. They can use them to protect themselves from clients,[16] to enhance their own power,[17] to manipulate their own status within the organization and protect themselves from further management demands,[18] and to sabotage the wishes of policy makers through work-to-rule tactics. It is one thing to specify the logically rational criteria for the patterned behavior required within an organization; it is quite another to deal with the interpretations and manipulations of these criteria by individual actors.

Management theorists have tended to respond to these and other problems by focusing on two broad issues. The first issue is the problem of coordinating the diverse tasks within a formal organization. For example, if the objectives of industrial firms include efficiency of operations and if task specialization is the logical expression of efficiency, then coordination of these tasks will remain a central problem for managers. The second problem is one of fitting individuals to their tasks. If there is a continual pressure toward greater efficiency, and if this can be effected by more routinized tasks, then managers will be faced continually with persuading individuals to adapt themselves to the specialized requirements of these tasks.

The emergence of a distinct occupational group of managers can be plotted at about the time of the worldwide depression in 1873–95. This was the era of take-overs of less successful companies and the expansion of large-scale corporations, such as Rockefeller's Standard Oil Corporation and the huge steel corporations in the United States and Germany. Coordination of tasks and allocating personnel were of concern then and they continue to dominate the thinking of managerial theorists now. The need for such organizations has been assumed. It has also been assumed that control must rest in the hands of a small minority of individuals. It is within this context that one of the first theories of management which explicitly attempted to form the industrial enterprise into a more efficient tool was articulated. This was the so-called "scientific" approach of F. W. Taylor. It has since been categorized as a "classical" approach to management.

The Theory of Scientific Management

F. W. Taylor, a mechanical engineer at the Midvale Steel Works in Pennsylvania, published his theory of management in 1911. It was his intention to replace the informal, intuitive style of administration with explicit principles of productivity. Once having articulated these principles, managers would only need to ensure that workers adhered to them. Taylor viewed the principles as scientific in the sense that they represented an ordering of tasks and individual behavior into a scheme which demonstrated improved efficiencies in attaining desired productivity rates. Such efficiencies were best expressed in terms of units of motion in relation to the minimum amount of time required for each unit. In this sense, both workers and machinery were viewed as components in the manufacturing process. Ideally, all decisions were removed from the worker and formalized into sets of principles. This approach is best illustrated in Taylor's own commentary:

> Under the old type of management success depends almost entirely upon getting the "initiative" of the workmen, and it is indeed a rare case in which this initiative is really obtained. Under scientific management the "initiative" of the workmen (that is, their hard work, their good-will and their ingenuity) is obtained with absolute uniformity and to a greater extent than is possible under the old system; and in addition to this improvement on the part of the men, the managers assume new burdens, new duties, and responsibilities never dreamed of in the past. The managers assume, for instance the burden of gathering together all of the traditional knowledge which in the past has been possessed by the workmen and then of classifying, tabulating, and reducing this knowledge to rules, laws, and formulae which are immensely helpful to the workmen in doing their daily work. In addition to developing a science in this way, the management take on three other types of duties which involve new and heavy burdens for themselves.
> These new duties are grouped under four heads:
> *First.* They develop a science for each element of a man's work, which replaces the old rule-of-thumb method.
> *Second.* They scientifically select and then train, teach, and develop the workman, whereas in the past he chose his own work and trained himself as best he could.
> *Third.* They heartily cooperate with the men so as to insure all of the work being done in accordance with the principles of the science which has been developed.
> *Fourth.* There is an almost equal division of the work and the responsibility between the management and the workmen. The management take over all work for which they are better fitted than the workmen, while in the past almost all of the work and the greater part of the responsibility were thrown upon the men. . . . [19]

Taylor's approach assumed an economic model of man; that is, that the primary motive of behavior was economic gain. The only variations in individual attributes which were relevant for management were the skills and aptitudes of individual workers. Thus the problem was to determine these aptitudes, match them to the tasks at hand which had been formulated in the most efficient manner, and motivate workers by basing their wages upon their output.

It is clear that under Taylor's approach managers were to dictate the terms under which work roles were to be carried out. Yet while managers were to be in complete control, the element of legitimacy, which Weber had argued was required for stable relations involving dominance, was provided by the belief in the correctness of "science." Further, the appeal to the "principles of science" removed managers from personal responsibility for their actions. They could, in effect, redefine themselves as merely agents acting in behalf of the science of production. Should workers themselves accept this interpretation, then it followed that conflict with managers would be eliminated. Of course, from a Marxian point of view, this would represent a clear case of reification accompanied by the alienation of workers.

Taylor's formulations, however, were not accepted as smoothly as he had hoped. In testimony before a United States congressional committee, he described how it took him three years to break the opposition of lathe operators in a steel plant. Not only did they fight to control their rates of production, they also, at last resort, destroyed parts of their lathes. It was only as a result of dismissals and fines for damages that the remaining workers conceded to the requirements of the more "rational" work designs.

Far from diminishing labor-management conflicts, the use of Taylor's approach heightened them. Workers could not be induced to play the role of robots as Taylor had implied. Yet once the principles were formulated, the continuing problems merely generated refinements of Taylor's approach, rather than completely new theories. The continuing pressures of competition reinforced the popularity of these principles for managers.

Intellectual descendants of Taylor concentrated upon three general areas: (1) increasing efficiency in human movement; (2) formulating more rational models of coordination among tasks; and (3) formulating principles that enhance the adaptability of individuals to the required tasks. Gilbreth's formulations of human motion units is an example of the first area of theoretical development. Gilbreth classified the basic motions of the body into units called "therbligs" (a reverse spelling of "Gilbreth"). These were then observed in actual work situations and reformulated for the individual worker, so that the most efficient forms of movement according to time values could be employed in any given task. Not only were specific movements charted, but also the relationship among movements, e.g., for every backward movement of the left leg, the right hand more or less naturally moves forward.[20]

Indicators of physical movements and energy expenditures have remained very much a part of contemporary theories and research on workers' productivity. Most recently such indices and scales have been applied to office work. Hand movements, leg movements, body positions, and eye travel time have all been catalogued into standardized units of time. This permits any task performance to be reconstituted into the most time-saving sequence of motions.[21]

The second area of concentration within the classical perspective deals with rational models of task coordination. This involves classification schemes for administrative units. The premise that guides these formulations is that maximum output should be accomplished with a minimum number of organizational partitions.[22] Two of the more basic organizing principles that have emerged from this premise are classifications of tasks by process and by product.[23] But these two principles may be in conflict. Grouping tasks only by department often means duplication of similar tasks carried out in each of the different departments. On the other hand, grouping tasks only by process often results in greater specialization with resulting problems of coordination and efficient use of labor. The dilemma is resolved at the point when the two principles become complementary rather than conflicting. This, in turn, depends on other factors, such as volume of work. For example, classifying typists by product (department) is preferred if the volume of work occupies them full time. If, however, a department cannot use their services to this extent, then they are to be classified by their specialty. The work of each department can then be allocated to a pool of typists.

The third area of theoretical development, the modification of individuals' behavior to fit the demands of their job requirements, is a logical extension of the concern for efficiency. These formulations have included tests for aptitude, for tolerance of strain, and for other factors which contribute to a sense of psychological well-being. In the United States, the problems of allocating men to different tasks in the army during the First World War spawned an interest in these endeavors. The findings from this research were later applied to industrial firms. In addition to psychological tests, research was carried out on a broad range of environmental stimuli which could affect workers' productivity. These included the effects of noise, colors in the workplace, music, different intervals of rest periods, illumination, the home environment, size of work groups, and other variables. The behavioral logic behind these tests assumed that if individuals were well selected for their tasks, once those factors were discovered which contributed to their sense of well-being, individuals would be willing to produce to their full capacity.

While the formulations of Taylor and his intellectual descendants now seem unduly simple-minded, it is a mark of their influence that their logic and methods continue. Their continued elaboration has finally brought about some significant shifts in theories of management. It was with the concern for maximizing the adjustment of individuals to their tasks that the most dramatic changes occurred. This finally resulted in what has been called the "human relations" approach to organizational dynamics.

The Human Relations Approach

From 1927 to 1932 Elton Mayo and his research team undertook a series of studies on worker motivation and output. The research took place in the Hawthorne plant of the Western Electric Company near Chicago. Before Mayo's studies, the National Research Council of the National Academy of Sciences in the United States had carried out experiments on illumination in the workplace. Because there appeared to be no relationship between brightness of illumination and worker output, Mayo's research group were highly sensitive to the role other variables might play in accounting for this. In an effort to control for extraneous factors such as shifting personnel, changes in the work roles, and fluctuations in work schedules, the researchers formed an experimental group of six women—five assemblers and one "layout operator." These workers were studied for two years in an isolated workroom.

The researchers followed all the procedures of an experimental design, except for the most crucial one—the use of a control group. In a before-and-after design, they measured the effects of different variable upon rates of productivity. These variables included rest periods, lunch times, number of work hours per day and workdays per week, wage incentives, and illumination. In addition, they recorded the effects of physiological variables such as fatigue, dexterity, intelligence, and menstrual cycles.

Members of the research team were well aware of the influence of sentiments and emotional attachments that existed among the workers. However, they utilized these factors as controls, assuming that they would remain constant as the other behavioral variables were manipulated. Their justification for studying the small group of women was that by establishing mutual confidence between themselves and the women, the reactions of their subjects would not be "distorted by general mistrust."[24] They also believed that it was important to select workers who were cooperative and who got along well with each other, so that their reactions to the experiments would be "normal and genuine."[25]

The research findings remained inconclusive. It is clear from reading the recorded observations of the women that behavioral variables such as rest periods, fatigue, monotony, and wages were important to them. Yet when these variables were each isolated and related to work productivity, they paled in importance. The reasons seem obvious now but were not readily apparent then. The manipulation of these variables was done in a context in which the observer continually encouraged the women to cooperate with the experiment. Further, he actively intervened in their work environment in an effort to maintain high morale. The workers were thus responding to him and their special status, rather than to the experimental variables. The researchers finally realized that, "In the process of setting the conditions for the test, they had altered completely the social situation of the operators and their customary attitudes and interpersonal relations."[26] This implied that the effects of experimental variables could not be predicted unless they were treated within the total context of meanings.

As a result of these interpretations, the research team shifted to interviews of workers throughout the entire plant. These interviews were directed at finding out the general level of morale, satisfactions and dissatisfactions in jobs, and the workers' personal histories and backgrounds. The results of this inquiry were also inconclusive. The researchers then set about to investigate the effects of social organization inside the plant, especially the role of informal groups.

As a consequence of these shifts in inquiry, management theory began to move away from Taylor's mechanistic model, away from the rational model of management with its emphasis upon behavioral imagery of man, towards an emphasis upon the industrial organization as a setting for individuals attempting to satisfy their social "needs" while performing their required tasks. The model of man in this approach is one who is largely irrational in the sense that he is strongly influenced by his interactions with others and that he exercises "rationality" only when confronted with choice situations in which he lacks group support.

Extended elaborations of this view have resulted in applied programs designed to train managers how to be sensitive to interaction patterns among workers, how to preserve the workers' self-esteem, how to probe for subtle covert meaning, and how to use this knowledge in order to gain more ready acceptance among workers for policy decisions. But an emphasis upon this approach immediately came into conflict with organizational requirements for efficiency and predictable behavior. Overconcern for workers' social welfare could not create the kind of task-oriented efficiency required of a formal organization .

The classical approach of scientism assumed that individual workers were motivated only by economic rewards. It merely remained for managers to demonstrate more efficient (rational) means for workers to attain their ends so as to meet the objectives of the organization. The human relations approach demonstrated that workers' motives were not that simple. In addition to seeking economic ends, individuals workers used the organizational setting for social support. Taylor attempted to keep the individual isolated; the human relations advocates attempted to capitalize upon the social dependence of the individual. To get individuals to adhere to organizational rules, managers were to foster socially rewarding experiences, not, as Taylor would have it, threaten the loss of livelihood if workers failed to comply.

Viewed in a broader perspective, it is apparent that in its extreme state of development, the "classical approach" became somewhat absurd. One outcome of the awareness that too much stress was being placed on baiting the individual worker was a philosophy of management that emphasized the importance of human relations. Yet the further development of this approach also led to distorted interpretations.

A Neo-Classical Approach

A third theory of management, first advanced in the 1950s and subsequently refined, can be labelled a "neo-classical" approach.[27] Like the scientific management school, it assumes a rational model of man in the sense of the individual behaving in such a way as to realize his own objectives. But unlike the classical approach, it does not restrict the objectives of individuals within the work organization only to economic ends. Rather, the individual is viewed as having many objectives, of which economic gain may only be one.

Both the classical and the neo-classical approaches are quite explicit in detailing methods of controlling individuals within the organization. The classical approach attempts to do this by removing decisions from individual participants. Advocates of the neo-classical school attempt to preserve the decision-making qualities of individuals, but they utilize behavioral methods to control the environment in which the decisions are made.

The neo-classical approach is ostensibly a synthesis of previous theories and principles of management. The synthesis itself is couched within a decision-making model. Organizations are seen as decision-making systems that have emerged out of collective efforts to achieve some objectives. Once in place, managers seek to reduce uncertainty by making the environment of the organizations subject to increased prediction and control. It is in this sense that both individuals and organizations are viewed as rational. They both have preferences, search procedures for uncovering available courses of action, and have the ability to choose among the alternatives. It remains for managers to ensure that the order of preferences for individual choices is made compatible with the organization; they can then provide the appropriate procedures for revealing the courses of action that can be taken. The final choice, given the compatibility of preferences, should thus serve the best interests of the organization.

The basis of authority for the neo-classical approach is expertise. Participants are to decide who is best qualified to solve a problem. At the same time, they are trained in the necessary skills to perform required tasks and they are provided with information by which they can make decisions which are relevant to the tasks.[28] Presumably, the effect is to promote a sense of integrity at all levels of the organization.

Neo-classicists maintain that individuals make decisions leading to some state of satisfaction rather than continuing to maximize their rewards. They engage in "satisficing" activity. That is, they tend to accept the first satisfactory course of action available, rather than continually weigh all the alternatives to achieve maximum returns. (Indeed they can never have all the information necessary to make decisions which maximize the returns.) However, satisfaction remains open-ended. Individuals are constantly being influenced in what they define as satisfactory. There may be a change in values associated with a given state of affairs, there may be a change in perceived consequences of action, and there may be changes in perceptions about the range of alternatives for action that are available.[29] Once individuals decide to participate in an organization, these changes immediately come into play. Organizational control is a matter of influencing perceptions. To do this, managers must take into account the environment of the organization, especially the general economic conditions and societal values.

According to neo-classicists, the types of influence impinging upon individuals within the organization include supervisory styles, strength of informal work group pressures, and the nature of rewards offered to individual participants (for example, schemes of promotion, economic rewards, etc.). Managers can modify these influences and ensure that individual decisions serve the ends of the organization by manipulating the division of labor, by standardizing procedures of operation, by clearly defining lines of authority, by ensuring clear lines of communication, and finally by training and indoctrination.

Yet individuals must also receive rewards for their participation in the organization, and these must be commensurate with their contributions. In effect, the organization transforms the contributions of individuals into inducements for their continued employment. Whether or not the inducements will be acceptable to individuals depends upon the value of the alternatives they see as open to them. In addition, the failure of their search behavior to reveal better alternatives, as well as the definite knowledge that only worse alternatives are available, lowers the expected levels of satisfaction for individuals. Satisfaction is further influenced by whether the individuals perceive that the "employment contract" is fixed or subject to change. If the latter is the case, internal conflict and bargaining will likely follow.

Since behavior is motivated by some perceived level of satisfaction, managers cannot assume that there is an unlimited potential for maximizing worker commitment and productivity. They must constantly be attentive to the perceptions of individuals within the organization. However, individuals are not necessarily concerned with all the issues relevant to the organization. This adds an additional element to be taken into account in gaining reliable participants. It is in this area of "indifference" that managers can exert control most directly.[30] Overall, it is for managers to determine the perceptions of individuals across a broad range of variables and then to apply the right balance of environmental stimuli and personal rewards.

In what remains as one of the most comprehensive statements of this behavioral approach to management, March and Simon culled from research findings 206 variables, which they believe influence different types of organizational participation.[31] These variables are classified into five categories: those relating to control and authority, those which serve as inducements to participate in the organization, those contributing to conflict, those which account for the limits of rationality as it relates to communication and coordination, and those which must be taken into account in planning and innovation. Managers can manipulate these variables in such a way as to get individuals to participate willingly in the organization and to ensure their allegiance once they do participate.

The neo-classical approach attempts to meet both the problems of developing organizational efficiency and individual commitment by emphasizing the role of decision-making and rationality. The logic roughly follows this sequence: (a) individuals are decision-making entities; (b) the opportunity for them to make decisions must be preserved; (c) organizations, by definition, require that the decision be "rational," i.e., serve the purposes of the organization; (d) orderliness must be preserved; which requires that there be (e) restrictions over the range of decisions to be made; hence (f) managers must ensure that the environment within which decisions are made is under their control.

In effect, this system results in manipulative maneuvers designed to induce individuals to participate within a highly restrictive environment while preserving their belief that they are behaving in a manner that maintains an acceptable level of satisfaction. In fact, as one critic pointed out, it is a short road from inducing cooperation by manipulation to outright coercion.[32] Workers may not reveal what they are ready to accept. Thus a bargaining relationship can easily emerge. When workers form their own community of interests, such bargaining can easily convert the neo-classical model of contributions by inducement to one of conflict contained by outright power.[33] Indeed, one can argue that this is the very basis upon which organized labor relates to management.

Later formulations of the neo-classical approach have utilized computer simulations as a means to account for all the variables impinging on the decisions made by individuals within organizations. But the emphasis is clearly away from the group-centered emphasis of the human-relations school to the isolated individual. Further, very little account is taken of the possibility for other, less manipulative forms of collective endeavor.

A Neo-Human Relations Approach

Just as the neo-classical approach represents a more comprehensive formulation of "scientific" management, thus reducing the impact of its inherent contradictions, so is the neo-humanist approach a response to the relatively naive formulations of Mayo and the Hawthorne researchers. In 1960 McGregor advanced an approach to management that again emphasized the social-psychological dimensions of organizational dynamics. But these went beyond the needs for social acceptance that had provided the main theme of the earlier human relations school.

McGregor believed that managers had been adhering too closely to the classical approach to management. Adherents to this position assumed that workers were inherently recalcitrant and were motivated only by economic gain. Acting on these assumptions, management tended to be punitive in their treatment of employees. After labeling this approach "theory X" McGregor proposed his "theory Y" in which management was to provide conditions by which individuals could achieve self-fulfillment within the contexts of their work roles. From this premise, it follows that management should operate on the basis of objectives rather than control. That is, it should matter less whether workers are rigorously adhering to rules and regulations than whether their tasks are being completed.[34]

McGregor incorporated the formulations of Maslow who, along with other "self-actualization" psychologists, had advanced the thesis that individuals progress, when there is opportunity to do so, along a hierarchy of needs. In Maslow's scheme, these needs were, in ascending order, the need for safety and survival, the need for social acceptance, ego and self-identity needs, the need for individual autonomy, and finally at the highest level, the need for self-actualization and creativity.[35] In this formulation, a higher order need cannot be satisfied until needs below it have been met. McGregor used a variation of this formulation to advance a theory of management which optimizes the possibility of individuals to meet higher order needs within the organization. In effect, the application of his scheme meant that individuals were to be located in positions according to the level of needs they were trying to satisfy.

A variation of this approach is that proposed by Argyris. He recognized a basic contradiction between the norms of efficiency of industrial organizations and personality needs of individuals. The more formally regulated the organization, the more frustration and conflict would result from thwarted needs of individual employees. Of course, there are several corrective responses. One is to alter the behavioral styles of management so that the organization becomes less coercive. Another is to reduce the degree to which work roles delimit the expression of personality needs of individuals. A third is to match the types of needs which specific individuals have with specific task requirements. Argyris would like to see all responses pursued, but he concentrates his concern upon the last one. He argues that individuals will contribute to organizational demands if there is some gain for them. The "gains" in turn are to be understood by taking into account individual needs.[36] He classified these needs on a scale representing infantile and adult needs. Thus, while infants begin as dependent and submissive, adults attempt to be independent and to control their immediate world. Where an infant has few abilities, an adult has many. Further, an infant may have shallow abilities, but an adult has developed a few in depth. Finally, infants have a short time perspective in that they respond to the immediate present, whereas adults develop a sense of longer term consequences. When there is an incongruity between the needs of individuals and organizational requirements, individuals are likely to experience "(1) frustration, (2) psychological failure, (3) short time perspective, and (4) conflict."[37] This dilemma can be resolved by determining the types of needs individuals are seeking to meet and then placing them in roles where this can best be done. Thus, those persons remaining at the infantile level can more easily adjust to roles requiring repetitive tasks, while those roles requiring creativity, decision-making, and responsibility are best met by individuals seeking to meet their adult needs. Failure to take these considerations into account results in apathetic or recalcitrant participants.

Argyris views organizations as systems which entail characteristics of individuals, of groups, and of relationships among groups. A competent system is one which is able to solve problems, make decisions, and implement the decisions effectively. This requires, in turn, individual participants who exhibit self-acceptance, trust in others, a sense of "essentialness" which is derived from the ability to express central needs and employ principal talents, and, finally a sense of psychological success. In addition, there should be an identification with group processes, general cooperation and trust among work groups, and valid information available.[38] For Argyris, managers should be oriented toward creating a cooperative endeavor in which individuals can meet their own psychological needs while contributing to the objectives of the organization. To the degree that this occurs, the need for formal expression of control decreases.

Likert's work represents another variation of this approach. His emphasis is primarily on styles of management. He argues that a manager must continually adapt his behavior to take into account the "expectations, values, and interpersonal skills of those with whom he is interacting."[39] Organizations which are most successfully managed, according to Likert, are those in which participants exhibit attitudes of cooperation and identify with the organization and its objectives.

Successful managers, Likert argues, have the ability to tap into individual motives, including those related to ego needs, security, curiosity and the desire for new experiences, and economic needs. Further, there is a high degree of communication among all units within the organization; measurements of organizational performance are used primarily for self-guidance rather than superimposed control. Likert emphasizes the necessity to instill a sense of worthiness in workers. To the degree that managers can link individual motives to the requirements of the organization, both satisfaction and productivity will follow.

If the neo-classical approach is manipulative in ensuring that individuals make the correct decisions, the neo-humanist approach also attempts to manipulate the organizational environment so that individuals can realize their higher-level psychological needs. Whether or not this implies facilitating decision-making abilities is somewhat incidental for the neo-humanist. What remains, however, is a basic contradiction between the organizational norms of efficiency and "human needs."

This contradiction is not resolved by the managerial theories we have considered, but it is made explicit in at least one managerial rating scheme. In order to create greater management "effectiveness," Blake and Mouton consider the relative emphasis managers place upon two concerns: organizational efficiency and human needs.[40] Plotted on two axes, with the vertical axis representing a "concern for people" and the horizontal axis representing "concern for production," a good manager scores high on both 9-point scales. Less effective managers may not score as highly on one axis relative to the other, or they may score low on both scales. Placement on the "grid" indicates the nature of the manager's orientation and this is derived by his scores on a battery of tests.

A manager who gives thoughtful attention to the needs of the people but neglects efficiencies of production scores "1,9" on the grid. If he emphasizes efficiencies of production to the neglect of the welfare of employees his score is "9,1". The aim is to train managers to instill trust, respect, and commitment among employees, while achieving maximum efficiencies in production, a "9,9" score.

Reddin has since added a third dimension, "effectiveness," by which he attempts to take into account the specific leadership requirements of particular tasks.[41] Thus, requirements to meet specific dead-lines mean primary emphasis should be placed upon efficiencies of production, whereas long-term projects require more concern with the welfare of individual participants in order to sustain their commitment. It is the requirements of the tasks that determine how managers should relate to their employees and thus how individuals should behave. Of course, this makes the focus of responsibility even more abstract, since the impersonal characteristics of "a job" justify the authoritarian role of managers and the style in which they wield their power.

In reviewing these theories of management, one theme remains dominant: those in management positions formulate and determine the conditions within which others shall participate. They direct and administer formal organizations rather than fellow participants. Of course, individuals who are managers are subject to a variety of constraints, but these are constraints that come with the exercise of authority, not as a consequence of being subject to that authority.

The fact that there are academic programs leading to graduate degrees designed for the express purpose of teaching managerial skills further reinforces this separation of functions and the subsequent monopolization of power. Thus, managers may be better viewed as free-floating professionals able to employ their expertise in any organizational setting, rather than as employees of particualar formal organizations. The earlier, thinly disguised power of Taylor's manager, operating according to "scientific principles," has been replaced by a more therapeutic approach. But the structure of authority remains and managers determine how it shall be employed.

Hegel had high hopes for the impersonal machinery of formal organizations. Marx saw their structures as a medium of power. Weber explained the manner in which that power was legitimated, in which it became a structure of *authority*. The metaphor which was originally employed to characterize the formal organization was the highly efficient machine. Taylor made this explicit by requiring workers to act in a highly routinized, machine-like manner.

When this had been carried to extreme lengths by researchers and theoreticians, the human relations approach was "discovered." The metaphor became transformed into one in which the manager served as a therapist, cajoling workers into being willing participants in the organization. The premises of scientific management were not so much replaced as modified. The neoclassical approach shifted the basis of its formulations to psychological behaviorism. The neo-human relations approach rested upon developmental psychology. But the elite status of managers remains. The exercise of their power merely becomes more subtle in these theoretical formulations.

The monopolization of power by elites may not be a problem in those societies in which inequalities are assumed to be part of the "natural" order of the social world, and in which authority, in Weber's terms, is based upon the values of tradition. But in capitalist societies, the existence of formally free labor implies the basic values of freedom and equality. To tolerate the existence of power elites is to contradict these values and the authority systems of formal organizations. It is a contradiction in which the *social* character of the formal organization serves the *private* interests of managers. The continual search for more effective management styles may be seen as an attempt to overcome this contradiction.

The question remains whether formal organizations can operate without the presence of a power elite. There are two responses to this question. The first response would be to simply remove the incentives for private gain from managers and declare their *motives* to be for the public good. The Soviet Union furnishes an example of this, where the managers eagerly accepted the principles of scientific management. But this form of declaration has not been convincing, and for Marxists remains a fundamental problem in the exercise of power, given the fact that the rational authority structures remain.

A second answer is to revise the authority structure so that workers at all levels in the organization contribute to the decision-making process. This is the approach of different models of "industrial democracy," variations of which exist in the workers' councils in West Germany, in participatory management in Yugoslavia, and within the consensual approach of the rural kibbutzim in Israel. There remains a fundamental dilemma, however. If efficiency of administration is to be stressed in the operations of large-scale organizations, to what degree can decisions depend upon public discussion and debate? Until the basic structures of authority are changed, the monopolistic exercise of power in the pursuit of efficiency will continue to be the dominant trend.

Solutions to the dilemma may require new metaphors to structure social organizations: seeing them perhaps as similar to husking bees or in terms of the social interaction that goes on at a peasant village well.[42] In this sense, the activity of production would serve the functions of social interaction and the development of a community of interests as much as it would produce goods. But given the complexity of contemporary production, coordination and direction are still required. How to accomplish this without creating a basis for a new power elite is a dilemma yet to be resolved.

Conclusions

The coordination of functions and tasks, and the cooperation of personnel remain the dominant problems confronting managers of complex, formal organizations. Theories of management attempt to deal with these problems. They reveal, however, a commitment to an authority structure in which managers themselves occupy an elite status quite independent of the effects of these theories when they are put into practice. (It should be noted that there is a considerable difference between the formulation and the practice of management theories.) This results in a fundamental paradox. Equality, especially equality of opportunity, may be stressed, but the terms of its expression are controlled by those in managerial positions.

The contradiction inherent in this position is not lost by personnel who are subject to these policies. While these theories are well-known among managers in Canada, the prevalence of labor unrest attests to the fact that they have been less than successful in their practice. The contradiction remains.

Attempts to justify this contradiction, if not resolve it, have been made by employing ideological expressions. These represent attempts to persuade individuals of the correctness of the managers' positions of power by recasting the problem into new contexts of meaning. These tactics are the concern of the chapter to follow.

Notes

1. Karl Marx, *Critique of Hegel's Philosophy of Right*, ed. Joseph O'Malley and trans. Annette Jolin and Joseph O'Malley (London: Cambridge at the University Press, 1970), p. 47.
2. Ibid., p. 51.
3. Karl Marx, *Capital: A Critique of Political Economy*, Vol. III (Moscow: Progress Publishers, 1971), p. 438.
4. Ibid., p. 444.
5. Max Weber, *Economy and Society*, ed. Guenther Roth and Claus Wittich (New York: Bedminster Press, 1968), p. 212. For an excellent treatment of Weber's analysis see Martin Albrow, *Bureaucracy* (London: Macmillan, 1970).
6. Weber, op. cit., p. 215.
7. Ibid., p. 213.

8. Ibid., pp. 220–221.

9. Ibid., pp. 956–958.

10. Ibid., p. 956.

11. Ibid., p. 973.

12. Ibid., p. 974.

13. Ibid., pp. 974–975.

14. Ibid., p. 111.

15. Robert Merton, *Social Theory and Social Structure*, rev. ed. (Glencoe, Ill.: The Free Press, 1957), p. 200.

16. Peter Blau, *The Dynamics of Bureaucracy*, 2nd ed. (Chicago: University of Chicago Press, 1963).

17. S. M. Lipset, *Agrarian Socialism* (Berkeley: University of California Press, 1950).

18. Michel Crozier, *The Bureaucratic Phenomenon* (Chicago: University of Chicago Press, 1964).

19. Frederick W. Taylor, *The Principles of Scientific Management* (New York: Harper and Brothers, 1911), p. 35.

20. Cited in Harry Braverman, *Labor and Monopoly Capital* (New York: Monthly Review Press, 1974), p. 173.

21. Ibid., pp. 173–182.

22. James G. March and Herbert A. Simon, *Organizations* (New York: John Wiley, 1958).

23. Luther Gulik, "Notes on the Theory of Organization," in *Papers on the Science of Administration*, ed. Luther Gulik and L. Urwick (New York: Institute of Public Administration, 1937), pp. 1–46.

24. F.J. Roethlisberger and William J. Dickson, *Management and the Worker* (Cambridge: Harvard University Press, 1939), p. 20. For a sharp critique of the Hawthorne studies, see Alex Carey, "The Hawthorne Studies: A Radical Criticism," *The American Sociological Review*, Vol. XXXII, No. 2 (June, 1967), pp. 403–416.

25. Roethlisberger and Dickson, op. cit., p. 21.

26. Ibid., p. 183.

27. See Herbert A. Simon, *Administrative Behavior* (New York: Macmillan, 1958). For an earlier "classic" statement, see Chester Barnard, *The Functions of the Executive* (Cambridge: Harvard University Press, 1938).

28. Herbert A. Simon, op. cit., p. 80.

29. March and Simons, *Organizations*, p. 52.

30. Herbert G. Simon, op. cit., p. 116.

31. March and Simon, op. cit., pp. 249–253.

32. Sherman Krupp, *Pattern in Organization Analysis* (New York: Holt Rinehart and Winston, 1961), p. 115.

33. Ibid., p. 116. See also Nicos P. Mouzelis, *Organization and Bureaucracy* (Chicago: Aldine, 1967), pp. 135–142; and David Silverman, *The Theory of Organisations* (London: Heinemann, 1970), pp. 204–210.

34. Douglas McGregor, *The Human Side of Enterprise* (New York: McGraw-Hill, 1960).

35. Abraham Maslow, *Motivation and Personality* (New York: Harper, 1954).

36. Chris Argyris, "Personality and Organization Theory Revisited," *Administrative Science Quarterly* (June, 1973), pp. 141–167.

37. Ibid., p. 144.

38. Chris Argyris, *Intervention Theory and Method: A Behavioral View* (Reading, Mass.: Addison-Wesley, 1970), pp. 47–48.

39. R. Lickert, *New Patterns of Management* (New York: McGraw-Hill, 1961).

40. Robert Blake and Jane Mouton, *The Managerial Grid* (Houston: Gulf Publishing Company, 1964).

41. Reported in Ann Rhodes, "Where are Canada's Most Effective Managers?" *The Financial Post Magazine*, June, 1977, pp. 23–29.

42. A suggestion made by Charles Perrow during a discussion period at the American Sociological Association meetings in Chicago, 1977.

chapter seven

Ideologies of Management

Introduction

In Chapter 3, I argued that the typical reaction of those persons in positions of authority who were threatened by the apparent discrepancy between values and authority systems was to construct conceptual linkages to overcome this gap. This linkage constitutes the defining characteristics of ideologies, which are symbols of meaning that are designed to justify or further the interests of a particular group of people. Ideologies come into play if a group of individuals intends to maintain authority in the face of opposition or wishes to change the structure of the authority.

In this chapter I wish to examine how ideological expressions have played a role in maintaining the authority of entrepreneurs and managers of production enterprises. I also want to delve into the methods used to convey these expressions, for in so doing, it will become apparent that the "theories" of management treated in Chapter 6 can also be seen to include many ideological elements.

On the Nature of Ideology

It is ironic that the term "ideology" was first used by the French philosopher-visionary Destutt de Tracy in 1797 to counteract what he believed to be the distorting effects of metaphysical assumptions. The term was used to connote a "correct" view of the world. De Tracy and his company of "ideologues" sought to ground all ideas in empiricism.[1] Yet today, "ideology" tends to convey an image of distortion.

There is a good reason for this transformation, for the group of ideologues attempted to set up an educational system which would ensure that individuals would develop the correct view—their view. Napoleon was first intrigued by them, but then cast them aside for political reasons, accusing them of merely furthering their own biases and hence merely substituting one distortion for another.

Marx and Engels, in *The German Ideology*, written in 1846, used "ideology" to characterize the distorting beliefs—distorting because they did not reflect the true character of class relations—that perpetuated the capitalist bourgeoisie. In effect, Marx and Engels were arguing that empiricism per se was an insufficient ground of knowledge. The empirical world was fundamental but the experience of it was mediated by social class. When the structure of class was no longer supported by the changed modes of production, "false consciousness"—or ideological beliefs—could continue to contribute to the perpetuation of class relations.

Currently, there is much discussion about the definition of ideology and what constitutes ideological statements. The most general definition is that the term denotes those beliefs, concepts, and statements which distort some aspect of reality in order to achieve some given end. What lies behind this definition is the question whether truth itself can be known without knowing who made the statements and toward what end. Further, the issue is not merely one of what might be called morality. "Morality" in this sense can be defined as the degree to which the actions of individuals (that is, behavior which is "meaning-full") are consistent with the values that they presumably share. For example, instances of inequality must be explained when they contradict the value of social equality. It is *explanation* that I want to view as ideological. Used in this way, the concept of ideology implies that beliefs may merely be justifications whenever there are deviations from some prior set of assumptions regarding truth or morality.

It follows then that questions arising from these conditions are questions of motives and intentions. What is of particular interest, however, is that such questions are a common part of contemporary western industrialized societies, and are most dramatically imposed within the political arena, where it is assumed that intentions and pronouncements do not necessarily match. Currently, many people maintain a skeptical stance toward pronouncements of business representatives, labor leaders, and spokesmen for professional groups and other vested interests. This skepticism in turn, one could argue, spawns additional ideological pronouncements as individuals seek to make sense out of these diverse interpretive statements and to justify their own interests.

Such a pervasive skepticism is a relatively unique historical event. This is not to say, as Mannheim has pointed out, that there have not been periods in which interpretations have been questioned and justifications required. Mannheim notes that the Sophists of the Greek Enlightenment were highly skeptical of the established order. He argues that this was a consequence of the conflicts in modes of thought between the dominant nobility and the more analytic approach of a growing urban artisan class.[2]

What is historically unusual in the Western world is that the conditions which made industrialization possible have also stimulated a continual orientation of doubt and hence its consequences—a need for justifications by those who are doubted. It is precisely this stance that was part of Weber's imagery when he analyzed the relationship between the Protestant Ethic and the legal-rational orientation of capitalist entrepreneurs. Further, many philosophers have labelled the period of early industrialization of the Western world in the nineteenth century the "Age of Ideology," an age in which the earlier trust in the rationality of man and the hope of a naive empiricism were being refuted by the political and social upheavals of the eighteenth and nineteenth centuries.

Marx clung to the hope of a better state of existence based upon a more sophisticated empiricism. To this he added the experiential effects of class relations. Weber carried the issue to the content of the subjective interpretations of experiences. Mannheim, who dealt directly and specifically with the issue of ideology, made class relations an incidental part of his analysis, arguing instead that the high degree of division of labor, the functional differentiation, and increased democratization had made the experiences of individuals within their own lifetime so highly diverse that interpretations of truth or morality had become amorphous. Individuals were required to continually assess and evaluate their own and others' actions by criteria which themselves seemed to change in different contexts.

Using Weber's study of religions as a model, Mannheim noted that people in caste-like societies can be committed to a single religion even though there may be variations in interpretation. There is nothing to threaten these beliefs as long as there is no mobility or radical shift in the experiences of individuals. With a stable authority system and with "social prestige accorded only to the achievement of the upper stratum" there is little cause for the dominant class to "call into question its own social existence and the value of its achievements."[3] As an effect of social mobility (up or down) or other forms of experiencing social change, individuals often begin to question the derivation and validity of the ideas of the dominant class.

In addition to these factors which create skepticism toward the ideas of a dominant ruling class, Mannheim also pointed out that in every society there is a group of intellectuals who interpret events that are commonly experienced. Intellectuals tend to acquire a well-defined position in stable societies.[4] Further, they tend to become increasingly scholastic as they gain a monopoly over these interpretations. As they systematize and elaborate upon these interpretations, they become more remote from the experiences and conflicts of everyday life.[5] This structuring process, Mannheim implies, eventually leads to the demise of not only the system of thought, but also to the group of intellectuals.

For Mannheim, the "decisive fact" of "modern times" is that the influence of such an organized group of intellectuals has been broken; as the marketplace rests upon free competition for goods and services, so it creates an arena for the competition among ideas and interpretations. "In this process, the intellectual's illusion that there is only one way of thinking disappears."[6]

With the stable referents for determining the validity of beliefs gone, a likely substitute referent, Mannheim argues, is the self and the act of knowing or cognition.[7] Yet this finally contributes to an extreme of subjective relativism. To surmount this problem there is the possibility of adhering to a model of consensual validation of experience, of arguing that only as experience can be reduced to a common language can there be some common mode of interpreting the world. Yet, according to Mannheim, this has turned out to be a highly restrictive approach which leaves out any evaluative element.

The functionalist approach has furnished another means to bypass the issue of relativism, but this too does not deal with the problem of evaluative judgments. To say something is a "function" of something else does not assess its effects. Thus, judgments remain relative while analyses are kept highly restrictive and void of moral content.[8] Analyses are still dependent on a consensus over the manner in which they themselves are to be carried out. Thus the problem of relativism remains. Such a dilemma is caught in Geertz's citation of what he calls a "paradic paradigm": "I have a social philosophy; you have political opinions; he has an ideology."[9]

This excursus on the problems best dealt with under the rubric of sociology of knowledge has shown that those beliefs and interpretations which are now defined as ideological are further aspects of the changes accompanying the process of industrialization.

On Power, Authority and Ideology

In a deft Weberian style of analysis, Mannheim pointed out that the institutional means by which the Catholic Church provided salvation to the individual believer was reduced to a private, subjective experience for the Protestant.[10] The individual's subjective consciousness rather than the Church became the arbiter of salvation. It was only a short step away from this sacred-subjective concern for salvation to a secular psychological concern for the self.

Gouldner picks up this theme in his work entitled *The Dialectic of Ideology and Technology*. He argues that the transformation in social conditions and in interpretations in the nineteenth century made individual actors the central driving forces of societal organization and change. They became the locus of power and hence were morally responsible for their actions.[11] Gouldner emphasizes that such a transformation grounded ideology in "an historically evolving, new sense of the potency of ordinary men and not just of great kings, generals, or the rich."[12] It is in this sense that he argues that ideologies are "person-constituting." They produce a "sense of potency" essential for "person-being."[13]

Ideological expressions then incorporate the dimension of power, while appealing to individuals as agents of that power. Yet this appeal must carry a connotation of legitimacy, which in effect transforms the dimension of power into an issue of authority. To accomplish this, ideologies must demonstrate some connection with a more generally accepted value, as they seek to motivate or to justify. "Ideologies," Gouldner writes," "reduce the dissonance between (1) the recognition that one is seeking a private advantage and (2) one's wish to be seen as pursuing courses of conduct that are justifiable."[14] Justifications are typically based upon images that convey the idea of an enhancement of the social welfare for individuals. It is in this sense that Gouldner views ideologies as implying "the possibility of rational public projects to change society, even if only to restore it to the *status quo ante* or to prevent further revolutionary change."[15] All ideologies, regardless of their particular political direction, imply that contemporary society can be improved.

If one argues that authority is "legitimized power," then it follows that the legitimacy must often be demonstrated in industrialized societies, since these are societies marked by diversity in the experiences of individuals and in their meaning systems. Ideological expressions aid this demonstration: they not only incorporate an emphasis on the legitimacy of a "public project," but they also delimit the range of evidence they present in order to be more forceful.

Mannheim distinguishes between two types of ideologically related expressions. He redefines ideology itself to refer to the interpretations of members of ruling groups who become so "intensely interest bound to a situation that they are simply no longer able to see certain facts which would undermine their sense of domination."[16] "Utopian" expressions, on the other hand, are counterideologies: they represent the orientation of oppressed groups that are "so strongly interested in the destruction and transformation of a given condition of society that they unwittingly see only those elements in the situation which negate it."[17]

This raised a moral problem for Mannheim, for he asks "how is it possible for man to continue to think and live in a time when the problems of ideology and utopia are being radically raised and thought through in all their implications?"[18] If this dilemma was not to be solved through some "supratemporal logic" in which truth remained at some abstract level, then, Mannheim thought, individuals would turn toward activism for the validation of their interpretations. Truth as an absolute becomes less an issue than do the tests of action and control.[19]

This effectively makes "truth" a function of power. Whereas Marx could return to his basic premise that truth is to be found in the experience of production and therefore ultimately with the experience of the working class,

Mannheim saw this as merely one of many interpretations of a truth which could never be known in any absolute sense.[20] There was, for Mannheim, no single social class that served as a guide.

While this posed an insoluble paradox for Mannheim, the two inter-related referents which Gouldner identified do remain—individual and power. (In a sense, they provide the basic referents for interpreting the problem of relativism.) The identity of these referents does not resolve the problem, but it does sensitize us to the principal strategies of ideological statements. In other words, if there are no assertions about ultimate truth to be made, then persuasive appeals will be directed to individual welfare and the power that is required to attain more desirable social conditions.

On the Construction of Ideologies

If ideologies can be characterized as those sets of symbols by which given groups or social classes seek to persuade others to adopt a cause or to justify their own existence, then it follows that those who construct such systems will attempt to draw upon values that are shared by a larger audience. For example, the Quebec provincial election of 1976 was won by the Parti Québecois primarily on a platform of good government rather than on the doctrine of "sovereignty-association." Obviously, everyone, regardless of his position on the issue of the association of Quebec with the rest of Canada, could support "good government," especially after the exposure of considerable corruption in the previous government.

Most analyses of ideological expressions have focused on the societal attributes that have given rise to them. This, for example, was the approach of Mannheim and of Marx before him. Both Mannheim and Marx noted that the ruling class had recourse to ideological expressions whenever their dominance was threatened. Whether one sees the general phenomena of ideology as class-linked or as a consequence of the general conditions which are produced by a fragmented society (i.e., a pluralistic model which stresses a multiplicity of interest groups) remains open to some debate.[21] What is not debated is the fact that ideological expressions are most prevalent during periods of stress and conflict, and that these periods themselves are frequent and intense in industrial capitalist societies. Less understood, however, are the *means* by which groups or classes are successful in gaining their ends through ideological expressions.

It was one of Weber's major theses that the content of belief systems, and one may add, ideologies, cannot be traced solely to forms of class relations within given societies. Rather, one must take the unique history of values into account. Because Marx took a critical stance against any autonomous existence of ideas or "consciousness," he was not concerned with the dynamics of ideological constructions as such. But the fact that he allowed for the possibility of "false consciousness" suggests that to understand the dynamics of ideological expressions, one must also analyze them in their own terms. Geertz, in noting the absence of analyses at this level, points out that too often the connecting link between causes of ideological expressions and their effects "seems adventitious because the connecting element— autonomous process of symbolic formulation—is passed over in virtual silence."[22] Geertz points out that in most analyses there is no attempt to relate particular ideological themes to other themes so that we may know the means by which ideologies can transform "sentiment into significance." H. M. Drucker, extending Geertz's critique, notes that "we have a tendency to put a work, say the *Communist Manifesto*, down side by side with a description of the supposed interests of the proletariat in the mid-nineteenth century and to say that the one served the other. How? This is what we need to study."[23]

In an attempt to isolate the principles of meaning which appear in ideological expressions, Gouldner argues that there is a "linguistic conversion" by which a new language creates a sense of alienation of the self from the existing social system and thereby permits this newly defined self to act against "the old world."[24] To accomplish this, recourse must be made to a broader system of interpretation, or what Gouldner calls "the paleosymbolic." By this he means the "shared ordinary . . . languages of everyday life learned during primary socialization as children."[25] Since "socialization" would imply the adoption of values, one may argue that the effectiveness of particular ideologies is contingent on the degree to which they incorporate elements of these values.

Of course, the necessity to appeal to these common elements means that the intentions of individuals who formulate ideological expressions may not be similarly held by their followers or by those whom they are seeking to persuade. For example, the call for individual freedom may be interpreted to mean either a justification for keeping unions from organizing workers, or as a rallying cry for the formation of unions. (Gouldner's example of this is that the call to behead the king may be taken by some to suggest discrediting all figures in authority.) Thus, ideological appeals, as they are interpreted by individuals in relation to their own particular experiences, may aid in the creation of social movements or in supporting existing authority systems, but the very heterogeneity of those who accept the ideological tenets fosters the possibility of dissension.

Despite these inherent problems, it is apparent that for ideologies to be effective they must (1) identify the nature and source of a problem of social existence; (2) define the individual as having the power and means to overcome the problem; and (3) appeal to commonly shared values. To achieve these ends, ideological expressions employ a wide range of symbolic devices to emphasize, form closure, and bring together discordant meanings in such a way as to create a new, internally consistent image.

Emphases of particular ideas can be accomplished by sheer exaggeration, of course (for example, it might be argued that unions pose a threat to the entire free enterprise system), but there are other more subtle ways of accomplishing this. Names of parts may be substituted for wholes ("Parliament Hill" for the Government of Canada), wholes may be substituted for parts ("the management" for a single administrative officer) or attributes of one thing used to describe another ("that union official has the stubbornness of a mule").

Unusually forceful images can be created by combining elements from two different contexts of meaning. The old Esso advertisement to "put a tiger in your tank" allows the consumer to make the connection between a tiger and a tank of gasoline, but it assumes that all car drivers want power from their automobiles and that a tiger epitomizes that power.[26] What emerges is a more forceful image than a detailed description of the advantages of Esso gasoline would be. However, for such images to be successful, there must be something known about the manner in which the elements are regarded. To tell someone that she is the "cream in my coffee" may have different effects, depending on whether coffee is preferred with cream or not.[27]

These symbolic devices constitute the use of metaphors. "The power of a metaphor," Geertz writes, "derives precisely from the interplay between the discordant meanings it symbolically coerces into a unitary conceptual framework and from the degree to which that coercion is successful in overcoming the psychic resistance such semantic tension inevitably generates in anyone in a position to perceive it."[28] Geertz further notes that metaphors that work become "apt analogies"; those that do not are merely "extravagances." A sufficient degree of "semantic tension" is required to increase the forcefulness of the metaphor—i.e., the relationship between the discordant meanings—but not enough to become absurd.

J. David Sapir has attempted to explain the ingredients of successful metaphors by noting that the discordant elements must share some commonalities.[29] But W. Percy has pointed out that often those metaphors which appear to be most effective are those which at first glance seem to include elements without any relationship; that, in any event, it is the tension produced by the discordant meanings which produces unusually powerful images.[30]

Slogans that have a hostile connotation are an effective method to increase tension before its resolution. The world of advertising is full of such examples. "Freedom Now!" (a rallying cry for civil rights groups) stimulates tensions, but then loses its original intent when used to sell feminine hygiene products. Similar approaches have been used by spokesmen for managers. When such tactics are successful, they not only intensify the dramatic impact, but also serve to co-opt, then defuse the original hostile intent.

On Managerial Ideologies

What is important in the examination of ideologies is to ask (1) what social conditions contribute to their expression, and (2) what semantic techniques are employed to maximize their impact upon a given audience. In their analysis of the "American business creed," Sutton et al. argue that the nature of the threats to businessmen determine the nature of the ideological expression.[31] Of the three broad factors which they argue influence ideological expressions, the "cultural," the "institutional," and the "motivational," the last is given the most emphasis in their analysis. The study itself was carried out within a limited time period, 1948–1949. From their analysis the authors conclude that the ideologies of businessmen do not change much in their content, but rather in the degree of emphasis which they place upon different themes—according to the nature of the threats.

More recently Seider analyzed the addresses of American corporation executives and discovered that executives from different industries emphasized different themes depending on their particular vested interests. Speakers from the aerospace industry tended to stress nationalism and patriotism, while those from the auto industry, banks, and utilities stressed classical laissez-faire themes. Representatives of the petroleum industry and the retail trades were the most likely to make reference to "social responsibility."[32] From this data, it is obvious that justifications for the authority structures of these industries vary according to the different types of threats from their social environments.

The classic analysis of the effects of societal and organizational change upon the expressions of both entrepreneurial and managerial ideologies is that of Reinhard Bendix. He captures the essence of the strains within authority systems when he writes that the few who command "have seldom been satisfied to command without a higher justification" while "the many have seldom been docile enough not to provoke such justifications."[33] Bendix compared the historical evolution of ideologies of managerial authority in Russia and the Soviet Union with those in England and the United States. His analysis of the latter two societies are most relevant to the ideological expressions of entrepreneurs and managers in Canadian society.

Implicit in Bendix's treatment of ideology are two perspectives. The first is based on what Mannheim viewed as a conception of ideology which characterized a total historical age. (This, of course, implies that the ideological perspectives which we now have are used to reinterpret history as being comprised of ideological "ages.") The second perspective—the "particular" in Mannheim's terms—traces the ideological expressions of specific groups, in this case, the managers of industrial enterprises. The two perspectives are interwoven in Bendix's analysis.

Bendix argues that before the emergence of a class of industrial entrepreneurs in England, the aristocracy legitimated their position of authority through an ideology of paternalism. They viewed themselves as responsible for the welfare of the lower classes. In effect the justification of this arrangement was based on an image of society as an extended family: the lower classes were childlike, while the ruling classes were like parents.

This orientation continued with the emergence of the industrial entrepreneurs who located their factories within stable communities. They could, in effect, assume the role of landed aristocrats in their treatment of workers. But the Enclosure Acts, the increase in population, and the need to locate factories near sources of energy and raw materials meant that such stable relations could not be sustained. These factors, combined with the new discipline required for factory work, left the traditional models and interpretations of class relations without support.

The shift in the traditional paternalistic metaphor began to occur, according to Bendix, at the end of the eighteenth century. Apologists for entrepreneurs began justifying their actions by two new statements, which were, in fact, common practice but were "startling when pronounced": (a) individuals must depend only upon themselves and their skills for their livelihood, and (b) members of the upper classes cannot be responsible for the employment of people or for the relief of the poor.[34] These statements, when brought into public consciousness created a paradox: "How could higher classes deny their responsibility for the poor and at the same time justify their power and authority over them? How could the poor be taught self-dependence without developing in them dangerous independence?"[35]

This dilemma was resolved by assigning causes and consequences to a combination of abstract uncontrollable laws on one hand and by offering a means to circumvent them on the other. Malthus's *Essays on Population* (1798) "proved" that "higher classes were unable to relieve the poor and that the poor must reform their habits if they were to escape starvation."[36] The poor had to learn to curtail their high birthrates. Thus, the only way the upper classes could help the poor was to "educate them" toward virtuous living. Vice and virtue became not merely religious issues but secular principles.

Note that this transition is yet another aspect of the Protestant Ethic and its secular expression as defined by Weber. Further, it represents a popular expression of the Enlightenment social theorists of the eighteenth century. These ideas had to do with general class relations and the organization of society as a whole. In effect, they applied not merely to workers and the poor, but they helped break the hold of the landed aristocracy over the growing numbers of industrial entrepreneurs. The emphasis upon personal responsibility and achievement not only relieved entrepreneurs of the responsibility for caring for the welfare of the poor, but it also questioned the legitimacy of the status of the aristocracy.

A strong note of optimism accompanied the emphasis on individual responsibility; optimism in the sense that individuals could not only escape the "laws" of poverty through self-improvement, but they could also surmount what had been rigid class divisions. Yet this too presented a paradox, for when translated into social positions, there was in fact a limit to the extent of self-improvement.

The metaphor which seemed to resolve this dilemma temporarily was one of "social darwinism." Individuals were to compete in order to better their own personal conditions, but it was to be recognized that each person had inherent limits, and in the end, just as species of animals survived by being the fittest, so did those in power survive and perpetuate their standing through their offspring. In the 1860s in the United States, Bendix notes, ruthless competition was taken to be a typical pattern of behavior by the ideologues of industry. Those who achieved were held to be deserving, while those who failed "were believed to lack the requisite qualities and they were enjoined to obey the men whose success entitled them to command."[37]

Workers were affected by the emphasis upon self-improvement, as we shall see in Chapter 8. But the entrepreneurs did not foresee the translation of these efforts into *collective* rather than individualized efforts. Bendix notes that at the very pinnacle of their social recognition as the prototypes of successful individuals, American employers were challenged in their authority by the collective strength of trade unions.[38] To combat this, employers argued for the freedom of the individual to work where he chose, under his own terms, without union intervention. It was an argument in support of the "open shop." The ideology shifted, but the virtue of hard work and the goal of success remained. In addition, the ideological pronouncements made it quite clear that a worker could not better his condition "unless he gained the 'confidence, respect, and cooperation of his employer.'"[39] This meant the impersonal principles which ensured success did not exist. Rather, it revealed the fact that it was the employers who wielded the power that determined work and class relations.

Once again a paradox stood revealed. Existing modes of production could not continue; employers could not maintain their positions of authority if an image of class conflict were to gain credence. It is within this ideological dilemma that scientific management attained prominence. Part of its appeal lay in its attempt to circumvent the inroads of unions by appealing to individualistic achievement. But the achievement was couched within a new metaphor based upon machine-like attributes of the productive organization. By assuming that both employment and good wages were desired, adherence to the scientific laws of a production "machine" would maximize the benefits for workers and for management.

Scientific management in effect sought to impose a new set of abstract principles by which the authority of management could be justified. In so doing, it aimed to deflect the attacks upon management *per se*. At the same time, as I pointed out in Chapter 6, it was consistent with the growing complexity of industrial enterprises which required increasing attention to developing and maintaining more rational structures.

Such attention to rational, increasingly bureaucratic structures presented another paradox. How could individual achievement be pursued if the rational structure of an industrial organization was to be preserved? The problem lay with the definition of achievement. As long as it implied the success of an independent entrepreneur or the image that the possibilities were nearly limitless, bureaucratic-like structures would be in direct contradiction. Within the increasingly dominant large-scale organizations, praise for abilities in the management of men and conformity to job specifications were far more appropriate than praise for autonomy, daring, and perseverance.[40]

Such a shift involved a new metaphor, one in which the industrial enterprise was viewed as a collective effort, a community of individuals each contributing to the common good. By the 1920s several writers had pointed out the need to treat individuals within the production enterprise as having strong social needs, including needs for social recognition and approval. The reinterpretation of the data from the experiments at Western Electric's Hawthorne plant added a "scientific" basis to these assertions. Where Taylor had seen the individual as autonomous, rational, and economically motivated, Mayo viewed him as group-oriented, largely illogical, and motivated by positive evaluations from his fellows.

Such an approach served to justify the authority structure within the enterprise by putting the expertise of assessing such needs in the hands of management. The disruptive effects of the virtues of achievement were replaced by stressing the qualities of understanding and cooperation. Achievement was to be through cooperation.

This formulation was especially significant because it was directed as much toward middle management as toward workers. Not only does such an approach attempt to defuse worker opposition, but it also preserves authority from conflicts among managers in different departments.

Just as early entrepreneurs extolled the virtues of rugged individualism while not actually tolerating these same traits within their own production enterprises, so later top management has not in fact carried through the full implications of the "human relations" approach. To do so would mean to lose discretionary decision-making. The ideological pronouncements gloss over these implications. It is not specified just who determines to what end there should be cooperation.

What is important is that the basic structure of authority—the system of meanings legitimizing the power of management—has been maintained, even though it has gone through several transformations and faced continual threats from labor and other groups. Ideological formulations have played a major role in the strategies employed to maintain management's power.

Ideological Expressions of Canadian Managers[41]

Bendix's description of ideological shifts provides an overview of the general sequence of justifications for authority structures within industrial enterprises. When one looks at the justifications used within Canada, one finds unique variations of these themes. Examples of these characteristics can be drawn from an examination of the news journal of the Canadian Manufacturers' Association, *Industrial Canada*. Before analyzing these shifts, it is worthwhile to have some understanding of the organization itself.

According to S. D. Clark, the origins of the Canadian Manufacturers' Association can be traced to a group of 62 manufacturers, merchants, and newspapermen who met in Toronto in 1858 in order to propose adjustments to tariffs that would better serve the interests of Canadian manufacturers vis-à-vis American manufacturers. Clark argues that this concern was prompted by a surplus of supplies and manufactures that were part of the aftermath of a railway building boom, which was then followed by a depression in the late 1850s. Manufacturers were caught in a squeeze between high overhead costs and declining output. It was hoped that higher tariffs would stimulate sales of home manufactured goods and stabilize prices.[42] The original strategy of the group was to apply pressure on government bodies and influential economic groups in order to effect changes in the tariff structure.

After several periods of reorganization, the body took on the title the Canadian Manufacturers' Association in 1877. By this time the organization sought to encourage export trade and to promote technical education. In 1900 the association was reorganized and branches were established in the major cities of Canada. During the early part of this century the association became a powerful force in the economic and political life of Canada. While branches existed throughout the country, the association in a very real sense represented the challenge of the industrial interests of Toronto to the financial establishment of Montreal. It was an attempt to break the hold of banking and transportation interests by presenting a united front to the federal government of Canada.

In addition, the association soon found itself in opposition to the advances of organized labor. It fought against the 9-hour movement (an event to be treated more fully in Chapter 8) and worried that governments within Canada were more responsive to labor than to manufacturing interests. However, as an association, its battles on behalf of manufacturers were fought by employing lobbying tactics on governments. Clark cites the case of the success of the association in opposing the Workman's Compensation Bill in Nova Scotia in 1915.[42]

As the larger companies developed their own programs, the association came to represent smaller enterprises. Yet the current ideologies of management tended to be reflected in its journal, *Industrial Canada*, even though there was often considerable divergence of positions taken over specific issues. Iron and steel enterprises, for example, were primarily concerned with raising tariffs, while the textile industry was concerned mostly with the threats of organized labor. Despite this diversity, the association encouraged the development of joint efforts—the formation of combinations—to halt the inroads of organized labor.[44] Yet after 1919 it softened its opposition because labor organizations also supported tariff protection.

Currently, the Canadian Manufacturers' Association does not represent the dominant interests of industrial enterprises. Viewed historically, however, it does provide an example of the use of ideology to protect the authority structures of entrepreneurs, and later, managers.

The analysis of the transformation of ideological themes was based on a content analysis of specifically ideological statements printed in *Industrial Canada* during the years 1901 to 1970. Issues of every fourth month of each year were sampled—January, April, July, and October.

The journal itself was primarily concerned with transmitting technical news and reporting on government policies. Articles that could be clearly defined as ideological in content were relatively few. They were apparent only in discussions of the labor movement and problems of industrial organization, and in inspirational articles. The relative infrequency of such articles is not surprising if one holds to the view that such expression will be most frequent only when those in authority perceive some threat to their position.

The analysis revealed that the content of the ideological themes shifted in a manner similar to that reported in Bendix's account. But before examining the nature of these shifts, it should also be noted that during those years in which strikes and lockouts were most numerous— periods in which there was the greatest threat to management authority—the frequency of ideological expressions was also greatest.[45] Such industrial conflict was most marked in the periods 1916–1920, 1936–1950 and again in 1956–1970.

The content of the ideological themes tended to be focused upon three main subject areas: (1) self-perceptions, (2) perceptions of workers and unions, and (3) strategies of management. Expressions of these concerns were interwoven throughout the 70-year period.

Self-Perceptions

During the earliest years, self-perceptions were couched primarily in terms of active individuals and disciplined leaders of men. For example, one author pointed out in 1912 that those in business should have "the capacity to get others to take pains" and in 1916 a representative article stated that "a man who has not mastered himself cannot master another."

Over time, increasing emphasis came to be placed upon responsibility to both the company and to the larger society. In 1925, for example, the president of the Association told his constituency to "go and explain to the people that you are not capitalists but simply trustees to those of your fellow man ...." Social benefits of industry were also stressed. Note the imagery in the following quote from 1918: "Without a moment's hesitation you cast upon the altar of civilization your whole future, not merely to make a world safe for democracy but to keep democracy safe for the world."

From 1931 up to the final years of the analysis, readers of *Industrial Canada* were reminded that "they have to fight to maintain the very foundation of society" (1931), and were advised to preserve democracy and personal independence (1939), to take on more responsibility in public life (1941), to make their industrial responsibilities compatible with their duties as citizens and members of family groups (1955), and to broaden their community involvement (1968). These are themes of inspiration, directed toward managers to reinforce the leadership image of themselves. The nature of the leadership changes but the authority remains.

Perceptions of Workers and Unions

More telling in their ideological implications are those expressions which dealt with perceptions of workers and unions, and strategies of management. The transformations in images of workers were very similar to those described by Bendix: from viewing workers as reluctant and slovenly persons to finally viewing them as work associates whose basic cooperative nature was being corrupted by unions. In 1909, for example, one author noted that workers tended to have "habits of deceit and slothfulness." In 1920 they were seen as "intelligent, fairminded, and patriotic." In 1937 workers were defined as "steady, contented people who want to live in harmony with other citizens, and to enjoy the ordinary amenities of home and community life ...." By 1945 they were "thoughtful and reasonable people." In 1949 they were human beings who had desires for "material improvement" and a greater share in power and authority. Workers, it was argued, wanted "freedom for themselves so that they can do things that they want to do." In 1970 workers were seen as similar to managers: both have ego needs, as well as needs for self-fulfillment, creativity, health, security, social acceptance, and related attributes.

The transformations in the images of workers are not merely the result of increased enlightenment. This is apparent when these themes are seen in relation to images of labor unions. The growing emphasis on viewing workers in a more humane manner represents a symbolic "flanking" maneuver which, in effect, undercuts the legitimacy of unions. Workers came to be viewed as worthy individuals at the very time that unions were viewed as corrupting influences. Up to the point where unions were finally viewed as permanent fixtures in the industrial scene, there was growing positive orientation toward workers while negative orientations were maintained toward unions.

The concern that unions were attempting to wrest control from management was expressed in the earliest issues of *Industrial Canada* and reappeared in 1940 and continued intermittently through to 1970. The early expressions of hostility toward unions were accompanied by statements that unions were acceptable as long as the "freedoms" of workers were preserved. The writers had the acceptability of company-sponsored unions in mind and they argued that in the general case Canadian unions should be incorporated and "governed by Canadian officials and free from foreign control." What this really meant was that unions could then be sued before a court of law and would not have access to the resources of American-based unions.

The attempt to speak for the protection of individual workers in the face of mounting union strength took on a variety of symbolic forms. In 1909 one writer argued that unions sapped the motivation of workers; and that with unionization there would be no inducement for greater efficiency or self improvement. The closed shop was held to violate the fundamental principle that a worker could sell his labor to "whomsoever he pleases."

Opposition to unions was most vociferous in 1912 and 1913. Unions were charged with committing conspiracies against employers, fostering class hatred, causing inefficiency in work, contributing to inflation in the economy, and paralyzing industry. But by 1918 the emphasis had shifted. New metaphors incorporating images of opposition into a new unified whole came into being. One author claimed that just as there is no opposition between the sun and its beams, so there need be no opposition between management and labor. In another metaphor, the same author viewed employers and workers as the blades of a pair of scissors which in their opposition came together to cut away misunderstandings.

During the Depression there was a marked absence of reference to unions. But before the end of the Second World War, the old themes resurfaced. Unions had won considerable gains in legal status during the war and employers were fearful that these would remain and contribute to increased union strength after the war. Critical themes were directed against collective bargaining and against closed and union shops. The latter union tactics were viewed as undemocratic because they constituted a "monopoly over labor." Yet nothing was said about management's control of labor. Suspicion toward unions remained a dominant theme through the 1960s, although collective bargaining had become more acceptable, a "bulwark, a protection, a defensive mechanism of the private enterprise system" according to one author. What came to be emphasized more than antagonism toward unions *per se* was an attempt to characterize union leaders as smug and unconcerned about the welfare of workers.

Strategies of Management

Themes that dealt with management strategies evolved from a behavioral model, in which better physical surroundings and economic incentives were stressed, psychological testing advocated, and educational programs supported, to an emphasis upon cooperation, good communications, and team-work with workers at all levels of the enterprise. In 1901 one writer argued that "Thoughtful attention to the comfort and education of the employees brings contentment to all." In 1907 a writer argued that by paying attention to the physical, intellectual, and moral welfare of his employees, an employer could realize increased output and better work. In 1914 better communication and improved interpersonal relations were stressed. But control of labor in 1920 remained very much an issue. One author argued that employers should provide their workers with the fullest information about the company to demonstrate to them the importance of cooperation and to gain their con-fidence and control through closer cooperation. Workers were to understand that "the matter of wages and hours of work are not governed by mere arbi-trary ruling of the boss, but are on the other hand, governed by economic laws . . . ." One should notice the juxtaposition of "confidence," "control," "cooperation," and the appeal to "economic laws." Implied here again is the metaphor of a mechanistic world, the premises of which are to be taken as axiomatic and beyond the understanding of those who are not managers.

The emphasis on gaining the confidence of workers continued into the 1940s. In these latter years, consistent with the influence of the human rela-tions approach, such confidence was to be won by treating workers as fellow associates. In 1949 one author argued that "you get people to do what you want them to do by kindness; by looking after them; by satisfying their needs . . . ." In the 1960s authors were writing that workers should be made to feel that they were important participants in the productive process. This was emphasized at the same time that unions were viewed as corrupting influences upon workers.

Throughout the 70-year period under analysis, the authority of management has remained. But the justifications have changed as organiza-tional structures have become more complex and as organized labor has exerted increasing influence upon management. The more recent emphasis upon equality—referring to workers as fellow participants and in terms that express a common purpose—carries, perhaps, a double message. On the one hand, it is of course aimed at resolving conflicts while maintaining authority. These ideological expressions are consistent with the management theories discussed in Chapter 6. On the other hand, these themes say something about the precariousness of managers' own positions—especially those in middle and lower management. Were they secure, there would be no need to employ these themes.

Thus what these themes also suggest is that the roles of managers are being threatened by continued rationalization and routinization. As less is re-quired of managers, especially lower level managers, except for their time in performing routine tasks, there appears to be more emphasis placed on being responsible while treating workers increasingly as colleagues. While ideological themes in the past were directed toward justifying authority in the face of infringements upon the value of equality, the current stress upon responsibility suggests an attempt to deal with the curtailment of managers' freedoms.

Conclusions

In this chapter I have sought to outline the principal attributes of ideologies and to suggest why ideological expressions appear to be more prevalent in industrialized societies and in those societies undergoing industrialization. Two referents, the individual actor and the notion of power (or control), appear to be universal elements in ideological expressions, whether they support or attack the social status quo. In utilizing these referents, ideological expressions employ a wide variety of linguistic devices in order to present images more forcefully. It is perhaps obvious that in relatively static societies ideological expressions are, by definition, relatively few. It is when authority systems are under attack that these expressions are made. For authority systems to be under attack suggests that they, in some way, are not consistent with the predominant values of a given society.

The shifts in ideological expressions which appeared in *Industrial Canada*, a journal of the Canadian Manufacturers' Association, were similar to those shifts described by Bendix. The most common linguistic devices used were simple exaggerations and metaphors. The self-images of managers changed from the autonomous achieving individuals to organizational teamworkers. Images of workers shifted from recalcitrants to malleable organizational components to "associates," while unions continued to be viewed as malevolent influences. Despite these changed images, there was never any question that managers should in fact relinquish some of their control.

Notes

1. Alvin Gouldner, *The Dialectic of Ideology and Technology* (New York: Seabury Press, 1976), pp. 11–12.
2. Karl Mannheim, *Ideology and Utopia* (New York: Harcourt Brace/Harvest, 1936), p. 9.
3. Ibid., p. 8.
4. Ibid., p. 10.
5. Ibid., p. 11.
6. Ibid., p. 12.
7. Ibid., p. 14.
8. Ibid., pp. 16–22.
9. Clifford Geertz, *The Interpretation of Cultures* (New York: Basic Books, 1975), p. 194.

    Following from Mannheim's commentary, one can see that it is no happenstance that contemporary philosophers themselves are currently occupied with problems of validity and bases for knowing. Morton White has called twentieth century philosophy "The Age of Analysis" and includes in it contemporary existentialists, pragmatists, logical positivists, and linguistic analysts. See Morton White, "The Decline and Fall of the Absolute," in *The Age of Analysis*, Vol. 2, *The Great Ages of Western Philosophy* (Boston: Houghton Mifflin, 1962) pp. 444–450. See also Nigel Harris, *Beliefs in Society: The Problem of Ideology* (London: C.A. Watts & Co., 1968), pp. 15–16.

10. Mannheim, op. cit., p. 34.

11. Gouldner, op. cit., p. 68.

12. Ibid., p. 69.

13. Ibid., p. 67.

14. Ibid., p. 219.

15. Ibid., p. 77.

16. Ibid., p. 40.

17. Ibid.

18. Ibid., p. 42.

19. Ibid.

20. This problem, a problem of relativism, is perhaps the major issue underlying contemporary sociological analyses. One response has been to focus on "situation analyses," by which an attempt is made to sort out the factors which influence given forms of action. The analyst in turn must be aware of the forces that have influenced him and his perspectives. It requires a stance of "reflexivity." It incorporates an attempt to objectify the self while analyzing what is being observed. Others argue for a "hermeneutic approach," by which truth is arrived at through contextual dialogue between the analyst and expressions of meaning, either written or spoken. Finally, some would begin with some definition of a desired state of the individual and direct their analyses to critical appraisals of societal structures which contribute or fail to contribute to that state.

21. It may be the case that the very experience of fragmentation draws greater attention to a class system which perpetuates it. Braverman, among others, views fragmentation as a condition which lends greater control to a ruling class. But this too may be a perspective born out of the state of fragmentation. If so, the issue is really one of relative degrees of power rather than absolute power of a ruling class. See Harry Braverman, *Labor and Monopoly Capital* (New York: Monthly Review Press, 1974).

    Ashford presents a persuasive argument that class-based theories minimize the effects of ideas. See Douglas E. Ashford, *Ideology and Participation* (Beverly Hills: Sage Publications, 1972), pp. 36–38.

22. Geertz, op. cit., p. 207.

23. H. M. Drucker, *The Political Uses of Ideology* (London: Macmillan, 1974), p. 47.

24. Gouldner, op. cit., p. 84.

25. Ibid., p. 225.

26. J. David Sapir, "The Anatomy of Metaphor," in *The Social Use of Metaphor*, ed. J. David Sapir and J. C. Crocker (Philadelphia: University of Pennsylvania Press, 1977), pp. 3–32. For a classic statement on the role of metaphors and other symbolic forms, see Kenneth Burke, *The Philosophy of Literary Form* (Baton Rouge: Louisiana State University Press, 1941).

27. Geertz, op. cit., p. 212.

28. Ibid., p. 211.

29. Sapir, op. cit., pp. 25–28.

30. W. Percy, "Symbol, Consciousness and Intersubjectivity," *Journal of Philosophy*, 15, (1958), pp. 631–641.

31. Francis X. Sutton et al., *The American Business Creed* (New York: Schocken Books, 1962).

32. Maynard S. Seider, "American Big Business Ideology: A Content Analysis of Executive Speeches," *American Sociological Review*, 39, (1974), pp. 802–815.

33. Reinhard Bendix, *Work and Authority in Industry* (New York: Harper and Row, 1956), p. 1.

34. Ibid., p. 73.

35. Ibid., p. 78.

36. Ibid.

37. Ibid., p. 258.

38. Ibid., p. 267.

39. Ibid., p. 274.

40. Ibid., p. 308.

41. Substantial portions of this section were previously published in the *Canadian Journal of Sociology*, 2 (1977), pp. 263–282. I am grateful to Bobbie Siu for his aid in the arduous task of gathering the data and in preliminary analyses.

42. S. D. Clark, *The Candian Manufacturers' Association* (Toronto: University of Toronto Press, 1939), p. 1.

43. Ibid., p. 34.

44. Ibid., p. 42.

45. Taking the years from 1901 to 1970 in five-year intervals, the frequency of strikes and lockouts was correlated with the number of ideological themes for each of the periods. A Spearman's rho rank order correlation coefficient was .758 with the probability of such a correlation less than .01.

Part Three

Labor's Response

chapter eight

The Trade Union Movement in Canada

Introduction

To deal with the trade union movement, I must refer once again to the descriptive phrase, "formally free labor." To be "free" may mean the ability to pursue one's own inclinations, but it can also mean the abdication of social responsibility in that pursuit. The social expression of this dual definition lies at the heart of the conflict between labor and management. Employers may advocate more freedom in order to pursue their own interests, but they may extend very little responsibility toward their employees.

The expansion of commerce and the emergence of the factory system created a wage-earning class of people who could not rely upon any social allegiances of their employers; nor could they depend upon their own productive skills, since they neither owned the means, nor determined the methods of production. Labor itself became a mere factor of production to be sold to the highest bidder in an uncertain market. As long as a surplus of labor existed, the employer could afford to limit his responsibilities to a minimum level, necessary only to maintain his own labor supply.

It is ironic that the process of industrialization itself was one in which small local masters, manufacturers, and shopkeepers were reluctant participants. Hobsbawm points out that these people were not committed to an economy of limitless expansion. Their ideal was one of "a small scale society of modest property owners and comfortably-off wage-earners, without great distinctions of wealth or power; though doubtless, in its quiet way, getting wealthier and more comfortable all the time."[1] Most capitalists, Hobsbawm argues, "took the new machine in the first instance not as an offensive weapon to win bigger profits, but as a defensive one, to protect themselves against the bankruptcy which threatened the laggard competitor."[2]

In general, manufacturers were often reluctant to employ machines because they represented large investments, the returns of which were not certain. Machines were most frequently adopted during periods of rising prosperity when employment itself was expanding. As a consequence, opposition to their use did not usually emerge until employment was directly threatened during periods of contraction in the demand for labor.[3] In Britain, the stimulus for continued competition came from the government, which in turn was influenced by commercially oriented elites. These elites gained from the investments which the government sought in its drive to win economic and political dominance in the world of trade.

From the point of view of wage labor, it made little difference if employers were reluctant participants in the competitive process that increased with industrialization. Workers felt the direct brunt far more dramatically than did the capitalist employers. Throughout the Western world, the history of industrialization is marked by accounts of riots and violence between workers and owners of production enterprises. In Canada, to note one example, work stoppages and violence were a continual problem in building the Rideau canal in Ottawa.[4] In effect, these incidents of conflict represent the reaction of individuals to the loss of their control over their work skills and to the tendency of employers to exploit their labor excessively. What requires a more detailed explanation, however, is the process by which these personal experiences were translated into organized social movements. Viewed in more theoretical terms, this transformation has to do with workers' attempts to resolve the discrepancy between the *values* of freedom and equality, and the authority systems of production organizations. These organizations further permitted an abdication of the social responsibility that the upper class once exercised in a feudal order.

In this chapter, I attempt to trace the origins and development of the Canadian labor movement and to offer some explanations for its characteristics. I shall first outline some principles of the general phenomenon of social movements and then use these as a means to understand the dynamics of labor movements in general and the Canadian labor movement in particular.

Some Principles of Social Movements

A social movement may be defined as a group of people "acting with some continuity to promote a change or resist a change in the society or group of which it is a part."[5] It is behavior that is non-institutionalized. That is, it is not a part of the established systems of meaning which make up the ongoing structure of society. In the general sense, this definition defines the nature of labor movements. Workers, experiencing the social dislocations which have accompanied the ongoing processes of industrialization, have engaged in many forms of dissent, but whether or not these actions resulted in sustained social movements depended on several fundamental factors. These are the following: (1) Individuals must perceive that they are existing in a socially and/or economically deprived state that is not justified by current values. That is, it is not deprivation as such, but *unjustified* deprivation. In the case of workers, such a perception is created when they compare their position of relative powerlessness with the positions of employers on whom they are dependent. The positions may be seen to be unjustified within the context of the values of freedom and equality.

(2) Before a social movement can be organized, there must be an awareness that other individuals share the same experience and interpret it in a similar manner. Without this knowledge, individuals may merely assume that it is their own behavior or their own unique interpretations that are the cause of their sense of deprivation rather than any "objective" conditions.

(3) There must be a utopian form of ideology which enables the individual to translate a personally felt sense of deprivation into the "public domain." Such an ideology identifies the causes of the deprivation, offers explanations for its continued existence, and provides a hope for its correction. In Mannheim's terms, the form of such ideological expressions is to be viewed as utopian because such interpretations emphasize elements of a social situation that justify attempts to change it. The appeal of such utopian ideologies, the degree to which people will accept them, depends upon the degree to which they can provide clear symbolic expressions which link together the experience of the deprivation with a generally accepted set of values and a plan of action. In the case of labor movements the dominant value has been egalitarianism, whether this is expressed in terms of more equal income or in terms of a greater share of control over the workplace.

(4) There must be leaders who can formulate objectives and plan strategy and tactics for change in such a way as to stimulate individuals to act as a cohesive group.[6]

(5) There must continue to be experiences that reinforce the validity of the ideology. What usually serves as a catalyst for the emergence of a social movement is a single dramatic event, such as unexpected repressive reactions on the part of employers. Peaceful demonstrators have often been attacked by policemen or guards acting on behalf of employers; these experiences, in turn, have fostered greater commitment of workers toward their objectives. The experiences must sustain a hope for change. Unless there is some sense of progress toward movement objectives, participants will leave.

(6) Once in existence, the characteristics and orientation of a social movement will be influenced by the type of response of powerful opposition groups. Some opposition is required in order to give the movement a cause for

being. But dominant groups supporting the status quo may attempt to absorb the social movement or make other accommodations to it. (This was a strategy employed by Bismarck in Germany in the 1860s and 1870s.) When this occurs, leaders of social movements must decide whether or not these responses in fact constitute the realization of their objectives. Of course, total opposition from powerful entrenched groups can decimate a social movement. Hence, it is necessary, as part of the movement's strategy, to seek to bring about changes without creating conditions that would destroy the movement itself.

Social movements in general, and labor movements in particular, will be most successful if their objectives are aimed at *modifying* existing social structures rather than destroying them.[7] This means modifications of structures of authority, for example, rather than a wholesale attack upon them. While the threat of revolution can be used as a bargaining point to accomplish more modest change, *successful* revolutions, although dramatic in their demonstration, are relatively rare.

Social movements may not be directed toward changing social structures as such, but rather toward changing the response of individuals toward them. Religious movements and movements stressing withdrawal and non-cooperation with the institutions of society are examples of this type of orientation. The spread of Methodism among the English working class during the early stages of the Industrial Revolution is one example of this type of orientation; it enabled many workers to endure, if not change, those conditions which were socially and physically so destructive.

Unless events can be interpreted as proofs of progress, social movements cannot be sustained. Experience and ideological interpretations must sustain a view that possibilities for change are always imminent. When individuals no longer see alternatives to their state of deprivation, apathy is likely to follow. Thus it is far easier to organize workers who have once experienced a higher economic and social status, or who are aware that individuals similar to themselves have experienced improvements in social and economic status, than it is to organize those who have always experienced poverty and uncertain working conditions and know of no concrete evidence that change is possible. Successful ideologies provide linkages between these experiences and hopes for future improvements.

Among the different labor organizations that have emerged in the course of the labor movement in Canada, those with reformist objectives have been most successful in remaining in existence. In part this is due to the response of dominant elites in business and government. As long as there is continued growth in the economy, business and government can afford to make concessions to labor without losing their influence. Stated in economic terms, everyone can gain something in an expanding economy while the proportional share remains the same. This does not mean that dominant elites will readily make concessions, but it does mean that they can *afford* to do so under such conditions.

Under conditions of a stagnant economy, however, gains by labor mean absolute costs to employers. Hence, the issues are cast in far more dramatic terms. During the initial stages of such economic conditions, there is not likely to be much unrest by organized labor since concerns for merely maintaining jobs supersede the concerns for improving conditions. But as the economy continues to stagnate, labor unions are likely to become far more radical in their demands, incorporating a greater degree of political change into their objectives. Yet, even while this is taking place, union membership may decline if individuals see no hope of improving their own conditions.

An Overview of the Major Debates Within the Canadian Labor Movement

Apart from the ongoing conflict with employers, the labor movement in Canada has been marked by internal debates and conflicts. Viewed in retrospect, there seems to be a consistent pattern in which leaders, once having created support for their particular positions, have had a tendency to become locked in them. Thus, the shifts in orientation within the labor movement have seldom been made by the same leaders. Rather, they have occurred when opposition groups have formed to challenge them. The emergence of opposition has usually occurred with changes in the composition and structure of industry and with shifts in the political environment.

The expression of the opposition has typically involved four major issues. The first has to do with the basis upon which workers should be organized: whether by craft (or skill), or by type of industry in which they are employed. Craft-based unions were the first to be organized; hence their leaders have occupied powerful positions and have been the most influential through most of the history of the labor movement. Those who represent the craft-based view have argued that it is the role of unions to protect skilled tradesmen against the encroachment of machine technology and the use of unskilled labor. Their logic rests upon a monopolization of skills. This form of organization implies that a large number of different unions can exist within a single enterprise, depending upon the division of crafts. This type of organization is probably at its most complex form of development in Great Britain, where single plants may be divided into a myriad of different union jurisdictions, each of which may require its own collective agreement with management.

Opposed to this view is the argument that workers should be organized on the basis of a particular industry, regardless of the craft. Thus, all workers in the pulp and paper industry should be in one union, all workers in steel corporations in another, and so on. As industries have become more mechanized, some skills have been made redundant; hence this orientation, although existing since the early stages of unionization, has become an important force only since the late 1930s. The logic employed to support this position asserts that the power of unions is to be gained from monopolistic control of workers as such, not merely skills.

A second controversial issue has been the *objectives* of the labor movement. While there is obvious commitment to the protection and improvement of the conditions of workers, there has not been agreement on what objectives to pursue to achieve these more abstract ends. The question is whether the interests of workers should be advanced without questioning the foundations of capitalist society, or whether the labor movement should attempt to create radically different social structures. The first reformist position has come to assume that labor organizations are part of a pluralistic society, in which groups of diverse interests compete against each other to protect and advance their causes. This, however, has not always been the argument of this position. Originally, those advocating this reform argument did so on the premise that such an approach was a strategic device by which the total reorganization of society would be gradually accomplished. To launch a total, frontal attack, they argued, would create strong opposition and thus block the long-range objectives of labor organizations.

The opposing, more radical view has argued that reformist tactics merely appease powerful groups—especially employers—and do not remove the basic problem, namely, the continued exploitation of workers. This view aligns itself with socialist ideologies and argues that low wages and poor working conditions are merely symptomatic of a society built upon processes of exploitation. Rather than restricting themselves to economic demands, supporters of the radical perspective have argued that unions should be politically committed to seeking society-wide change.

The reformist approach has been dominant in Canada, in part because its objectives have been more focused and more easily related to the concrete experiences of individuals. Telling a worker that his personal experiences are due to societal conditions has relatively little impact. Telling him that his wages are too low is more closely related to his experience. The reformist orientation has also been more dominant because it has been a more tolerable approach to employers and governments in Canada. Finally, the influence of the American labor movement has reinforced this orientation.

A third issue has been the *strategies* to be employed in obtaining objectives. This issue debates whether employers should be confronted directly or whether progress is best made by attempting to influence government policies. Unions may approach either governments or employers from a reformist or a radical stance. During the early stages of the Canadian labor movement, labor organizations tended to direct their energies toward governments. Later they focused on employers. These issues of strategy have been controversial, especially in the earlier stages of the labor movement, and more recently in the debates on the proper role that labor should play with respect to the federal government.

A fourth issue of contention has been the degree to which Canadian workers benefit from membership in *American-based unions*. Initially the appeal of these "international" unions was the belief that the spread of industrialization transcended political boundaries, and thus workers of diverse national identities had more in common through their class identity than they did with their own countrymen of a different class.

More practically, ties with American unions offered additional leverage against American companies spreading into Canada. Canadian workers could have access to the services and economic resources of the large American unions. Yet, many Canadian unionists came to believe that the American headquarters of these unions were insensitive to problems unique to Canadian labor. Further, they have argued that such ties have been one more example of American dominance over Canada, and that these alliances have prevented the development of a labor movement more consistent with Canada's geographically scattered labor force, governmental structure, industrial characteristics, and other unique attributes.

American courts have defined local unions as integral administrative units of a national or international union. Individual members of the local commit themselves to the constitution of the larger unit. From the American point of view, Canadian locals have no rights except those assigned to them by their international unions. Canadian courts have usually supported this interpretation.[8] These legal interpretations make it very difficult for Canadian unions to sever their ties with American international unions.

It will be seen in the account to follow that conflict within the labor movement became most intense when opposing positions on these major issues became mutually reinforcing. For example the most conflict-ridden periods occurred when craft-oriented, international organizations based in the United States and committed to restricted economic objectives by pressure group tactics and bargaining with employers, were challenged by autonomous Canadian industrial unions, who were oriented toward major structural changes and employing tactics of opposition against governments, as well as employers.

Early Stages

In Canada, the first indications of workers' movements are in the late eighteenth century, with accounts of work stoppages by voyageurs and St. Lawrence River pilots.[9] Workers' organizations began forming during the late

1820s. In 1830 there was a shoe workers' union and a tailors' lodge in Montreal. By 1833 printers and carpenters had established unions in the same city.

The formation of labor organizations, or unions, represents the beginning stage of a social movement in which individuals perceive that their best interests are served through collective action. The labor unions for which there are the clearest records are those in the typographical trades.[10] The International Typographical Society No. 91 of Toronto has documents that go back to 1832, and has been in continuous existence since 1844. The journeymen and foremen who organized the society did so in order to protect themselves against lowered wages and against the extended use of apprentices to perform the work of journeymen. Further, they were being threatened by foreign tradesmen, whom employers actively recruited in order to reduce their labor costs. Related to these concerns, of course, was the potential loss in status previously accorded these skilled tradesmen. Note the following statement recorded in 1832:

> Owing to the many innovations which have been made upon the long established wages of professors of the art of printing, and those of a kind highly detrimental to their interests it was deemed expedient by the Journeymen printers of York, that they should form themselves into a body, similar to societies in other parts of the world, in order to maintain that honourable station and respectability that belongs to the profession. . . . [11]

The declarations of the Canadian typographers were seldom militant and certainly not revolutionary. In this, there were practical considerations: conflicts involving skilled workers in both Britain and the United States often erupted in violence. Thus, Canadian employers were highly suspicious of labor organizations and the workers were well aware of the potential reactions of employers. The statement quoted earlier was undoubtedly designed to reassure employers that the purpose of the Society was "the mutual interest of employers and employed." The society endeavored to be more reassuring when, in 1844, it declared that it was "united to support not combined to injure."[12]

In the early period of labor organization, many trade union principles and objectives were imported into Canada from Britain. In some cases this resulted in the creation of formal organizations. The Amalgamated Society of Engineers, with headquarters in England, formed locals in both Canada and the United States. By 1851 it had branches in Toronto, Hamilton, Kingston, and Montreal.[13] The Amalgamated Society of Carpenters and Joiners, another English federation, was the first permanent organization in Hamilton, Toronto, and London.[14]

English and Scottish labor theorists shaped the early ideological expressions of the early Canadian organizations. These were primarily socialist in nature, stressing the necessity for workers to control the production process. However, techniques of organizing workers were soon influenced by

Americans. In large part, this was due to the proximity of the two countries and the large volume of workers crossing back and forth across the boundary. In 1859, for example, the Toronto Typographical Society received a letter from the National Typographical Union in the United States suggesting that the Toronto society affiliate with it. It did not accept the invitation, but the two unions did exchange information regarding trade and employment conditions and lists of members in good standing. They also honored membership cards held by their respective members. Meanwhile, in the 1860s the strongest completely autonomous Canadian unions were to be found in the ship-building trades, and among bricklayers, bakers, and tailors.

During this same period, Americans themselves established unions in Canada. These included the Iron Moulders Union of North America with branches established during the years 1861–1863 in Montreal, Hamilton, London, and Toronto; the National Typographical Union, which organized branches during the 1860s in St. John, Montreal, Ottawa, Halifax, Hamilton, and London; the cigarmakers, who established a local in Montreal; and the International Journeymen Coopers who established branches in Ontario.

In the transportation industry, the American-based Brotherhood of Locomotive Engineers established branches in Belleville, Hamilton, Montreal, Halifax, Toronto, and London during the years from 1864 to 1868. The Brotherhood of Railroad Conductors had a branch in Montreal and three in Ontario in 1868. In the early 1870s the Brotherhood of Locomotive Firemen, another American union, began organizing in Canada.[15]

Perhaps the most intriguing of the American-based organizations was the Knights of St. Crispin. This was an organization of shoemakers that expanded into Canada soon after its founding in Milwaukee in 1867. As in most early labor organizations, its members were skilled craftsmen, but instead of attempting to prevent the use of machinery and the employment of unskilled labor, it sought to maintain the right to train new workers in the use of machinery.

The objectives of the American unionists in establishing organizations in Canada were to prevent the emergence of competition from cheaper, unorganized Canadian labor and to create transnational organizations to oppose employers operating in both countries. For their part, Canadian workers welcomed the resources of American unions. Further, with the constant movement of workers back and forth across the Canadian-United States border, little importance was placed on the significance of this political boundary.

It is important to note that nearly all the early workers' organizations emerged among skilled tradesmen. These were workers who had already met the first conditions necessary for the development of a social movement, namely, an awareness that their status was being threatened or that they were suffering unjust economic and social deprivation. Further, the close sense of community that had existed among those engaged in trades of similar skills meant that they readily saw their condition not as a privatized personal experience but as a social problem.

The Canadian Labor Union and the Nine-Hour Movement

Labor organizations through the 1860s tended to remain restricted to their own trades. There was cooperation within specific trades, especially among locals within international unions, but little inter-trade communication existed except for the occasional social gathering. City confederations were the usual extent of inter-organizational cooperation.

In the 1870s a growing awareness of common interests among different trades led to greater inter-trade contact. The Toronto Trades Assembly, founded in 1871, brought together journeymen coopers, three lodges of the Knights of St. Crispin, and the Toronto Typographical Society Number 91. This organization was responsible for holding the first meeting of labor delegates from different labor centers and played a major role in influencing early legislation. Finally, it was largely instrumental in forming the Canadian Labor Union.

The sequence of events which led to the formation of this labor federation centered around attempts to limit the length of the working day to nine hours. Similar campaigns were being mounted in Great Britain and the United States. It was quite normal in Canada and in other industrialized countries for workers to be at their jobs for 10 or 12 hours a day. Agitation for a shortened workday began in 1869 when the Typographical Union of Toronto requested that their employers reduce the number of hours worked from 60 to 58 hours a week. This request, although extremely modest, was refused. The union thereupon set up a committee to "disabuse" employers of "some erroneous ideas they have conceived as to the loss they will suffer by granting the concessions."[15] But the employers refused to meet with the committee.

In 1872 the union asked for a conference with their employers to discuss and settle their differences. Again they were refused. Meanwhile, the bookbinders asked for a nine-hour day and offered to accept reduced wages in exchange. They too were refused. Printers then called for a strike on March 25, 1872, and on April 14, a major demonstration was held in Toronto. It included a parade of 13 unions and over 2000 people, representing iron moulders, bricklayers and masons, cigarmakers, coopers, coach makers, blacksmiths and machinists, bakers, varnishers and polishers, the Knights of St. Crispin, the Amalgamated Engineers, typographers, bookbinders, and "employees of R. Hay and Company." The parade ended with a meeting swollen to some 10 000 persons who heard an address by J. S. Williams, president of the Toronto Trades Assembly.[17] The following day, the Master Printers' Association, an employers group, pressed legal charges against members of the original organizing committee and all twenty-four members were arrested, and accused of seditious conspiracy. That evening another demonstration was held to protest their arrest.

These events were particularly significant because they were dramatic demonstrations of the common plight of workers in diverse trades. What became apparent to all workers was that not only did they lose their battle for a shortened workday, but there was also no legal protection for their organizations. The British Trade Union Act of 1871, which granted unions legal status, had no effect in Canada. The Nine-hour Movement was a catalyst for bringing diverse trades together and the experiences of the Toronto demonstrations revealed that there were far broader issues at stake—namely the question of the legal rights of workers. To raise questions about legal rights is to raise the issue of social responsibility. It became readily apparent that employers were under no obligation to demonstrate such responsibility toward workers. Still, social reformers and several influential newspapers such as the *Toronto Leader*, the *Montreal Star*, and the *Hamilton Standard* had been supporting legislation to legalize unions and union menbership. The *Toronto Globe*, published by George Brown, remained adamantly opposed.

On April 18, 1872, John A. Macdonald supported a bill in Parliament almost exactly like the British Trades Union Act. In large part it was a move by the Conservative government to win the political support of workers after Brown, a Liberal, had, through his Toronto newspaper, taken his stand opposing the workers. Macdonald's bill passed in Parliament later that same year.[18]

The Canadian Labor Union emerged from these events as the first inter-trades organization. It was formed by the unions involved in the events in Toronto and it represented a tangible expression of a common purpose. The very quick response of Macdonald apparently influenced the founders to press for more favorable legislation. In doing so, they sought to use means

> consistent with honour and integrity to so correct the abuses under which the working classes are labouring as to insure to them their just rights and privileges to use our utmost endeavours to impress upon the labouring classes of this country the necessity of a close and thorough organization. . . . [19]

Organizers of the Canadian Labour Union struggled to keep it a going concern in the face of very hostile employers, only a superficial degree of government protection, and a severe economic depression which began during 1873, the year of the confederation's founding. But the odds were overwhelming. Membership in the central body declined after its first year until the union was dissolved in 1877. At its last annual convention there were barely sufficient members in attendance to constitute a quorum. During the brief lifespan of the union, some members had argued that it should be a coordinating and supportive body for its individual local union members. Others, however, who carried a majority view argued that it should serve primarily as a means to influence governments to invoke more favorable legislation. Both views have continued to be issues in the debates over union movement strategy.

In the early period from the 1840s to the 1870s, the objectives of labor organizations were extremely utopian. For example, at the time of its founding in 1855, the Quebec Typographical Society included in its aims the hope of maintaining among its members, "the lines of the most brotherly amity, and to instruct and perfect them in the art of typography." While committed to protecting wage levels, regulating employment of apprentices, and dispensing aid to sick members and to families of those who had died, the Society also sought to stimulate educational and social advancement. In 1860 it established a library of over 1000 volumes and frequently sponsored lectures.[20]

Another instance of the early utopian objectives of unions is found in an editorial in the *Ontario Workman* in 1872, in which the author argued for a "thorough system of State education," legislative reforms, and the development of cooperative principles which would supersede the "present system" as it has "superseded the serf system in the past." The author further called for a system of arbitrating labor disputes which would eliminate the necessity of strikes.[21] The experience of dramatic social changes fostered visions of new social forms soon to be brought into place if individuals had the energy and ability to create them. It is important to remember that, even though there was intense suffering during this period, it was also a time of optimism which influenced tradesmen in unique ways. It is also worth remembering that this was a time of intense intellectual ferment throughout the Western world, when social philosophers, social reformers, and religious leaders attempted to influence the new social structures in the process of being formed. It was during this period that Karl Marx was developing his analysis of capitalist society.

Continued Growth and the American Presence

After the depression of 1873, organizing activities at the local level increased and closely followed the pattern of industrial development. By the late 1870s and early 1880s most transport trades, building trades, and coal miners had been organized. With the exceptions of the organization of coal miners in Nova Scotia, the building trades in the East, and clothing trades and public employees, most of the growth in the number of labor organizations came from foreign-based unions. By 1887 the most influential labor organizations were the American-based unions of typographers, bricklayers, iron moulders, and cigar makers; the American Brotherhood of Carpenters; and the British-based Amalgamated Society of Carpenters and Joiners.

The most spectacular growth occurred in the early 1880s with the expansion of the American-based Knights of Labor in Canada. By the end of that decade it had 250 Canadian locals which in turn were organized into 7 district assemblies. The objectives of the Knights were unique, in that they were far broader than those of unions organized along the lines of specific skilled trades. The Knights hoped to change the basic structure of capitalist society by forming a cooperative society. Membership was open to everyone except "doctors," lawyers, businessmen, and "purveyors of intoxicants."[22] The organization stressed that individual greatness was to be measured by industrial and moral worth rather than by wealth. It was the duty of members of the organization "to secure for the workers the 'full enjoyment of the wealth they create, sufficient leisure in which to develop their intellectual, moral and social faculties, all the benefits of recreation and pleasure of association; in a word, to enable them to share in the gains and honours of advancing civilization.'"[23]

In the United States the membership in the Knights of Labor declined from a high of 729 677 in 1886 to approximately 74 635 in 1893. There were several reasons for this: the organization's objectives and membership covered too wide a spectrum to effect much organizational discipline; the hostility of employers to it was especially severe; and it was later opposed by the tightly organized craft-based American Federation of Labor. But in Canada, assemblies of the Knights continued to remain in existence until 1902 and vestiges of the assemblies continued for some time thereafter. They were most strongly established in Quebec.

The Trades and Labour Congress

By the 1880s leaders of the Toronto Trades and Labour Council believed that in order to combat the growing size and power of industrial enterprises, a large coordinating body of labor organizations was required. In 1883 the Council sponsored a meeting attended by delegates from local unions and Knights of Labor assemblies throughout Ontario. Its purpose was to simply hold discussions on problems that the delegates regarded as important. In 1886 a second meeting was held, attended by delegates from Ontario and one delegate from the Knights of Labor in Quebec. During this meeting the Trades and Labour Congress of Canada was formed

The general aims of the TLC were to bring about legislation more favorable to the trade union movement and to reduce conflicts and jurisdictional disputes among affiliated unions. It sought to be a national coordinating body operating according to delegate vote. Assemblies of the Knights of Labor and individual labor unions were permitted one delegate if they had 200 members or less, 2 delegates if they had up to 400 members, and 3 delegates if they had over 400 members. Trades and labor councils of specific areas, district assemblies of the Knights of Labor, and central labor unions incorporating several local unions were each permitted 3 delegates.[24] This form of organization was influenced by the British Trades and Labour Council. Meanwhile the American Federation of Labor was being organized along similar lines in the same year as the founding of the TLC.

By 1889 the success of labor unions in having their own candidates elected to the British Columbia legislature influenced delegates at the TLC convention to pursue a similar course at the national level.[25] A candidate from the ranks of labor subsequently ran for office in Winnipeg and became the first labor representative in the federal parliament in 1900. Support for political involvement was anything but unanimous. Most locals in the Trade and Labour Congress had ties with American unions and most of these, in turn, had affiliations with the recently formed American Federation of Labor. The guiding philosophy of the AFL was "pure and simple unionism," for which political involvement was thought to be a distraction to the workers' real interests.

It is necessary at this point to elaborate briefly on the context within which the AFL pursued this strategy. The American Federation of Labor was born out of the intense sectarian debates among American socialists in the United States from the 1870s to 1890s. (Underlying these debates, of course, was the issue regarding the meaning and expressions of freedom and equality.) The most important organization to emerge during this period was the Socialist Labor Party, organized in 1877 and dominated by inflexible "Lasalleans." These theorists, most of whom were immigrants from Bismarck's Germany, argued that labor should attach itself to political programs, forcing governments to legislate social change more favorable to workers.[26]

Others opposed this view, claiming such political orientation would merely lead to a more powerful state which, in the long run, would be in opposition to the worker's welfare. Further, it was argued that such an orientation was ill-suited to the American context, in which individualism, rather than class identity grounded in a feudal past, was the dominant social reality.[27] Samuel Gompers, an active participant in these debates and head of the Cigar Workers' International Union of America, argued that labor's interests were best served if the objectives were limited to immediate benefits for workers. His was a militant stance aimed directly against employers. In 1886 he and Adolf Strasser played major roles in founding the American Federation of Labor, which was aimed at opposing the doctrinaire socialists. Gompers served as the president of the AFL for all but one of its first thirty-eight years of existence. The strategy of the Federation was to incorporate unions of skilled workers and thus to confront employers with a united force to back their demands.[28] Gompers's aim was to mold both a nationwide and international organization of sufficient discipline and clarity of purpose to challenge the growing industrial combines.[29]

As a leader of the AFL, Gompers believed that a pragmatic orientation was necessary for the survival of the labor movement, and that organized labor should seek a secure place within capitalist society in order to be in a position to transform it by demanding a share of power.[30] He held to a form of organization which emphasized strict jurisdictional boundaries based upon craft specialties. In response to those who argued for a greater involvement in the political arena, Gompers maintained that political change would come as an ultimate consequence of his approach, but not from a direct attack on political institutions. There were concrete events that reinforced Gompers' stand. These included the disastrous effects of the Haymarket Square battle and the subsequent execution of leaders of the Black International in Chicago in 1886, and the losses suffered from a strike against the Pullman Palace Car Company in 1894. Further, the Knights of Labor, with their broad objectives and heterogeneous membership, declined rapidly in the face of more focused, pragmatically oriented workers' organizations.

Linkages Between the Trades and Labour Congress and the American Federation of Labor

Since the Trades and Labour Congress included unions which were affiliated with American-based unions and since most of these were affiliated with the American Federation of Labor, the Congress had from its inception very precarious grounds upon which to formulate its own programs. The first formal contact between the TLC and the AFL came in 1896 when the secretary-treasurer of the TLC, George Dower, sent a letter to Gompers complaining of a newly enacted American alien law designed to limit the entry of cheap labor from the Orient. The law was also hindering the flow of Canadian labor to the United States. Gompers replied that he sympathized with Dower's concerns, but that it would be difficult for the AFL to support the free flow of Canadian labor into the United States while at the same time supporting the bill. Gompers invited the TLC to send a fraternal delegate to attend the AFL convention later that year. Although representatives of the British Trades Union Congress appeared, none from Canada attended.

A year later the issue of dues paid by Canadian affiliates to their American-based union became an issue of contention between solely Canadian unions and those with headquarters in the United States. The problem came to light when the TLC sought to get financial support from its affiliates in order to maintain a legislative committee in Ottawa. Very little support was forthcoming, since the Canadian affiliates were restricted in their expenditures by their head offices in the United States.

The Trades and Labour Congress was caught not only with a financial problem, but also with one that had jurisdictional implications. Member unions affiliated with American unions were not paying dues to the TLC at the very time that the TLC needed finances to support lobbying programs and organization drives. This meant that the loyalty of the American affiliates was directed more to the AFL than to the TLC. The executives of the AFL, realizing that the concern about the dues payment could damage their drive toward an international organization, finally agreed to pay the TLC a small annual grant to aid in its work. In return, the TLC agreed to exchange fraternal delegates with the AFL. Thus, in an effort to maintain the membership of the American affiliated unions and to gain additional financial support from the AFL, the TLC opened the way for a close relationship with the American Federation of Labor.

Despite these close links, the TLC did maintain some characteristics distinct from the AFL. It was more inclusive in its membership, it tolerated dual union membership (for example, membership in both the TLC affiliated unions and the Knights of Labor), and it encouraged active programs to support political candidates as spokesmen for labor. The unifying strategy of the TLC, composed as it was of American affiliated unions, Canadian unions, and assemblies of the Knights of Labor, was to seek improvement through political action and favorable legislation. The strategy of the AFL, on the other hand, was to confront employers directly and to seek immediate economic benefits.

The uneasy relationship between the two confederations continued until the 1902 TLC convention in Berlin, Ontario (now Kitchener), when, with the American affiliated unions controlling the majority of votes, the representatives attending the convention voted to oust the assemblies of the Knights of Labor, as well as those national unions which represented the same crafts as international unions, and those unions which sought active political involvement, especially in alliance with the Socialist Party.[31] The American affiliated unions were following the directions of their head offices. Ostensibly, the issue for Gompers and his supporters in the AFL was that workers' loyalties were split if they belonged to more than one federation; hence their strong objection to dual unionism. In fact, it was a maneuver of power against the Knights of Labor, autonomous Canadian unions, and the fledgling Socialist Party. Those sympathetic to the AFL argued that theirs was the "new socialism." To take part in the political process was merely to lend support to "capitalist forces." Thus, they maintained, labor should follow an independent route, "to reward friends and punish enemies." Their concern was to avoid identification with existing parties and to remain independent from what they regarded as the overly intellectual theoreticians of the Socialist Party.[32] Commenting on the tactics of the AFL, the Executive Committee of the TLC supported the AFL orientation by declaring during the 1905 convention that "If the labormen of Canada generally, would act in the same way, it would be but a short time before independent labour candidates would occupy seats on the floor of Parliament in large numbers."[33]

The Trades and Labour Congress remained the major labor federation in Canada until 1956. But other organizations and the conflicts among them and with the TLC have given the labor movement in Canada its distinctive characteristics. Controversies regarding the membership of Canadian workers in American-controlled unions have remained dominant throughout the history of the Canadian labor movement.

The Canadian Federation of Labour

The delegates who had been evicted from the TLC in 1902 immediately met to form a new coordinating body which they called the National Trades and Labour Congress. The founders opposed the AFL because of its pragmatism and because they regarded the AFL as maintaining a superior rather than a parallel relationship with the Canadian-based Trades and Labour Congress.[34] Their original aim was to build a strong national-based labor federation out of the Knights of Labor assemblies and existing national unions. In 1908 the name was changed to the Canadian Federation of Labour. In the same year, the Canadian locals of the International Typographical Union seceded from the TLC and joined the new organization. In 1910 an organization of Nova Scotia miners joined and the Provincial Workmen's Association also became affiliated.[35] However, attempts by the new federation to organize the shoe and leather, printing, and mining industries were unsuccessful.[36]

The stated aim of the CFL was to achieve protection for the Canadian worker through more favorable legislation. The preamble to its constitution, which was adopted in 1908, stated that the Canadian workers required protection "both in their relationship to capital in the hands of the organized employing class, and in the autocratic domination of trade unionism and its policy exercised by the present system of internationalism."[37]

Consistent with its support for autonomous national unions, the federation supported higher tariffs from 1903 to 1907, in contrast to the stand taken by the TLC. In 1903 it demanded to be recognized by the federal government as the only legitimate Canadian congress of workers. At different times it sought an end to the check-off system of dues payment, where an international union was the bargaining agent. It also sought more rigid enforcement of the Alien Labour Law from the federal government as a means to control the number of Americans coming into Canada under the employ of

American enterprises.[38] Finally, it embarked upon a campaign to adopt a union label for the goods its members manufactured and thus to encourage consumers to purchase only its marked products.

During its formative years, the bulk of the membership came from the old Knights of Labor assemblies in Quebec. But by 1919 most members came from Ontario and included affiliates from Alberta and British Columbia.[39] The federation had been losing its Quebec membership to a more locally sensitive movement, the Catholic Social Action, which had been in existence since 1907. As a consequence of its activities, a separate workers' council made up of CFL unions and other unaffiliated unions was established in Quebec City in 1918.[40]

The Canadian Federation of Labour declined soon after 1923. Its demise was hastened by the TLC's strong opposition to its objective of establishing national autonomy while attempting to incorporate a wide range of orientations within its organization and its strategy of enticing already organized unions into its fold rather than devoting more resources to organizing the unorganized. Finally, its approach toward affecting favorable legislation as a means to further its aims lacked the immediacy of effect that the international "business unions" were able to convey in their tactics of direct confrontation with employers. By 1927 remnants of the CFL joined with other dissident national unions to form the All Canadian Congress of Labour. I shall have more to say about this organization later.

The Western Canada Labour Conference, the One Big Union, and the Winnipeg General Strike

In 1918 the TLC had been experiencing more divisions within its ranks. Regional factionalism was a major cause of the dissension; this in turn reflected differences in industrial structure. Manufacturing was dominant in Ontario and Quebec. Here, international unions had been firmly established along craft lines for nearly fifty years. In the West, extractive industries, including mines, timber, and pulp and paper, were the principal industries. Union activity in the West had been more recent; hence there were more models for members to choose from in developing their organizations.

Unions from the eastern provinces who were affiliated with the TLC tended to support international, craft-based organizations and to focus on rights of collective bargaining, with additional attention directed toward obtaining favorable government legislation. In the West, especially in British Columbia, workers tended to favor industrial-based forms of organization and to be opposed to the American-dominated craft unions. The more militant western unions favored more political action and in some cases advocated total opposition to the existing political structure of Canada.

The formal confrontation between these two groups occurred during the TLC convention in Quebec City in 1918. The convention issues focused primarily on the cooperation of the TLC executives with the federal government's war policy. Unionists from the West tended to be opposed to this, and also noted that most of the representatives who had met with the government were members of the international unions. Further, the delegates from the West wanted the TLC executives to take a more adamant stand against the continued importation of labor from the Orient.

The issues remained unresolved and after the convention the delegates from the West met to formulate ideas and policies for the "reconstruction" of a federation they regarded as acting too closely in the interests of employers. In addition, of course, there had been the opposition to conscription expressed before and during the First World War by various labor representatives. Indeed, the war had proved to be a bitter experience for labor throughout the industrialized world, since it destroyed the growing movement for a world labor federation.[41]

Dissident delegates who met after the end of the official convention were careful to point out that their intentions were not to move toward secession or toward dual unionism.[42] They had hoped to sponsor a reform movement. Later in November, 1918, the planning committee of the group announced a conference to be held on March 13, 1919.

Meanwhile, throughout the western industrialized countries, conservative politicians were alarmed over the successes of the Communist Revolution in Russia. The avowed intention of the Communist party to foment a world revolution added to these fears. In the United States, the International Workers of the World, with its radical critique of American society, was especially threatening to supporters of the status quo. Canadian politicans were also concerned. The federal departments of Labour and Justice investigated the activities of the IWW in Canada, but found no evidence that the organization had engaged in obstructionist tactics during the war. Yet, the Borden government required every alien over sixteen, of enemy nationality, and residing in Canada, to be registered on the government rolls. This had an immediate effect upon the western miners, since a significant proportion of them were Ukrainian, Russian, or Finnish. Invoking the wartime Industrial Disputes Investigation Act, the government restricted freedoms of speech, association, and publication, and the right to strike.[43]

This curtailment of liberties merely reinforced the view among many unionists that cooperation with the Borden government was useless. The Winnipeg Trades and Labour Council took a vote in favor of calling a general strike to protest against the government's no-strike decree. Ninety-two percent of the union membership voted in support of this tactic. Support also came from Calgary and Edmonton. The Winnipeg Council then informed the federal government of the possibility of a strike, whereupon the government backed down on its intention to prosecute five labor leaders who had advocated the strike.

The Western Canada Labour Conference, proposed by the planning committee of the dissidents of the Quebec City TLC Convention, was endorsed by the Winnipeg Council, the Alberta Federation of Labour, the United Mine Workers, the Vancouver Council and, meeting in Calgary just prior to the proposed council, the British Columbia Federation of Labour. During the conference in March, 1919, the original intent to develop a program for the TLC convention to be held later that fall was superseded by demands for a separate organization. The convention resolutions committee recommended reorganization of labor along industrial lines and went on to condemn capitalism, craft unionism, and lobbying tactics. It further proposed that members sever their ties with international unions.[44]

On the following day, the conference policy committee recommended that a new labor organization, the One Big Union, be formed, and that steps be taken to implement its formation. In addition, resolutions were passed condemning the federal government and calling for the restoration of freedoms of speech, press, and assembly, the release of all political prisoners, the removal of restrictions on workers' organizations, and support for a six-hour day and thirty-hour week. (The rationale for the last proposal was the necessity to ensure high employment levels during the postwar reconstruction.) The delegates went on to support a general strike, if employers did not implement this last demand by June 1.

The delegates also supported resolutions calling for a political system of soviet control by representatives from industries, rather than maintaining the existing parliamentary system. They supported the principles of "proletarian dictatorship" and went on to register their support for the Russian Bolshevik and German Spartacist revolutions and demanded the withdrawal of all allied troops from Russian soil. All these resolutions were to be put before members of existing labor associations for their ratification. But while the referendum among locals was being conducted, the Winnipeg General Strike occurred at the end of May.

The Winnipeg General Strike

The Winnipeg General Strike is especially significant because it represents an event that sparked massive resistance to the initial successes of the more radical wing of the labor movement. It is important to remember, however, that the initial issues in the strike were anything but radical. The general strike itself was an outgrowth of two strikes which were based on the issue of "the right of the workers to bargain collectively through union structures of their own choice."[45] These strikes involved the building trades unions and the metals trade workers at the three metal shops. Both groups sought to coordinate local demands through central councils representing each group—the Building Trades Council and the Metal Trades Council. The employers, represented by the Builders Exchange and the Metal Trades Contractors, would not recognize the councils and maintained the position that they would deal only with individual unions.

The two groups of unions thereupon informed the Winnipeg Trades and Labour Council of their plight. The issue regarding the freedom of unions to choose their own bargaining structure had sufficiently important implications for the Council that it polled its affiliated unions to determine whether or not they would be willing to engage in a general sympathetic strike on behalf of the Building Trades and the Metal Trades councils. The returns indicated that 8667 union members supported the proposed strike with 645 opposed.

The general strike began on May 15, 1919. Within two hours the whole industrial and commercial life of Winnipeg was paralyzed. However, essential services were maintained. While the police had voted to strike, they were asked by the Labor Council to stay on duty in order to maintain law and order. Water works, fire protection, and milk deliveries were also maintained. Returned soldiers also supported the strike. While the affiliated membership in the Winnipeg Trades and Labour Council numbered only 12 000, an estimated 35 000 workers were involved in the strike.

In response, business interests organized a "Citizens Committee of 1 000" and, with the full support of the Federal government, made it clear that there would be no bargaining unless the strike was first called off. The committee further called for the deportation of aliens on strike and obtained amendments to the Immigration Act which permitted such deportations to occur without trial.

The strikers organized a series of demonstrations in order to show their strength and to protest the arrest of their leaders. The Committee of 1 000 kept the justice department and the RCMP informed of these developments and when the workers held a silent parade on June 21, special police, mounted RCMP, and units of both the militia and the regular armed forces attacked. In the melee that followed one person was killed and dozens were injured.[45] The Strike Committee thereupon called an end to the strike on June 25, 1919.

In effect, the Winnipeg General Strike was an enactment of the general unrest among western workers. The conditions contributing to this mood were high inflation, grievances over the imposition of conscription during the war, and the impact of news of scandals involving huge profits made by individuals and corporations during the war. Further, unemployment was high among returning soldiers and farmers were suffering from falling wheat prices.

The fears of Bolshevism which swept through the American West and up into Canada must have been an important factor in accounting for the government's strong reaction. The federal government's response was directed by Arthur Meighen, Minister of the Interior and acting Minister of Justice during this time. He was instrumental in employing orders-in-council to ban selected publications and political organizations. A number of aliens were also arrested. Earlier, on May 1, 1919, a committee of the House of Commons had been appointed to draw up a new section of the Criminal Code. It was, in effect, copied from the United States Espionage Act and from American statutes against criminal syndicalism. The committee proposed that the penalty for sedition be raised from two to twenty years. The act itself was rushed through Parliament between June 27 and July 5, 1919.

The act made unlawful any association whose purpose was to bring about "governmental, industrial or economic change within Canada by force or violence or which teaches or defends such use of force or violence."[47] It provided for the seizure of all property belonging to or suspected to belong to such an association. This could be done without warrant by any person authorized by the Commissioner of the Royal Canadian Mounted Police. Crimes punishable by 20 years imprisonment included acting as an officer of such an association, selling, writing or publishing anything representative of it, becoming and continuing to be a member of it, wearing a badge or button indicating membership in or association with it, and contributing to or soliciting dues for it. In addition the act provided for deportation of any alien advocating violence. Naturalized citizens could have their certificate revoked if convicted, and British subjects could be deported if they belonged to "prohibited or undesirable classes."[48]

These responses strengthened the resolve of the western labor movement. Meanwhile political moderates appalled by the Winnipeg General Strike and the conservative reactions, defeated the Conservative party in the 1921 general election and brought about reforms within the Liberal Party. In the long run the labor movement itself benefited from the Strike, but not its more radical wings. It is also likely that these events laid the groundwork for the eventual founding of the Co-operative Commonwealth Federation Party in 1932 and 1933.[49]

While the Winnipeg General Strike caught the planners of the One Big Union by surprise, the events probably contributed to the union's membership growth, even though they refused the request of the Winnipeg strikers to mount sympathy strikes in other cities. But this growth was relatively short-lived. The One Big Union was unable to influence eastern unions, it suffered from attacks from employers' associations, and it had even more difficulty withstanding the aggressive organizers from international unions and the opposition of the Trades and Labour Congress.

The All Canadian Congress of Labour

While the embattled One Big Union was suffering membership losses, other unions were breaking away from the Trades and Labour Congress. The Canadian Brotherhood of Railway Employees led by A. R. Mosher and M. M. Maclean had been ousted from the TLC on charges of dual unionism. The two leaders had argued that there could be no viable Canadian labor movement as long as the TLC refused to affiliate those Canadian unions who had members from the same trades as already incorporated by international unions.

Under the auspices of Mosher and Maclean, delegates from other dissident unions met to form a new federation. At the founding convention in 1927 were delegates from the One Big Union, remnants of the old Canadian Federation of Labour, the International Brotherhood of Electrical Workers, the Electrical Communication Workers of Canada, the International Commercial Telegraphers Union, the Canadian Association of Railroad Enginemen, the Toronto Printing Pressmen's Union, the Mine Workers Union of Canada, the Federation of Bricklayers, Masons and Plasterers of Quebec Province, and the National Union of Theatrical Employees.[50]

The aims of the new organization were to organize workers into autonomous bodies along industrial lines, to educate workers of the necessity to engage in political action, and to work for legislation which would bring immediate improvements for workers. The new congress supported existing national unions and embarked on an organizing campaign of its own.

However, the new federation, the All Canadian Congress of Labour, ran into difficulties almost immediately. Mosher, the head of the Congress, held to a reformist philosophy. His principal concern was the national identity of Canadian unions. But other affiliated unions were primarily concerned with more radical objectives and placed more emphasis upon political confrontation to realize those objectives. Thus members of the One Big Union were not strong supporters of the relatively conservative policies of the ACCL executives. Further, in 1930 the Mine Workers of Canada left the ACCL to affiliate with the Communist Workers' Unity League and later with the United Mine Workers of America. In sum, the objectives and policies of the ACCL were too narrowly defined and too conservative in contrast to the orientation of many of its affiliated unions. By 1935 most of the activities of the ACCL were directed toward publicizing the labor movement and seeking favorable legislation. These aims, of course were similar to those of the TLC. Finally, even though the ACCL declared itself to be an industrial-based organization, nine out of the sixteen unions attending the 1935 convention were craft-based unions.[51]

In 1936 those members of the executive board who were from the One Big Union and the secretary of the ACCL concluded that the coming convention should not be held. President Mosher declared this to be insubordination and the One Big Union, the Amalgamated Building Workers, and members of the electrical workers union were purged from the congress. Thereafter, the ACCL continued in a weakened form although it gained a few new members from the hosiery, furniture, and other industries.[52] By 1939, the federation was largely a spent force.

Despite these difficulties, the relative success of the Canadian national unions is indicated by the fact that nearly half of the organized workers in 1935 belonged to them. In large part, this was due to the increased organization among semi-and unskilled workers—a sector of the labor force which tended to be neglected by the TLC.

The federations to which most of these industrial-based unions were affiliated were the All Canadian Congress of Labour, the Canadian and Catholic Confederation of Labour founded in Quebec in 1921, and the Workers' Unity League formed in 1930 among workers in mining, clothing, lumber, and textile industries. The WUL was under communist leadership and was the most radical of the three major groups. It was the only union which sought to organize the unemployed and to use strikers against both employers and governments.[53]

The Growth of Industrial Unions

The strength of an autonomous Canadian union movement appeared to be based upon an industrial form of organization. But while industrial unions increased in Canada during the late 1930s, Canadian control declined. There were several factors that contributed to this development. One was the issue of communist involvement in the Canadian labor movement, and the strong reaction to it not only by business and industrial interests, but also by politicians and many leaders within the union movement itself. Even though in 1935 the Communist International called for a united front among the working classes to "destroy fascism" and headquarters in Moscow ordered the Workers' Unity League to disband and its unions to affiliate with the TLC, the Communist issue remained very much alive.

With hostility against organized labor running strong in the 1930s, those who argued for an industrial-based form of organization welcomed additional resources and collaboration. These appeared to come from the United States. This period was one of the most momentous in the history of the labor movement in both Canada and the United States. It was a time of reassessment of the role of labor in the economy by leaders of industry and governments; yet at the same time some of the most anti-labor positions ever experienced by the labor movement were taken. Further, intense rivalries and factional disputes occurred over jurisdictional issues among labor organizations.

In the United States the problems of the Depression created a changed perspective of labor's role among many influential economists and leaders in government and industry. This was a change in the definition of labor, from a cost factor in production to a matter for welfare and supportive legislation designed to encourage an increase in employment and subsequently an expansion of the consumer market.[54] To that end, the American government instituted labor legislation which provided the legal groundwork for a strengthened labor movement and measures for workers' welfare. Since price competition among industrial enterprises was ruinous under Depression conditions, the government relaxed its sanctions against the formation of monopolies, while big business agreed to support more favorable labor legislation.

One major outcome of this new perspective was the passage of the National Labor Relations Act in 1935 (the "Wagner Act"), which banned company-sponsored unions, and forbade employers to discriminate against union members and to refuse to bargain with unions who represented the majority of their workers. While the act was at first widely ignored by industry, the Supreme Court upheld its constitutionality in 1937 and thereafter unions received greater legal protection than they had ever experienced before. Workers now had the right to organize themselves, to bargain collectively through representatives of their own choosing, and to engage in concerted activities for purposes of collective bargaining and other forms of mutual aid.[55] During this time unions made spectacular gains in membership.

Yet, while this act provided greater legal support for unions, employers were at the same time employing the most vicious tactics to weaken the labor movement. There was a pervasive use of undercover agents, with one author estimating that there was one spy in each of the 41 000 locals in the United States, at an estimated cost of $800,000,000 per year.[56] Hearings before the congressional Civil Liberties Committee from 1934 to 1936 revealed that most major corporations employed labor spies and that several even maintained huge stocks of munitions and private police forces. (Youngstown Sheet and Tube, and Republic Steel Corporation were two companies that had the most spectacular arsenals.)

Those unions which made the most gains in membership during this time were industrial-based organizations. Within the AFL, union leaders who supported the industrial-based unions formed the Committee for Industrial Organization (CIO) in an effort to broaden the scope of the AFL organization. When they were rebuffed during the 1935 AFL convention, the Committee and its affiliated unions, led by John L. Lewis of the United Mine Workers, were expelled from the Federation in November 1936.

Despite these strong reactions, the CIO organizing drives were extremely successful. This did not escape the attention of those Canadian labor leaders who were committed to the industrial basis for organization. They subsequently sought help from the CIO to mount similar campaigns in

Canada. When aid could not be provided, they organized CIO locals on their own and then sought and received recognition from the American-based CIO headquarters. The attraction of CIO affiliation was that it conveyed to employers, many of whom were representatives of American corporations, an image of a powerful international labor organization commanding huge resources.

The conflict between workers and employers was also intense in Canada during the later 1930s. Between 1936 and 1937, one half of the total time loss due to strikes occurred in those industries in which union recognition was the main issue. A strike of automobile workers in 1937 in Oshawa, Ontario against the General Motors Corporation marked a turning point toward an increased growth of industrial unions. Four thousand two hundred recently organized workers struck for a period of two and a half weeks, from April 8 to 26. Their demands included union recognition, wage increases, and additional benefits.[57] Members of the new union identified themselves with the CIO-affiliated United Automobile Workers of America. The American-owned company refused to deal with the union, ironically because its negotiation committee included an international representative from Detroit. The Premier of Ontario, Mitchell Hepburn, viewed the strike as the work of "foreign agitators" and mobilized police and military and civilian personnel into a paramilitary force of 400 men to deal with the "crisis."[58]

The newly formed union, for its part, had no financial backing from the American-based CIO. While the Americans dispatched a very effective organizer and sent public messages of support, it appears that the *belief* that American economic resources were behind them, rather than the reality, was a strong force in maintaining the workers' commitment to the work stoppage. No support came from the TLC. After two and a half weeks, the strike ended with workers gaining some wage increases, a reduction in the work week from 55 to 44 hours, and a few other minor concessions. But there was no company recognition of the United Auto Workers, the CIO affiliate.

While this was a loss for union recognition, the event did demonstrate that unskilled workers in large mass-production industries, most of whom were in Ontario, were ready to join more powerful labor organizations. However, the extreme, nearly hysterical, response of Premier Hepburn of Ontario, the opposition of business and manufacturing interests, the apprehensions of the large public whose fears of communist infiltration were being reinforced by politicians, and finally the opposition of many craft-based unions and the All-Canadian Congress of Labour (ACCL president Mosher had praised the actions of Hepburn in keeping out agents of "foreign domination")—all combined to retard the growth of industrial unions until the later years of the Second World War. The Canadian labor movement lacked the legal support enjoyed by its American counterpart. The relative size, strength, and especially the legal status of Canadian unions as a whole lagged at least ten years behind the unions in the United States.[59]

Meanwhile, at the national level, the Trades and Labour Congress found itself in a difficult position because of the formal division in the United States between the CIO-affiliated unions led by John L. Lewis of the United Mine Workers and the traditional craft-based unions which controlled the AFL. The AFL had expelled the industrial-oriented unions in 1936 and put pressure on the Trades and Labour Congress to do the same in Canada. The rationale for the split was that the CIO affiliates were guilty of dual unionism. For the TLC to eliminate these unions was to weaken the Canadian movement. On the other hand, to retain them was to risk the loss of those unions loyal to the AFL.

As early as 1911, TLC delegates, meeting at the annual convention in Vancouver, endorsed the principle of industrial unionism. But subsequent conventions reduced the impact of the resolution with the argument that the traditional craft-based unions were not opposed to industrial-based unions as long as they did not infringe upon those sectors already controlled by the traditional craft unions. Obviously, with the changing structure of industry, this position became more ambiguous and harder to defend, Further, because the TLC was committed to jurisdictional divisions by skill, it was unable to adopt more flexible tactics to meet the changes in labor force composition—changes that were a direct consequence of the impact of huge, mass-producing enterprises, such as those in the automobile, steel, and rubber industries.

Confronted with the consequences of the American split, the Congress, at its convention in 1937, adopted a motion to make known to the Americans their plight—that the split would greatly weaken the Canadian movement. In the actual vote, representatives of craft-based unions, which had most to lose by incorporating the new industrial form, were either opposed to the motion or sought assurances of protection of their own jurisdiction.

The TLC offered to serve as mediator between the two American factions. However, a Canadian delegate at the Houston convention of the AFL nullified this offer after he had condemned the CIO-linked unions. He was expressing the popular fears of that time, that the CIO unions were merely vehicles for the spread of communism. The American CIO in the meantime declared itself an organization separate from the AFL. The TLC was left without room to compromise.

After polling the members of its executive council, the TLC executives suspended the following CIO-linked organizations in 1939: the United Mine Workers of America (72 locals, 15 000 members), the Amalgamated Clothing Workers of America (20 locals, 4000 members), the International Union of Fur Workers (11 locals, 750 members), the International Union of Quarry Workers (1 local, 54 members), the United Auto Workers (1 local, 200 members), the Steel Workers' Organizing Committee (8 locals, 1120 members), and the Mine, Mill and Smelter Workers (3 locals, 1100 members). Support for the ouster was far from unequivocal. Those opposed to the suspension argued that American issues should not be permitted to dominate

Canadian labor policy. But ultimate authority remained entrenched in the craft-based unions who held to existing jurisdictional lines, arguing that increasing strength should be based upon international affiliations by craft designations rather than within Canada by industry. What they failed to recognize was that the structure of industry and hence the composition of the labor force had changed while they remained committed to a restrictive ideology that was fast becoming outmoded.[60]

The Canadian Confederation of Labour

In October, 1939, Canadian representatives of the CIO-affiliated unions who had been expelled from the Trades and Labour Congress met and formed a separate organization with the sanction of the American CIO president, John L. Lewis. To reduce the impact of communist influence within its ranks, the Canadian-based CIO unions sought a merger with the All Canadian Congress of Labour. For their part, leaders of the ACCL believed that the Congress could benefit from the financial and organizational strengths of the CIO affiliates. However, they agreed to the CIO proposal only if the new organization stated, as part of its official policy, the need for an independent Canadian movement. CIO affiliates assented, and in 1940 a new organization, the Canadian Confederation of Labour, was founded.

Before the merger, leaders of the ACCL had received support from and shared much of the reformist and socialist political philosophy of the Cooperative Commonwealth Federation party. It was this philosophy rather than the communist that came to dominate the CCL. Actually, had the Amalgamated Clothing Workers not joined the merger at the last minute, the communist faction would likely have taken over the new organization.

As it emerged, the CCL came to be controlled by the wealthy and relatively conservative unions: the Canadian Brotherhood of Railroad Employees (Mosher's union), the United Mine Workers, the Amalgamated Clothing Workers, and later, the United Steel Workers. The Congress remained more an uneasy coalition than a cohesive organization, since each faction sought to pursue its own ends. The conflicts were expressed in terms of two issues: the issue of continuing affiliation of communist-dominated unions and the issue of autonomous Canadian unions versus those with US affiliation.

With respect to the first controversy, the United Electrical Workers proved to be the most troublesome union. Although the ostensible reasons for conflict were non-payment of dues and "libeling Congress officials," these incidents were mostly contrived by leaders of the CCL. The real concern was communist leadership of the union. (Between 1943 and 1949 the union was suspended from the CCL six times before it was finally ousted.) Communist leaders, forced out of other unions, had became officials of the United Electrical Workers, hence strengthening this union's communist orientation.[61]

The CCL also found the United Auto Workers a troublesome affiliate. The Congress was itself in a position of ambivalence during a major UAW strike against Ford in 1945 because of the UAW's communist dominance on the one hand, and Ford's attempt to destroy the union on the other. The anti-communist leaders on the CCL executive—Mosher, Conroy, and Millard—were opposed to the strike. But the leaders of the UAW and especially its rank and file supported it. Some writers have argued that the strike itself was engineered by the communists to further their own ends. Others have argued that the strike and the tactics used were independent of such influence.[62] The truth is probably a combination of the two interpretations. The Ford strike itself brought into the open the fundamental conflicts between the two factions that had been submerged during the war. Pressure to oust the communist leadership from the UAW continued, but what was likely more effective in reducing this influence was the general anti-communist hysteria manifested throughout Canada and the United States, and more particularly the growing loss of support for communist leadership among the membership following the Berlin blockade and the *coup d'état* in Czechoslovakia.

While the moderate forces gained control of the CCL, the second major issue—internationalism versus nationalism—was not resolved. In fact it remains an ongoing issue of contention within contemporary labor federations. There are two aspects to this issue that illustrate the problem of control: finances, and an appropriate stand on political policies. Under the terms of the merger, the CIO-affiliated unions continued to send their monthly per capita tax of five cents to their headquarters in Washington. The CIO headquarters agreed to then rebate two cents of this tax back to the Congress. In 1941 Mosher, the president of the CCL, argued that the Canadian affiliates should pay their two-cents share directly to Canadian headquarters. While seemingly an insignificant issue, it was of symbolic importance in that it removed one element of dependence upon Washington. (In actual fact, there is some evidence that once the CIO unions were established, the American headquarters actually subsidized the Canadian affiliates. It was not until the Second World War that Canadians suffered net losses of the flow of funds from Canada to the United States.)

But Mosher's other proposals were rejected. He had proposed that newly organized unions should come under the sole control of the CCL rather than be allied with the American based CIO; that all unions under 1000 members should be under CCL control; that publications used in Canada should be of Canadian origin; and that the international unions should emphasize affiliation with the CCL rather than ties with the CIO.[63]

Abella writes that the CIO leadership in Washington saw no reason for supporting these proposals. They did not accept the notion that the Canadian unions were any more unique than state organizations. In Canada, the conflict between the national unions and the CIO affiliates within the CCL was further intensified by basic differences on objectives and strategies. The reformist orientation and the tactics of moderation by elements from the old All Canadian Congress of Labour came into frequent opposition with the CIO affiliates, who tended to be somewhat more radical in their objectives and more militant in their strategies.

In 1941 Conroy was elected as Secretary-Treasurer. CIO unions supported him because he had come from a CIO-affiliated union, the United Mine Workers. But he turned out to favor a nationalist stance. He argued successfully with the American executives that the CCL should collect the full five cents per capita dues, after he threatened to alert Canadian customs officials that some CIO affiliates were ignoring wartime regulations regarding the export of money into the United States. In addition, several jurisdictional disputes were resolved by the CCL without the intervention of the American-based CIO headquarters,

Yet, in 1945 Conroy had to fight a hard battle to get the Canadian organization seated at the World Labour Conference in London. With the support of the CIO, the conference attempted to deny the right of Canadian representation, arguing that Canadian unions were merely affiliates of American organizations.

The insensitivity of the American headquarters to its CIO affiliates is illustrated by the continual stream of directives sent to the CCL. Abella reports that Conroy responded to most of these with humorous replies. For example, when he received a telegram asking for a "solid labor vote for Roosevelt" as president,

> Conroy replied that Canadians were quite satisfied with their system of government, but if the Americans really wanted to trade President Roosevelt for Prime Minister King, then a deal could conceivably be worked out. In the next year when Haywood [president of the CIO] urged Congress unions in Canada to "communicate to their senators their support of Henry Wallace as secretary of commerce," Conroy pointedly responded that Canadians had no desire to interfere in American affairs "though the contrary could not be said for some Americans."[64]

These exchanges continued for some seven years, from 1944 to 1950, with Conroy insisting that the Canadian Congress of Labour was not merely a state federation and was not to be treated as one.

Internal conflicts within the CCL reflected the conflicts between the CCL officers and the CIO headquarters in Washington. The United Steel Workers had emerged in the late 1940s as a major force within the CCL. It was the largest union in terms of membership and it was the wealthiest. It financed many of the organizing and political and educational campaigns, and led in the drive for more influence of international unions within the CCL. Thus, while Donald McDonald, a representative of the national unions, was elected president in 1952, the international unions controlled the executive council. As a consequence, the council passed amendments that took the power of appointment from the secretary-treasurer and put it in the hands of the council. Further, the dues structure of directly chartered unions was raised to the same level as the international unions, thus eliminating one incentive for workers to join national unions. After 1952 the international unions controlled the major policy decisions of the CCL. This did not necessarily mean outright control from American headquarters. But it did result in an orientation which minimized the importance of uniquely Canadian problems. Canadian leaders of international unions not only had to deal with the requirements of their Canadian constituencies, but they also had to make sure that their decisions were consistent with the overall policies of their American headquarters.

The Canadian Labour Congress

Meanwhile, in the United States it had become apparent to executives of both the CIO and the AFL that a more united labor front was necessary. There were several reasons for this. First, the political climate under the Republican control of Congress became less amenable to labor. Postwar legislation moved toward greater supervision of union-management and employment practices. The Taft-Hartley Act in 1947 curbed growing union control over employment practices, picketing, and boycott tactics. It also instituted increased regulations over strike procedures.

Second, awareness grew even among AFL leaders that, in the changing structure of industry, the old craft-based philosophy of union organization was losing ground to employment realities. Craft jurisdictions were increasingly more difficult to justify in the face of the expansion of mass production enterprises.

Third, the CIO had become greatly weakened after eleven national unions were expelled because of their alleged communist leadership. With the change in leadership from Green of the AFL and Lewis of the CIO, to Meany and Reuther of the two respective organizations, the way was paved for a merger. The two union bodies amalgamated in 1955.

In Canada, the forces toward reunion had always been relatively strong, mainly because the great geographical and industrial disparities in relation to a relatively small labor force made the need for a co-ordinating body more obvious. After the American merger, the international unions in Canada were free to endorse a Canadian confederation. The two bodies came together in 1956 and formed the Canadian Labour Congress. Currently the congress is the dominant labor federation in Canada.

The Structure of the CLC

The CLC, in its role as "the voice of labor," is now the principal body representing labor interests to the federal government. For example, it acted on behalf of its affiliates in opposing the federal government's wage and price controls, when they were first put into effect in 1975. (Of course affiliate unions have also made their own representations to the federal government.)

For its part, the federal government finds it more efficient to relate to the CLC than to separate unions. In some cases it may ask the CLC to intercede in a labor dispute. For example, this occurred when the Treasury Department asked the CLC to use its influence to end the postal workers' strike in November, 1975. The then CLC president, Joe Morris, refused. Nevertheless, in an effort to end the impasse, the Postmaster General later had talks with a member of the executive council.

The officers of the CLC are distributed throughout the country with a national director and an assistant headquartered in Ottawa and a second assistant in Montreal. In each of the regions—the Atlantic provinces, Quebec, Ontario, the Prairie provinces, and the Pacific region—there is a regional director and between four to eight representatives, depending upon the number of union members. Through these representatives, the CLC attempts to mediate jurisdictional disputes among its affiliates, provides information services, and, in the case of directly chartered unions, participates in collective bargaining processes.

Figure 1 illustrates the basic organizational structure and functions of the organizational components of the CLC, as well as its relationship to the AFL-CIO. Typically, union members belong to their locals which, in turn, are affiliated with national or international organizations. The day-to-day activities are conducted by local unions. These include filings for grievances and ensuring that contract agreements are upheld.

Most local unions are, in turn, parts of national or international unions. These larger units direct the policies and strategies for collective bargaining. Most of them are represented in the CLC or in the major labor federations in Quebec. Most international unions have ties with both the CLC and the AFL-CIO. The CLC acts primarily as an official public outlet for announcing policies formulated during the convention and for expressing the orientations of member unions. In addition, the CLC, like other labor federations, acts as a coordinating body for affiliated unions and provides research and educational services.

Not illustrated in Figure 1 are a few local unions that have a direct charter with the CLC with no intermediary links and some international unions not affiliated with the CLC. In addition, the figure does not show additional units which may be organized by province or city. These are local assemblies of unions in specific areas, which vary in the degree of authority

FIGURE 1   **Organizational Structure of the Canadian Labour Congress by Flow of Revenues and Services, 1974**

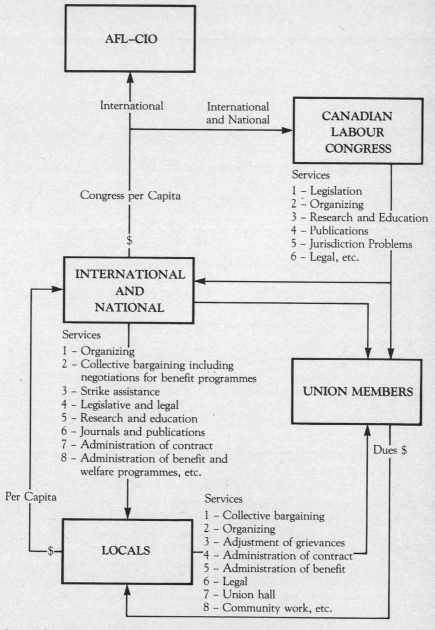

Source: *Corporations and Labour Unions Returns Act* (Ottawa: Queen's Printer, 1976).

they exercise. For example, both the British Columbia Federation of Labour and the Quebec Federation of Labour are somewhat unusual with respect to the power they are able to wield over their affiliates and the degree of autonomy they exercise within the organizational structure of the CLC.

It is important to recognize that the CLC is not a highly centralized, monolithic organization. Its authority depends upon the resolutions that are passed during its biennial conventions. While authority (legitimate power) resides within the electoral process, actual power remains with the unions. They wield their influence through the presence of their representatives on the Executive Council and the Executive Committee. (The Council is the official governing body between conventions; the Committee oversees the administration of the CLC.) Traditionally, beginning with the era of the TLC and later manifest in the CLC, the larger international unions have influenced the policies of the Congress. In the past, this has meant that the decisions made in the Council were often influenced by the American headquarters of the international unions. Thus, the strains between American and Canadian interests have always been felt at the highest level of trade union confederation.

Yet, it should be added that the international unions vary in the degree of control American-based headquarters exercise over their Canadian affiliates. Unions whose CIO affiliation predates 1956 have tended to be more autonomous from their American parent organizations than those affiliated with the AFL. Further, the larger Canadian affiliates of international unions tend to be more autonomous than the smaller ones. Crispo noted in 1967, however, that among 100 international unions operating in Canada, only 20 had established separate and distinctly Canadian organizations.[65] Large industrial unions like the United Steelworkers, the United Automobile Workers, and the Food and Allied Workers represent this type of union.

The proportion of Canadian members in American-based unions declined from approximately 90 percent in 1911 to about 51 percent in 1935. It increased to 63 percent in 1940 and to over 70 percent from the late 1940s to the mid-1960s. With the organization of public service workers, the proportion dropped to a little over 51 percent in 1975. An additional factor in the latest decline was the withdrawal of several industrial unions from their American affiliation. These shifts are illustrated in Table 1.

The shift in membership has meant that national unions have become more powerful within the CLC. The most influential of these come from the more recently organized public service sector and are organized on an industrial basis. That national industrial-based unions have been gaining in strength over the years is indicated in Tabel 2. Since most of these unions are affiliated with the Canadian Labour Congress, the data in the table reveal some of the important centers of power within the Congress.

Table 2 also reveals a historical pattern in which the largest unions, regardless of their federation affiliations, have emerged in the more concen-

TABLE 1 **Canadian Membership in International Unions as Percentage of Total Union Membership, 1911–1978**

Year	Total Union Membership (x 1000)	Canadian Membership in International Unions (x 1000)	Percentage of Total Membership in International Unions
1911	133.1	119.4	89.7
1915	143.3	113.1	78.9
1920	373.8	267.2	71.4
1925	271.1	199.8	73.7
1930	322.4	230.9	71.6
1935	280.6	143.6	51.2
1940	362.2	227.0	62.7
1945	711.1	471.0	66.2
1951a,b	1 028.5	726.6	70.5
1955	1 268.2	893.8	70.5
1960	1 459.2	1 052.0	72.1
1965	1 588.8	1 124.7	70.8
1970	2 173.1	1 359.3	62.5
1975	2 875.5	1 478.6	51.4
1978	3 277.9	1 553.5	47.4

a Data on union membership for all years up to and including 1949 are as of December 31. In 1950 the reference date was moved ahead by one day to January 1, 1951. While no figure is shown for 1950, the annual series is, in effect, continued without interruption, e.g. the 1951 date actually refers to the latest data of 1950.

b Newfoundland included for first time in 1949.

Sources: For years 1911, 1915, 1920, 1970, 1975, 1978: *Labour Organizations in Canada* (Ottawa: Canada Department of Labour, 1912, 1916, 1921, 1971, 1976). For years through 1965: *Union Growth in Canada, 1921-1967* (Ottawa: Canada Department of Labour, 1970) p. 95.

trated and labor-intensive industrial sectors. In the earlier years, the largest unions were to be found among railway employees. But more recently, the United Steelworkers of America and the United Automobile Workers (now the United Automobile, Aerospace and Agricultural Implement Workers of America), both industrial-based unions, have become important centers of power. Still more recently, the two unions in the public sector, the Canadian Union of Public Employees and the Public Service Alliance, have emerged as important voices in the labor movement. Indeed, CUPE is now the largest union in the CLC. (It should also be kept in mind that in terms of absolute numbers, these unions are far larger than those in the 1930s and earlier.)

Despite these shifts, craft unions still wield considerable influence. The largest of these have been in the construction trades. Note, for example, the Carpenters (now officially known as the United Brotherhood of Carpenters and Joiners of America, and an affiliate of the CLC) who have tended to maintain their strength throughout the history of the labor movement.

TABLE 2 Unions Having at Least 3.5 Percent of Total Canadian Union Memberships, 1911–1971

Unions	Affiliation	'911	1916	1921	1926	1931	1936	1941	1946	1951	1956	1961	1966	1971
1. Mineworkers	AFL/TLC: CIO, 1938; CCL, 1940: CLC, 1956	9.7		6.4	5.4	5.5	5.1	4.8						
2. Trainmen		6.1	6.7	4.6	5.2	4.3								
3. Maintenance of Way	AFL, 1921	5.9		3.8		5.6	3.8							
4. Carpenters	AFL, 1914	5.9		3.6		3.7				3.7	4.2	4.5	4.1	
5. Bricklayers	AFL, 1916	5.0												
6. Can. Bro. of R.R. Employees (1940: CBRT)	ACCL, 1929; CCL, 1940: CLC, 1956					3.6			3.5					
7. Firemen and Enginemen		3.8	4.1											
8. Western Fed. of Miners		3.9												
9. Street and Electric Railway Employees	AFL/TLC			3.6										
10. Machinists	AFL/TLC	3.8	4.4					4.3			3.5			

	Affiliation													
11. Clothing Workers	AFL/TLC: CCL, 1941; AFL-CIO/CLC, 1956	4.4												
12. Telegraphers	AFL/TLC		3.7											
13. Railway Carmen	AFL/TLC		3.7	4.5	4.3									
14. One Big Union Ind.;	ACCL 1929, CCL, 1940			6.8	7.8	7.4	4.7							
15. Steelworkers	AFL/TLC; CIO, 1938; CIO/CCL, 1940. AFL-CIO/CLC, 1956								4.2	5.3	5.2	5.7	6.9	7.9
16. Autoworkers	AFL/TLC; CIO, 1938 CIO/CCL, 1940 CLC								6.0	5.8	4.8	3.9	5.6	4.7
17. Can. Union of Public Employees	CLC								4.8	N.A.	3.2	5.2	7.5	
18. Public Service Alliance of Can.	CLC										4.0	5.7	4.9	5.9
19. Quebec Teachers Corporation														4.2
Total Union Membership (x 1 000)		133	160	313	275	311	323	462	832	1 029	1 352	1 447	1 736	2 231

Sources: *Labour Organizations in Canada* (Ottawa: Dept of Labour, 1912–1972).

The Canadian Labour Congress exerts very little authority independent of its member unions. Indeed, while most characteristics of the Canadian labor movement can be captured in an account of past federations, it is important to remember that in most cases these were amalgamations of separate unions agreeing among themselves over one or more issues. They represented alliances rather than power centers. This may be changing, however. One effect of the institution of the Anti-Inflation Board has been an emphasis on the Canadian Labour Congress as the principal voice of labor. Should a tripartite association among the federal government, business leaders and the CLC emerge,the federation might be strengthened, relative to individual unions, even more. This power, however, would likely be contingent on the response of unions in the public service sector—whether they will continue to push for advantages which already exceeded those of unions in the private sector in 1978 or whether they will consent to ally themselves with a united front. What can be expected, however, is that the CLC will play an increasingly sophisticated role as both a service body for labor unions and a pressure body in relation to governments and industry.

Continued Growth of Union Membership

Despite the various controversies surrounding the development of the labor union movement in Canada, there has been a steady increase in the proportion of non-agricultural paid workers who have become union members. This is shown in Table 3. From only 5 percent of the non-agricultural paid labor force in 1911, 38 percent were members in 1977.

It is somewhat difficult to compare union organization trends among different industrial sectors because the statistics have not always been reliable and there have been changes in sector classifications. There is evidence, however, that since the 1950s union membership has generally increased in the sectors of manufacturing, construction, transportation, communication and other utilities, and trade. Union membership has fallen off somewhat in the sectors of forestry and mining. Since the 1960s, rather dramatic increases have occurred in public administration and in other services. In 1962 the percentage of workers in these two sectors who were members of unions was 22 and 9.5 respectively. In 1976 these figures had increased to over 67 percent and nearly 23 percent. The percentage of union membership for the sectors included in the *Annual Report of the Minister of Industry, Trade and Commerce under the Corporations and Labour Unions Returns Act* for 1976 is as follows:[66]

Public Administration	67.4%
Construction	52.1%
Transportation, Communications and other utilities	50.0%

Forestry	42.0%
Mines, Quarries, and Oil Wells	39.7%
Manufacturing	43.5%
Fishing and Trapping	73.5%
Service Industries	22.6%
Trade and Commerce	8.5%
Finance	2.7%
Agriculture	.3%

In 1960, Daniel Bell, commenting on the American labor movement, argued that union membership would not likely surpass about a third of the non-agricultural labor force.[67] Since there are close parallels with the Canadian labor movement it is worth considering the changes that have occurred since that time. The gist of Bell's thesis was that union membership drives were most successful among blue-collar manual workers, particularly in in-

TABLE 3   **Union Membership as Percentage of Non-Agricultural Paid Workers, 1911-1978**

Year	Union Membership (x 1000)	Union Membership as Percentage of Non-Agricultural Paid Workers*
1911	133	4.9
1921	313	16.0
1925	271	12.3
1930	322	13.1
1935	281	14.5
1940	362	16.3
1945	711	24.2
1951a,b	1 029	28.4
1955	1 268	33.7c
1960	1 459	32.3
1965	1 589	29.7
1970	2 173	33.6
1975	2 884	36.9
1978	3 278	39.0

*Figures in this column up to and including 1930 represent *total* non-agricultural workers.

a Data on union membership for all years up to and including 1949 as of December 31. In 1950 the reference date was moved ahead by one day to January 1, 1951. While no figure is shown for 1950, the annual series is, in effect, continued without interruption, e.g. the 1951 date actually refers to the latest data of 1950.

b Newfoundland included for the first time in 1949.

c Figures on Non-Agricultural Paid Workers are, for all years up to and including 1952, as of the first week in June. Data for subsequent years are as of the first week of January.

Sources: Frank Denton, *The Growth of Manpower in Canada* (Ottawa: DBS, 1970), p. 40; and *Labour Organization in Canada* (Ottawa: Canada Department of Labour, 1976, 1978).

dustries such as manufacturing, mining, railroads, construction, and public utilities. Union membership would grow to a limited extent, he believed, in distribution fields such as trucking, but he did not see much increase in the trade and service fields. Further, any increase in growth in these fields would be offset by a general decline in the size of the labor force employed in the manufacturing sector.

Bell could see little growth in union membership among white-collar workers. His reasons were that where white-collar workers were in firms which employed a unionized blue-collar labor force any increase in wages granted to them was usually also applied to white-collar workers. But more importantly, he believed that for status reasons, white-collar workers were reluctant to identify themselves with largely blue-collar organizations and that in any event given the then high turn-over rate of women white-collar workers they were not likely to be interested in union membership.

Bell did not foresee that women would become less transient in employment or that the differences in status would be eroded by the increasingly routine and segmented nature of white-collar jobs and that differences in wages would subsequently be diminished. The processes of rationalization in authority structures continue into clerical work and lower management, hence union membership is becoming more attractive to these workers for reasons very similar to those that influenced craftsmen to organize over a hundred years ago. In Canada, these factors have played a dominant role in the increased union membership among school teachers, bank tellers, retail sales clerks, clerical workers in some firms and large union membership in the public service sector. The Public Service Alliance and the Canadian Union of Public Employees play a strong role among public service workers and exert considerable influence in the Canadian Labour Congress. (These two large unions are in part a consequence of a more favorable stand of federal and provincial governments toward unions in general.)

A review of the evolution of the Canadian labor federations is presented in outline form in Figure 2. The location of the federations in the figure approximates in a very rough way their general orientations on three of the four major issues: craft versus industrial organization; reformist or radical stance; and national or international ties. Eventually, most federations had a mix of strategies, focusing upon both employers and governments.

Not included in the figure are unaffiliated labor organizations. In 1973 these unions accounted for approximately twenty percent of the union membership. (Unaffiliated unions include not only those that never joined with the CLC, but also those that have been expelled or suspended. This latter group includes the Seafarer's International Union of Canada, and internationally-affiliated Teamsters and United Auto Workers.) The development of the labor federations should be seen within the context of the changing structure of labor markets and the shifts in the political environment.

FIGURE 2   The Development of Canadian Labor Federations

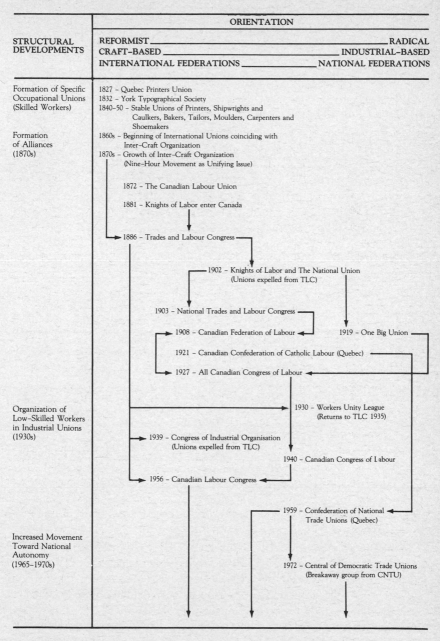

Adapted from: Rosemary Warskett, "The Structure and Ideology of the Canadian Labour Movement: 1830–1940," Unpublished Paper.

Since 1956 the dominant union federations in Canada have been the Canadian Labour Congress, and, in Quebec, the Confederation of National Trade Unions. (I shall deal with the Confederation in the next chapter.) Table 4 presents the distribution, by affiliation, of unions and union membership in Canada.

TABLE 4   **Union Membership by Type of Union and Affiliation, 1978**

Type and Affiliation	No. of Unions	Membership	
		Number	Percent
International Unions	88	1 553 477	47.4
AFL–CIO/CLC	69	1 281 495	39.1
CLC only	5	165 131	5.0
AFL–CIO only	7	10 573	0.3
Unaffiliated Unions	7	96 278	3.0
National Unions	121	1 637 626	50.0
CLC	23	743 886	22.7
CNTU–(CSN)	9	177 239	5.4
CSD	3	25 406	0.8
CCU	13	26 007	0.8
Unaffiliated Unions	73	665 088	20.3
Directly Chartered Locals	251	26 493	0.8
CLC	111	13 300	0.4
CNTU–(CSN)	4	516	*
CSD	136	12 677	0.4
Independent Local Organizations	170	60 372	1.8
Total	630	3 277 968	100.0

* Less than 0.1 percent.

Source: *Labour Organizations in Canada, 1978* (Ottawa: Department of Labour, 1978).

As noted previously, in 1975, local unions affiliated with international unions accounted for 51.4 percent of the total union membership. The total number of local unions involved was 4787. Nearly all were affiliated with the American-based AFL-CIO unions and most of these, in turn, were affiliated with the CLC. The remaining unions with international ties were affiliated with the CLC, but with no other federation, or had links with the AFL-CIO but not with the CLC. Finally there were some international unions that had no ties with any federation.

Most of the national, completely Canadian unions were affiliated with the CLC, but a fairly large number remained unaffiliated with any federation. The remaining membership among solely Canadian unions was claimed by the Confederation of Canadian Unions, and by major federations in Quebec; namely, by the Confédération des Syndicats Nationaux, by the Centrale des Syndicat Democratiques, and by the Corporation des Enseignants du Québec (not indicated in the table), an independent local organization.

Directly chartered unions are those which have been directly sanctioned by a national federation rather than a national or international union. Only slightly more than six percent of the membership belong to these unions. Finally, there remain the totally independent locals which claim two percent of the total union membership.

Local unions formed at the plant level are the basic units of organized labor and conduct the day-to-day activities. They deal, for example, with workers' grievances against management. Actual policies and strategies of collective bargaining, however, tend to be directed by the national unions or the Canadian affiliates of international unions.

Labor federations act primarily as official public outlets for announcing the policies and orientations of the member unions. These policies are formulated during conventions. In addition, the federations act as coordinating bodies for affiliated unions and provide research and educational services. Federations differ in the authority their head offices can exercise over affiliated unions. Currently, for example, the administrative bodies of the CSN in Quebec exercise more control over their affiliates than do their counterparts in the CLC.

Conclusions

Viewed in broad historical terms, the labor movement can be seen as a collective response to the personal experiences of tradesmen whose status, skills, and bonds of community were being reduced and destroyed by the process of industrialization. In the workplace, the constraints of social responsibility of an earlier era were replaced by highly specific contractual agreements in which employers were subject to very few liabilities. Unskilled workers had also reacted to these changes through work stoppages and other opposition tactics, but it was some time before they became effectively organized. The lack of identification with an occupational community, such as that experienced by skilled tradesmen, appears to be an important factor in accounting for this difference.

Employers tend to view labor as a cost factor of production. Consequently, there is always a tendency to exploit labor either on the job or indirectly through the uncertainties of unemployment. Yet this orientation has been somewhat mitigated by the organization of labor unions, which have in-creasingly been able to control the terms of employment. Further, employers have had to recognize that workers are also consumers and thus they must, at least to a minimal degree, support measures that will enhance this latter role.

For the worker, the union means more than merely improvement of wages or the processing of his grievances. (Actually, the ratio of workers' wages and salaries to company profits has remained surprisingly constant. Higher costs have simply been passed on to consumers.) It provides him with a continuing source of protection and advancement of his rights on the job.[68]

Notes

1. E. J. Hobsbawn, *Labouring Men: Studies in the History of Labour* (London: Weindenfeld & Nicolson, 1964), p. 13.
2. Ibid., p. 14.
3. Ibid., pp. 12–14.
4. Rosemary Warskett, "The Structures & Ideology of the Canadian Labour Move-ment 1830-1940," unpublished paper, May, 1974.
5. Ralph H. Turner and Lewis M. Killian, *Collective Behavior* (Englewood Cliffs, N.J.: Prentice-Hall, 1957).
6. Neil Smelser, *Theory of Collective Behavior* (New York: Free Press of Glencoe, 1962), p. 16.
7. Robert Ash, *Social Movements in America* (Chicago: Markham Publishing Co., 1972).
8. Stuart Jamieson, *Industrial Relations in Canada*, 2nd ed. (Toronto: Macmillan, 1973), pp. 53–54.
9. Charles Lipton, *The Trade Union Movement of Canada, 1827–1959*, 2nd ed. (Mon-treal: Canadian Social Publications, Ltd., 1968), p. 23.
10. This is true for most industrialized countries. It remains unclear, however, whether this is simply because record-keeping was more likely among typographers than among other skilled workers.
11. H. A. Logan, *Trade Unions in Canada: Their Development and Functioning* (Toron-to: Macmillan, 1948), p. 23.
12. Ibid., p. 25.
13. Ibid., p. 28.
14. Ibid., p. 28.
15. Ibid., p. 30.
16. Ibid., p. 39.
17. Ibid.
18. Lipton, op. cit., p. 32.
19. Logan, op. cit., p. 44. See also Lipton, op. cit., pp. 37–39.
20. Ibid., p. 34.
21. Ibid., p. 47.
22. Martin Robin, *Radical Politics and Canadian Labour, 1880–1930* (Kingston: In-dustrial Relations Centre, Queens University, 1968), p. 20.

23. Ibid., pp. 19–20.

24. Logan, op. cit., p. 57.

25. Robin, op. cit., p. 63.

26. Daniel Bell, *Marxian Socialism in the United States* (Princeton: Princeton University Press, 1967), pp. 36–39. See also Michael Harrington, *Socialism* (New York: Bantam Books, 1973), pp. 147–151.

27. Harrington, op. cit., p. 148. Harrington cites Engels who had argued that the analytic model which the German emigrés had brought to the United States was ill-suited for the unique historical conditions there.

28. Donald D. Egbert and S. Persons, eds., *Socialism and American Life*, Vol. 1 (Princeton: Princeton University Press, 1952), pp. 140–141.

29. Robert Babcock, *Gompers in Canada: A Study in American Continentalism Before the First World War* (Toronto: University of Toronto Press, 1974), p. 211.

30. Bell, op. cit., p. 37.

31. Robin, op. cit., p. 67. Before the convention, David Carey, who had been a fraternal delegate to the AFL convention in December 1900, stated that the Americans had taught him that labor "must be governed by labour pure and simple and that politicians should be left 'severely alone'."

32. Ibid., pp. 68–69.

33. Ibid., p. 69.

34. Logan, op. cit., p. 370.

35. Ibid., pp. 165–192. Logan reports that the Provincial Workmen's Association had originally been formed among Nova Scotia coal miners in 1879. It later expanded its membership to include glass blowers, iron workers, and boot and shoe workers. In 1892 it announced that membership was open to all trades and laborers. It later included railway employees, steel workers, tramwaymen, quarry-men, dockworkers, and retail clerks. However, many of these groups seceded, so that by 1907 the organization was primarily a miners' union again. It remained in existence until 1917, when it merged with the United Mine Workers.

36. Norman J. Ware, "The History of Labor Interaction," *Labor in Canadian—American Relations*, ed. H. A. Innis (Toronto: Ryerson Press, 1937), p. 28.

37. Logan, op. cit., p. 376.

38. Ibid., pp. 375–376.

39. Ibid., pp. 370–372.

40. Lipton, op. cit., pp. 223–224.

41. Ibid., pp. 162–166.

42. Robin, op. cit., p. 163.

43. Ibid., p. 166.

44. Ibid., p. 174.

45. Norman Penner, ed., *Winnipeg 1919: The Strikers' Own History of the Winnipeg General Strike* (Toronto: James Lewis & Samuel, 1973), p. ix.

46. Ibid., p. x.

47. Ware, op. cit., pp. 36–37.

48. Ibid.

49. Penner, op. cit., pp. xxii–xxiii. Penner believes that the strike enhanced the political position of labor. However, he argues that it led away from "revolutionary

ideology and strengthened reformism." A major cause for this shift was that because Canadian capitalism still had a great capacity for growth, liberal democracy gained ground at the expense of Toryism. Thus, the labor movement gained moderate sympathizers rather than recalcitrant opponents.

50. Ware, op. cit., p. 38.

51. Ibid., p. 39.

52. Logan, op. cit., p. 345.

53. Irving M. Abella, *Nationalism, Communism and Canadian Labour: The CIO, The Communist Party, and the Canadian Congress of Labour 1935–1956* (Toronto: University of Toronto Press, 1973).

54. Richard A. Lester, *Economics of Labor*, 2nd ed. (New York: Macmillan, 1964), pp. 94–95.

55. Broadus Mitchell, *Depression Decade: From the New Era to the New Deal, 1929–1941* (New York and Toronto: Rinehart and Co., 1948), p. 278.

56. Ibid., p. 281.

57. Stuart M. Jamieson, *Times of Trouble: Labour and Industrial Conflict in Canada, 1900–66*, Study No. 22 (Ottawa: Task Force on Labour Relations, Information Canada, 1968), p. 252.

58. Ibid., pp. 255–259.

59. Ibid., p. 259.

60. Logan, op. cit., p. 367.

61. Abella, op. cit., p. 145.

62. Discussed in Abella, p. 146. Abella disagrees with Horowitz who argued that the strike was engineered by the communists. See Gad Horowitz, *Canadian Labour in Politics* (Toronto: University of Toronto Press, 1968).

63. Abella, op. cit., p. 170.

64. Ibid., pp. 183–184.

65. John H. G. Crispo, *The Role of International Unionism in Canada* (Montreal: Private Planning Association of Canada, 1967). See also John H. G. Crispo, *International Unionism: A Study of Canadian-American Relations* (Toronto: McGraw-Hill, 1967); and Ed Finn, "The Struggle for Canadian Labour Autonomy," *The Labour Gazette*, November, 1970, pp. 767–774.

66. *Annual Report of the Minister of Industry, Trade and Commerce under the Corporations and Labour Unions Returns Act, Part II: Labour Unions* (Ottawa: Statistics Canada, 1978), p. 74. See also *Union Growth in Canada, 1921–1967* (Ottawa: Information Canada, 1970). The percentages are probably conservative estimates since they are based upon total employment which include managerial and professional workers who are generally ineliglible for union membership.

67. Daniel Bell, *The End of Ideology* (New York: The Free Press of Glencoe, 1960), pp. 214–215.

68. A. Flanders, *Trade Unions* (London: Hutchinson, 1968); Andrew Levison, *The Working Class Majority* (New York: Penguin Books, 1975).

chapter nine

The Labor Movement in Quebec

Introduction

Regional variations, coupled with differences in types of industry, have played an important role in shaping the Canadian labor movement. But the characteristics of Quebec society and its relationship with the rest of Canada and North America have produced particularly unique effects. Thus, the labor movement in Quebec requires separate treatment. The role of labor unions is of special interest as the latest in a historical sequence of institutions, classes, and social movements that have been committed to preserving the autonomy of French culture. As a result, much of the orientation of labor unions has been defensive in nature and fused with either institutionalized religion, or more recently, with nationalist aspirations. Quebec unions have come to be more politically oriented, encompassing broader goals, while unions in the rest of Canada have tended to focus more narrowly on economic issues.

Currently the following major union federations exist in Quebec: the Federation des Travailleurs du Quebec (Quebec Federation of Labour), which is the provincial representative of the CLC; the Confédération des Syndicats Nationaux (Confederation of National Trade Unions), which is the most politically influential of the labor organizations; the Centrale des Syndicats Democratiques (Central of Democratic Trade Unions), formed by a more conservative faction which broke away from the Confédération des Syndicats Nationaux; and finally, the Corporation des Enseignants du Quebec (Quebec Teachers Corporation), which is closely allied in its policies with the CSN.

In this chapter I want to emphasize those features which give the Quebec labor federations their special characteristics. Briefly stated, they are the following: the role played by elites, both religious and secular, after the British Conquest; the effects of industrialization that was dominated by Anglophones; the decline in political influence of the Church and the growth of provincial government power; and the role of intellectuals in the Quebec labor movement. These features should be seen within the context of a working class reinforced in its identity by its unique ethnic, religious, and language characteristics and its location within a specific geographical area.

Antecedents

In nearly every account of the history of Quebec the Catholic Church plays a major role. Rioux, for example, writes that even before the British Conquest in 1760 the Church was the dominant institution: "To understand the type of society which developed under French rule, we must realize that the influence of the Church, and from 1635 onwards, that of the Jesuits especially, was much more constant and decisive than the influence of the political metropolis."[1] Thus, any account of the development of the labor movement in Quebec must acknowledge the role of the Church.

After the British Conquest, with the destruction of the French commercial class and the civil administration, the British sought the cooperation of the Church in order to maintain a stable society. For their part, leaders of the Church were ultramontanists and ruled with a zeal born of Counter-Reformation fervor.[2] The Church elites directed their allegiance to Rome rather than to Paris and viewed Quebec society as being more religiously pure than French society, which was then experiencing the effects of secular ideologies. This meant that most Canadiens in what is now Quebec never saw themselves as merely colonists from France in a way that parallelled the self-perceptions of British immigrants.

Under British rule, the elites of Quebec were composed of British officers and colonial administrators, local Catholic bishops, and a few French-Canadian manorial lords. The terms of the agreement between the British and the Canadiens included a guarantee of French language and religious rights and the continuation of the French civil code. Meanwhile, Anglo-American merchants in Montreal had been pressing for an elective assembly within the Government of Canada (what is now Quebec) in order to protect their interests. This assembly was instituted under the terms of the constitution of 1791 and was eventually to provide the means by which Francophones gained political power in the province. But for most of Quebec's history, the Church with its local and national organizations, provided the principal institutional structure.[3]

The elites of the Catholic Church regarded the preservation of French culture as a means to preserve the Catholic religion. Throughout the nineteenth century, they viewed Quebec as an island of moral and civil excellence in a sea of Protestant materialism. They emphasized values that encouraged close family bonds, community loyalty, and the general virtues of rural life. Beginning with Confederation in 1867, the Church elites tended to support the Quebec wing of the Conservative party, which controlled the provincial government for nearly ten years. The federal Conservatives were staunch supporters of the British Empire and were mercantilist in their economic orientation. However, the Church viewed an alliance with the party as tolerable. It gave Quebec society stability and order, and the Church elites were able to mount effective administrative programs which served to preserve Quebec culture and hence the Catholic religion.

However, this rather tenuous relationship was marked by increasing distrust of the English, especially after the execution of Louis Riel, the Métis leader hanged for murder and for leading an insurrection in Saskatchewan. Anglophones viewed Riel's execution as an act of preserving the Confederation. For the Francophones, however, the execution fuelled suspicions that the English were committed to annihilating the French culture in Canada. There was added support for these suspicions: when it entered Confederation in 1870, Manitoba granted minority rights to the 14 percent of its population who were French-speaking, but by 1890 these rights were all but lost.

As a consequence, the Church shifted its political support first to an independent political party, then back to the Conservative party for another six years, and finally to the Liberal party. The Liberal party was favored primarily because it advocated increased autonomy for individual provinces and a pattern of economic development for Canada that would be more independent of ties with Great Britain. The Liberals held power in Quebec for forty years from 1897 to 1936.

The Role of the Church in the Quebec Labor Movement

By the end of the nineteenth century, population pressures and the secularizing influences of industrialization became primary concerns of the Church elites. One problem was the spread of American labor organizations, which had been active in Quebec for nearly twenty years. As we have already seen, the Knights of Labor had made inroads into the province in 1881 and many assemblies continued to exist in Quebec for a considerable time after the demise of the federation in the United States.[4] The American Federation of Labor and unions associated with the Canadian Trades and Labour Congress had also been active and had established a large enough membership to cause considerable alarm within the Church.

In formulating their response to these secular developments, the Church elites relied heavily upon the encyclical letter of Pope Leo XIII, the *Rerum Novarum*, written in 1891. The encyclical followed the same intellectual tradition that had opposed the individualism which the French Revolution had spawned and, later, in the nineteenth century, was characterized by the individualism of industrial capitalist societies. The solution to the social ills of industrial capitalism, according to the adherents of this tradition, was to form social units similar to the guilds of the Middle Ages. These units would help protect the individual against the social irresponsibility which the values of freedom and equality merely seemed to justify. Leo gave added emphasis to this movement by recommending the creation of workers' associations or "corporations," as guilds had once been called in Pre-Revolution France. "History attests," Leo wrote, "what excellent results were effected by the artificer's guilds of a former day."[5]

Leo rejected both capitalism and socialism—the former for its lack of social concern, the latter because of the militant atheism expressed at that time. He offered no concrete program for sweeping reform, except to advocate the formation of occupational associations and to support the intervention by the State in order to raise and protect the standard of living of depressed classes of people.

It is perhaps important at this point to briefly examine the meaning of the term "corporatism" or "corporativism," for it has frequently been associated with fascism. According to *The New Catholic Encyclopedia*, the Catholic conception of corporate structures is one whereby these different groupings—comprised of individuals in similar occupations or industries—maintain an autonomous and self-governing status and provide representations to the State. The fascist version, on the other hand, views such units as merely *organs* of the State. The State thus becomes the supreme authority, with the corporations its political units.[6] In both conceptualizations the individualism of industrial capitalist societies is curbed. The social costs of freedom and equality are diminished through social security and a sense of social responsibility.

The elites of the Quebec Church interpreted the papal directives within the context of Quebec society. They reemphasized the importance of the community and the family and encouraged the further development of agriculture-based communities. They further supported the foundation of workers' syndicates as a means of checking the expansion of secular unions. Later, in 1907, they created formal confessional unions. But these unions were not simply imposed on the workers. Many of the workers themselves favored such organizations since members of the clergy often provided important services for them as mediators and arbitrators of disputes. For example, in 1900 a Mgr. Bégin served as an arbitrator in a strike and lockout in the shoe industry in Quebec. In 1906, the Archbishop of Montreal served as arbitrator in a strike of leather workers.[7] Still there were some misgivings among some workers who feared that the Church would follow a course of conservative paternalism.

This more active role of the Church in the labor movement was part of the larger concerns of Church elites which included the flow of Francophones to the United States; the suspicion that the English Canadians were intent upon reducing the French Canadians to a small, powerless minority; the continued disregard for school and language rights of French Canadians living in other provinces; the effects of Great Britain's foreign wars, which required Canada and Quebec to contribute soldiers and materiel; growing anticlericalism, especially among American-dominated labor unions; and finally, apprehension over increasing control of Quebec industry by English Canadians and Americans.[8]

It should be remembered that this was a time of very rapid economic development, especially during the period from 1896 to 1914. Prior to this time, the general economy had gone through a period of depression, with the shipbuilding and logging industries in decline, and a lowered world demand for grain. Yet taking into account the period from 1890 to 1910, the Gross National Product of Canada, including Quebec, increased by 122.7 percent in constant dollars. The number of persons employed in manufacturing doubled; output per employed person increased by 11 percent; and per capita income in constant dollars increased from $240.00 to $434.00. (Constant dollars are based upon the years 1935-39.)[9] Raynauld has argued that by 1913, Quebec, along with Ontario had achieved its economic "take off."[10]

Under such conditions, the authority of the Church was being severely threatened. If economic expansion was taking place in Quebec, it was occurring in even more dramatic terms in the United States, and this enticed many Québécois to go south. In an effort to prevent the secularization and alienation of workers the Church brought together the confessional unions and organized them into the Confédération des Travailleurs Catholiques du Canada (the Canadian Catholic Confederation of Labour). Established in 1921, the Confederation was modelled largely after the Catholic labor organization in Belgium. It was both nationalistic and religious in orientation. It opposed international unions, having defined them as secular, materialistic, and foreign, sought to protect Quebec autonomy, and supported a form of corporatism, whereby workers would share in the profits of the company, with employers admonished to be fair and benevolent in their management.[11] But its most forceful orientation was in its negative stance: it was anti-socialist, anti-communist, anti-international union, anti-American, anti-English, anti-Protestant, and anti-foreign capital in the province.[12]

Opposition to international unions was especially forceful. For example, Church authorities in 1913 called for workers to get rid of them "if they wished to keep their Catholic faith." In 1938, a Father Ares wrote in the *Petit catéchisme d'éducation syndicale* that the Catholic worker was permitted to choose a non-denominational union only if it were necessary in order to prevent severe suffering, such as losing the only job available to him, and a sympathetic sociologist wrote in 1939 that international unionism was no more a guarantee of order than the revolutionary individualism from which it emerged or the communist orientation toward which it led.[13]

The CTCC approved of strikes only as a last resort. It seldom cooperated with other unions in the province, and because the Quebec government favored it, the Confederation remained a close political ally for over twenty years. Employers tended to prefer the CTCC because it was more docile than the international unions. Most unions affiliated with the CTCC were in the building and construction trades. Both the provincial government and the Church were also heavily involved in this sector. In 1931, after the onset of the Depression, Pope Pius XI announced his encyclical, the *Quadragesimo Anno*. This was a reinterpretation of the *Rerum Novarum* in which the Pope denounced capitalism and called for a redistribution of private property. He further advocated the formation of occupational associations: "The aim of social legislation must be the establishment of vocational groups."[14] Again, the Quebec Church responded to this by encouraging the development of cooperatives, and advocating government regulation of foreign-controlled industry and outright government ownership of key industries, especially utilities. Spearheading these movements for reform was the Ecole Sociale Populaire. Underlying these programs was thorough skepticism toward individualism and the social inequities which the liberal values of freedom and equality seemed to support.

In his 1937 encyclical, *Divini Redemptoris,* Pius XI stated that "A sound prosperity is to be restored according to the true principles of a sane corporative system which respects the proper hierarchic structure of society."[15] When translated into the Quebec context, this further reinforced the efforts of Church elites to hold in check and control the secularizing influences of industrialization and urbanization. Yet these influences also contributed to the intellectual underpinnings for later, more radical, orientations of the Quebec labor movement. Ironically, what had been the conservative programs of the Church became the intellectual roots for a left-leaning, politically oriented labor movement.

It should be noted that the conditions giving rise to the Church's involvement in the labor movement in Quebec are similar to those in other societies in which the Church has been the dominant institution for a minority group. Barnes notes that Christian trade unionism appears to be of greatest significance when "it is one of the defense mechanisms of an embattled minority."[16] Thus he observes that there have been particularly strong Catholic trade unions in the Basque country in Spain, among the Flemish in Belgium, and among the Catholic population in the Netherlands.

The Secularization of the Quebec Labor Movement

In addition to the efforts of Church elites to maintain the integrity of Quebec society, there were also influential people who attempted to accomplish similar aims but for different reasons. These were individuals who sought both more freedom from the strictures of the Church and the preservation of the cultural integrity of French society in Quebec. It seemed obvious to them that unless the process of industrialization were encouraged within the terms set down by persons acting in the interests of the French-speaking population, emigration would continue as the surplus rural population sought more lucrative jobs elsewhere. Further, there was the fear that Quebec itself would become completely dominated by foreign interests.

In the early part of the twentieth century, different versions of this orientation found expression in politically oriented journals, in universities, and, of more consequence, within the provincial government. Members of the provincial government, after the election of the Liberal party in 1897 in Quebec, encouraged industrial expansion and investment within the province. Later, during the period from 1920 to 1936, the Liberal government offered generous incentives to encourage additional investments from both indigenous and foreign sources. However, foreign interests played a dominant role since there was little Quebec capital available, and financial institutions dominated primarily by Anglophones favored loans to English rather than to French-speaking entrepreneurs. A consequence of this investment policy was that while the Francophones came to dominate the polity, Anglophones controlled the economy. This division has been a major source of tension between the two ethnic groups.

It is within this context that the Quebec labor movement should be seen, namely, as a three-way pull of conflicting interests: the Church was concerned with religious and cultural integrity; the secular political elites were concerned with economic growth as well as with the preservation of cultural integrity; while economic interests were the preoccupations of the Anglophone community.

For much of the history of the Quebec labor movements, the proportion of workers who were members of unions remained relatively small. In 1935, only 9 percent of the non-agricultural paid workers (about 50 000) in Quebec were members of labor organizations.[17] (In the whole of Canada 14.5 percent of the workers were members of unions.) At that time, 74 percent of the union members in Quebec were members of unions affiliated with the CTCC.

In the latter part of the 1930s, the aggressive organizing tactics of CIO-affiliated unions resulted in a rapid growth of union membership, but with a proportionate decline of membership in CTCC-affiliated unions. This growth accompanied the changing composition of the labor force as mass production industries expanded. By 1941 nearly 20 percent of the industrial wage earners were members of unions, but only 38 percent of these were affiliated with the CTCC. In 1943, while union membership continued to grow, the percentage of members affiliated with the CTCC dropped to a low of 28 percent.[18] Despite the efforts of the Church, increasing numbers of industrial workers were joining secular unions, most of which were CIO affiliates.

Tied to an ideology involving a strong element of protectionism, the leadership of the CTCC responded to these developments by attempting to resist the inroads of the secular, mostly American-based unions, rather than defending the interests of workers against the exploitation of employers. Yet not only were these unions losing ground to the CIO affiliates, they were also suffering from the more aggressive recruitment policies of unions affiliated with the Trades and Labour Congress (the Féderation Provinciale du Travail du Québec). This aggressiveness was also a response to the success of the recruitment tactics of the CIO unions.

After the Second World War, the continued expansion of mass production industries created a more diverse and urban labor force. Meanwhile, Quebec labor law followed a North American pattern in that only a single union, chosen by simple majority vote, was permitted to represent employees of an enterprise. This often meant that either the CTCC was prevented from acting as a bargaining agent, or that it represented a significant body of workers who either were not permitted to be full participating members because they were not Catholic, or who, even if they were Catholic, did not share the social philosophy of the union.[19]

The CTCC had been the product of the Church elite and its leadership had been culled from the ranks of the clergy. But with the changes in industrial structure and the inroads made by international unions, it became clear to those most intimately involved in the labor movement that the perspectives of the federation were too narrow in terms of membership policies and too vague and idealistic in terms of objectives. Yet the cultural integrity of Quebec remained an important issue.

Graduates of the Faculty of Social Sciences of Laval, a church-supported university, began moving into leadership roles. Most of them had been members of Catholic youth organizations, had lived through the Depression of the 1930s and had experienced the rapid expansion of industrialization. Educated in a clerical tradition, they were socially conscious and reform-minded.[20]

The model proposed for meeting the challenges of the 1940s was the leftist Catholic labor movement emerging out of postwar France. In 1946, Gérard Picard, a journalist, became the CTCC president. Drawing upon the academics from Laval, he embarked upon an aggressive organizing campaign and directed the federation toward attaining better working conditions, greater government protection for the rights of workers and a program advocating a restructuring of industrial administration that would permit more worker control. The era of a patient, enduring, and defensive leadership of the CTCC was drawing to a close.

However, the antecedents of this shift are more complex than this brief description would imply. To gain a more complete picture, we must be familiar with the intellectual debates among the political elites and account for those conditions which marshalled support among the workers.

The economic policies of the Liberal party, based upon a laissez faire philosophy, reached their most extreme expression during Taschereau's administration from 1920 to 1936. In addition to the incentive programs designed to attract industrial investment, the provincial government opposed public control of utilities and had only a minimal concern for issues raised by labor unions, especially by those not associated with the Church. Only reluctantly did the Taschereau administration introduce measures that permitted union organization and collective bargaining and established minimum wages and standards for proper working conditions.[21]

This laissez faire Liberal policy resulted in a solid entrenchment of large industrial interests in the Quebec economy headed almost entirely by Anglophone and foreign companies. With the coming of the Depression, nationalists, including those from church-sponsored organizations, saw this as evidence of the effects of foreign control in particular and of inherent weaknesses in the capitalist system in general. In the 1930s strong criticism came to be directed not only against foreign ownership and the expansion of capitalism, but also against the Liberal party which had encouraged this development.

It was in the context of these concerns that a group of Liberal party members, having become dissatisfied with the party's economic policies and the tight control of Taschereau, broke from the party and formed L'action Libérale Nationale. In 1935 this group joined with several Conservative party members to form the Union Nationale party. This became the party of Maurice Duplessis, which, with the exception of the period from 1939 to 1944, remained in power until 1960. During its formative years, the Union Nationale, influenced in large part by the left-wing stance of Paul Gouin from L'action Libérale Nationale, appeared to be both progressive and nationalistic—a party appealing to the concerns for Quebec's cultural integrity and to the voters' economic insecurities.

The Duplessis Era

Duplessis proved to be a more astute politician than the more inexperienced left-wing members of the Union Nationale. While the latter spoke out against the presence of the "trusts" in the Quebec economy, Duplessis attacked the graft and corruption of the former Taschereau regime, and while the left called for new structures to contain the excesses of capitalism, Duplessis, selecting only the anti-socialist stand of the papal encyclicals, argued for strong centralized authority under the label of corporatism. This eventually came to mean strengthening the power of the provincial government with the support of small business and the extractive, and pulp and paper industries. Duplessis claimed that every encouragement should be given to the development of French-Canadian enterprises, but he did nothing to control the operations of large foreign interests, and he reversed his earlier pledge to nationalize a private utility company, the Beauharnois Light, Heat and Power Company.[22]

The government of the Union Nationale was pragmatic and exercised patronage to the Church and rural electoral districts. Duplessis reemphasized the merits of a rural, religiously-based society under strong paternal leadership. Yet he maintained a base of power with the large foreign-dominated industrial interests. While he had claimed that the lot of the working class would be improved and strengthened, he came to be an opponent of the labor union movement.

Despite these policies, Duplessis was able to retain a high percentage of voter support. While most of his backing came from rural areas, he was also able to sustain a high degree of support from urban districts. Quinn, marshalling data from Quebec cities of 20 000 or more, shows that for the three election periods of 1948, 1952, and 1956, the Union Nationale almost invariably had the majority of the vote. (Only about a quarter of the English community in Montreal supported the party. Quinn suggests this was because of the U.N.'s refusal to align itself with the federal government's war policies.)[23] Further, Quinn also presents data from working-class electoral districts in Quebec City and Montreal, and from the more important industrial towns in the province. Even in these areas the U.N. party usually obtained a majority or close to a majority of the vote.[24] The continued support for Duplessis is at first surprising in view of his conservative policies. Yet, seen within the context of the Depression, his programs seemed to offer relatively easy solutions to complex problems—problems whose effects were being experienced by nearly everyone.

It should be kept in mind that the strategies adopted by the Union Nationale were not unique. Political leaders in other societies were also grappling with the effects of the worldwide Depression. This was a period when the role of governments in most industrialized societies expanded to previously unknown degrees. Economic recovery was offered under strong centralized governments. In addition, the fear of Communist take-overs goaded many world leaders to take strong authoritarian actions. Indeed, during their early years in power, Mussolini, whom Duplessis admired, and Hitler, who impressed Mackenzie King, were viewed by many observers as enlightened leaders in an era of economic and social dislocation.[25]

Unions as a Political Force

The increase in the percentage of wage earners who were union members in Quebec followed those percentages in the other provinces fairly closely. In 1949, 24 percent of the Quebec workers were union members while in Ontario, 23 percent were organized. For Canada as a whole, 29 percent of wage earners were organized. American unions continued to be successful in attracting union members in Quebec, despite the attempt of the Church to direct the labor movement toward religious and nationalist ends. These secular unions, unencumbered by adherence to broad social and religious principles were able to meet many of the daily economic needs of workers. Nevertheless, when critical events challenged concerns unique to the Quebec worker, the secular unions were often found wanting. There was little balance between the extreme and unrealistic panaceas of the Church and the overly pragmatic orientation of the American dominated unions.

Picard and his associates had set the CTCC-affiliated unions on a radical course, one which, like Duplessis' earlier pronouncements, made reference to the papal encyclicals. But, whereas Duplessis had emphasized the anti-socialist stand of the encyclicals and interpreted corporatism to mean strong state control, Picard argued for a radical reform of industry in which workers were to participate in making management decisions. Thus, in the face of rivalry from international unions and a hostile provincial government, the CTCC gradually emerged as a radical force of opposition to government policies.

The event which dramatized the open break between the Duplessis regime and the CTCC was the Asbestos Strike of 1949. The circumstances leading up to what were actually a number of strikes in asbestos mines in Asbestos and Thetford, Quebec, began when negotiations over wage contracts between the CTCC and the major asbestos companies finally broke off without resolution in January of 1949. Following the efforts of a conciliator from the Quebec Department of Labour, managements and the local union affiliate of the CTCC, the National Federation of Mining Industry Employees, Incorporated (Fédération nationale des employés de l'industrie minière incorporés) agreed to submit the case to arbitration. However, because of what was perceived to be a bias in favor of management in a previous arbitration case, union members voted on the night of February 13 to refute the agreement and go out on strike the following morning. The most dramatic events of the strike occurred in Asbestos. On February 15, the Minister of Labour sent a telegram to Jean Marchand, General Secretary of the CTCC, condemning the strike and announcing that he, the minister, would form an arbitration board to settle the dispute if the workers would first return to work. In addition, the minister stated that should the strike continue he would notify the Labour Relations Board of its illegal nature and ask the Board to consider withdrawal of the union's certification.[26]

On February 18 after workers had received their pay cheques from company offices for work done before the strike, they occupied the offices of the Johns-Manville Company. The company, in response, obtained an injunction against the union which ordered the union to stop illegal picketing and to end its "illegal" activities. The company also filed a $500,000 suit for damages against the local union at Asbestos, the National Federation of Mining Industry Employees and the CTCC. On February 19, a contingent of the provincial police arrived and three days later the town council lodged a formal protest against their presence. On February 22, the union was decertified. The events that followed often gave an appearance of a small-scale civil war. In March a railroad line was dynamited; in April the police imposed a curfew on the town of Asbestos. Meanwhile, the Johns-Manville Company had been importing strikebreakers into the mines. During this time scuffles often broke out between strikers and "scabs" and the provincial police continued to make arrests. In May, strikers blocked the roads leading to Asbestos in an effort to stop the entry of strikebreakers. On May 6, the Riot Act was read prohibiting "unlawful" assembly. Arrests of some one-hundred eighty people were made on the streets, in public places, and even in a number of houses.[27] Finally on Sunday, May 8, the Riot Act was lifted.

Efforts to resolve the dispute were made by members of the clergy beginning May 11, but it was not until June 13 that the Archbishop of Quebec, Mgr. Roy, gained success in his role as a mediator among the parties in the dispute: the provincial government, the Johns-Manville Company, the CTCC and its mining union affiliate. The strike ended on the first of June 1949 with the company increasing wages by ten cents an hour and guaranteeing work to all employees without discrimination.[28] But final signing of collective agreements did not occur until the beginning of 1950.

A major consequence of the Asbestos Strike was a shift away from the abstract idealism of earlier years to more pragmatic applications of a labor-oriented political philosophy. A sense of urgency served to strengthen the labor movement as a whole. Additional conflicts reinforced the more pragmatic direction. These occurred in the textile plant in Louisville in 1952 and in the copper mines at Murdochville in 1957. Federation leaders shifted their philosophy of trade unionism from church-inspired corporatism to secular socialism, while borrowing the organizational tactics of the secular international unions. A formal separation of the federation from the Church occurred in 1960 and the federation was reorganized under its present name, the Confédération des Syndicats Nationaux (The Confederation of National Trade Unions). (Earlier in 1955, the federation had denied the right of Church chaplains to exercise veto powers over union resolutions.) The new CSN immediately embarked upon a class analysis of Quebec society. In a sense, it was a secular expression of previous analyses of Quebec society authored by individuals sympathetic to the Church. The difference, however, was a much more hard-hitting approach, stressing the exploitation of the working class not only through foreign control of the Quebec economy but also by the existence of capitalism *per se*.

A second consequence of the events from 1949 to 1957 was the attempt to form closer ties among the dominant unions. In 1955 the Quebec unions affiliated with the Canadian Congress of Labour joined with the Trades and Labour Congress to form the Quebec contingent of the Canadian Labour Congress. This alliance formed the Féderation des Travailleurs du Québec (the Quebec Federation of Labour). During that same year, the CTCC voted in favor of the principle of labor unity with the CLC. In 1956 it adopted the principle of affiliation with the CLC, on the condition that its identity be preserved. But while both sides agreed to some type of affiliation, final plans were never consummated.[29] One major reason for this was the strike of Francophone producers against the Canadian Broadcasting Corporation in 1959. The CLC failed to support the producers, even though they belonged to a CLC-affiliated union. As a result, the producers withdrew from the CLC and affiliated with the CTCC. This not only drove the CTCC further from an alliance with the CLC, but also alienated the Quebec Council of the CLC, the Féderation des Travailleurs du Québec.

By 1965 the membership of the CSN was equal to that of unions affiliated with the FTQ. One major reason for this growth was a provincial law that permitted government workers to be unionized. But the law, passed in 1964, specified that such a union could have no political party affiliation. This effectively excluded international unions who were affiliated with the CLC since the Congress had earlier endorsed the New Democratic Party.[30] The newly organized workers within the CSN included hospital workers, employees of Hydro Quebec, and government functionaries. Figures from 1970 illustrate the significance of the workers in the public sector within the CSN. Of a total of 244 365 members, over 55 000 were hospital workers, 26 000 were workers in public utilities and nearly 32 000 were civil servants. These workers constituted 46 percent of the CSN membership.

Since 1960 the CSN has been a key vehicle for the expression of national unionism in Quebec. With its new aggressiveness, it has been largely responsible for setting the course of the trade union movement in that province. Highly effective organizing campaigns were initiated during the presidency of Jean Marchand from 1961 to 1965. Marchand formed the Confederation into an extremely effective centralized power. Yet the nonsupportive stance of the provincial government and the absence of trained leaders at the local level exacerbated internal conflicts.[31] Wildcat strikes, slowdowns, and walkouts marked this period.

Marchand left the presidency in 1965 to enter federal politics. Marcel Pépin assumed his office with a restricted definition of the CSN in relation to affiliated unions. As a result, the Confederation became less centralized, permitting local unions more autonomy in defining their own objectives. During this time, Pépin sought to push forward more effective bargaining and to meet the immediate needs of the unions. This decentralization was formalized at the CSN convention in 1968. Thus, the structure of authority of the Confederation reverted to a form similar to that which existed before 1961. Local unions became responsible for organization, education and collective bargaining, while the Confederation provided special services, such as research, publications and communications.[32]

Since 1968 the CSN has again become more centralized in its authority structure. One reason for this is that confrontations with the provincial government require more coordination in order to mount a more compelling bargaining position. As a result, the political orientation of the CSN has been reinforced, while grievances in the public sector have taken on political connotations.

Inter-Federation Competition

The pattern set by the CSN over the past twenty years has influenced the mode of operations of the FTQ. Thus the FTQ has not dared to be content to merely represent the Canadian Labour Congress in Quebec. It has assumed the role of interpreting the objectives and needs of the Quebec worker, not only to the CLC, but also to the provincial and federal governments. Responding to the aggressive tactics of the CSN, the FTQ has itself assumed additional power over its local affiliates and has demanded additional power within the CLC. It has also sought to maintain its image of a federation able to bring resources from the United States headquarters to bear upon the unique needs of Quebec labor.

As we have seen, the structure of the CLC and its provincial federations follows the example of union organizations in the United States. These organizations depend on their member unions for their authority, and, as a result, do little more than represent the union movement before governments and provide services such as research, publications, and financial resources to their member unions. The FTQ, however, represents union members of a different linguistic and cultural group. Further, it has been faced with a social movement of nationalism directed not toward traditionalism and rural values, but one tied directly to, and allied with, the processes of industrialization. While ruling elites in Quebec have shifted from an ideology of conservatism to liberal capitalism, union leaders have moved from corporatism to socialism. Yet all these orientations have been expressed within the context of preserving French culture.

Leaders of the CSN have been the most forceful apologists of socialism, but officers of the FTQ have responded similarly in an effort to maintain and expand union membership in their federation. Since its member unions are affiliated with American-based unions, the leaders of the FTQ must demonstrate that it is meeting the needs of Quebec workers. At the same time, they must also rationalize their foreign ties, both American and English-Canadian.

There is another reason for greater union political militancy in Quebec. Because most of the unions in English Canada are affiliated with the CLC, there is nearly complete immunity from inter-union raiding. But in Quebec no such agreements exist between the two dominant labor federations. In order to compete with the CSN, the FTQ has had to support not only nationalist sentiments but it has also exercised greater authority over its member unions and has maintained a greater degree of autonomy within the CLC compared to other provincial federations.[33]

Political Aggressiveness of the Quebec Labor Movement

The aggressiveness of the Quebec labor federations in the late 1960s and early 1970s can be viewed not only as a manifestation of the continuing theme of self-preservation of Quebec society, but also as an indictment of capitalism itself. It is an expression of labor leaders' reactions to the earlier "Quiet Revolution" of the middle classes. The explanatory thesis of this revolution is that as a consequence of the Duplessis regime, the public service sector provided the main routes of mobility for the French-speaking middle class. When these became saturated and blocked, pressure came to be placed upon the private sector in industry.[34] From the point of view of labor leaders, however, the ensuing debates were misplaced. To open the channels of mobility to French speakers without changing the nature of the industrial system would merely mean substituting English-speaking managers with French-speakers. A few individuals might benefit from such a transformation, but not the collective welfare of industrial workers. In their view, the structure needed to be changed rather than revised.

The first clear political expression of Quebec union ideology occurred in 1966 when the leaders of the CSN announced what was to become a series of documents dealing with social criticism and union strategy. The Confederation stated that its aim was not only to seek an increase in working benefits but also to eventually bring about industrial democracy, with workers taking an active part in management decisions.[35]

A second manifesto was announced in 1968, in which the role of workers as consumers was emphasized. The CSN announced its concern with a variety of social problems and committed itself to a program of consumer counselling, support for tenants' associations, debt counselling, etc.[36] These declarations were directed against social injustices and couched in terms of Quebec nationalism.

Riding on the crest of the new wave of nationalism emanating first from a new middle class, the CSN became the vanguard of the Quebec labor movement. FTQ leaders soon picked up this theme. In 1969 liaison was established between the two federations and plans for possible mass action on behalf of workers and for general social reform were discussed. In October 1971 a lockout by the French language newspaper *La Presse*, owned by the conglomerate Power Corporation, proved to be the catalyst that brought together the CSN, the FTQ, and the Corporation des Enseignants du Québec (Quebec Teachers Corporation).

The issues that prompted the newspaper lockout and subsequent strike were technological change and job security. Management refused to negotiate jointly with the four different unions over their contracts. Work stoppage for union members occurred after the legally required negotiation period had ended. Some commentators believe that the real target of management was the more left-wing journalists. It was the hope of management, they argue, that the journalists would refuse to cross the picket lines the typographers had set up and thus would lose their jobs. This would permit management to follow a new more apolitical policy and to hire journalists who would remain politically neutral.[37]

The hard line taken by *La Presse* was interpreted by union leaders as evidence of an anti-union axis between government and big business. Leaders of the three federations called for a mass demonstration. *La Presse* then announced it would temporarily cease publication. The mayor of Montreal, Jean Drapeau, entered the conflict by enacting an anti-demonstration bylaw that had earlier been declared illegal (*ultra vires*) by the Quebec Supreme Court. However, Drapeau justified its invocation by stating that the law was under appeal.

The demonstration took place despite Drapeau's interpretation of the bylaw, and some 15 000 people marched through the streets of Montreal. In the process, the marchers were confronted with police who attempted to disperse them. In the ensuing fight many were injured and one woman died.

These events served to radicalize the union leaders even more. A mass rally at the Montreal Forum on November 2, 1971, further solidified the Common Front. Meanwhile during the fall and winter of 1971, the three federations published working papers to be acted upon during the forthcoming conventions. The CSN paper entitled *Ne Comptons que sur nos propres moyens* (It's Up to Us), followed a Marxian analysis and pointed out Quebec's dependent position in North America. Commenting upon the "Quiet Revolution" of the 1960s, the authors further argued that the government policies to gain greater control over selected industries in electric power, forestry, mining, petroleum, and manufacturing represented little more than the substitution of *outright foreign control by indirect control mediated through a Quebec bourgeoisie.*[38] As a solution to the continued exploitation of workers, the document supported a socialist economic structure, whereby the workers would decide on goals and the rate of economic development, while the State would be relegated to decisions determining the allocation of investments.[39]

In the document published by the Quebec Teachers Corporation entitled "Phase One," the authors defined the role of teachers as "ideological workers" which linked them to the working class. No longer were teachers to perpetuate the ideology of the "ruling class."[40] Pointing out that strikes were too costly and benefited only the "bosses," the authors of this document argued that teachers in unison with workers should take their fight to the social and political arenas rather than restrict themselves only to economic issues.

Of the three documents, the FTQ's working paper was unusual in its militancy. Entitled "The State is Our Exploiter," it pointed out the role of the state as a source of incentive for private enterprise. It further analyzed the causes of unemployment.[41] The paper, in its introduction, pointed out that contrary to popular belief the direct involvement of the state in the economy leads not to socialism but to a reinforcement of capitalist domination. In reviewing its past history in the labor movement, the authors explained that the FTQ had been successful in achieving narrowly defined economic goals, but that this approach could never solve a basic issue in capitalistic society, the continued exploitation of workers.

These documents, all working papers, represent a clear departure from the orientation of most existing unions in the rest of Canada. The orientation is not unknown within the labor movement, but the Quebec statements are unique in the unanimity expressed by the major federations.

The crisis in the fall of 1971 quickly became a political issue of the labor movement in Quebec. It became concretized in the negotiations between the civil servants and the provincial government. Leaders of the Common Front of all three federations first sought to form one central bargaining unit for all the unions represented in the public sector work force. They further attempted to win concessions on the total amount of money available for all salaries, with the hope that they would then decide how it was to be distributed. If these initial economic conditions were met, they were then prepared to permit the provincial government to bargain separately with individual unions on working conditions and job security.[42]

The Front also wanted several principles adopted, such as equal pay for equal work, regardless of sex, region or sector in which the job was performed. They sought an 8 percent raise to keep up with the cost of living, the establishment of a $100 minimum wage per week for all workers, greater assurances of job security, and increased worker participation in the operation of services in such a way as to meet more closely the needs of the public.[43]

Teachers were especially concerned about job security, since, as a result of the government's rationalization program, between 5 000 to 7 000 of them were in danger of losing their positions. As for the $100 a week minimum wage, it was an important objective for the unions, since it would establish a precedent which they could employ for bargaining in the private sector.

On March 9, 1972, the Front called a strike vote. Seventy-five percent of the votes were in favor of rejecting the government's offer of a 4.3 percent wage increase and gave approval for a general strike. The Front then called for a one-day strike for March 24. It was postponed because of a snowstorm, but when the strike actually occurred on March 28 the government served injunctions against Hydro-Quebec workers and psychiatric and chronic care hospital workers. In effect, these injunctions declared the strikes to be illegal. The government then raised its wage offer by .4%. On its side, the Front compromised its demand for an immediate $100 a week minimum wage and offered to spread the demand over a period of the three-year contract. This was rejected by the government.

With this stalemate the Front leaders decided to organize an unlimited general strike for April 11. Essential services, however, were to be maintained. The government immediately served injunctions on the hospital unions—an act most likely to arouse public opinion in favor of the government's position. Workers at some twenty hospitals chose to ignore the injunctions, arguing that they deprived them of their right to strike—a right guaranteed by the Quebec labor code.

The strike lasted from April 11 to April 21. It was probably the most massive strike in Canadian history. During that time, thirteen hospital workers were sentenced to jail terms and assessed fines for ignoring the injunctions. On April 21, the National Assembly passed a bill (Bill 19), which legislated the civil workers back to work. Resistance was weakening within the ranks of the CSN. Three members of the five-man executive voted to accept the law and return to work. And when workers were asked to vote on whether to continue the strike, an insufficient number voted to give the Common Front leaders justification to continue. On April 21, the Front leaders announced their decision to end the strike. On May 8, the leaders of the three federations, Laberge of the FTQ, Pépin of the CSN, and Charbonneau of the CEQ, (the Quebec Teachers Corporation), were sentenced to one year in jail for counselling hospital workers to ignore the back-to-work injunctions. In May the three dissenting members of the CSN executive council led a breakaway group to form La Centrale des Syndicats Démocratiques (The Central of Democratic Trade Unions). Three months from the date of its founding, it claimed slightly less than 19 000 members.

The existence of this splinter group is significant in terms of the major strains that continue to exist within the Quebec labor movement and that have existed in varying degrees within the movement in the rest of Canada. These have to do with the strategies for change—whether to pursue continued economic advancement through collective bargaining ("Gomperism") or whether to seek complete structural change through political militancy. The recently formed CSD represents the former commitment. Leaders of the CSN, the FTQ and the teachers' federation have taken the latter course,

especially when they have had some assurance of support from their membership.

It may be of further significance to note that the leaders of the CSD
came up through the ranks of labor, while Pépin and his predecessor in the
CSN were university graduates. Indeed, there never has been a break in
university-trained leadership in the CSN. This implies that academic-trained
elites have played a more important role in the Quebec labor movement than
has been the case in the rest of North America, and that their orientation, in
contrast to their counterparts of the other enduring labor federations in
North America, has consistently been guided by more encompassing
ideologies of change.

After the sentencing of the leaders of the three federations, strikes and
demonstrations occurred in towns throughout the province of Quebec. Yet
this unrest was relatively short-lived, as it became obvious that the government was continuing to hold to its hard line in attempting to control labor
unions, especially those who represented public service workers. Laberge,
Pépin, and Charbonneau accepted release on bail two weeks after they had
been sentenced. Since the Common Front strike, the leaders have taken a
more modest approach in their negotiations with government and private industry. Yet similar movements still remain highly possible as the government
continues to move in the direction of greater planning and more centralized
control in the different industrial and public service sectors. It is clear that
with such active government involvement the labor movement in Quebec is
likely to remain active in the political sector. A strike against the government
becomes a political act; as a result, union leaders will continue to be actively
involved in political issues as they affect the worker.

The election of the separatist Parti Québécois on November 15, 1976,
has raised new questions for the labor union movement in Quebec. Will this
change in government mean the beginning of a new order more compatible
with the ideology of Quebec labor leaders? Or will this merely mean the continuation of a capitalist society, but one exercising more autonomy in its
political decisions?

Conclusions

An analysis of the Quebec labor movement deserves more attention than I
have been able to devote to it. Nevertheless, this account should be sufficient
to demonstrate the variations in development due to prior features of authority structures and value commitments.

The major point I have tried to make in this chapter is that the minority
group status of the French Canadians within their own "home" environment
has greatly influenced the characteristics of the Quebec labor movement. By

"minority group" I am not referring to numbers of people, but to access to positions of power. Clearly, in an industrialized society the principal basis of power is in the economic sector. It is precisely this sector in which the French Canadians have been in the minority, particularly within Quebec itself.

The Québécois never dismissed industrialization as such, although Church leaders were fearful of its secularizing effects. It quite obviously represented a chance for mobility and higher living standards. But controlled by alien interests, it also represented a threat to the very existence of Quebec culture. Hence, the Catholic Church played an early and key role in setting the course of the labor movement. The current characteristics are certainly not what early Church leaders had in mind, but there is a thread of continuity between their notion of "corporatism" and the current emphasis upon "socialism"—a sense of community of interest in preserving French culture.

It should also be noted that the Quebec labor movement is unique within the North American context with respect to the important role intellectuals have played in union leadership. Concerns with protecting an abstraction like "culture," as well as the ability to articulate such concerns, are not likely to come from persons who are constantly engaged in manual labor and who must worry about immediate economic needs.[44] On the other hand, those who take on the role of relating abstract concerns to everyday life can be very effective if they have institutional supports for both their roles and their message. The Church, as an institution, laid the groundwork for such supports in Quebec.

The shift of the labor force from extractive industries located in relatively small communities to an urban labor force employed in mass production industries left the Church elites ill-equipped to deal with new problems. Further, the apparent success of secular international unions contributed to a decline in the influence of the Church. Yet the continuity of intellectual leadership has already been provided by the development of Church-sponsored university-trained elites. While this ultimately contributed to the secularization of the movement, the universities, especially Laval, provided the supports formerly furnished by the Church.

I have concentrated upon the indigenous components of the Quebec labor movement, not because international unions were unimportant, but rather because those unions which ultimately combined to form the CSN were the principal sources of influence that have made the Quebec labor movement unique. It should perhaps be reemphasized that the development of the Quebec labor unions is not to be viewed as distinct from other processes of change. I regard the latest phase in the labor movement developments as a working-class response to the experience of the "new" Francophone middle class of the late 1950s and early 1960s. As Guindon has observed, these individuals, drawn into expanding public bureaucracies, have had their aspirations raised, only to be blocked by the dominance of English-speakers in the private sector.[45] The result has been a renewed commitment to becoming "masters in their own house." The lessons of this experience, as well as the combination of factors I have pointed out in this chapter—of religious and ethnic differences superimposed upon lower class occupations, which in turn have taken place within a clearly defined geographical area; of grievances analyzed by a highly articulate elite—have been to produce a more politically radical and articulate labor movement than exists anywhere else in North America.

Notes

1. Marcel Rioux, *Québec in Question*, trans. James Boake (Toronto: James Lewis and Samuel, 1971), p. 20.

   This work and that of Hubert Guindon have been particularly influential in providing the general orientation to this chapter.

2. The term "ultramontanist" ("beyond the mountains") refers to the belief in papal supremacy over other secular rule. The concern for preserving the power of the Catholic Church began in the fifteenth century and became especially virulent during the religious wars of the sixteenth century. It was opposed not only to heretical Protestant movements, but also to the national monarchies, both of which were undermining papal authority. In 1870 at the first Vacation Council the dogma of papal infallibility was defined as part of Catholic belief—a victory of Jesuit-supported ultramontanism.

3. Mason Wade, *The French Canadians, 1760–1867* (Toronto: Macmillan, 1968), pp. 47–88.

4. Trudeau believed that one of the reasons for the endurance of the Order of the Knights of Labor in Quebec was because its broader political objectives to change the structures of society were compatible with the aspirations of many French-Canadians. See Pierre Elliot Trudeau, "The Province of Quebec at the Time of the Strike" in *The Asbestos Strike*, ed. Pierre Elliott Trudeau, trans. James Boake (Toronto: James Lewis & Samuel, 1974), p. 59.

5. "Corporativism," *The New Catholic Encyclopedia*, Vol. 4 (Toronto: McGraw-Hill, 1967), p. 343.

6. Ibid., pp. 343–344.

7. Trudeau, op. cit., p. 59.

8. W. F. Ryan, *The Clergy and Economic Growth in Quebec* (Québec: Presses de l'Université Laval, 1966), pp. 257–258; and Wade, op. cit., p. 338.

9. Ibid., pp. 27–28.

10. Cited in Ryan, ibid., p. 30.

11. Trudeau, op. cit., pp. 22–23.

12. Ibid., p. 210.

13. Samuel H. Barnes, "The Evolution of Christian Trade Unionism in Quebec," in *Industrial and Labor Relations Review*, Vol. 12, No. 4 (July, 1959), reprinted in Aranka E. Kovacs, *Readings in Canadian Labour Economics* (Toronto: McGraw-Hill, 1961), pp. 58–74. See especially p. 61.

14. *The New Catholic Encyclopedia*, op. cit., p. 345.

15. Ibid., pp. 343–344.

16. Barnes, op. cit., p. 59.

17. Hubert Quinn, *The Union Nationale* (Toronto: University of Toronto Press, 1963), p. 86.

18. Ibid., pp. 204–205.

19. Ibid., p. 62.

20. Ibid.

21. Ibid., p. 32–33.

22. Ibid., pp. 76–77.

23. Ibid., pp. 98–99.

24. Ibid., p. 101.

25. Trudeau cites a statement by Cardinal Villeneuve which illustrates the fascination with strong leaders in an era of considerable social uncertainty: "As for fascism, (Mussolini) has made a great contribution to saving the peace of Europe by his presence in Munich. The Italian mode of government involves certain dangers, it is true, but one should not forget that the democratic form of government involves certain dangers as well." Trudeau, op. cit., p. 16.

26. Gilles Beausoleil, "History of the Strike at Asbestos," in *The Asbestos Strike*, ed. Pierre Elliott Trudeau, trans. James Boake (Toronto: James Lewis & Samuel, 1974), p. 147.

27. Ibid., p. 171.

28. Ibid., p. 175.

29. Gérard Dion, "The Trade Union in Quebec," in *University of Toronto Quarterly*, Vol. 27, No. 3 (April, 1958), p. 379.

30. Sheilagh Milner and Henry Milner, *The Decolonization of Quebec* (Toronto: McClelland and Stewart, Carleton Contemporaries, 1973), p. 187.

31. Fraser Isbester, "Quebec Labour in Perspective, 1949-1969," in *Canadian Labour in Transition*, ed. Ulric Miller and Fraser Isbester (Scarborough, Ont.: Prentice-Hall, 1971), p. 262.

32. Ibid., p. 265.

33. Paul Bernard, *Structures et Pouvoirs de la Fédération des Travailleurs du Québec* (Ottawa: Queen's Printer, 1970).

34. For the classic statement of this thesis, see Hubert Guindon, "Social Unrest, Social Class and Quebec's Bureaucratic Revolution," in Queen's Quarterly, Vol. LXXI, No. 2 (1964), pp. 150-162. For a further extension of this analysis see Guindon, "The Modernization of Quebec and the Legitimacy of the Federal State," in *Modernization and the Canadian State*, ed. D. Glenday, H. Guindon, and A. Turowetz (Toronto: Macmillan, 1978).

35. See the presidential address to the Convention of the C.S.N. In C.S.N. *Procès Verbal*, 1966.

36. C.S.N. *Procès Verbal*, 1968.

37. Nick Auf der Maur, "October 1971: Labour Comes to the Fore," in *Quebec: A Chronicle, 1968-1972*, ed. Robert Chodas and Nick Auf der Maur (Toronto: James Lewis and Samuel, 1972), pp. 91-107.

38. Translated by Penelope Williams and reprinted in Daniel Drache, *Quebec—Only the Beginning* (Toronto: New Press, 1972), pp. 1 90. See especially p. 37.

39. Ibid., p. 57.

40. Translated by John Chambers, Ibid., pp. 97–148. See especially p. 115.

41. Translated by Claude Hénault, ibid., pp. 149–270.

42. Auf der Maur, op. cit., p. 113. See also Milner and Milner, op. cit., p. 207.

43. Auf der Maur, ibid.

44. For additional evidence of this assertion, see C.S.N. *Rapport du Comité des Douze,* 45 Congrès de la C.S.N., 11 au 17 juin 1972. I am grateful to George Shano for calling this to my attention in his paper, "The Radicalization of the Labor Movement in Quebec," unpublished, n.d., Concordia University.

45. Guindon, "Social Unrest, Social Class and Quebec's Bureaucratic Revolution," op. cit., pp. 150–162.

chapter ten

The Institutionalization of Labor-Management Relations

Introduction

For most of the history of unionization in Canada, the battles that have been fought have been over the legal rights of unions as organizations. Since the forms of social relationships in capitalist societies rest heavily upon legally-backed contractual relationships, such rights represent an index of institutionalization.

The term "institutionalization" refers to those relationships among collectivities of individuals or formal associations which have become routinized and thus exist within a set of rules and regulations that have been commonly agreed upon. To refer to the institutionalization of labor-management relations is to deal with the transformation of the labor movement from its social movement characteristics to an organization having legal rights in its interaction with management. As a result of the pressure from labor unions to achieve this status and then to use it for improving the conditions of workers, non-union members have benefited as well. It is chiefly through court decisions and government legislation that this has been accomplished.

Changing Contractual Relations

Federal Legislation

In Chapter 8, I made reference to the shifts in the basis of employee-employer relationships with the coming of industrial capitalism. Continuing further on this theme, it is worth noting that during the initial stages of industrialization social relations once appropriate to a feudal society continued to be invoked against workers within industrial enterprises. But it was the obligations that serfs once had toward their masters that were stressed, not the responsibility of masters. Chapter 7 dealt with the manner in which this interpretation was advanced and transformed through ideological manipulation.

This early tradition had its influence in Canada. When the committee members of the Toronto Typographical Union were arrested in 1872, the court ruled that since there were no precedents to the case, the defendants were subject to the English law of 1792. Citing English statutes, the judge ruled that "combinations of workmen" were illegal if they sought to lessen hours of work, fix or raise wages, decrease the quantity of work, quit work before it was finished, induce others to end their employment before the expiration of their contracts, refuse to be employed, and to influence others not to be employed.[1] This interpretation was based upon the premise that each person had a relatively permanent social location and subsequently should be obedient to its demands. Subordination to authority was thought to be a natural condition of the social order.[2]

In effect, the feudal definition, cast within the context of industrial capitalism, meant that workers were to follow the new system of authority, but without the supports of security that existed within feudalism. Industrial entrepreneurs came to define labor as a *factor* in production, which existed independently of the individual's personal welfare. That is, the abstract concept of "labor" became a reality defined in terms of costs involved in the production process. Viewed in this way, individuals could be replaced, but not "labor." Indeed, individuals were to mold themselves into the new definitions of labor. They were to work during stated hours and to follow set routines while at their place of work. Employers were responsible only for their wages.

Since there were no legal precedents for defining the rights of individuals in their roles as employed production workers, the resolutions of labor-management conflicts rested upon case-by-case rulings of individual courts. These rulings tended to favor employers and retarded the development of legal machinery that would permit the recognition of workers' rights for self-protection. Certainly there were no provisions of this nature in the British North America Act of 1867. Yet there were clear references to procedures for forming corporations, filing bankruptcies, declaring insolvencies, and establishing patents and copyrights. These provisions protected the rights of business and industrial enterprises, but not the workers within them.

In addition to favoring employers, it has been the general case that courts have tended to favor the jurisdictions of provinces while restricting federal powers. This has added to the complexities of labor legislation and has undoubtedly been an influential factor in the fragmented nature of the Canadian labor movement.

Legislation designed to safeguard the rights of individuals in their roles as employees has been slow and halting in its development. Jamieson notes that even now, while governments will intervene to settle disputes and prevent strikes, presumably in order to protect the public "from interruptions in production and distribution of goods and services," employers remain free to reduce or cease production, displace workers from their jobs by introducing technological changes and lay them off temporarily or discharge them permanently, whenever it is economical or profitable to do so."[3]

Still, a range of legal rights has been won by the labor movement. Their gradual accumulation began in 1872 after the incident involving the Toronto typographers with a court decision that workers had a legal right to form associations. The Federal Trade Union Act and the Criminal Law Amendment Act of 1872 declared that workers' associations were to be defined as voluntary associations; hence workers had a legal right to be members. To define early unions in this manner meant that they had a status equal to other associations, such as social clubs and religious organizations. They were thus exempt from charges of criminal conspiracy—a charge often laid by employers against workers associations—even though they may in fact advocate measures that could restrain trade. This act, noted in Chapter 8, followed a similar act passed in Great Britain the year before.

The Canadian law merely declared unions to be legal associations. It forbade any acts of violence, intimidation, and coercion, and other acts which prevented entry into a plant. It did, however, permit peaceful picketing. In 1875 and 1876 the Act was amended by adding a clause that standing near a place of business was not to be construed as "watching and besetting" as long as it was merely for purposes of transmitting information. In 1892, however, this clause was removed after an opinion of the Minister of Justice found that it was redundant. But with its absence, interpretations of what constituted legal picketing varied widely among different courts. Frequently they read into the law a Parliamentary intent to remove legal protection from the act of picketing.[4] The clause permitting picketing was reintroduced in 1934 and again stated that "watching and besetting" were not unlawful as long as they were done merely to obtain or communicate information. But those actions which prevented individuals from entering a plant remained illegal.

Attempts to legislate the resolution of conflicts between workers and employers soon followed the Act of 1872. The first of these were initiated by provincial legislatures who followed the example of Australia. These acts provided for local boards of conciliation to be set up when such a course of action was agreed upon by both workers and employers. The boards were designed to resolve conflicts before strikes on the part of workers, or lockouts on the part of employers could occur. Ontario enacted such a bill in 1873 and Nova Scotia, Quebec, and British Columbia soon followed. However, in most cases these acts were of little consequence, since it was extremely difficult for the parties to arrive at such agreements. The acts were soon repealed.

In 1900 the federal government enacted similar legislation under the Conciliation Act ("An Act to Aid in the Prevention and Settlement of Trade

Disputes and to Provide for the Publication of Statistical Industrial Information"). The act was a consequence of the investigative report on the conflicts within the mining industry in British Columbia. It resulted in the establishment of the Federal Department of Labour, which was then responsible for collecting and publishing labor statistics. The Minister of Labour was empowered to inquire into the causes of any dispute, arrange conferences between parties in the dispute, and appoint a conciliator or a board of conciliation at the request of either the employer or the workers. He was also empowered to appoint an arbitrator, but only upon application of the parties to the dispute. Finally, he was granted the power to recommend to the government the appointment of commissions to conduct investigations of conflicts between workers and management.

It is helpful to make a clear distinction between "conciliation" and "arbitration." Conciliation is an attempt to settle disagreements by marshalling data to clarify the issues, meeting with the parties to sort out the major objectives, and setting conditions by which the two parties can work out a compromise. A conciliator or a board of conciliation acts as a liaison agent between labor and management. (The term "mediation" is often used to refer to conciliation.) To submit to arbitration, however, is to present the two positions before a juridical body. After hearing the evidence from both sides, the arbitrator or board of arbitration hands down a decision which labor and management have either previously agreed to follow or which they are legally bound to obey.

In 1903 the federal legislature introduced the element of compulsion in resolving labor-employer disputes in its Railway Labour Disputes Act. The law provided for a three-man conciliation board, one person to be chosen by each party in the dispute and the third to be chosen jointly. It also provided for compulsory investigation to "compel testimony under oath, and the production of documents essential to a knowledge of the true situation."[5] The emphasis was upon conciliation, but there was a provision made for a board of arbitration if both parties agreed. In 1906 the Acts of 1900 and 1903 were combined and extended and these, in turn, were superseded by the Industrial Disputes Investigation Act in 1907. (Meanwhile, Quebec had already instituted a Trade Disputes Act in 1901, which provided for conciliation and voluntary arbitration in all industries. This remained in effect until 1964.)

The Federal Industrial Disputes Investigation Act of 1907 was designed to apply to disputes involving ten or more persons who were employed in those industries subject to federal jurisdiction: mining, transportation, communications, and public utilities. It provided for a tripartite board of conciliation and investigation and for legal power to investigate disputes and to compel submission of testimony and evidence. If negotiations broke down, it required that an additional period of time must elapse before there could be a work stoppage—a "cooling off period"—while investigations were under way. The major role of the board was to be conciliation, but if this failed, it was given power to pass judgment on issues and parties in dispute. Finally, the Minister was empowered to appoint a member to the board if either part failed to nominate one and to appoint a chairman in case of disagreement. During the First World War, this act was replaced by the Emergency War Measures Act, which required compulsory arbitration. Further, strikes and lockouts were made illegal. All industries were covered by this act.

After the war, the Emergency War Measures Act was rescinded. However, as a result of the intense labor unrest during this period, particularly the Winnipeg General Strike of 1919, the federal government passed legislation extending the authority of the Minister of Labour under the Federal Industrial Disputes Investigation Act of 1907 to all industries. The Minister was empowered to establish boards of conciliation and investigation for enterprises in all industries in which there was a possibility of strikes or in which strikes were already in progress. In 1925, however, this act was challenged in the courts and in the Privy Council on the grounds that the federal government was again acting beyond its proper constitutional jurisdiction. The act was subsequently amended to apply only to disputes earlier defined to be within the jurisdiction of the federal government. The amendment contained an added feature in that it could be extended to apply to industries under the jurisdiction of provinces if they passed legislation permitting this authority. During the period from 1925 to 1932, all the provinces except Prince Edward Island passed new laws which allowed this extension of federal jurisdiction.

In 1939, at the beginning of the Second World War, the federal government again extended the Industrial Disputes Investigation Act via orders-in-council. This act covered defense-related industries. It required compulsory conciliation during disputes, a "cooling off" period before initiating a strike or lockout, and it instituted special measures to impose wage ceilings, job freezes, and compulsory transfer or allocation of labor in essential industries.

By 1942 a nationwide labor code had developed in piecemeal fashion that included recognition of the right of workers to join unions, the encouragement of collective bargaining, and the previously mentioned compulsory conciliation of disputes. But even at this late date, there were no federal provisions for certifying unions to act on behalf of workers or for requiring employers to recognize and bargain with worker organizations having the support of their members. This meant that unions could hold legal status as voluntary associations, but there was no assurance that they could be negotiating agents for workers.

It was not until 1943 that the federal government passed an order-in-council that finally made provisions for certification of unions to act on behalf of workers. These provisions were modelled after the American National Labor Relations Act of 1935 (popularly known as the Wagner Act). The order guaranteed the right of workers to organize, the right to select their units for collective bargaining (that is, workers, rather than employers, defined the groups to be covered by agreements), the certification of bargaining agents, compulsory collective bargaining, and a provision for labor relations boards to investigate and to correct unfair labor practices. This order-in-council provided the basis for most postwar industrial relations legislation in Canada.

After the war, in 1948, the federal government again restricted its jurisdiction to the industries of mining, transportation, communications, and public utilities. In 1970 the Canadian Labour Code superseded the 1948 Act, although it incorporated the major provisions of the 1948 law. Like other federal acts, it applies only to those industries under federal jurisdiction, but adds to it "any other operations that Parliament declares are for the general advantage of Canada or two or more of its provinces."[6] There is also "enabling legislation" which permits the Code to be applied to industries under provincial jurisdiction should their legislatures adopt it. The Code further provides that "employees and employers have the right to organize and bargain collectively and that trade unions may be certified as sole bargaining agents for employee groups."[7] It provides for assistance in collective bargaining by conciliation officers and boards, and also provides for arbitration of disputes dealing with the meaning or violation of collective agreements. Conditions for each party to observe prior to embarking on a strike or lockout are also detailed.

In addition, the act provides for a Canada Labour Relations Board made up of appointees of the Governor-in-Council. The board certifies unions and bargaining agents, and, at the request of the Minister of Labour, investigates complaints regarding processes of collective bargaining. More specifically, it exercises statutory and regulative powers which deal with bargaining rights, investigation, conciliation and disposition of complaints relating to unfair labor practices, definition of technological changes which are likely to affect the terms, conditions, and security of employees, disposition of complaints relating to technological changes, declaration of unlawful strikes and lockouts, and provisions for advice and recommendations relative to statutory and regulatory powers of the Board.[8]

Provincial Legislation

The provinces, especially during the period from 1945 to 1950, passed labor relations acts, almost all of which contained provisions protecting the rights of workers to organize and to bargain collectively. As with federal legislation and earlier moves in the late 1930s, these included workers' rights to determine bargaining units and to select their bargaining agents. These measures also called for the investigation of unfair labor practices. There were variations of these provisions among the provinces. These included definitions of bona fide unions as opposed to company-formed unions. Saskatchewan provided for voluntary rather than compulsory conciliation. Prince Edward Island lacked government legislation for conciliation and arbitration of disputes. In Quebec and Prince Edward Island there were restrictions placed upon unions' freedoms to negotiate closed shop agreements, and in Quebec there were more restrictions placed on union activity in general compared to other provinces. Not until 1964 were Quebec's labor statutes liberalized to match those of the other provinces.

To date, provincial legislation covers industrial relations in a manner similar to federal legislation. Alberta, Ontario, and New Brunswick also have provisions for accrediting employer organizations in the construction industry and British Columbia has similar accreditation provisions that can apply to all industries. These acts are a consequence of efforts to standardize collective bargaining in these sectors. In most cases, both labor and employers must comply with conciliation or mediation procedures before a strike or lockout may take place. Further, every agreement must have provisions for settling disputes that arise during the term of the agreement and for prohibiting strikes and lockouts during that time. However, these provisions, as will be shown, have frequently not accomplished the purposes for which they were intended.

All provinces also have prohibitions against what they define as unfair labor practices. Alberta, British Columbia, and Ontario have limitations on hours to be worked per day and per week. (In Alberta and British Columbia it is 8 hours per day and 44 hours per week. In Ontario it is 8 hours per day and 48 hours per week with one-and-a-half times the regular rate to be paid on work done, with a permit, beyond the 48-hour week.) Manitoba and Saskatchewan do not limit daily and weekly hours, but require payment of one and a half times the regular rate if work continues beyond 8 hours per day and 44 hours per week in Manitoba, and 8 and 40 hours in Saskatchewan. Most provinces have special statutes regulating working hours in specific industries, such as construction.

All provinces have minimum wage laws, which cover most occupations except farm labor and domestic service. Newfoundland, however, has legislation that includes farm labor and Ontario minimum wage laws cover some farm-related occupations. All provinces have legislation governing vacations and holidays (the general standard of vacations is two weeks per year), discrimination in hiring, conditions of employment and trade union membership, apprenticeship and job training, and industrial safety and workmen's compensation in cases of accidental injury at work or disablement from industrial disease.

With respect to employers terminating employment, the following provinces have legislation specifying the period of advance notice: Nova Scotia, Saskatchewan, Prince Edward Island, Manitoba, Newfoundland, Ontario, and Quebec. In addition, employees are required to give advance notice on leaving their jobs in Newfoundland, Nova Scotia, Prince Edward Island, Quebec, and Manitoba. Finally, maternity protection and postnatal employment legislation exist in Ontario, British Columbia, New Brunswick, Nova Scotia, and Manitoba.

Grievance procedures are usually included within the terms of collective agreements or, in some cases, imposed by law. These provide for the resolution of conflict resulting from the application and interpretation of the initial contract agreements. They are basically rights of appeal for individual union members through representation by their union to management.

Individual Rights and Contractual Relations

The transformation of the values of security to those of freedom and equality has meant that the individual, rather than the larger social order, becomes, with industrialization, the dominant "good." Society comes to exist for the benefit of the individual, not the individual for society. This is reflected in the growing importance of formal contractual relations. The assumption behind these relations is that individuals have at least a minimal degree of freedom of choice. At the same time they also assume that the agreements are of limited scope in terms of commitments. A worker in a factory contracts for the sale of his labor, but he does not expect that his relationship with the employer should include other social contexts. The limitations of the terms of commitment to the work role has a further consequence, in that it assumes that the individual has some degree of freedom to pursue his own ends, even while the ends of the enterprise are being served.

These assumptions, however, do not take into account the conditions under which the freedom of choice is to be exercised, nor does it recognize that the terms of the contract, at least for employment, permit one party to have exclusive rights of authority over the other. For workers, then, freedom of choice is severely limited in terms of both alternatives to employment and conditions of employment.

For workers to become organized, collective measures had to be adopted by which individual freedoms could be expressed under more favorable conditions. (One cannot be free without having control.) However, from the point of view of employers and courts, especially during the nineteenth century, workers' organizations were power blocs operating in restraint of trade by controlling the deployment of labor. It was essential for employers to regard workers as individually contracting their labor for sale, since labor, as a factor of production, could then be "costed" on an additive basis, and could be increased or reduced by adding or firing individual workers. To view labour *en bloc* was to lose control over both supply and the nature of its use.

The Trade Unions Act and the Criminal Law Amendment of 1872, in responding to the crisis brought about by the Toronto typographers, sidestepped the fundamental issue by asserting that workers had the legal right to organize, but they did not recognize the union itself as the legal representative for individual workers. This nominalist definition has meant that there has always been an area of ambiguity in the interpretations and rulings of courts over the rights of individuals versus the rights of an association. What has evolved is that while workers' associations were originally formed to bring about improved economic conditions and improved conditions in the workplace, the conflicts have mostly been fought over the role of unions, both in terms of whom they represent and their legal status. The labor codes developed during 1942 and 1943 and again in 1970 fostered the idea that unions had a legal status insofar as they were recognized as agents for workers in collective bargaining. Such a legal status was reinforced by recognizing the rights of unions to enforce a closed or union shop, and to insist on the wage check-off system of dues payment.

Yet the ambiguity remains, and is reflected in the nature of court decisions. When unions become relatively strong, courts tend to shift the nature of their deliberations from a straight contract law basis to the view that "moral, ethical and economic considerations" are at stake. This in turn has resulted in greater surveillance of individual rights within the unions.[9] This ambiguity is also reflected in the consequences that unions face in defying a court injunction at the federal level prohibiting a strike. Both the union and its individual members can be fined. Another aspect of this ambiguity is the interpretation of the value of freedom. It can be held that unions should be free to determine the qualifications for membership in the interests of preserving the existence of the association and in serving the welfare of its members. But individual members, it can be argued, should also be free to decide upon union policies, to change their associations. In short, there remains the problem of freedom granted to unions to control their own membership and organizational policies versus the preservation of the freedom of the individual.[10] Yet these questions are seldom asked of employers because it is presumed that individuals choose to submit to the control of their labor, while unions are presumed to be acting on behalf of the welfare of individuals. It is a curious paradox that while unions have been attempting to improve the welfare of workers within the industrial organization, they have at the same time often been accused of violating individual rights. Seldom, however, have similar charges been laid against employers.

Institutionalized Relationships: The Significance of Collective Bargaining

The series of court decisions and legislative acts that I have reported deal almost solely with the containment of conflict. Jamieson has pointed out that during the first sixty years of labor legislation, government policy has been preoccupied with simply preventing disorder rather than "protecting the rights, liberties and prerogatives of one or the other contending parties."[11] In contrast, due in large part to the New Deal policies during the Depression in the United States in the 1930s, there was an earlier attempt to define the rights and prerogatives of labor and management. However, since the Second World War, Canadian governments have paid more attention to organized labor in its confrontation with employers. This is most clearly expressed within the context of regulations governing collective bargaining.

Labor organizations are now accepted as legitimate entities, although ambiguity remains over whether they are to be regarded as voluntary associations or as legal entities having rights and responsibilities beyond that of their members. The resolution of conflict with employers is governed by law. Obviously, for collective bargaining to be effective, employees must have the right to form associations, to engage employers in negotiation (bargaining), and to invoke economic sanctions. While all three of these components were once illegal, they are now protected by law.[12] Hence governments in Canada have become involved in the very basic assumptions upon which collective bargaining rests.

The formal process of collective bargaining within a company usually begins after requests for negotiations have been made by either the union or management. Representatives from both sides exchange proposals regarding new agreements. Negotiations then begin by first dealing with the range of issues to be considered and then with the actual terms of the new contract. If these negotiations break down, most Canadian labor laws require that the two parties submit to the process of conciliation before a strike or lockout is invoked. (Conciliation is not obligatory in British Columbia, Alberta, Saskatchewan, or Manitoba.)

Strikes or lockouts may be averted if the two parties agree to submit to the process of arbitration. After the case is reviewed by a single arbitrator or board of arbitrators, a judgment is handed down on the contract terms. Judgments by arbitration are usually binding; that is, they permit no alteration or future recourse in negotiations until the end of the term for the existing contract. Governments frequently step in to ensure that the terms of collective agreements are binding. This is done through provincial and federal labor relations boards.

During the period from 1970 to 1974, 39 percent of the collective contracts for firms of 500 or more employees were established by bargaining alone. Forty percent of the contracts were settled after conciliation or mediation, 6 percent were settled by arbitration, 14 percent were settled after a strike or lockout, and 1 percent were settled by other means.[13] Thus, in Canada, most collective contracts are the products of bargaining or conciliation and mediation.

The process of collective bargaining itself represents a controlled environment within which conflicting demands may be resolved. This does not mean that labor-management relations will be peaceful, nor that there may not be opposition to governments and government legislation, as events continually show. What it does mean is that unions are protected by law and the law recognizes the legitimacy of the conflicting claims of labor and management, as long as the claims do not entail fundamental political rearrangements. It both protects and restricts the right of labor unions to engage in economic sanctions within specified limits.

This means that both parties recognize a basic set of values that forms the basis for collective bargaining. The values of freedom and equality have been expanded to include labor, forcing employers to grant them the very arguments they themselves used during the early stages of industrialization. The attempt of workers to act on these values has continually forced management's hands. Workers, and especially organized labor, have challenged employers' definitions of labor as merely a "factor" in production.

Further, forced to take these values into account, governments now act to (1) make available the offices of disinterested persons at the request of both parties in conflict to assist, through mediation, in resolving disputes; (2) provide machinery for binding arbitration at the volition of both parties; (3) require intervention by a mediator at the request of either party and the further requirement that both parties must deal through the office of the mediator; (4) impose on both parties an obligation to accept the services of a conciliator or mediator; (5) publicize the results of an inquiry, thus marshalling public opinion toward a resolution; and (6) take outright possession of the enterprise.[14] This institutional arrangement is informed by a basically optimistic belief that solutions can be found through dialogue between representatives of labor and management.

However, there are paradoxes that remain in the process of ensuring the expression of freedom and equality for workers. These have to do with the values as applied to individual workers and as applied to unions representing their interests. Currently, laws dealing with labor unions encompass three main areas: (1) regulations governing collective bargaining, certification, negotiations, strikes and lockouts, and enforcement of collective agreements; (2) limits to lawful picketing and boycotting—watching and besetting, trespassing, etc.; and (3) the internal affairs of unions—relationships between individual workers and unions and among union organizations.[15] As I noted before, the laws have been most ambivalent with respect to the internal affairs of unions. When courts define conflicts as issues among union members, unions themselves have been treated as unincorporated associations governed by common law. This means that individuals rather than unions are subject to the law. What is basically at stake is the issue of individual rights.

At the other extreme, however, in viewing unions as legal entities, statute law has permitted the imposition of restrictions upon individuals. As statute law, manifest in specific regulations, has played a larger role, the notion that unions continue to manifest social movement characteristics is difficult to uphold. Given these legal interventions, the closed shop, the union shop, union hiring, and the check-off systems of dues payments are legal rights granted to unions. However, it must be pointed out that they are coercive measures directed toward the individual as well. Such measures are not different in kind from those which have commonly been legally enforced by employers. Indeed, given these and other measures of union discipline, employers gain from unions a disciplined work force and greater assurances of industrial peace between contracts. The unions gain organizational and financial security.[16] To be sure, these gains are bargaining points, assurances should suitable agreements be made; but having been made, they change the basic mode of confrontation.

Conflict: A Continuing Issue

Despite the institutionalization of labor-management relations and the central role that collective bargaining plays in it, conflict still remains. This will continue as long as there are disparities in the distribution of economic rewards and in authority relations. Further, there is some evidence that some legal requirements involved in collective bargaining may heighten rather than reduce conflict. The required "cooling off" period during the process of conciliation often only increases demands. Both parties may wait for the recommendations of conciliation boards in hopes that their decisions will benefit their cause. With this in mind, both sides tend to begin negotiations with exaggerated demands and conditions, on the assumption that the final outcome of the entire process will meet their more realistic expectations. The time involved in resolving disputes thus becomes longer and the conflict more intense than might otherwise be the case without this clause.[17] It should be noted that since unions cannot strike during the period of a contract, negotiations are extremely important. For example, without cost-of-living clauses in their contracts, labor would be unable to maintain real earnings through the threat of strike during a contract period in which the cost of living continues to rise. Employers, on the other hand, have a freer hand in allocating their economic returns.

   While the existing unions and labor federations are now accepted components of Canadian society, conflict with management, governments, and among labor unions themselves remains a frequent occurrence. Most incidents of conflict are expressed within the local plant. Disputes over wages and working conditions are usually resolved as part of the collective bargaining process when new contracts regarding the terms of employment are worked out.

   There still remain many other expressions of conflict that are not easily identified because they are not part of the formal system of conflict resolution. These expressions include wildcat strikes, workers' sabotage of the production process, work slowdowns, sick leaves, absenteeism, and so on. Overall, strikes account for only a small proportion of time loss at work. Absenteeism due to sickness of various types accounts for approximately four times the time loss due to strikes or lockouts.

Despite these differences, strikes remain the most dramatic and the most costly expressions of conflict to unions and to individual members, and they still account for the more serious expressions of discontent. Further, they continue to be the major weapon of the unions in confrontations with management. During the period from 1968 to 1974, among nine leading industrialized countries, Canada's rate of time loss due to strikes and lockouts was exceeded only by Italy.[18]

Unions as Service Agencies

The shift from the social movement characteristics of labor unions to increased institutionalization of labor-management relations has involved both rewards and costs for labor. Certainly the rewards have come from a general recognition of unions as legitimate entities and as a force to be taken into account by both employers and politicians. The process of collective bargaining has become sufficiently routinized so that problems of union recognition and representation, and the ground rules for negotiation are no longer issues to be hotly debated.

However, the costs to the social movement characteristics of labor unions have been high. Increasingly, as ongoing formal associations in their own right, unions have taken on the characteristics of agencies offering services *to* workers rather than expressing the collective will and commitment *of* workers. There is an irony here, typical of most social movements which have attained legitimation. In the course of establishing formal relations with previously existing institutions, the internal structures of the social movement organizations also tend to become increasingly formalized. This development has occurred within labor unions. The result is that the measures of effectiveness employed by union executives are centered upon rational models by which unions provide their services. This tends to objectify the union structure, taking it outside the realm of personal commitment for most workers. Workers in turn come to assess unions on the basis of their effectiveness, measured in terms of financial costs, time expenditure, and complexity of procedures; criteria employed to evaluate any other social agency.

These characteristics, typical of service agencies, can be illustrated by the fact that union executives often face difficulties in maintaining commitment among the union members. Attendance at union meetings is usually low and only reaches significant proportions when contracts are under negotiation. Further, union members do not always follow the recommendations of their executives, but tend to evaluate them in relation to their own objectives. A higher proportion of union members have never experienced the social movement characteristics of unions and this further reinforces the view that they are organizations which provide services rather than foster commitment.

There is always the possibility that commitment to a collective identity will be revived among workers. But this will depend upon the nature of the issues in contention and the responses of leaders of the parties involved. The labor movement remains in a state of tension. It has taken on the attributes of rational authority structures while seeking to attain the collective ends of workers. The question remains whether or not the concrete expressions of the value premises of freedom and equality can be made compatible with these formal attibutes.

Conclusions

The process by which labor-management relations have become institutionalized is a process of elaboration and revision of systems of authority. Unions first had to gain recognition and legitimacy; then norms for collective bargaining were established; and finally legislative acts were created by which basics rights and perquisites of workers were defined. The gaining of a place of legitimacy has itself occupied over half of the history of labor unions in Canada. Part of this is undoubtedly due to the degree to which the structure of industry itself has shifted, from a multitude of small enterprises to increasingly larger units of production. With this shift has also come a decline in jurisdictional disputes; thus unions have been able to form more cohesive bodies in their confrontations with management. Yet, once having gained a greater degree of legitimacy, unions are often caught in a problem of role definitions: are they agencies merely providing services to workers which they could not otherwise provide for themselves, or are they social movements which represent a groundswell of commitments from individual members?

The development toward greater institutionalization has increased the active participation of governments at both the federal and provincial levels. Departments of Labour have been created and government legislation regarding minimum wage rates and working conditions has been passed. Additional government regulations, such as wage and price controls, have increased this involvement. Finally, the increased number of public service workers who have become union members has put pressure on governments to shift their positions from roles of arbitrators to those of antagonists in bargaining with unions. One consequence of this is that the dominant labor unions are likely to become far more influential in the political sector.

It should be noted that there is often the tendency to assume that defining interaction as "institutionalized" implies a relatively static state of role relationships. In fact, however, institutionalization, particularly in labor-management relations, has merely meant that there are agreements regarding the range of issues over which there are grounds for dispute and that there are limits to the modes of expression of these disputes. But even these agreements remain tentative assumptions. Collective bargaining, for example, does not entail issues regarding changes in the entire economic and political structure, but it could. Nor does it assume overt violence. Yet this too is always a possibility. If there is evidence of bad faith in the basic premises of the institutionalized relations, the whole structure is in jeopardy.

Notes

1. H.A. Logan, *Trade Unions in Canada: Their Development and Functioning* (Toronto: Macmillan, 1948), p. 402.
2. Philip Selznick, *Law, Society and Industrial Justice* (New York: Russell Sage, 1969), p. 123.
3. Stuart M. Jamieson, *Industrial Relations in Canada* (Toronto: Macmillan, 1973), p. 141.
4. A. W. R. Carrothers, *Collective Bargaining Law in Canada* (Toronto: Butterworths, 1965), p. 17.
5. Jamieson, op. cit., p. 119.
6. *Canada Yearbook: 1973* (Ottawa: Information Canada, 1973).
7. Ibid.
8. See *Organization of the Government of Canada*, 1974, Section 3900–4114.
9. Carrothers, op. cit., p. 521.
10. Ibid., pp. 519–521.
11. Jamieson, op. cit., p. 116.
12. For a detailed account of how these rights were won, see Carrothers, op. cit., pp. 11–59.
13. André Beaucage, *An Outline of the Canadian Labour Relations System* (Ottawa: Labour Canada, March, 1976), p. 32.
14. Carrothers, op. cit., pp. 8–9.
15. Ibid., pp. 501–514
16. Selznick, op. cit., pp. 148–149.
17. Jamieson, op. cit., p. 126.
18. Joseph Smucker and Will Van Biljouw, "Industrial Diversity and Strikes: An Inquiry," Paper presented at the Annual Meeting of the Canadian Sociology and Anthropology Association, Frederiction, N.B., 1977. See also, Will van Biljouw, "Industrial Diversity, Patterns of Organization and Strikes: An International Comparison," M.A. Thesis, Concordia University, 1978.

chapter eleven

Ideology and Working-Class Consciousness

Introduction

Working-class consciousness has interested theorists ever since the mid-nineteenth century. The term has a variety of connotations. What it usually implies is that members of the working class share a sense of solidarity that is oriented against the vested interests of employers in particular and the bourgeoisie in general. The issue is of considerable theoretical importance because it points to a source of change—Marx would argue *the source* of change—in the social organization of industrial society.

In the past it was believed that unions could provide the infrastructure for the development and spread of working-class consciousness. But this relationship, when it has occurred, has seldom been sustained, except under unique conditions such as those suggested in the examination of the Quebec labor movement. Why this is so has remained a subject of considerable debate. Since the issue involves the role of ideology, both the ideological concerns of the dominant labor federation and the nature of class consciousness itself need to be examined.

Ideological Transformations of the Canadian Labour Congress[1]

In Chapter 7, I dwelt at some length on the nature of ideologies, pointing out their historical content and the techniques they employ for persuasion and justification. In that presentation I stressed the conservative nature of ideologies when they are employed to justify authority systems. The focus now is upon ideologies which justify programs for change. They are, in Mannheim's terms, "utopian" insofar as they emphasize negative elements of the existing social system while advancing programs for correction through social change. If the dominant labor unions, such as those within the Canadian Labour Congress, represent the voices of labor, and if they have become legitimate components of society, then we need to know how they have been able to accommodate this status with an earlier commitment to social change. This should further provide some clues regarding the relationship of the union movement to the formation and maintenance of working-class consciousness.

In examining the content of the ideologies that attempted to advance and justify the different strategies within the Canadian labor movement, one must take into account once again the relationship between those values of freedom and equality that marked the growth of industrial capitalism and the rational authority structures that characterize the typical modes of production. The discrepancy between these two structural components is most apparent among workers who cannot exercise these values within the production enterprise.

The exploitation of workers within the production enterprise has been a sufficient cause for worker unrest. But ideologies have served to provide organizing principles for removing the cause. What has fostered the ideological interpretations, solutions, and plans of action has been the reinterpretation of the application of the values of freedom and equality. When the early bourgeoisie expressed these values, they intended them to apply only to those who had shown themselves to be "worthy." When applied to the working class, these values meant that workers were to be obedient to employers. The values, then, were to be earned according to the criteria of the bourgeoisie, not freely granted. The ideologies of labor movements reinterpreted these values in such a manner as to challenge the control by employers.[2] If the employers required workers to earn the right to act upon these values, workers challenged employers to justify their right to control their expression. In their ideologies, employers claimed that they had achieved their authority through individual competition, which, they argued, followed from the values of freedom and equality. Since, for employers, freedom was expressed by competing in the marketplace for the sale of goods, the resulting consequences, with their stress upon efficiencies of production, were a denial of the expression of these values for workers.

The ideologies of labor unions sought to establish those conditions by which these values could be expressed by individual workers. These had to do with greater freedom over the exercise of the production process and greater equality over the distribution of the economic rewards. Collectivist means were required to preserve these individual rights.

In the process of gaining legitimacy, the ideological concerns of labor unions have undergone continual transformations. These have been due both to conflicts with employers and governments and to intramural conflicts among groups within the labor movement. In the previous chapters on the Canadian labor movement, I have pointed out the role of ideology as an integral part of the initiation and maintenance of workers' movements. The role of ideology appears to be especially pronounced in the case of the Quebec labor movement, in which the convergence of ethnic identity, religious differences, and a distinct geographical location, served to reinforce the salience of social and economic deprivation in the consciousness of Quebec workers. The role of ideology in English Canadian labor movements has been somewhat more complex. With a labor force less homogeneous than in Quebec, ideological expressions have had to undergo continual modification in order to incorporate diverse interests and to maintain an image of success and continuity among labor unions and federations.

In the early stages of the labor movement, ideologies advocating the complete reorganization of society and espousing radical alternatives occupied a prominent place among the variety of competing organizations. But they were immediately faced with the problem of demonstrating that they could bring about the changes toward which they were commited while being judicious in their tactics. This often resulted in abstract radical expressions, while the actual programs of labor organizations were quite pragmatic.[3]

I have described in previous chapters the occasions when more radical labor organizations have made an impact upon the Canadian labor movement. The ideology that has prevailed in English Canada, however, is one of reformism, enunciated first by the Trades and Labour Congress and then by the Canadian Labour Congress. In part, this approach was a response to the violence experienced by union members in the United States and to some extent in Canada. An illustration of this reformist approach is the statement of the president of the Trades and Labour Congress in 1902. In his address to the convention, he noted that "to others, reformers as they may be, who believe in revolutionary principles, it is no doubt a source of regret that this body is becoming such an important factor in the country. Against trade unionism there ought to be one source of opposition, and that only would be organized capital."[4]

But a reformist ideology does not ensure continued success of a labor organization. Leaders of the TLC and the CLC have continually had to face the fundamental problem of justifying the existence of the congress. As it has evolved from its social movement characteristics to becoming a component of the institutional order, many contradictions have had to be resolved in order for the congress to maintain its viability. Some of the more pronounced contradictions include the following: (1) seeking a greater share of economic rewards for union members without changing the basic framework of social institutions; (2) incorporating American-based unions into the congress without losing a Canadian identity; (3) attempting to influence both federal and provincial governments while maintaining an independence from firm political alliances; and (4) maintaining an image of a progressive organization while taking on the role of a legitimate social institution.

Major Ideological Concerns

The attempt to resolve these and other contradictions by ideological expressions is indicated by an examination of presidential addresses and reports of the executive council to the annual and biennial conventions of the Trades and Labour Congress and, after 1956, the Canadian Labour Congress. A sampling of convention reports in which these presentations were recorded was based upon every fourth year during the period 1898 to 1974.[5] Themes were classified according to contextual interpretations. These yielded five major concerns: (1) Themes classified as "Problems" were the most numerous. They stated problematic issues without offering solutions, and included reminders about hostile employers, anti-labor legislation, economic conditions, and divisions within the Congress. (2) "Achievement" related themes were next most numerous. They recounted what had been accomplished with respect to organizational growth, economic benefits won, influence upon governments, the attainment of greater legitimacy, and comments about the social welfare of the general population. (3) "Objectives" stated what the president hoped the Congress would accomplish. Those included in this classification called for greater political influence, greater organizational growth, and more economic benefits for individual union members. (4) "General commentaries" was the fourth most frequent type of theme. These described the general state of affairs, the economy, and world events. (5) Finally, there were "Tactical" themes, which defined the manner in which objectives were to be won. A frequency count of these themes is provided in Table 1.

In addition to the numerical frequency of the five major concerns, one should also note the frequency of individual themes that occur within the five categories. There are three which are especially important: those that stress union organizational matters, those that stress political influence and concerns, and those that stress economic issues. Although they were couched within different contexts of meaning as indicated in the five major concerns, these three represent the major themes addressed by spokesmen for the congress.

The relative importance of ideological concerns through the years is indicated in Table 2. Expressed in terms of importance for the sampled years which were organized into five time periods, one can note the shifts in concerns as the congress evolved into a position of legitimation. Inspection of the table reveals a proportionate decline in the frequency of "achievement" and "tactics" themes, and a proportionate increase in "objective" themes. The frequency of "problems" remained relatively the same and "commentary" themes were most frequent during the Depression years.

Equally important were the shifts in the subsidiary themes. In order to illustrate the shifts in ideological orientations with the institutionalization of the Canadian Labour Congress, these need to be treated within the context of the changing major concerns. Consider first the concern with "achievements." Most of these themes were expressed during the period from 1898 to 1926, and the achievements which were most frequently mentioned were those that indicated that the congress (the Trades and Labour Congress

TABLE 1 **Percentage and Number of Themes in Sampled CLC Reports**

Subthemes	Major Themes					
	Achievements	Objectives	Tactics	Problems	Commentary	Other
Union Organization	34 (18)	26 (11)	27 (7)	23 (15)		
Political Influence	34 (18)	11 (6)	38 (10)	14 (9)		
Economic Benefits	4 (2)	14 (6)		33 (21)	13 (4)	
General Welfare	10 (5)	22 (9)				
Legitimation	10 (5)					
Management share		5 (2)				
Strikes			12 (3)			
Hostile Employers				8 (5)		
World-wide Concerns					40 (12)	
Other	8 (4)	19 (8)	23 (6)	22 (14)	47 (14)	100 (9)
Total	100 (52)	100 (42)	100 (26)	100 (64)	100 (30)	100 (9)

Source: Joseph Smucker, "Reformist Themes in the Canadian Labour Congress," *Sociological Focus.* Vol. 9, No. 2 (April, 1976), p. 163.

TABLE 2 **Proportionate Frequency of Themes by Intervals of Four Sampled Years***

	Achievements	Objectives	Tactics	Problems	Commentary	Other	N	Total
1898–1910	.28	.11	.21	.21	.17	.02	47	1.00
1914–1926	.38	.03	.14	.38	.03	.03	30	.99
1930–1942	.12	.18	.06	.23	.35	.06	17	1.00
1946–1958	.20	.29	.09	.22	.09	.11	45	1.00
1962–1974	.19	.23	.08	.35	.13	.01	84	.99
N	52	42	26	64	30	9	223	

Source: Joseph Smucker, "Reformist Themes in the Canadian Labour Congress," *Sociological Focus*, Vol. 9, No. 2 (April, 1976), p. 164.

at that time) as a force was making inroads into the government and had considerable political influence. For example, in 1898 the president noted with satisfaction the election of a union official to Parliament. In 1906 the president noted that throughout the world there was evidence that workers were taking part in governments and that this was occurring in Canada as well. In 1910 the president announced that "success crowned the efforts of your executive to secure the amendment of the Industrial Disputes Investigation Act of 1907." In 1922 texts of exchanges of letters with Mackenzie King regarding the recognition of railroad unions were read and additional memos to the government were cited as evidence of the influence of the congress. In 1926 the president reported that legislation regarding workmen's compensation was in advance of the Unites States, thanks to the efforts of the congress. While these examples may appear to be merely statements of fact, they are also ideological in the sense that they are couched within a context of meaning that emphasized the ability of members, as a body, to achieve significant changes. The "wisdom" and "vigilance" of members were continually cited during this period.

In the sampled period from 1946 to 1974 there were only five references to influence on the government or legislators. In addition, these had a vastly different meaning than the eighteen themes expressed during the sampled years from 1898 to 1926. For example, in 1958 the annual "memorandum" presentations to the federal government were justified merely on the grounds that "they, the government, can't plead ignorance." Such a statement is a far cry from the assertions of influence in the earlier years. In 1962, while the president noted that the Canadian Labour Congress had assisted in forming the New Democratic Party, he further counselled that "support for the NDP is a decision each affiliate should make and each individual should make."

If achievement themes focusing upon political influence declined over the years, themes emphasizing the growth and development of the congress as an organization increased. In the early period from 1898 to 1926 , citations regarding gains in membership were the most frequent themes. In addition, there were tributes to ties with international unions. For example, in 1910 the United Mine Workers, an international union, was cited for "its great fight in the Eastern coal fields." By the 1950s through to 1974, there was little rhetoric involved in citing the attributes of the congress. Rather, there were reports on gains in union membership, organizational changes, membership drives, the development of additional services such as research, course offerings, and so on. These shifts are significant in that they represent indices of the institutionalization of the Canadian Labour Congress. The social movement characteristics, in which achievements in the political sector are emphasized, are replaced with achievements stressing organizational merits and expertise.

Themes dealing with "tactics" revealed a similar pattern. While the total number was relatively few, the dominant subthemes also dealt with political influence and organizational structure and growth. The former were predominant in the period from 1898 to 1926, while the latter were most frequent during the period from 1946 to 1974. In the early period, among the tactical themes were calls to finance tests of labor legislation, and pass legislation prohibiting the importation of Chinese labor, and in 1914, calls to combat anti-labor legislation, support Vancouver miners and marshal support for minimum wage legislation. In the later period the emphasis was upon developing new techniques for collective bargaining, aiding individual unions in recruiting members, especially among clerical workers, and supporting anti-poverty programs.

If the two concerns are combined so that the shifts in themes dealing with government influence and with organizational growth and structure are heightened, the following pattern results. (See Table 3.)

TABLE 3 **Shifts in the Major Themes Involved in "Achievements" and "Tactics"**

Period	Major Themes		
	Political Influence	Union Organization	
1898–1926	22	9	31
1946–1974	7	14	21
	29	23	52

$x^2 = 5.74$
$p < .05$

What is significant about these shifts is that, once in place, the organizational structure and attributes of the labor congress increase in importance relative to the original aims of influencing governments.

Themes dealing with "objectives" increased in number and scope during the period under review. Again, one can note the ideological transformation as the social movement characteristics take on the attributes of a legitimate organization. Involved here are themes which define objectives but do not specify what should be done. Of the total 31 themes, all but 9 occurred during the period of sample years from 1946 to 1974. In the earliest period, the objectives focused upon an 8-hour work day, which would have a beneficial effect upon "social, intellectual and moral conditions." In addition, in 1910 the president pointed to the necessity for labor to have a direct voice in creating the laws which govern workers. In the later period, from 1946 to 1974, the range of objectives increased markedly. For example, in 1958 the president listed the following "needs": vigilance toward the government, extending social welfare legislation with respect to the unemployed, old age pensions,

pensions for the blind and disabled, workmen's compensation and a national health plan, a change in the system of taxation, making the union movement better known in secondary schools, retraining workers to deal with automation, national, rather than provincial, responsibility for education, slum clearance and more low rent housing, and the need for more purchasing power.

In 1970 the president stated that there must be continuing efforts to organize the unorganized and that strength at the bargaining table was not a "sufficient answer if trade unions are to achieve their goals." He called for increased involvement in the political arena and pointed out that "we must . . . work in close alliance with all other institutions in Canada which share at least some, if not all, of our goals. Isolation is too costly a luxury for us to indulge in." He went on to list some ten areas of social welfare which included poverty, medicare, good housing, "restoring the atmosphere," "transformimg broadcasting into a medium of expression of an authentic Canadian viewpoint," and "strengthening human rights."

Such a diversity of objectives portrays an image of an institution that is fully integrated into the larger society and that can serve a great variety of interests. These themes suggest that there is virtually no limit to the ends that can be served by the congress. They further cast the CLC into the role of the "loyal opposition," commenting upon issues that touch upon nearly all aspects of Canadian society. Taken at face value, it would be difficult for an individual not to support such an organization, regardless of his class or political proclivities.

The relatively large number of themes classified as "problems" were evenly distributed throughout the sampled years. This is not surprising when one considers the difficulties experienced by the labor movement. But what is of interest is the manner in which these are expressed as the congress took on the role of an important component in the institutional framework of Canadian society. "Problems" in the early years included those dealing with government legislation, especially with respect to the importation of foreign labor, and the divisiveness within the labor movement as a whole. Divisiveness and intramural conflicts remained a concern throughout the time period.

In 1902 the president denounced those who advocated revolutionary principles. In 1906 the issue was the effrontery of the AFL in classifying the Canadian Trades and Labour Congress as a "state" federation. In 1922 the president again warned convention delegates against an "active minority furthering revolutionary objectives which would just as surely bring about their ultimate destruction." The addresses in 1930 and 1934 included references to competing federations and asserted that the Congress represented the true expression of Canadian labor. In 1946 internal strains were reflected in the allegiances of unions whose headquarters were based in the United States: "While we do not look or hope for any ill-feeling from any of our affiliated unions, it is our duty to protect our sovereign rights." Concerns were also expressed about the dangers of outside radical elements and the divisiveness of jurisdictional disputes in 1962, 1966, and 1974. Further, in 1974 the reemergence of nationalist sentiment among individual union members caused the president to caution delegates against becoming irrationally committed to disaffiliation with American-based unions.

More numerous in these last years were themes dealing with economic conditions. In 1962 the president called for an improvement in the standard of living. "Unless this can be done," he argued, "we will have difficulty demonstrating our way is better than that advocated by the Communists." "The fact remains," said the president in 1970, "that the working people are called upon to bear the brunt of the inefficiencies of our economic system." He further argued that reforms in taxation did not go far enough and the government had failed to meet the nation's housing needs. In 1974 the address was unusually forceful: "Income distribution which has always been grossly inequitable, is now worse than it has been in 20 years . . . all real wage and salary gains made in 1971 and 1972 were wiped out completely by rapidly escalating prices in 1973." To remedy this, the president called for "increased militancy at the bargaining table." Notice, however, that the overall structure of society is not questioned.

More recently, in 1974, the president of the CLC saw multi-national corporations as a major threat to the political independence and collective bargaining rights of Canadian workers: "If ever there was an indictment to be made of the capitalist system and the governments which support it, this is surely a classic example." Yet, despite the militancy, the address itself was a wide-ranging commentary, touching upon all the major social problems in Canadian society. Except for a renewed emphasis upon astute collective bargaining, no remedial strategies were advanced. In effect, the militancy encouraged by mounting dissatisfactions of workers in the 1970s was tempered by broadening the scope of the issues while concentrating upon institutional means—collective bargaining—to resolve the inequities most directly experienced by workers.

A final group of themes was "general commentary." These were proportionately most numerous during the Depression years. It is significant that it was also during this time that union membership dropped. In view of the pervasive effects of the Depression, there was little that the reform-oriented congress could do but express the general concerns of workers. Thus, these themes dealt with the difficult times, problems in the economy, the welfare of the nation, and world events.

I mentioned earlier that four contradictions appeared to be unusually pronounced in the history of the TLC-CLC. They are partially resolved by the manipulation of ideological themes. The emphasis upon collective bargaining reduces the severity of the contradiction in seeking a greater share of economic rewards without threatening the basic institutional structure. When the problem of American controlled unions in the congress emerges, caution is encouraged, backed by a threatening image of potential chaos. Encouraging unions and individual members to act on the basis of their own political commitments permits the congress to avoid boxing itself in with firm political allegiances while attempting to influence governments. Finally, by expanding the scope of objectives to be supported, the congress maintains an image of a progressive organization within its institutional setting. But even more significant is the transition from the rhetoric of a social movement to an enumeration of services and organizational achievements.

The connecting link between the social movement characteristics of the congress and its institutionalization in Canadian society is a redefinition of its role as a platform for articulating corrective causes. It is not that the CLC practises duplicity, but rather that it cannot in fact actively play the two roles simultaneously. Ideological expressions help alleviate the inherent strains. When more radical rhetoric is couched within the context of a legitimate organization, it serves more as a warning than as a threat, although there is always the possibility that the rhetoric of criticism will serve as a basis for action.

Kwavnick has argued that the leaders of the Canadian Labour Congress have had an "obsessive concern" to win legitimation as the sole voice of labor.[6] Having won it, they have also abandoned whatever radical elements the labor movement may have possessed. Yet this is to insist that labor movements *ought* to have been more radical. Evidence from the Canadian experience and from other societies indicates that radical movements are not likely to succeed unless there is a greater degree of collaboration between groups of different socially demarcated sectors. The failure of this collaboration suggests the very reason for the success of reform movements. But it does raise the issue about the role of unions in developing working-class consciousness.

The origins of the labor movement are to be found in the experiences of the wage earners selling their labor to others who own the means of production. These experiences are also the source for working-class consciousness. But the fact that the dominant labor federations in most industrialized societies are reformist in their orientation raises the question not only about the relationship between unions and the development of a working-class consciousness, but also about the nature of the working-class consciousness itself. If, for example, reformism in the labor movement merely means improving the ability of workers to attain a greater proportion of the economic rewards of capitalism, does this characterize the orientation of the working class as a whole, or is this reformism to be taken merely as one component of a more encompassing working-class consciousness? On the other hand, do more radical ideological orientations in which workers seek greater control over authority structures capture the essence of working-class consciousness as it presently exists? These questions require a closer examination since they are crucial to the debates surrounding Marxian analyses.

On Working-Class Consciousness

The notion of working-class consciousness incorporates the two Marxian concepts of "class-in-itself" and "class-for-itself." "Class-in-itself" refers to the degree to which workers interpret the entire range of their experiences within the framework of their economic dependence; "class-for-itself" goes on to assert that workers' interests are in direct conflict with those of the bourgeoisie or owning class. Class consciousness is thus dependent on a unique set of interpretations about the social world, which in turn guides individuals' actions.[7] This further implies that such a Marxian interpretation is based upon an extension of the values of freedom and equality in which their expression is to ultimately benefit the entire society, not merely a given class of individuals at the expense of another class. The early bourgeoisie limited the expression of these values to themselves, interpreting them as freedom from a feudal order and equality in relation to a landed aristocracy.

It was Marx's belief that there could be no improvement in the exploitative ills of capitalism as long as workers sought merely the individualistic, self-centered expression of the bourgeoisie. The freedom of the individual ultimately required the freedom from classes, since classes fostered self-aggrandizement and personal greed with their resulting social inequities in the distribution of wealth and social power. What was required to overcome this was to foster a realization that self-interests could not be attained in any ultimate sense until the individual fused his own interests with those of his "species being," i.e., with the totality of society or social man.[8] The issue, stated in more concrete terms, is finally an issue of a consciousness of producers rather than of consumers in an industrial capitalist society. The class of workers, as producers, is ultimately the source by which class structure itself is to be ended.

Mann outlines the Marxist interpretation of a working-class consciousness by presenting it in terms of four stages of development: (1) the identity of oneself as a member of the working class, enacting along with others a distinctive role in the production process; (2) the perception that the employer and his agents and collaborators constitute an enduring opponent to oneself; (3) the acceptance of the first two conditions as the defining characteristics of one's total social situation and the whole society in which one lives; and (4) a conception of an alternative society which can be obtained through struggle with the opposing forces.[9] The two things to notice in this formulation are the major role played by ideology, and the fact that, as these conditions develop, class consciousness is tantamount to a proposal for revolutionary change.

Marxian theorists assume that since the working class bears the full brunt of the exploitative effects of industrial capitalism, its members should in fact be the source of radical change. For these theorists, failure to support such a movement suggests a "false consciousness," in the sense that individuals have not adopted interpretive systems which match their own experiental world or point to ultimate solutions for the problem of interpersonal exploitation.

Yet the solutions require a distancing of the self in two senses: (1) in the sense of imagining the absence of exploitative relations, and (2) in the sense of imagining an identity of self in relation to an entire society or mankind in general rather than to one's own private world or to a specific class. Thus the terms of reference are to be changed from self-worth as associated with a system of exploitation (one's gain must be another's loss) to self-worth as a consequence of some model of self-actualization independent of class identity. (Such a future state is necessarily obscure since it is yet to be realized.)

What has exasperated Marxists is the failure of workers in industrialized societies to go through the ideological shifts, from discontent with the inability to realize the values of freedom and equality, to collective action which removes the barriers to their expression, to a new society in which their expression is without their exploitative consequences. The orthodox view of the sequence of events which fosters these shifts is that, as industrial capitalism advances, the restrictions on workers become more severe, resulting in a class consciousness of a revolutionary orientation and finally an "explosion" of action against the prevailing system.

Exasperation with the failure of the working class to realize their "own best interests" has been a continual theme in Marxian analysis. Steven Marcus notes, for example, that, in the first English translation of *The Condition of the Working Class in England* in 1844, Engels omitted the original dedication to the "English Workingman" apparently as a result of his disappointment with the English proletariat, whom he believed regularly "disgraced itself" by voting and behaving against what he believed to be its own best interests.[10] Since then there have been a variety of explanations for this apparent failure. A few examples follow.

Lukacs points to the emergence of a "fetishism of commodities" as the factor intervening between the experience of the workers and their failure to adopt a radical ideology. As a consequence of the division of labor in the production process, individual workers lose their sense of control over the goods which they produce. The commodities thereupon take on attributes of an independent reality subject to their own laws of the marketplace. This causes workers to mistake the abstract impersonal world of commodities for their own best interests. Not only do they come to view the ownership of commodities as marks of personal value, but they also view themselves as commodities.

While this would seem to be an inescapable condition, Lukacs does hold out hope for the eventual emergence of a class consciousness. While workers may see themselves as commodities, defined as quantities of labor within units of time, such conditions can be converted into consciousness. For Lukacs, this can occur when workers are aware that they are not isolated individuals, but part of a larger process of which the contemporary forms of production are merely part of a particular historical event, and when they realize that "social facts" are not objects but relations among individuals. When these conditions are met, a class consciousness can develop that transcends immediate realities. Since consciousness includes an historical awareness, one can presume that other social forms are possible.[11] It is the role of intellectuals to create this awareness.

Marcuse also follows the argument of the effects of segmentation of the production process in the use of his term, "technological rationality."[12] By this he means the predominance of thought that is ruled by criteria inherent in the production system. This defines the terms on which individuals and groups compete among themselves; since these tend to be highly restrictive, they close off the possibility for organizing radical social movements.

Althusser, adhering more closely to an economic Marxism, argues that, while in the last instance the modes of production determine the forms of other sectors in society, each sector develops along the lines of its own internal logic, and, in the process, develops its own contradictions.[13] Only when these contradictions become mutually reinforcing can individuals develop a class consciousness and hence a commitment to radical alternatives. But there is no way to predict when this is likely to occur.

Finally, Brecher, taking the Marxian idea of "praxis" seriously, argues that the material conditions are sufficiently developed for the emergence of a radical working-class consciousness.[14] But this will occur only during the experience of opposition, such as a mass strike oriented toward achieving greater worker control. Mutual trust among workers develops during such experiences; this trust, in turn, leads to a sense of solidarity, from which a working-class consciousness emerges. Thus, overt acts of opposition further reinforce the development of a radical class consciousness. Existing trade unions, such as the American trade unions, are not the means for this expression since, he argues, they have accepted the rules for bargaining for greater economic gains rather than striving for outright control of the production process. The distinction between unions and workers is an important one, but Brecher's formulation sets up a continual dilemma in determining the collective will of workers and whether or not unions are in fact to be taken as divorced from this will.

Conditions Giving Rise to Working-Class Consciousness

While many Marxists have attempted to determine why the working class fails to develop a consciousness that is consistent with what they interpret to be the best interests of the working class, other analysts have sought to ascertain the nature, causes, and consequences of the consciousness that does exist. The research appears to be fairly consistent in finding that while workers in different capitalist industrialized societies may not be committed to the predominant values of capitalism, it does not follow that they necessarily embrace an opposing ideology.[15]

Michael Mann, in his review of the research in Great Britain and the United States, concludes that there are two types of interpretations that are widely endorsed by the working class: those expressed in concrete terms that correspond to their daily experiences, and those related to an image of the social world which entails a simple division between the "rich" and the "poor." But there is, he claims, "no real political philosophy uniting these themes."[16] Even where such a philosophy is offered, as in the case of the Communist-dominated Confédération générale du travail, the largest trade union in France, Hamilton found that union members voted for the Communist party, but showed little interest in the party organization.[17]

Drawing primarily from research in France, Great Britain, the United States and, to some extent, Italy, Mann concludes that the development of class consciousness among workers is less a function of the characteristics of capitalism than it is a consequence of "external" factors, that is, those which are associated with feudal elements that remain within capitalist societies. (Examples of these include a land-owning aristocracy, widespread nepotism, little mobility, and so on.) Mann argues that where this has been most strongly the case, such as in France and Italy, working-class consciousness is much more apparent.[18] What this implies is that capitalism, in its most *ideal* expression of open competition, precludes the formation of restrictive classes and hence the development of a working-class consciousness.

The research of Hamilton and Leggett provide examples that support this observation. In attempting to explain why the French working class tended to be leftist in its politics despite relatively high levels of affluence in some sectors, Hamilton found that those urban workers originally from rural areas were most likely to hold to this orientation. These were workers who had already been familiar with agrarian radicalism, which in turn had been born out of their experience in which land ownership and agricultural production had become highly controlled.[19] In the workers' shift from farm tenancy and village shops to urban factory work, Communist-dominated unions, already in place in the urban settings, provided the most ideologically compatible means by which the disorienting shifts could be explained. Continued infusions of workers from the countryside maintained the vitality of the unions. Hamilton further noted that similar associations of agrarian radicalism with urban leftist movements occurred in Italy, Spain, and Finland. The connecting links were workers shifting from radicalizing experiences in the countryside to the urban setting. The important point to be made about Hamilton's findings is that Comminist-dominated labor unions provided an ideological content for interpreting the disorienting experiences of workers recently arrived from the countryside. Where no coherent forms of ideological expression exist, these experiences may merely result in militancy devoid of any coherent rationale. This is implied in the research done by Leggett.

In his research among automobile workers in Detroit, Leggett discovered that those workers who were most militant tended to come from rural areas and to be black. From his findings, he argues that the crucial factor accounting for their militancy was "uprootedness." That is, their social identities and reference points were drastically changed in the process of their move to a new social context. Leggett cites additional references to support his findings and interpretations. Engels, he notes, once observed that workers express a high degree of revolutionary consciousness "during the early period of industrialization when changes come rapidly and discontinuously to an inexperienced working class."[20] He also cites the analyses of early industrialization by Adam Ulman and by G. D. H. Cole, both of whom observed that revolutionary thought tends to be strongest during periods of immiserization or hardship that are most severe for workers during the early stages of industrialization. Finally, Leggett cites Trotsky, who argued that the most militant workers were peasants who had recently been employed in factories. They, rather than the urban proletariat, had been the least successful in adapting to rapid economic and technological changes in Russia.

The evidence then suggests that sudden changes—"uprootedness"—experienced during a lifetime is a key factor in fostering militancy. The conversion of militancy into a coherent radical commitment requires that an organization or at least individuals who are committed to a radical ideology be in existence prior to the experience. Otherwise there is no guarantee that militant workers will be committed to movements which fit the Marxist interpretation of "class consciousness." The Communist Labor Federation in France provided precisely this role.[21]

Robert Cole found that, in Japan, well-formulated Marxist ideology espoused by an intellectual class provided a perspective for workers opposed to the near absolute control by management. Cole argues that the ideology had been adopted by many workers more for its symbolic value of opposition than for its intrinsic meanings. When workers' personal livelihoods were threatened, they ceased to support the ideology. Further, a competing ideology, the Soka Gakkai, a religious-nationalistic movement, had more recently emerged and this had also attracted disaffected workers.[22]

These findings imply that the radically oriented class consciousness which Mann has been at pains to find is non-existent among workers who have undergone only the continuing experience of production work in industrial capitalist societies. The most militant workers are likely to be those who have recently been "uprooted." Yet the political directions of their militancy may remain indeterminate. The implications of this last assertion are captured in Maurice Pinard's observations of voting behavior among the working class in Quebec: ". . . in the absence of (1) a well-developed class consciousness, and (2) class organizations which go beyond the economic problems to encompass the social and political life of the working class, this unincorporated class is as likely to support a conservative movement as a progressive one, whichever is most available, when their conditions lead them to revolt."[23]

It would appear that the premises of movement ideologies make little difference to individual members under conditions of social dislocation. What is important is that credible links can be made between the dominant values, the experienced world, a cause, and a solution. It is conceivable that nationalistic-fascist ideologies may be just as likely as socialist or communist ones.

Where there has been a long experience with the effects of industrialization, there appears to be less likelihood that class consciousness of the Marxist orientation will develop. Of course, this presumes no further drastic social disruptions. It is doubtful that this can be safely asserted. It is possible that further social disruptions will occur with further shifts in the exercise of authority over production systems.

Meanwhile, individuals may be aware that their work is unsatisfying and that they are being exploited, but they are able to construct a variety of interpretations that explain their conditions and permit them to tolerate them. As Brecher puts it, "people will try to adapt to even the most unpleasant situation if it seems stable and they feel unable to change it—that is why they are not in a state of revolt continuously."[24]

Unless there is a shared perception among a collectivity of individuals that a chance for a change exists and that this can only be accomplished by acting in concert, the values of freedom and equality may heighten the awareness of inequities while at the same time place a crushing burden of responsibility upon the individual in acting upon them. In their sensitive analysis of the existential effects of social inequality, Sennett and Cobb have revealed how individuals in the United States, where premiums are placed upon individual achievement, suffer a personal sense of loss if they have not been upwardly mobile, while others often bear a sense of guilt if they have. The people whom they interviewed tended to resolve this dilemma by disassociating themselves from the roles which expressed social inequities.[25] (They were just "doing a job.") Where classes are clearly identified and interpreted as a function of "the system," this responsibility is removed and at least personal dignity among one's class peers can be maintained. These observations suggest that class identification can provide a sense of security for the individual. As such, it can negate efforts to effect change in the structures which rest upon social inequities. This suggests, then, that only under special conditions will class identity foster the kind of class consciousness that Marxists have hoped for.

This presents another dilemma for Marxists. Marx had hoped that individuals could see that they were ultimately responsible for social structures and that they could initiate changes in those structures. But individuals are just as capable of taking personal responsibility for having "failed." Class identity eliminates this problem and, in so doing, may just as easily serve to negate change toward greater freedom and equality, even while the rhetoric of equality is expressed.

On Militancy and Reformism

I pointed out earlier that militancy among workers is not restricted to commitment to radical ideologies. The labor unions in the United States, for example, have been primarily reformist in their orientation but have been at the same time some of the most militant in the world. Similarly, Canada, most of whose unions are reformist, also has one of the highest rates of time loss due to strikes and lockouts among the industrialized capitalist countries. On the other hand, the Communist-dominated labor federation in France has been comparatively subdued.

The factor that appears to contribute most strongly to a high degree of militancy is the existence of a fragmented labor market that encourages comparative assessments among workers and labor unions. Further, these conditions appear to be special cases of more general principles which account for other social movements as well. Pinard argues from his data that social movements are more likely to occur under conditions in which there is a fragmented society of discrete social arenas, rather than within a social context characterized by a homogeneous mass of alienated individuals.[26] However, while social movements are more likely under these conditions, their orientation is most likely to be *reformist*. *Radical* movements are most likely to exist when the various contexts of experience mutually reinforce a sense of injustice during periods of relatively sudden social dislocation. As I noted earlier, these are conditions most likely to occur during the early stages of industrialization, but they can also emerge during periods of severe economic crisis.

In addition to the effects of segmentation on both the frequency of acts of militancy and the likelihood of reformist ideologies, there are also the effects of the state of economy. When the economy is expanding, unions are more likely to become militant in their *economic* demands as they seek to maintain or improve their economic returns. Under such conditions, employers tend to be more amenable to making concessions in order to avoid setbacks in their positions relative to their competitors. The proportion of earnings labor receives can remain the same, but the absolute amounts increase with an expanding economy. When the economy is stagnant, increases in economic concessions to labor mean severer losses to employers. Further, these losses are more difficult to recoup from consumers. Hence, employers tend to become more adamant against labor demands. When this occurs, the issues for unions are more likely to shift from gaining increased economic benefits to challenging the authority structures themselves. It is highly possible that Canadian workers, having experienced relatively high levels of affluence, are not as likely to remain as apolitical as they were in the Depression of the 1930s should a sudden economic crisis occur now.

On Criticisms of the Canadian Labor Movement

Some academic analysts and commentators have accused the Canadian labor movement in general, and the Canadian Labour Congress in particular, of becoming conservative, content to maintain legitimacy in relation to governments and the general populace. They often interpret strikes as an index of militancy misdirected—away from political objectives of transforming society to merely gaining a greater share of the rewards of capitalist society.[27]

Such a condemnation of contemporary labor organizations overlooks the historical reasons for the direction the movement has taken, given the perceptions of its leaders. It should be remembered that the failure of the Knights of Labour caused early labor leaders to fear a dissipation of labor movement energies. The membership of the Knights was interpreted to be too broadly based and its objectives too ill-defined. Second, there has been a long-standing distrust against tying in too closely with political parties, even when they identify themselves with the interests of labor. Political parties seek to expand their constituencies and, in doing so, labor has come to be suspicious of the consequences. Labor has been sympathtic toward efforts at establishing parties amenable to its interests, but has never supported such parties completely. There was not much labor support for the Cooperative Commonwealth Federation party, and although the CLC played an active role in the founding of the New Democratic Party, support for it has not been unequivocal. Further, union membership voting records in past federal elections have revealed only a minority support for the NDP. In the 1979 general election, even though the CLC publicly endorsed the NDP, this appeared to have had relatively little effect in influencing workers' votes.[28] Specific issues, such as wages and working conditions, will unify a union movement; but broader political objectives in which the issues and consequences are more obscure serve to divide it. The failure of workers to wholeheartedly back labor-oriented political parties is not restricted to the Canadian labor movement. It is also found in other industrialized capitalist countries.[29]

As I have noted previously, the Canadian labor movement has been heavily influenced by those American labor unions which early adopted the Gomperist position that the best interests of the labor movement were to be served by remaining separate from any political movements. These unions concentrated on specific objectives directly related to the workplace. The rationale for this approach was the belief that the larger social welfare issues would be resolved in a step-by-step process, beginning with improving the conditions of work. Thus, the AFL did not associate itself with a variety of social reform groups, especially those supporting anti-monopolistic legislation. On this particular issue, it saw economic concentration as inevitable and that ultimately, labor unions, having gained a secure place within the capitalist society, would, when powerful enough, transform society by demanding a share of the concentrated power.[30]

It should also be pointed out that the very nature of the market system as it operates in capitalist society produces economic pressures which "set aims and determine methods which are consistent with a freely competitive economic system."[31] The options for labor movements have thus been restricted by these conditions. (Analogously, the options for socialist countries in a world market have also been restricted to market terms.) Within this frame of reference, the Canadian union movement has clearly been beneficial to workers. However, one can anticipate new options as either changes occur in the structures of industry or basic contradictions reveal the necessity for organized labor to change its orientation. One development to observe is the effect of a greater proportion of workers under direct government employment, in public service, and in nationalized industries. Under such conditions, economic issues become more directly linked to political policies and political power can replace earlier economic aims. (The labor unrest in the early 1970s in Quebec provides evidence for this assertion.)

If there is little proof that class consciousness exists, at least as defined by Marxists, there is also little evidence that unions represent a unified collective expression of the dissatisfactions which continue to be experienced by workers. Rather, these dissatisfactions tend to be private, their existence revealed by absenteeism and general restiveness within the production enterprises. Unions appear to serve more as brokerage agents, offering services to workers while defining what workers can reasonably expect. These are necessary services, but they do not appear to ameliorate the full range of the workers' dissatisfactions. Although it is significant that unions have become a means to serve individual interests of workers, they have yet to provide the means by which these interests can be fused with the collective welfare of mankind in general. It is *this* transformation which Marx hoped would come about.

Notes

1. A substantial portion of the analysis of the ideology of the CLC appeared in Joseph Smucker, "Reformist Themes in the Canadian Labour Congress," *Sociological Focus*, Vol. 9, No. 2 (April, 1976), pp. 159–173. I am grateful to Rosemary Warskett for critical comments and aid in data collection and analysis.

2. In addition to the labor movement, the conflicts that were required to gain a wider application of these values can be documented by the franchise movements among people who owned no property, among women, and among minority groups.

3. Jane Masters, "Canadian Labour Press Opinion, 1890–1914: A Study in Theoretical Radicalism and Practical Conservatism," M. A. Thesis, University of Western Ontario, 1969.

4. Proceedings of the Trades and Labor Congress, Berlin, Ontario, 1902.

5. The analysis of ideological content presented some problems of reliability. During the sampled years, 1906 through 1922, the president merely gave welcoming addresses. The "Report of the Executive Officers" was thus included for analysis during these years. Further, in the sampled years, 1926 and 1934, the presidential addresses were paraphrased in the reports of the convention proceedings. Finally, the style of the speeches differed in both length and detail. In general, the presentations did not reveal the full extent of conflicts within the Congress. They were directed primarily toward minimizing rather than exacerbating those conflicts.

6. David Kwavnick, Organized Labour and Pressure Politics (Montreal: McGill-Queens University Press, 1972), pp. 217–219.

7. Anthony Giddens, The Class Structure of the Advanced Societies (London: Hutchinson University Library, 1973), p. 113.

8. For a more comprehensive analysis of this theme see Robert C. Tucker, The Marxian Revolutionary Idea (New York: W. W. Norton & Co., 1969), pp. 30–32.

9. Michael Mann, Consciousness and Action Among the Western Working Class (London: Macmillan, 1973), p. 13

10. Steven Marcus, Engels, Manchester and the Working Class (New York: Random House, 1974), p. xii.

11. George Lukacs, History and Class Consciousness (London: Merlin Press, 1968), pp. 168–181.

12. Herbert Marcuse, One Dimensionsal Man (Boston: Beacon Press, 1964).

13. Louis Althusser, For Marx, trans. B. Brewster (New York: Pantheon, 1969), p. 99.

14. Jeremy Brecher, Strikes! (San Francisco: Straight Arrow Books, 1972), pp. 233–242. See also Stanley Aronowitz, False Promises (New York: McGraw-Hill, 1973), pp. 4–8 for a discussion of these approaches.

15. See, for example, Eric Nordlinger, The Working Class Tories (Berkeley: University of California Press, 1967); Robert McKenzie and Alan Silver, Angels in Marble (London: Heinemann, 1968); Irving Richter, Political Purpose in Trade Unions (London: George Allen and Unwin, 1973); Michael Mann, "The Social Cohesion of Liberal Democracy," American Sociological Review, Vol. XXXV, No. 3 (June, 1970), pp. 423–439, and Michael Mann, Consciousness and Action, op. cit. Aronowitz, op. cit., pp. 258–260, reminds his readers that early industrial workers joined unions in order to share in the capitalist expansion, not to bring about its downfall.

16. Michael Mann, "The Social Cohesion of Liberal Democracy," op. cit., p. 436.

17. Richard Hamilton, Affluence and the French Worker in Fourth Republic (Princeton: Princeton University Press, 1967), p. 31.

18. Mann has also examined the effect of strikes on class consciousness. He finds that in Great Britain and the United States, where employer and union representatives meet face-to-face in processing most strikes, a "bargaining mentality" is developed. In Italy, where there is an absence of regular channels of communication between unions and employers, strikes are more likely to take on an insurrectionist

character. Conditions similar to Italy also exist in France. See Michael Mann, *Consciousness and Action Among the Western Working Class*, op. cit., p. 49.

19. Richard Hamilton, op. cit., p. 275.

20. John C. Leggett, *Class, Race, and Labor: Working Class Consciousness in Detroit* (New York: Oxford University Press, 1968), pp. 69–75.

21. Hamilton, op. cit., p. 275.

22. Robert Cole, *Japanese Blue Collar: The Changing Tradition* (Berkeley: University of California Press, 1971), pp. 266–269.

23. Maurice Pinard, *The Rise of a Third Party: A Study in Crisis Politics* (Englewood Cliffs, N.J.: Prentice-Hall, 1971), p. 85.

24. Brecher, op. cit., pp. 244–245.

25. Richard Sennett and Jonathan Cobb, *The Hidden Injuries of Class* (New York: Alfred Knopf, 1972).

26. Pinard, op. cit., p. 194.

27. See for example, Kwavnick, op. cit., p. 219.

28. Gad Horowitz, *Canadian Labour in Politics* (Toronto: University of Toronto Press, 1968), p. 41. Horowitz reports that in 1962 only 22 percent of the union membership supported the NDP party. A CLC survey of union support for the NDP in the 1968 elections revealed that only about 20 to 25 percent of the 603 affiliated unions who responded played an active role on behalf of the NDP. In the 1979 federal election, four out of five, or 80 percent of unionized workers voted for either the Liberal or Conservative party. See Ed Finn, "Why Labor Failed to Help NDP," *The Gazette*, Montreal, June 2, 1979.

29. Most of the research on working class voting patterns has been done in Britain. In addition to the works by Nordlinger, McKenzie and Silver and Richter cited earlier, see David Butler and Donald Stokes, *Political Change in Britain* (London: Macmillan, 1969); Bob Jessop, *Traditionalism, Conservatism and British Political Culture* (London: George Allen and Unwin, 1974); and W. G. Runciman, *Relative Deprivation and Social Justice* (Berkeley: University of California Press, 1966). See also, Michael J. Sullivan, "Sources and Varieties of Working Class Conservatism: A Late Reconsideration of an Ancient Debate," unpublished paper, McGill University, 1978. For an early statement of the issue, see Selig Perlman, *A Theory of the Labor Movement* (New York: Kelley, 1968), p. 144.

30. Daniel Bell, *Marxian Socialism in the United States* (Princeton: Princeton University Press, 1967), p. 37.

31. V. L. Allen, *Power in Trade Unions* (London: Longmans, Green, 1954), p. 29.

Part Four

The Experience of Work in Rational Authority Systems

chapter twelve

The Experience of Working

Introduction

In the previous chapters, I attempted to analyze the major social structural trends in industrialization in Canada by focusing on the interplay between values and authority in production systems. The context in which these two structural components are most dramatically experienced by individual actors is in their work. In this chapter, I want to deal with the role of work and how individuals perceive it and respond to it.

The *Financial Post* reported in its October 22, 1977 issue that "more than 125 million man-days are lost in an average year to industry beyond approved leaves of absence, vacations, paid holidays, strikes and lock-outs." This, the author stated, represents 11 times the loss by strikes and lockouts alone. While much of this loss is a consequence of illness or family problems, the author of the report estimated that 50 percent of the lost time could be recovered by more "vigilant managers." As it has been, on any average working day, more than 530 000 employed workers do not report for work in Canada. The fact that the author of this article called for more managerial vigilance suggests that for many people the authority systems for production do not support the values of freedom and equality.[1]

Strikes and lockouts are organized forms of expressing dissatisfaction with different aspects of the work role. What the above report indicates is that each worker also endures or enjoys his work experience in his own private manner, the expression of which is not necessarily dependent upon organized action. Dissatisfactions are often parts of a solitary hell, relieved occasionally by hostile acts against the organization. Many people view their work as merely an activity to be endured yet one that is required to earn a living.

The questions that I want to raise in this chapter have to do with the current importance of work in the expression of the values of freedom and equality. The question is not only whether in fact these values can be realized in the world of work, but whether work remains the most important arena of experience by which the relevance of these values is tested. It is conceivable that other non-work activities have superseded or will supersede the central role work has occupied in the lives of individuals since the Industrial Revolution. If there is unhappiness in the work that people do, will economic rewards—wages, pensions, health benefits and so on—be sufficient to keep them committed to the experience of work? If organizations tend to make work routine, are there alternatives to which people can turn in order to live fulfilling lives while "making a living" or does the work role remain the central life experience for them?

The Concept of Work

Currently, discussions of work often sound like discussions of sexual intercourse; not only is it an act of reproduction but it should also be enjoyed. Such ideas of work (like ideas of sexual relations) are certainly not universal when viewed historically or cross-culturally. Tilgher, in his historical survey of the shifts in the interpretations of work in western societies, has pointed out that the importance we place upon working and the work role is a relatively recent phenomenon. The "right to work" would strike many ancient Greeks as a curious demand. Indeed, they saw work, especially physical labor, as something to be avoided since it brutalized the mind and thus made it unfit for contemplation and the practice of virtue. The ancient Hebrews, while viewing work as painful drudgery, saw its necessity as a means to expiate man's sinful state. Early Christians saw labor primarily as a way to ward off the corruption of earthly pleasures.[2] As we have seen in Chapter 3, Luther invested the work role with the virutes of a "calling," and thereby raised the religious worthiness of nearly all occupations to the level of the priest. The doctrines of Calvin, according to Weber's interpretation, indirectly added further impetus to the value of working.

If hard work, in its physical manifestations, has not always been viewed as desirable activity, it is likely that industriousness of some sort has been valued. Greek philosophers prized industriousness in thought and in political participation. Further, while they did not view physical labor as desirable in itself, they undoubtedly rewarded the hard-working slave more generously than the indolent one. To be industrious in contributing to the maintenance and well-being of a social group is always highly regarded by its members.

That individuals should be evaluated primarily by the work that they do and how they do it has been, of course, a central theme in industrialized societies. Work has been the primary means by which individuals structure and act upon their expectations of themselves and of others. The very existence of industrialized societies has depended upon work roles linked together by contractual relations and designed for the production of goods and services. However, the changes in the structure of authority toward greater segmentation and formalization have made it more difficult for individuals to derive important meanings from work, other than as a way of gaining a living. This has occurred at the very time social critics, commentators, and apologists for managers argue that the performance of work is crucially important for society as a whole. The segmentation has increased the degree of functional interdependence and this in turn has raised administrative costs when individuals fail to meet their role requirements. Thus more attention and expenditure of energy must be directed toward controlling individuals in their work. This requires an increasing proportion of formal rules (in contrast to mores and folkways) and less tolerance for ambiguities.[3] This means that there can be very little moral content in the experience, since "morality" becomes merely a matter of obeying abstract rules, rather than exercising judgments on what is being produced and for what purpose. The rationalization of production has drained the work role of any sense of community effort or obligation. There is a totally different set of meanings involved in other types of work activities like neighborhood barn-raising or husking bees, to use Wilensky's examples. As Bennett Berger puts it, "our value system does not provide us with the moral vocabulary to defend much of the behavior and many of the roles which the social structure requires."[4] But perhaps this is merely irrelevant theorizing. We need to have some empirical evidence to support these claims.

Research Findings on the Experience of Work

There exists a vast amount of literature, both analytic and descriptive, on the experience of working. Where historical comparisons have been made, many authors have conjured up romantic notions about the joy people once experienced in their work. But these notions often turn out to be based upon a mythical image of a happy medieval craftsman, which is then compared to a stereotypical automobile assembly line worker, embittered by his routine, meaningless endeavors. Work as an activity required to gain a livelihood has been a mean experience for most people throughout history. But what is unique in industrialized societies is that the work role occupies a central place in the social identities of persons, while at the same time requiring unremitting commitment to the principle of working. The question is whether too much is expected of the work role within organizational settings which require progressively less of most individuals' capabilities. If this is true, then there exists a crisis stemming from a discrepancy between the expectations or hopes of what work should be on one hand and the authority structures on the other.

There are five general areas of research on the experience of working within industrialized societies in which the findings have been relatively consistent and which provide some answers to the general issues posed above. These are findings on (1) work satisfaction, (2) the importance placed upon working in general, (3) commitments to specific jobs, (4) rewards which individuals desire from their work, and (5) psychological and physical reactions to the demands of work. I shall deal with each of these in turn.

Work Satisfaction

When responding to a single question whether or not they are satisfied with their current jobs, "with all things considered," the vast majority of workers usually indicate that they are satisfied. This finding has been repeated in different countries at different times over at least a 25-year period.[5] For example, in 1949 Centers reported that in his sample of Americans, 82 percent of the professionals and 72 percent of unskilled manual workers reported that they were satisfied with their "present job." A more recent tabulation of findings of American Gallup Polls indicates that an overwhelming majority of white employed persons answered that they were satisfied. (A lower proportion of black persons reported that they were satisfied, however. This suggests that membership in a minority group which has been both socially and economically suppressed affects the findings.) The summary of these surveys is presented in Table 1.

TABLE 1 **Tabulation of Gallup Polls on White and Non-white Employed Americans Regarding their Satisfactions with their Work Roles**

Year	Percent Satisfied		Percent Dissatisfied		No Opinion	
	White	Non-white	White	Non-white	White	Non-white
1949	69	55	19	33	12	12
1963	90	54	7	33	3	13
1965	87	48	9	38	4	14
1966	87	69	8	18	5	13
1969	88	76	6	18	6	6
1971	83	68	9	21	8	11
1973	80	53	10	22	10	25

Source: "Job Satisfaction and Productivity," *Gallup Poll Index No. 94* (April, 1973). Reported in George Strauss, "Is there a blue-collar revolt against work?" in James O'Toole, *Work and Quality of Life: Resource Papers for Work in America* (Cambridge: MIT Press, 1974), p. 43.

Data from Canada reveals the same pattern of findings. In the "Work Ethic Survey" published by the Department of Manpower and Immigration in 1975, 82 percent of a sample of 1959 Canadians revealed that their jobs were at least "somewhat enjoyable." (Fifty percent reported that their jobs were "very enjoyable" and 32 percent reported that they were "somewhat enjoyable." However, it should be noted that nearly 34 percent of the sample were unemployed when they were surveyed.) In another survey of 6920 Canadians, 46 percent reported that they were "very satisfied" with their present job and 42 percent reported that they were "somewhat satisfied" for a total of 88 percent at least somewhat satisfied.[6]

Gallup Poll data taken among male Canadians in 1963 revealed that all the respondents in professional occupations were satisfied with their work role, 92 percent of the managers reported that they were satisfied, and 88 percent of both white-collar and blue-collar respondents indicated that they were satisfied with their role.[7]

At first glance, these findings are somewhat startling when seen in relation to strike behavior, on-line sabotage, and absenteeism. Personnel managers and apologists for industrial organizations frequently cite these findings to support their positions that the plight of the exploited employee has been over-dramatized. Even an American vice-president of the AFL-CIO stated in 1973 that there was an "invalid conclusion that today's generation of young workers is rejecting the world of work ... the real significance of studies showing that one worker in five finds fault with an aspect of his job is that 80 percent are satisfied."[8] This raises a perplexing question. Why, given the relatively high rates of absenteeism, high turnover rates and industrial sabotage, do workers respond as they have?

In 1965 Kornhauser reported that when a number of *different* questions about job satisfaction were asked of Detroit factory workers, 67 percent of the young and 73 percent of the middle-aged *skilled* workers reported that they were satisfied with their work. Among *ordinary semi-skilled* factory workers, 54 percent of the young and 66 percent of the middle-aged workers were satisfied, while among workers required to do *machine-paced repetitive work*, 23 percent of the young workers and 40 percent of the middle-aged workers reported that they were satisfied. (Young workers were between the ages of 20 and 29. Middle-aged workers were between 40 and 49 years old.)[9] These findings indicate that the type of job influences indices of satisfaction when questions tapping different aspects of the work role are asked, rather than just one question dealing with "satisfaction." Without additional probing questions, researchers and pollsters are in danger of confusing satisfaction, derived from coming to terms with limited options, with "happiness."[10] Further, while type of job makes a difference in responses, there is also a difference accounted for by age. Young workers tend to be more critical of their jobs than are middle-aged workers.

The fact that older workers are more likely to indicate that they are satisfied with their jobs suggests that those who had been dissatisfied had left for other jobs, or that, with age, workers came to accept the jobs they did have, to lower their expectations, and come to terms with circumstances they could not alter. They may not be particularly happy but they maintain a modicum of satisfaction—a satisfaction born of coming to terms with lost hopes. I shall have more to say about the implications of these findings later.

Importance Placed upon Working

A second area of research which has significance for interpreting how individuals view their work role indicates that workers at all occupational levels regard the idea of working—in distinction to their present jobs—as an important activity. The classic finding in this regard is that of Morse and Weiss in 1955.[11] In responding to the question whether or not they would continue working, even if they had inherited enough money to live comfortably without having to work, 80 percent of a national sample of 393 American male workers stated that they would continue, although the proportion declines with age. When asked if they would want to continue working in the job they *currently* held, 61 percent of those in "middle class" occupations said they would, while only 34 percent of those in "working class" occupations would continue in the same job. Among the farmers in the survey, 69 percent indicated that they would continue in their jobs. Clearly, the value placed upon working was very strong, but the commitment to the currently held job varied considerably.

The reason why the respondents would continue to work differed by occupational level. Those in "middle class" occupations were more likely to state that it was the rewards which came from interesting work and the feelings of accomplishment that would keep them working. "Working class" respondents, on the other hand, stated that working was a means to keep themselves occupied, to fill what otherwise might be empty time. Table 2 illustrates the pattern of these responses.

TABLE 2 **Reasons for Continuing Work.**

Occupational Group	Interest or Accomplishment	To keep Occupied	Other	N
Middle Class	44%	37%	19%	57
Working Class	10	71	19	144

More recent surveys tend to support the findings discovered by Morse and Weiss over twenty-five years ago.

In the Canadian survey cited earlier, 70 percent of the male respondents and 73 percent of the female respondents agreed at least "somewhat" or "strongly" that they work "more because I like to than because I have to."[13] Among the total sample, 56 percent disagreed "strongly" and 28 percent disagreed "somewhat" with the statement that "To me, work is a way to make money and I don't expect to get any special satisfaction or enjoyment from doing it."[14] Further, when asked to respond to the statement, "I would like to work a little while and then get by on Unemployment Insurance," 95 percent of the respondents in the Canadian Work Ethics survey disagreed.[15] In general, working is still highly valued, even though the reasons may differ somewhat by occupational level. Unfortunately, the Canadian study does not distinguish the responses by occupational level.

Commitment to Present Jobs

I have already cited research evidence that there is a difference between the commitment to working *per se* and satisfaction with present jobs. People appear to believe that work is an important experience, but many do not find their own particular work role to be satisfying. In a survey reported by Blauner in 1960 only 16 percent of American unskilled auto workers would choose the same job if they had a chance to make the decision again. In contrast, about 70 percent of the professionals would make the same choice.[16]

In the Canadian survey, 60 percent of the respondents indicated that they would "take (the) same job without hesitation" in answer to the question, "Knowing what you know now, if you had to decide all over again whether to take the job you now have, what would you decide?" But we do not know how this breaks down by type of job. When the question was posed free of all restrictions—"If you were free to go into any type of job you wanted what would your choice be?"—only 50 percent indicated that they would choose the same job.

It is apparent that many people would not remain in the same jobs if they had a chance to make a change. The commitment that they have depends on the type of work they do. Overall, the strongest predictor of an individual's attitude to his job is its status relative to other occupations. This social ranking, in turn, is highly correlated with the amount of control individuals can exercise within their jobs[17]

Rewards Desired from the Work Role

The fourth area of consistent research findings has to do with those attributes individuals desire most from their work roles. Respondents in the Canadian study mentioned "interesting work" most frequently—even more than wages.

This, in turn, was highly associated with statements indicating "an opportunity to develop special abilities," "being given a chance to do the things one does best," and "being given a lot of freedom in deciding how to do the work."[18]

Blumberg, in his survey of research on the effects of "job enlargement," reports that in nearly every study, workers have welcomed such changes if they believed that their actual control over the performance of their jobs would be increased.[19] He points out that the consistency of these research findings is rarely achieved in social research. "Actual control" is the crucial element. Merely increasing requirements does not increase satisfaction with the job. Indeed, it can have the opposite effect. Further it is also clear that individuals dislike total open-endedness. Administrators, engineers, and scientists appear to have greater dissatisfaction with their jobs when there is a high degree of role ambiguity.[20]

Psychological and Physical Reactions to the Demands of the Work Role

The fifth and final set of consistent research findings demonstrates a strong correlation between work requirements and psychological and physical health of workers. Research on physical health indicates that job factors are as good predictors of the state of health as are personal habits such as smoking, cholesterol intake, and degree of physical activity or are even better predictors of the state of health than personal habits.[21] The manner in which an individual comes to terms with his job demands is a crucial element in this regard. House argues that this is the important explanatory link in the relationship between job demands and states of health. For example, higher cholesterol counts have been found among those individuals who feel that they have not enough time to accomplish their work and who doubt their ability or suspect that they may fail. Positive social support can diminish these effects.[22]

How an individual comes to terms with the demands of his job also influences his standing on measures of *mental health*. Kornhauser's research remains a classic in this regard. His findings revealed that those factory workers in his Detroit sample who were performing repetitive machine-paced work are least likely to have a high degree of mental health according to his measures.[23] Only 10 percent of the young workers performing this type of work showed signs of being mentally healthy, while 26 percent of the older workers in this type of job revealed similar mental attributes. Those workers who had recently come from farms were least likely to have a high degree of mental health, regardless of the type of work that they did within the factory.

For those workers in skilled occupations within the factory, 58 percent of the younger ones scored high on mental health, while 56 percent of the older workers scored at this level. Among a different sample of white-collar workers, 75 percent of those classified as "younger" scored high on the mental health scales, while only 59 percent of the older workers had similar scores. The data on white-collar work suggests that early occupancy in white-collar occupations encourages expectations of higher achievements that will be met in time with disappointment.

Education level also influenced the findings on mental health. Those with relatively high education in high skill-level jobs had better mental health than those with low educational levels in low-skilled, repetitive jobs. ("High education" in this regard means high school graduation.) A slightly higher proportion of those in low-skilled, repetitive jobs who had relatively high educational levels had better mental health than those in similar jobs with low educational levels. Kornhauser believes that even though individuals at this skill level tend to have a low level of self-esteem and low satisfaction with life in general, those with higher education levels were able to derive some means to assimilate this in a manner which permitted them to maintain higher levels of personal morale and sociability. Further, good childhood experiences contributed to a better ability to cope, regardless of the nature of the job. Yet, overall, the more routine and repetitive the job, the lower the level of mental health.

A corollary to these findings are those of Kasl. He reports that individuals who find some attributes of their job with which to be satisfied have better mental health than those who have found nothing to encourage some degree of satisfaction. Such attributes are likely to be found by an individual when he perceives that there is no escaping his job.[24] However, this interpretation overlooks other factors. Mental health, as defined in these studies, seems to imply merely adjustment. The terms of adjustment may be quite severe. Hinkle reports that in a longitudinal study of women employees of Bell Telephone Company in the United States, those who were especially well adjusted to their work as measured by absences, company dispensary data, and psychiatrists' ratings tended to be "unmarried, led a routine, dull, withdrawn existence and refused to get involved with other people."[25] Whether the work that they did caused this syndrome or whether such individuals were first attracted to the work remains a moot point.

Meissner, in analyzing the effects of technical and social organization of the workplace, argued from his data on workers in a British Columbia lumber and planing mill, that the nature of the work role influenced social behavioral characteristics outside the work role. This was measured by the manner in which individuals used their leisure time. Individuals whose jobs were constrained by technologically induced requirements were less likely to engage in leisure time activities which require "planning, coordination, and purposeful action—activities typically associated with membership in voluntary associations"—than those whose jobs were not so constrained. But they were more likely to spend their leisure time in "sociable and expressive activities" with their friends and associates. Workers who were required to labor under socially isolating conditions, regardless of the technology, also spent less time in "organized and purpose-directed activities." In addition, they tended to spend their free time more frequently in socially isolated activities, such as fishing, etc., than those workers who carried out their tasks in more socially integrated work contexts.[26] Yet, since there are no data showing before and after effects of these job characteristics, it still remains unclear whether the nature of the work role is the cause of the use of leisure time, or whether some process of selection is operating here. (There may be some individuals who prefer working and using their leisure time alone.) Nevertheless, the correlation remains, and if such work experiences cannot be proved to be the cause, they certainly reinforce such syndromes. Descriptive case studies, such as Terkel's collection *Working*, are replete with expressions of exasperation by those locked into uninteresting work, even as they seek a justification for their entrapment.[27]

Implications of the Research

From this review of the research findings it seems clear that most people still uphold work as an important arena of experience. People tend to think that, ideally, the work role should be the means by which they can express their own abilities and develop their own potentialities, and that it should enable them to make some contributions to their own social world. It is the arena within which the values of freedom and equality are put to the test.

Of course, it may be the case that working is not inherently the only means to obtain these objectives, but in industrialized societies, by definition, the role of work has been the major means to accomplish these ends. Those activities which encompass "work" are vast, but what principally defines them is that they are activities by which individuals earn their livelihood. The subsidiary definitions attached to this are that the rewards of working, both economic and social, are indices of the worth of an individual.

Despite the fact that working continues to be the dominant testing arena for the values, the evolving systems of authority increasingly prevent individuals from acting upon them. The following quote from a worker in an automotive plant in southern Ontario illustrates this point:

> Oh it can drive you. It can really drive you after a while, especially with all the repetition. You're a robot. You're a number, "who are you? I don't know, I'm 3518." Getting written-up, getting into trouble is the only way you get recognition. A "pinkie" is an award - they still remember your badge-number and name. You gotta lead a wild-cat if you wanna be a foreman. Sabotage too, that helps break the monotony. Sure. How many guys in there are divorced because they are working there. It's a great place to become an alcoholic - 7 days a week, 12 hours a day. How greedy are you? Sure, I hit the sauce pretty bad for a while till the wife threatened divorce. But they treat it like a game. I would like an apprenticeship. I really want an apprenticeship bad. I love working with my hands. I put in for one—they had three openings. I figured that would be my college education, that's where it's at for me. But I didn't get it and I know why —it's my

union involvement. They make a game of it, when it's not really a game. It's people, human lives you're dealing with. These people aren't games. It's a corporate game. It's the corporation that counts and nothing else. Production is all they care about. Everything else—safety, quality, people—they couldn't give a shit. That frustrates me when I start thinking about that. I don't daydream anymore. I save that for when I go to bed at night—going hunting or what have you. Oh yeh, that's a real freedom. The last time I went up to the woods I told my wife before I went I might not come back and she knows I'm serious. Things are just moving entirely too fast. I guess that's the reason for escape. We are rushing . . . pushing buttons we're busting our ass to create new objects to save time so we can spend more time figuring out how to save more time. It's just out of control.[28]

What is interesting in this account is that the respondent regards work as an important activity, insofar as it is meaningful, utilizes his skills, and contributes directly to the general welfare of others. These are all attributes which require the practice of the values of freedom and equality. But he, like many workers, must settle for less, for extrinsic rather than intrinsic rewards, for income earned rather than for the actual activity of work itself. "People," writes Beynon, "develop a pretty accurate idea of their own life chances, of the odds they face and hopes that they can realistically entertain."[29] Note the comments of another southern Ontario worker, whose initial aspirations of work end in self-denigration:

I do like going to work. I do honestly like going to work where it's a job where I can say, you know, I'm gonna work on so and so. I'm gonna do this. I'm gonna eh . . . wire up a new panel. Maybe I'm lookin for an ideal situation, you know. Maybe it's being selfish. I don't know. But I'm looking for an ideal situation where I look forward to going to work. Whereas now there's no looking forward. I get up . . . like last night and eh . . . I just felt, you know, "Jesus Christ, I go in there." And as soon as I go in I've got a built-in animosity before I even start. The first person who upsets me is gonna get . . . the length of me tongue. I think the only way I'm gonna get it is to create somethin for meself. To do somethin for meself. Then I often wonder, "well, what would you be like if you employed say 4 electricians and one of them didn't turn in the work. What would you be like? Would you then turn around and slap down on one of them?" So there again, which way are you? You just circle.[30]

This leads to a second observation. Most individuals at all job levels prefer to be in occupations where they can exercise some creativity and control over the context of their work. From his review of case descriptions of work experience in Britain, Parker enumerates the factors creating work satisfaction and those causing dissatisfaction. Those factors which contribute to feelings of satisfaction are as follows: creating something, using skills, working wholeheartedly, using initiative and having responsibility, mixing with people, and working with people who know their job. Causes of dissatisfaction according to Parker's listing, are doing repetitive work, making only a small part of something, doing useless tasks, feeling insecure, and being too closely supervised.[31]

A third observation can be made from the account, as well as the surveys, that except for the most unchallenging work, individuals make an effort to find some aspect of their job which provides them with a degree of satisfaction or at least some means to adjust to their work experience. But this may be at the cost of a lowered self-esteem and lowered aspirations.[32]

Fourth, specific work roles are not necessarily the primary central life interest for many individuals, even though the value of working is upheld. The more repetitive and unchallenging the job, the less likely would workers choose it again if they had a second chance. In many of these cases, the family tends to take precedence in a person's priorities. Parker provides some evidence that individuals who work in service occupations which require direct contact with other persons as clients are more likely to regard their occupations as a central life interest than those engaged in "business occupations" which have little contact with individuals except in an instrumental manner.[33]

Fifth, the discrepancy between the dominant values and the rational systems of authority within the work setting takes its toll on mental and physical health. The research findings are consistent in indicating that the more routine the work, the poorer the general state of mental and physical health. Different occupations may be more conducive to certain health problems, but, overall, the more routine jobs are more likely to erode an individual's well-being.

It should be clear by now that even though most people view working as important for themselves and for others, there is little possibility for most of them to experience the value of freedom and equality within the work context. Organizations designed for efficient production do not permit the degree of personal control over work activities that is essential in acting upon these values. Workers are left with the responsibility for their own fates that these values imply, but they do not have the social means to express them. Thus, most workers remain in a double bind: not only are they relegated to the routine tasks of producing, but they must also carry the personal responsibility for remaining in these tasks. The continued threat of unemployment further reinforces this dilemma. Given these facts, the only way to make work tolerable is to maximize the income that can be attained, or to lower one's aspirations, or to do both. The following quote from Milton's research in the southern Ontario factory illustrates this point:

> It's not the place. It's not the place so much. It's the system that it runs under. I can't just ... I can't take the system. The system I just hate ... because them people in that place have the power to turn around to any one individual whether he be a gentle individual or whether he be a militant individual and turn around and actually ruin that guy's life by putting one thing on his record up in an office. Another firm phoning up and saying, "look what's this? "well it's so and so and so and so" and it's fabricated. You have got no defence against it. They don't treat people as they should treat people. They treat people as far as they're concerned as if they are minions. They are there to do their bidding. There's a way of running a business and thinking of humanitarian problems at

the same time. You don't run a business purely to get a dollar out of a guy and the next thing you know there's something wrong with his family and you say, "ah, he's got family problems. Fire him." I'll tell you my ideal, the idealism I have is to have so much money in the bank I wouldn't have to work. But if I'm gonna work, I'm gonna work for the best money. Every man's his own man now. Everyone is sort of . . . you survive by animal instinct again. You've got to turn around and start fighting again. And I don't like that. I don't wanna have to do that—not a man of my age. I did that when I was a kid.[34]

Goldthorpe, et al. found that British workers in the Vauxhall automobile plant in England sought work there for the express purpose of earning relatively high wages. This, in turn, permitted them to attain a better lifestyle outside the factory gates.[35] Chinoy, in his classic study of the automobile worker, cited the manner in which occupational aspirations of long-term workers become displaced to "achievements" in acquiring commodities.[36] A certain amount of psychological compensation may be "earned" by workers projecting their aspirations onto their children. Data gathered in the United States in 1969, in which 30 percent of employed fathers were categorized as "blue-collar" workers, were compared with the fact that 34 percent of first-year students in junior colleges and 26 percent of first-year students in four-year colleges were from blue-collar families.[37] If it is true that higher education remains the principal route of mobility, then these statistics indicate significant proportions of working-class families whose children provide a hope for the future. (However, at the very time when proportionally more individuals in both the United States and Canada are obtaining higher degrees, their value decreases since they are no longer scarce and subject to strong demand.)

The Dilemma of Work in Industrial Society: A Conceptual Consideration

Given the dilemmas experienced in the world of work, the question can well be raised whether of not work activity can continue to remain the central area of experience. Since there is evidence that many workers have already diminished the importance of their own work roles, the question is whether alternative contexts exist within which the principal values and authority systems can be made more consistent. Bennett Berger believes that there has been so much importance placed upon the role of work that there remains no "moral vocabulary" by which to entertain an alternative.[38] One can argue, for example, that greater importance should be placed upon participating as a citizen in the larger community, but this option is not likely to be pursued if there are no social rewards equal to those which have accompanied middle-class occupations. Without such alternatives, individuals can only pursue escapist activities or withdraw into private experiences.

If apologists for capitalism continue to stress the central importance of the work role, so do Marxists. Marxists continue to emphasize the importance of work because it is the keystone of their theoretical edifice. Through work the individual contributes to the rest of society and thereby realizes his own full potential. So insistent are Marxists on this point that, in their eyes, individuals who view work in instrumental terms evidence "false consciousness" and are "estranged" from their species being.[39] This creates its own paradox, for as P. D. Anthony points out, the greater the degree to which the importance of work is stressed, the greater is the attention directed toward "the dehumanizing characteristics which have always accompanied it."[40] This further reinforces its alienating features. Yet to deny its importance is to reduce the motivation to work. Capitalism can only maintain such motivation by a gloss of ideology which stresses the expression of individual freedom and equality, even while it is being delimited within the workplace. Marxism, on the other hand, invests the work role with those attributes by which individual and societal purposes are fused. The same industrial work roles may have to be carried out in both communist and capitalist societies, but the difference lies in the authority systems by which they are controlled. The resolution of the problem of alienation for the Marxist is to be found in systems of production which bring together individual and social welfare. What this means in practice, however, remains unclear. It can, in fact, be merely a guise for elitism.

As we have seen in Chapter 1 "alienation," as Marx used the term, is coupled with the idea of objectification. For Marx, it was first necessary for individuals to objectify their social creations in order to control them. In industrial capitalism, however, the modes of production have been objectified, but are under the control of only the capitalists or employers. Further, the control itself is founded on false grounds, since the benefits which the employers derive are in the form of money and commodities that are gained merely for themselves while serving an objectified system. In fact, the capitalists themselves are also alienated. Workers experience alienation most acutely since they are under the control of capitalists. The social forms, the authority systems, as systems, rule their lives. Their plight is made even more poignant by Marx when he maintains that this in turn reduces individuals to the level of instinct-driven animals. Thus, their estrangement from man-made institutions is complete.[41]

The solution to this dilemma rests with the end of capitalism, since there will be no single class of owners who benefit, albeit in an alienated manner, from the work of others. Work will be for the common good. It is important at this point to note that the argument rests upon the control of work activity rather than the content of work. Marx does not appear to advocate a return to craft-like activities. He rather asks that the motives for working, the control of work, its products and their use be for the good of everyone, for the larger society, rather than for a specific class of persons. This can only occur if the authority systems are changed.

But these objectives are extremely abstract, and, as the history of labor movements has shown, they are not likely to sustain a social movement for change. Many Marxists hope that the focus on more narrowly defined class identities, when tied to the more abstract principles of contradiction, will become the means to escape this dilemma. When this is translated into actual labor union practice, the thrust of this orientation has more often been diverted into a competition between labor and management for narrowly defined rewards of production, namely the distribution of surplus profits. This merely sustains the state of alienation for individual workers, since the issue of control in their worlds of work remains beyond their grasp.

It makes little difference if industrial organizations are managed by private interests, by the "state," by a "workers' party," or by "the people"; as long as control is centralized and authority is not held accountable to those who participate in the organization, the alienating features of the work role will remain.[42] When this is coupled with segmented work roles, the dependency of workers on the organization is increased, resulting in more frustration and acts of anarchic rebellion that are costly not only to the enterprise, but to workers as well. The Marxist hopes that the resulting tensions will work themselves out in class conflict and result in a new order. The more pessimistic Weberian views the process of rationalization and abstract justifications as mutually reinforcing, relieved only occasionally by charismatic outbursts. But these need not to be the only alternatives. There may be other options.

Models of Industrial Democracy

The growing discrepancy between the values of freedom and equality and dominant contemporary authority structures has resulted in a variety of experiments designed to overcome its effects. One solution is to focus on the immediate work environments of workers in what Abrahamsson has called "socio-technical participation." This involves the participation of workers in the design and control of the tasks which management wants accomplished. Workers can determine how the tasks are to be allocated and in what manner they are to be performed. The Volvo-Kalmar factory in Sweden introduced this model by taking workers off the assembly lines and forming them into assembly stations where they decided how automobile chassis and bodies were to be put together. The parts were individually transported to each of the stations. This removed the workers from the dictates of assembly lines, but the increased degree of control over their work process remained limited.[43] Satisfaction with their revised work roles was initially high, but it is doubtful whether this positive attitude can be sustained once the distinction between assembly line work and work in assembly stations is lost.

A second approach is to argue that the union structure should be the main vehicle by which workers can influence their work process. This model is based upon an adversary system in which it is assumed that centralization of control will occur regardless under what system— socialist or capitalist—work organizations are formed. What is required is a viable opposition to management in the same sense that democratic governments have opposition political parties. Should unions become directly involved in management, they would lose their role as a "loyal oppposition" and thus take the autocratic characteristics of an unfettered management. This model involves the assumption that the interests of workers and management are by definition irrevocably opposed, regardless of the justifying values within which authority is carried out. Therefore, workers can gain control over their work roles only through the pressure tactics employed by unions against management. But opposition does not necessarily guarantee a solution to the problem of alienation, nor, by definition, can it ever do so within this model. Workers are not to become part of management, but only members of an opposition group by which the centralization of control is presumably to be made less onerous. What is lacking, as Blumberg points out, is the question of accountability. As long as managers are not *directly* responsible to workers themselves, the stance of opposition can merely heighten rather than reduce the problem.[44] This is further reinforced if unions themselves are not ready to take on the responsibilities of management. Individual workers are thus left with only the security of union protection from management excesses. They are not permitted the right of control over their own work-related activities.

A third model of industrial democracy is one that is in existence in West Germany. It involves having representatives of workers sit on the decision-making bodies of the industrial enterprise. Like the second model, it assumes opposing interests between management and workers but has them represented in a model of "co-determination." This system began in the years immediately after the Second World War, in which workers' representatives were to serve as watchdogs of management in the steel and coal-mining industries. In these industries, and to a lesser extent, in other industries as well, workers are given a voice in management equal to that of shareholders on a supervisory board of the corporation, but there can be no interference with the actual practice of management.[45] In addition, "workers councils" also exist in most industries in West Germany. These are made up of workers' representatives and act as consultative bodies to management. They have been given a voice in personnel matters, including promotions, hiring, and layoffs. The difficulty with this model is that it is a very abstract structure in relation to the individual's own work experience. Of course grievances can be registered, and there is evidence that these have reduced organized unrest from strikes and lockouts, but there is no immediate evidence that the worker indeed has control over the work process and its ends.[46]

The clearest example of workers' personal involvement in every aspect and at every level of decision-making is in the kibbutz communities in Israel.

These are relatively successful models but there is continual reinforcement for individual involvement. The communities are mostly based on agricultural production, they are small and relatively isolated, there is a communal style of life throughout all daily activities, and the cohesion is reinforced by common religious commitments. But, as Jenkins points out, these benefits are lost to hired workers.[47] Further, when the kibbutz model has been attempted in industry, through the labor organization, the "histadrut," the effects have not been encouraging. This failure has occured both in companies where there is co-determination with management and in companies wholly owned by the labor organization. Organizational exigencies have seemingly doomed the success rate of this model because of the abstract nature of control.[48] In the applications of this model to industrial production, management has tended to become separate from individual workers, serving interests not directly related to them.

In Yugoslavia, both workers' councils and unions exist, with the councils exercising power over the unions and over the management of enterprises themselves. The council, an elected body, which has limits to the number of years any one member may serve on it, is responsible for all policies of the enterprise, including the right to elect and recall members of the management boards.[49] In contrast to the experience of other models, this seems to be relatively successful. But one may well ask whether this is because of a supportive social environment throughout communist Yugoslavia. Further to say that the Yugoslavian experience is "relatively successful" is not to say that it has been a total success. In many cases, workers' management has not worked at all; the director or the party or the union may have had control. But Blumberg, in surveying the evidence, argues that at least the formal structure and the ideology are conducive to genuine workers' control and it remains for workers to exercise it.[50] He argues that if the effects of rational industrial organizations are to narrow the vision of the worker, the workers' councils are a means to broaden it. It remains for the workers to exploit this opportunity. However, one would expect that with such a supportive social environment both within and outside the production enterprise, this particular model would be even more successful. The limited success of this approach suggests that if control, rather than the specific content of the work role, is the more crucial aspect of worker alienation, still less abstract models need to be put into effect.

Oakeshott, although admitting that the success rate of different models of industrial democracy is not very impressive, believes that viable models of industrial democracy can be developed to resolve the problem of worker alienation and dissatisfaction. After surveying the historical and comparative record of attempts at industrial democracy, he argues that the many disappointing results have been primarily due to the failure to recognize that management functions are still needed and that these require separate and unique skills. What labels are attached to management is of little consequence; what is crucial, however, is the accountability of management to workers. Models based on fundamental opposition between workers and management cannot possibly be successful, he argues, because opposition, by definition, prevents the possibility of workers being the referents for accountability. Oakeshott claims that a flow of authority from the bottom upwards is required. This means that control is exercised primarily on behalf of workers, not on behalf of ownership, especially as it typically exists—beyond the control of workers.[51]

Oakeshott cites the example of workers' cooperatives started in the Basque province of Spain, in Mondragon, in 1956. Among the different cooperatives that now exist are Spain's largest producer of refrigerators and one of Spain's foremost producers of machine tools.[52] What distinguishes these cooperatives from the Yugoslavian model is that each worker has a capital investment in the enterprise. Further, the management, while answerable to the workers, is as highly skilled and competitive as other management-oriented enterprises. Of further importance is the fact that the initiative for these enterprises came from the workers themselves rather than from some other vested interest group. Thus, there was no suspicion of manipulation. Finally, the cooperatives exist within a supportive social milieu.[53] This milieu is the Basque province, which has long been marked by an embattled ethnic minority, historically relegated to inferior economic and occupational positions. In a sense, these cooperatives are also a consequence of some social attributes that contribute to social movements.

Oakeshott believes that unless models of industrial democracy are constructed in Britain, the implacable opposition between labor and management can only lead to mutual destruction and the downfall of Britain's economy with dire consequences. He argues for cooperatives of participants who invest their time, labor, and money in common production endeavors. Management would be accountable to the participants in the organization, not to outside controllers. The question, of course, remains whether these authority structures can be installed in an age of huge multi-national corporations with highly efficient centralized control structures. Yet at the same time, unless the authority structures are changed to conform more to the actual exercise of the values of freedom and equality—contradictory though those two values may be—we can expect continued problems with labor unrest and workers' dissatisfactions. The human toll will also increase as the dulling tasks, devoid of any individual control, reduce the individual to a state of apathy that comes from dependency, relieved occasionally by outbursts of intense hostility.

In Canada, as in Britain, organized labor has traditionally opposed models of industrial democracy because of its traditional role of adversary to management, first as a result of its battles to gain recognition, then in its stance as a collective bargaining agent. Unfortunately, this has merely meant the gaining of concessions over the conditions and financial rewards of employment—not over its control. The paradox is that for the individual workers, control over the personally meaningful events is one of the attributes that they desire most.

Conclusions

While the definition of work might include any activities which are of value to others, most research has focused almost solely upon those activities involved in the production of goods and services. Further, most of the research assumes that the role of work is of major importance for individuals and that this goes beyond merely earning an income.

Both Marxist theorists and apologists for management continue to stress the importance of work: the former because they view work as the key role for the reproduction of social forms and because it is the most important link between the individual and society; the latter because of their need to maintain a committed labor force. What is ironic about this emphasis is that it continues while rationalization, the use of machine technology, and the centralization of authority not responsible to workers have all created such narrowly defined contexts of work itself that it is nearly impossible for *individuals* to continue to believe in its importance. This occurs not only in jobs related to manufacturing, but it can also be found in all other industrial sectors in both blue-collar and white-collar occupations.

Even at a management level, work roles are undergoing transformations that limit the scope within which individuals can experience a sense of control over their activities, even though managers do not suffer the same degree of economic insecurity as blue-collar workers. Kanter, in her study of behavior among management personnel in a corporation, points out that for most individuals in these jobs, there was a complete disengagement of the self from work roles. They saw their positions merely as way stations in their attempts to move upward. Those persons who were "winning" were concerned more with their mobility chances than with performing their jobs. Those who were "losing" were more disaffected with their jobs than they would have been had they never been promised the chance for mobility. The overall consequence was that there was little responsibility practised in their jobs, there was a low degree of commitment to their work, and a general orientation of cautious conservation influenced their decision.[54] In his summary of the accounts of Americans in a wide variety of occupations, Terkel suggests that the specter haunting most of these people is a fear of obsolescence—an obsolescence which follows the same logic as the planned obsolescence of commodities.[55]

I wish to suggest in this chapter that the pattern of change in the authority structure of production organizations makes it increasingly difficult to practise the values of freedom and equality within the work role. These values are implied in discussions dealing with "control." Given the nature of the evolution of organizations and technology, pronouncements that work should be "meaningful" are likely to remain just that—pronouncements.

It is perhaps significant that the most successful models of industrial democracy are those in which workers hold management accountable and participate at all levels of the authority structure. Meanwhile in western industrialized societies there is evidence that many workers have already diminished the importance of their work roles. This being the case, the question needs to be raised whether other social contexts can more adequately provide for the exercise of the dominant values. It may be that the brutalizing or numbing effects of the work role are in part a result of a lack of other contexts that carry an equal amount of moral "loading." If little social recognition is given to raising a family, participating in the community, refurbishing neighborhoods, or other "non-work" activities, the effects of routine work will remain that much more pervasive in an individual's life patterns.

Notes

1. Richard Osler, "The 'Days Off' That Cost Firms Billions a Year," *The Financial Post*, October 22, 1977, pp. 1 and 4. Osler reports absenteeism accounted for 12.7 days off per year for each worker. Eighty percent of the absences are accounted for by illnesses.

2. Adriano Tilgher, *Homo Faber: Work Through the Ages* (Chicago: Regnery, 1958).

3. Harold Wilensky, "The Uneven Distribution of Leisure: The Impact of Economic Growth on 'Free Time'," in *Work and Leisure*, ed. E. O. Smigel (New Haven, Conn.: College and University Press, 1963), pp. 107–145.

4. Bennett Berger, "The Sociology of Leisure," in Smigel, op. cit., p. 32.

5. Alexander Stewart and Robert M. Blackburn, "The Stability of Structural Inequality," *The Sociological Review*, Vol. 23, No. 3 (August, 1975), pp. 481–508. See also Frederick Herzberg et al., *Job Attitudes: Review of Research and Opinion* (Pittsburgh, Pa.: Psychological Service of Pittsburgh, 1957).

6. M. Burstien et al., *Canadian Work Values: Findings of a Work Ethic Survey and a Job Satisfaction Survey* (Ottawa: Department of Manpower and Immigration, 1975), pp. 25, 29.

7. Computed from Gallup Poll data reported in William A. Westley and Margaret W. Westley, *The Emerging Worker* (Montreal and London: McGill-Queen's University Press, 1971), p. 33.

8. "Blue-Collar Blues Overrated: Sociologists Misread Attitudes of Young Workers on Jobs," *AFL-CIO News*, January 27, 1973, p. 5.

9. Arthur Kornhauser, *Mental Health of the Industrial Worker* (New York: John Wiley, 1965).

10. Stewart and Blackburn, op. cit., pp. 500–503.

11. Nancy Morse and Robert Weiss, "The Function and Meaning of Work and the Job," in *American Sociological Review*, Vol. 20, No. 2 (April, 1955), pp. 191–198.

12. Ibid.

13. Burstien et al., op. cit., p. 19.

14. Ibid., p. 19.

15. Ibid., p. 22

16. Robert Blauner, "Work Satisfaction and Industrial Trends in Modern Society," in *Labor and Trade Unionism*, ed. Walter Galenson an S. M. Lipset (New York: John Wiley, 1960), pp. 339–360.

17. See Robert Blauner, *Alienation and Freedom* (Chicago and London: University of Chicago Press, 1964); Theodore Caplow, *The Sociology of Work* (New York: McGraw-Hill, 1954); John Goldthorpe et al., *The Affluent Worker in the Class Structure* (Cambridge: Cambridge University Press, 1969).

18. Burstien et al., op. cit., p. 29.

19. Paul Blumberg, *Industrial Democracy: The Sociology of Participation* (London: Constable, 1968), p. 123.

20. Bruce Margolis and William H. Kroes, "Work and the Health of Man," in *Work and Quality of Life: Resource Papers for "Work in America"*, ed. James O'Toole (Cambridge, Mass.: MIT Press, 1974), p. 141.

21. James S. House, "The Effects of Occupational Stress on Physical Health," in James O'Toole, op. cit., pp. 145-170.

22. Ibid., p. 155.

23. Kornhauser, op. cit., p. 14. Good mental health was defined by Kornhauser to be the "development and retention of goals that are neither too high nor low to permit realistic successful beliefs in one's self a worthy effective being . . . ."

24. Stanislav Kasl, "Work and Mental Health," in James O'Toole, op. cit., pp. 184–186.

25. L. E. Hinkle, Jr., "Physical Health, Mental Health and the Social Environment: Some Characteristics of Healthy and Unhealthy People," in *Recent Contributions of Biological and Psychosocial Investigations to Preventive Psychiatry*, ed. R. H. Ojemann (Iowa City: State University of Iowa, 1959), pp. 80–103. Cited in S. Kasl, op. cit., p. 179.

26. Martin Meissner, "The Long Arm of the Job," in *Industrial Relations*, Vol. 10, No. 3 (October, 1971), pp. 239–260. For an earlier formulation of the relationship between work and the use of leisure see Harold Wilensky, "Work, Careers, and Social Integration," *International Social Science Journal*, 12 (Fall, 1960), pp. 543–560.

27. Studs Terkel, *Working* (New York: Avon, 1972).

28. From the research data collected by Brian Milton, "Styles of Alienation: A Theoretical-Empirical Examination of the Marxian Theory in a Study of a Group of Canadian Factory Workers," Ph.D. Dissertation, University of Waterloo, Forthcoming.

29. Huw Beynon, *Working for Ford* (London: Allen Lane, Penguin Books, 1973), p. 113.

30. Milton, op. cit.

31. Stanley Parker, *The Future of Work and Leisure* (London: Granada, 1972), pp. 45–47. See also Ronald Fraser, ed., *Work: Twenty Personal Accounts* (Harmondsworth: Penguin, 1968).

32. William A. Faunce. *Problems of an Industrial Society* (New York: McGraw-Hill, 1968), pp. 90–95. Faunce relates the problem of self-esteem maintenance to alienation. See also Leonard Goodman, *Do the Poor Want to Work?* (Washington. D.C.: Brookings Institute, 1972), p. 112.

33. Parker, op. cit., pp. 68–71.

34. Milton, op. cit.

35. John H. Goldthorpe et al., *The Affluent Worker: Industrial Attitudes and Behaviour*, Vol. 1 (Cambridge University Press, 1969).

36. Eli Chinoy, *Automobile Workers and the American Dream* (Garden City, New York: Doubleday, 1955).

37. Robert Schrank and Susan Stein, "Yearning, Learning, and Status," in *Blue-Collar Workers: A Symposium on Middle America*, ed. Sar Levitan (New York: McGraw-Hill, 1971), pp. 318–341.

38. B. Berger, op. cit., p. 32.

39. This interpretation is derived from excerpts from Marx's *Economic and Philosophic Manuscripts of 1844*. See Robert Tucker, ed., *The Marx-Engels Reader* (New York: W. W. Norton Co., 1972), pp. 61–62.

40. P. D. Anthony, *The Ideology of Work* (London: Tavistock Publications, 1977), p. 145.

41. Daniel Bell points out that by the time Marx wrote *Capital*, "exploitation" replaced "alienation" as a key concept. Cited in J. A. Banks, *Marxist Sociology in Action* (London: Faber and Faber, 1970), p. 41. See also Shlomo Avineri, *The Social and Political Thought of Karl Marx* (London: Cambridge University Press, 1968), p. 106.

42. For an insight into the problem of non-accountability in Yugoslavia, see the interview with Yugoslav writer Mihajlo Mihajlov, "What Should Be Fought For," *The New York Review of Books*, Vol. XXVI, No. 2 (February 22, 1979), pp. 34–36. For a recent account of the ideological gloss developed for American managers, see Richard Sennett, "The Boss's New Clothes," Ibid., pp. 42–46.

43. Bengt Abrahamsson, *Bureaucracy or Participation: The Logic of Organization* (Beverly Hills, Calif.: Sage Publications, 1977), p. 190.

44. The adversary role of unions in Britain has been supported by Hugh Clegg. For a synopsis and critique of this position, see Paul Blumberg, op. cit., pp. 143–145.

45. David Jenkins, *Job Power: Blue and White Collar Democracy* (Baltimore, Maryland: Penguin Books, 1974), p. 117.

46. Ibid., pp. 121.–122.

47. Ibid., p. 86.

48. Ibid., pp. 86–91.

49. Blumberg, op. cit., p. 202.

50. Ibid., p. 217.

51. Robert Oakeshott, *The Case for Workers' Co-ops* (London: Routledge & Kegan Paul, 1978), pp. 27–28.

52. Ibid., p. 166.

53. Ibid., p. 243.

54. Rosabeth M. Kanter, *Men and Women of the Corporation* (New York: Basic Books, 1977), pp. 139, 163.

55. Terkel, op. cit., p. xxii.

chapter thirteen

Current Crises and Future Options

Introduction

In dealing with the processes of industrialization, I have attempted to examine the nature of the transformations that have taken place in the structure of the Canadian economy, in the development of production enterprises, in the labor movement and its organizations, and in the social contexts of the role of work. Along with these developments there have been widening discrepancies and shifts in the interpretations of the values of freedom and equality. In this final chapter, I want to examine some broad effects of these changes and suggest some problems that accompany them.

Industrial Capitalism and Supporting Values

There was a time in the seventeenth century when social philosophers believed that economic competition among individuals was a means of channelling off their socially destructive emotions. This interpretation was also applied to nations. For example, Montesquieu argued that international trade could eliminate wars of imperialism since mutual needs could be met through buying and selling. Further, the rational calculations that business enterprises came to require were believed to check the "passions" of influential elites and thus prevent them from acting in an arbitrary manner.[1] In tracing the intellectual traditions that have interpreted the relationship between man's nature and social cohesion, Hirschman discovered that what was once regarded in the medieval ages as the most base of "passions"—greed and avarice—when coupled with "reason" came to be the means by which social philosophers believed that individuals could realize their own ambitions while controlling other socially disruptive "passions," such as ambition, the lust of power, and sexual lust.[2] In his analysis of the intellectual transformations that converted gaining money from a base to an exalted activity, Hirschman points out that not only did Weber's Calvinist employ this change in attitude as a means to gain some assurance of his salvation, but political elites also welcomed such a change as a means to win some degree of peace from continual political upheaval and social strife.

This process continued, with elaborations, in the shift from mercantilism to industrial capitalism. The view that wealth could be created, and thus was infinite, gained a central place in justifying economic activity. The individualism of an earlier Calvinism was coupled with the values of freedom and equality and thereby enabled early entrepreneurs, commercial and industrial capitalists alike, to pursue the acquisition of wealth in good conscience. They were free of feudal mores that denigrated economic activity on one hand while requiring the wealthy to be responsible for the welfare of the poor. Thus, they could in good conscience recruit and control workers on the basis of narrowly defined, work-related criteria alone, while accumulating capital for their own investments. In addition, the stress upon equality held out the hope for future rewards to workers and justified to entrepreneurs their attempts to acquire the same social status as that of the established landed aristocracy.

The idea of creating wealth is linked to the principle of the marketplace in industrial capitalism. According to this principle, individuals, in pursuing their own private gains, will contribute to the benefit of everyone. (In form, this is not unlike the medieval European notion that if each individual were to seek honor and glory for himself, society as a whole would benefit.)[3] Adam Smith, who argued for the benefits of unfettered personal pursuit of economic gain, hedged his position by assuming that such actions would be guided and restrained by principles "derived from morals, custom, and education," and, if these were insufficient, legal restraints could be employed.[4]

While early industrial capitalists may not have been rigorous in the application of this code toward workers and those whom they defined as outside their community of interests, these were important elements that made possible the floating of loans, the establishment of terms of sale, and the expansion of production. Further, rational accounting systems could be devised, transfers of property could be facilitated, and stable legal systems could be promoted.[5]

In England, workers, cut off from their social ties by land enclosure acts and poor laws, came to be dependent upon this system. Forced to sell their labor-time rather than merely the products of their labor, they could be organized, with varying degrees of success, into rational components of the production systems. Yet what remained a basis for this rational organization was the assumption that individual efforts would contribute to the welfare of everyone, provided that there was a trust in those who occupied positions of authority. As we have seen, this proviso was the principal theme in the rhetoric of managerial ideologies. It was to be assumed that managers knew what was best for the organization, for the workers in their place of employment, and for society as a whole.

A similar and more recent assumption, it has been argued, was also incorporated in Keynes's approach to controlling the wild fluctuations of the economy.[6] In this formulation, the state modifies the rules of competition and limits the opportunities in the marketplace. However, this assumed that managers of the economy would put into effect a "higher morality." Keynes's thesis, resting upon an older paternalistic view of the English upper class, regarded directors of collective bodies—of enterprises and labor unions—as individuals who would, or at least should, maintain a similar orientation. But this cannot be assumed. When the values of freedom and equality are acted upon by a wider population—which franchise movements document—then the moral prerogatives of managers and directors are themselves under attack; managers and directors stand revealed as serving their own interests first, with the larger social interests only of subsidiary importance. It is perhaps significant to note that just as the rationality involved in commercial enterprise was thought to curtail the passions of non-commercial elites, so was rational management thought, at the turn of this century, to curb "the greed of the capitalists."[7]

What has developed then, especially in the context of the North American market, is that competition itself has supplanted any higher social morality; the values of freedom and equality have come to be focused only on the individual to the detriment of the larger society. Keynes's "directors" tend to act on behalf of their own vested interests rather than those of the larger society. Economic competition, once viewed as a constructive way to release the "baser" passions, is now being questioned. The "passions" in fact may have become *more destructive*, even though they are expressed in a more calculating and rational manner. The moral principles that were to have guided the course of competition have been replaced by the confrontation and bargaining for advantage of corporations and associations acting ostensibly on behalf of individuals but often themselves becoming competitive actors. Under these conditions, it is doubtful whether one can still defend the position that society is the net gainer—and hence individuals within it—of individual competition.

If these observations are correct, then the contemporary social and economic malaise in advanced industrialized capitalist societies can be viewed as a disjuncture between the earlier definitions of the justifying values and the consequences of competition, guided as it is by rational calculating actions, and incorporated in rational authority systems.[8]

On the Changing Consequences of Competition

Economic Competition and Rational Authority Systems

The system of open competition in the economic market may work quite well for a given society when actors in all stages of the production process and in the act of consumption are relatively equal in their competitive stance. The cost of goods and services will be held to the level at which they can be most efficiently produced in relation to demand. Individual wealth can be gained to the degree that more efficient means are found for the production of goods. As demand increases, everyone benefits, if the growth rate of the population does not exceed that of the economy and if the rewards from more efficient production are distributed throughout the population. Inequalities in wealth can be tolerated as long as economic growth continues. Individuals can become more wealthy in absolute terms, comparing their income or ownership of goods to an earlier, more impoverished time, if not in terms relative to others who are more affluent. To the degree that individual competition can be said to lift the population beyond the subsistence level of existence, the society as a whole can be said to benefit. Such activities contribute to the public good. That is to say, not only are private lives of individuals improved, but the *context* in which they live is also enhanced. Improved methods of transportation and communication contribute to the public good, as do improved nutrition and health standards and improved housing and clothing.

Yet the process of economic competition, once in place, does not stop. Competition for markets stimulates producers to employ more efficient methods of production. This in turn stimulates the trend toward greater rationalization in the organization of the forces of production. As we have seen, this implies a division of labor in which work roles are simplified and routinized, and machines take over the performance of an increasing number of tasks. Further, rationalization implies a drive to control uncertainties at all stages of the manufacture and sale of commodities. This is required not only for efficiencies of production, but also to provide assurances for returns on investments. Two processes then operate in a mutually reinforcing manner: *economic competition* for the manufacture and sale of goods, and *rationalization*, which is the means by which economic competition is made more efficient. The values of freedom and equality provide the justification for the economic activity, while rational authority systems are the means by which it is carried out.

When unequal advantages emerge as a result of the concentration of economic power, the advantages to be gained for the few are heightened while those for many become less. In response to such inequalities, government bodies have created legislation, supervisory bodies, and government corporations. These are designed to preserve the competitive characteristics of the economy and thus curtail the effects of unequal economic power. Governments in Canada operate at two levels in their controls. They monitor the behavior of industrial, utility, and financial corporations and they also watch over the labor union movement. There are also protective regulations designed for individuals. These include minimum wage laws, unemployment insurance, and regulations governing health standards on the job and so on.

In effect, governments have sought to maintain growth rates of the Canadian economy by ensuring that conditions are preserved to foster competition among enterprises and individuals. However, in pursuing these ends, the process of rationalization is also reinforced, as governments themselves seek more efficient means to carry out their functions.

Formal rational organizations can be viewed both as one of the consequences of economic competition and as one of its corollary processes. We have seen in Chapter 12 how rationality, when applied to the industrial enterprise, imposes its own social realities upon individual actors. The work experience is constantly subject to routinization and segmentation at the very time when ideological spokesmen for both management and labor emphasize the importance of work. Within the work organizations rational authority structures encourage competition for increased rewards, whether in the form of wages or promotions. Personal evaluations themselves are based upon rational criteria. With respect to collective bargaining, the adversary system in Canada further intensifies competition through the efforts of unions to achieve increased rewards through rational means.

The dual effects of economic competition and rationality also influence individuals' lives outside the work organization. Their lives must be organized so that they are coordinated with the work world. This further fosters a rational orientation as individuals must calculate the costs and benefits of choices of action for given amounts of available time. One consequence is an increased demand for services that can be performed more efficiently outside the home. These include the more mundane services provided by city governments, such as street cleaning and road repair, garbage removal, and police protection, as well as services offered by private sources, such as child-care, laundry cleaning, food services, and counselling services of all types.

If it is true that economic expansion has also been accompanied by a proliferation of rational authority systems, then the question can be raised whether or not the benefits continue to flow to *both* individual actors and the public good. One could argue that the question is premature in the case of Canada since there remains considerable potential for continued economic expansion. Yet, the degree of concentration of Canada's industrial sectors and the proliferation of rational government controls suggests that the question is not ill-timed. The point I wish to argue is that, given the values of freedom and equality that predated the process of industrialization in Western Europe, the constraints imposed by rationalization foster an increased concern by individuals for their own welfare rather than the welfare of the public; in fact, such privatization of experience is becoming detrimental to the public welfare. (This suggests that such effects of rational authority structures are less severe where planned or command economies are imposed upon societies in which security and subsequently inequality had previously been the dominant justifying values. Socialist political economies which employ widespread rational authority systems appear to be more successful when they follow hard on the heels of feudal-like, or colonial social systems.) One way to understand the manner in which this transformation has occurred is to examine more closely the aggregate effects of the pursuits of individuals to increase their own personal welfare.

The Competition for "Positional Goods"

As wealth for the majority of a population increases, the satisfaction to be derived from any given commodity becomes less a function of the commodity itself and more a consequence of the conditions for its use. This introduces a set of problems in what Hirsch calls the market for "positional goods." These problems hinge upon the question of whether the conditions for the use of commodities can be created with the same degree of ease as the commodities themselves. If they cannot, then the self-oriented expressions of the values of freedom and equality, reinforced by rational authority structures, cannot be sustained since the attainment of these conditions by some must be at the expense of limiting them for others.

Hirsch approaches this problem by arguing that within the economies of western industrialized societies, two types of markets have developed. The first is oriented toward the attainment of wealth that is created and thus can be expanded. He notes that from the beginning of industrial capitalism in the western economies until about the First World War, the market principle of individuals seeking to maximize their own wealth contributed not only to their own welfare but also to the public good. The "unseen hand" of Adam Smith's marketplace appeared to be a beneficent principle.

The second market is one in which there is competition for "positional wealth." Hirsch means the term "positions" to represent competition for the desirable conditions by which commodities can be used. As the wealth in material commodities increases, there is also increased pressure to acquire more desirable "positions." This, however, exacts costs upon the public good. If everyone in an apartment block has acquired a sophisticated stereophonic sound system, individual enjoyment is contingent upon whether or not others are using their systems at the same time. Thus, a personal acquisition takes on public consequences. The only way a person can be assured that he will be able to enjoy his sound system at a volume level of his own choosing without interruption is for him to be able to rent an apartment with totally sound-proof walls or to live in a single dwelling unit. If everyone seeks these conditions, then the costs for the use of this particular commodity are bid up. Those who cannot afford these extra costs must live in an environment of reduced public good, even while acquiring an increase in personal material wealth. Or to put this in other terms, optimal conditions for use become more scarce as greater material wealth deteriorates the general conditions for use.[9]

Hirsch's definition of the market for positional wealth, expressed in more general terms, is that it is wealth which involves "all aspects of goods, services, work positions and other social relationships that are either (1) scarce in some absolute or socially imposed sense, or (2) subject to congestion or crowding through more extensive use."[10] Although Hirsch does not spell out the implications of this definition, it would seem to entail absolute and socially defined limits of space and time, and the socially defined limits of power, status, and what constitutes intrinsic satisfactions.

With regards to space and time, not only is space required to enjoy commodities, but time must also be available for such satisfactions. For the affluent urban dweller, a vacation home in the country may be desirable, but to ensure satisfaction from it, he must not have neighbors who live too close to him and he must have the time to enjoy his possession. As more individuals become affluent enough to seek these conditions, the conditions themselves increase in price since they are limited in supply. Of course, individuals may accept less favorable conditions—cottages crowded among small lots—but even these increase in price with increased demand. Individuals may then seek more secluded areas further away from the city, but this increases the costs in time, space, and transportation.

Related to the limits of time and space in the "positional market" are the limits to the achievement of desirable occupations. As we have seen, the work role is still held to be of prominent importance for individuals in industrialized society, but it is a role that is expected to provide intrinsic satisfactions as well as desirable social status. Further, those occupational roles which offer high social status are almost invariably roles which offer higher income, which in turn puts individual incumbents into more favorable positions in competing for the conditions of time and space.

Like material wealth, the number of occupational positions increase during the early stages of economic development.[11] This in turn stimulates occupational mobility. The benefits of both markets are more easily attainable during this time. However, the relative growth rate in the number of *favored* positions tends to decline with industrialization, even though more positions may be created. (The additional positions are a function of more segmentalized organizational roles.) This heightens the competition for more favorable positions, and in the process, raises the costs for individual applicants in attaining those attributes which employers or professions most highly desire. If the costs were commensurate with the overall social rewards (i.e., if the allocation of occupational positions matched relative qualifications), then there would be net benefits for everyone. But in fact, while the number of qualified persons increases, employers are in a position to raise requirements for applicants to all occupational positions. This means that the value of these qualifications for any one person *decreases* relative to the number of other individuals who have also acquired them. The value of a university degree decreases as the proportion of the population which has attained the degree increases. If a degree is a prerequisite for employment, employers in effect use the university as a screening device, passing off the costs for recruitment on to the public, government-supported sector. Meanwhile, university graduates will hardly be happy with organizational roles that are subject to greater routinization. The consequence can be greater unrest within these organizations.

The positional market, whether it is in terms of obtaining greater time and space, or power and intrinsic satisfactions in the world of work, operates, beyond a given point, on a "zero-sum" principle: to maintain positional advantages, others must be kept from attaining them. One can enjoy stereophonic equipment only if others living nearby do not play their equipment at the same time. One can enjoy isolated rural surroundings only if others are not seeking the same enjoyment. One can best utilize a university degree only if there are relatively few others who have one.

As costs for positional goods increase through increased demand and decreased supply, competitors must increase the efficiency by which they can gain and maintain desirable conditions. This contributes to the development of special services. For example, experts may be hired to advise candidates on how to present themselves for job interviews. Special training sessions in interpersonal relations may be undertaken to ensure success on the job. These extra services may be interpreted as components of an expanding economy if they are viewed as additive functions. But the overall contributions to the "public good" is doubtful. Hirsh points out that less tangible social costs may be involved in attaining and maintaining desirable conditions. For example, the person who attains a high occupational position may lose the social benefits of a stable neighborhood community. He may find it necessary to bid for commercial services which were formerly an integral part of non-economic social relationships.[12]

One can construct the following caricature to illustrate the point: an individual may, in order to preserve his position, hire an expert to choose a gift for his spouse, rely on another for vacation plans, entrust his child to still another to educate him in social skills which themselves may be viewed as marketable, hire a catering service to provide dinner for "friends" who themselves may be evaluated in terms of one's positional advantages, subscribe to a news summarizing service in order to carry on an "intelligent" conversation, and work out a salary scheme in payment for each family member's contributions to housework if one has not hired a maid. Finally, he may hire an analyst in lieu of lost social support from friends. But the process does not stop with this particular individual. It raises the stakes for other individuals who seek the same objectives since, presumably, they too must engage many of these services in order to attain a desirable "position."

Competition and the Consequences for Freedom and Equality

The paradox involved in the competition for positional wealth is that as more people gain the prerequisites to attain it, more can be demanded of them. If too many persons attain the positions, then the positions become devalued since their value depends upon scarcity. As more individuals buy automobiles, the satisfaction of driving a car decreases as traffic jams become more frequent and taxes increase to pay for highways. As proportionately more individuals acquire university degrees, the value of those degrees tends to decline, while employers can demand them as a prerequisite for jobs that formerly did not require them. The costs for everyone are increased as the few bid up the prices for desirable positions.

This has severe effects upon "losers," as more is demanded of everyone merely to stay in the running. More material is required for the poor as those with more wealth bid up the costs of positional advantages. As more importance comes to be placed upon higher educational requirements, even as the value of the degree declines, more individuals can ill afford *not* to continue their schooling. As the use of automobiles has increased, the quality of public transportation services has tended to decrease thus requiring more persons to depend upon the car. Shopping in nearby small grocery stores becomes curtailed as shopping centers are able to offer cheaper goods to those who can afford transportation costs and cold storage space for large stocks of foodstuffs. The positional advantages of a significant proportion of the population, in terms of space, time, and power, make the costs of losing more severe. This is because of the greater costs extracted from the public good, which everyone must pay for.

The failure to take into account the public costs, particularly as they are expressed in competition for positions, is reflected in the remedial programs that emphasize consumption, growth, and expanding employment. The aggregate statistics used to measure the welfare of the economy rest upon a summation of individual acts, not upon total benefits. An increase in the proportion of the population who owns cars, stereophonic equipment, and television sets may indicate an aggregate measure of economic growth, but it does not measure the costs of traffic congestion on super-highways which in turn disrupt neighborhoods, and it does not account for the social costs of the disruption of individual privacy from unwanted sounds. A more dramatic example can be drawn from the hidden costs of physical pollution—a more common theme among those concerned with the public good. A polluting steel mill may reveal economic benefits as hardware services are required to preserve houses from its corrosive effects, as sales increase for laundry detergents, and as health services increase. Yet nobody could argue that the social welfare of the inhabitants is thereby increased. What an individual enterprise may gain does not necessarily contribute to the public good.

The competition for material goods and the competition for positions is mutually reinforcing. Increased material wealth increases the demand for more favorable positions. But more favorable positions, in turn, require more material wealth as supply becomes limited and costs increase. The problem is that while the enactment of the values of freedom and equality may have been appropriate in gaining material wealth, their role as justifying values becomes suspect when applied to competition for position. Yet the competition continues.

Formal Rationality and the Constriction of Values

In his thesis on the influence and continued development of "formal rationality," Weber argued that in its pure form formal rationality is without "substantive" content. It represents, in effect, an approach in which the actor selects an end and those means which are most efficient and effective to achieve it. While early propositions regarding freedom and equality provided the moral justification for this approach to the world, rationality has, in turn, brought about an increased narrowing of the expression of these values.

Consider the effects of the rational authority structure. The ideological expressions of managers of industrial enterprises may stress the values of freedom and equality in an effort to recruit individuals into work organizations, but the continued elaboration of rational forms of organization through the use of machine technology and the segmentation and routinization of work roles do not support these values. As a consequence, their expression has been modified. Equality, for example, can mean the encouragement to compete for the scarce rewards of higher paying jobs rather than an equal distribution of those rewards. It can mean the encouragement of competition for positions without ensuring that the "starting points" for individuals are equal. Freedom can serve more to justify the irresponsibility of those who control capital than to preserve civil rights.

Routinization and segmentation limit the experiential world of the individual and consequently restrict the means by which his own acts are seen to contribute to the consequences of the larger organization. Or, to put it another way, the connections between an individual act and its social consequences become highly diffuse. Thus, the primary reference point for assessing actions becomes increasingly the individual actor and less the collectivity. For example, *The Economist* reported that in a study of the consequences of corporate take-overs and diversification in Great Britain, the aims of managers were served in expanding their empires, but shareholders and employees suffered "positive harm."[13] The isolation of their own roles even within the organizations reinforced the managers' own self-serving aims to the detriment of other constituencies. The embezzlement of large sums of money through computers in large financial companies has increased. But those who have been convicted frequently argue that theft from a corporation is not the same as theft from a person. The same rationale has been used for shoplifting in supermarkets. The point is that rationalized forms of behavior, whether in the work organization or in the supermarket, act as barriers in the relationship between an individual's own personal act and the public consequences. Indeed, for the individual there may well be no connection. There are no community interests to honor, only abstract rules and regulations; this appears to be true for many individuals whatever their position may be in the organization, or whatever their relationship to it.

Government policies have not alleviated these problems. The policies that have been enacted in order to control the problems of the economy tend to merely shift individualized competition from the economic to the political sector as different individuals and interest groups seek to maximize their rewards by anticipating government decisions and the effects of the policies. Rational pursuits for self-defined ends obscure the consequences for society as a whole. The satisfaction of the interests of particular social units, whether individuals, enterprises, or specific governments, does not necessarily add up to a more desirable social existence for everyone. Further, the shift from competition in the economic sector to increasing involvement in the political sector means the competition for "goods" that are even more limited—namely, power and influence. Because these are relatively fixed "resources," competition is likely to become more disruptive to the interrelationships among groups representing the vested interests of individuals.

Still, it must be pointed out that it is not at all clear at what point encouraging competition for private gains detracts from, rather than contributes to, the public good. As Hirsch poses the question, at what point are business enterprises to shift from competing among themselves to cooperating with government anti-monopolistic laws? If individuals are to maximize their own rewards when does this detract from the public good? At what point do the actions of labor unions detract from rather than contribute to the public good? At what point are corporations to be concerned with the national interest if they are also to maximize their profits?[14] If one actor, individual, enterprise, or labor union, does decide to act in behalf of the public good, what guarantee is there that others will act in a similar way?

It can be argued that governments and the law should provide this guarantee, since these are designed to protect the public good. However, these external controls can also be used for private advantage. To the extent that they are used, they raise social costs. Insurance claims can be filed for staged accidents. Injunctions can be invoked against workers to prevent a strike. There are cases in the United States where suits have been filed against schools for failing to properly educate a student and one individual filed a suit against his parents claiming that they were remiss in their parental responsibilities. There are, in addition, malpractice suits brought against doctors, and the invariable suits filed against airline companies whenever there is an accident. If the claims are decided to be legitimate, social costs increase both in terms of financial costs and in terms of further weakening the bonds of social trust.

In the absence of values that tie an individual's actions to their social consequences, laws are obeyed not because of one's commitment to their intended purpose, but because the discovery of their violation may be personally more costly. Of course, from the individual actor's point of view, if there are no rewards for acting on behalf of the public good, there is no point for him to act in any other terms.[15] Thus, self-oriented behavior is again reinforced. This suggests that if there is a problem of alienation, it is not so much because the work role has failed to provide "intrinsic meaning." Rather, it is because rational authority systems obscure the means by which the individual can relate his own activities to the larger society.

Sennett, in his provocative work *The Fall of Public Man*, provides another variation on this theme. He argues that as a result of the traumas accompanying the transition from late feudalism to nineteenth century industrialization, individuals who had the means, attempted to shield themselves "from the shocks of an economic order which neither victims nor victors understood."[16] For the emerging bourgeoisie, the family became a refuge from a seemingly chaotic world. It became idealized as a context in which "order, authority, and security" could reign. But with such an interpretation, it also became a "moral yardstick by which to measure the public realm."[17] The resulting severe judgments of public life as morally inferior tended to lead to a loss of will to influence it, and this in turn led to further retreat into the private world.

This orientation toward the private world has not ended. Currently, individuals who do participate in the public realm, such as politicians, for example, often are judged by their personal attributes rather than by the public effects of their actions. (Members of the news media are well aware that their stories will have greater interest to their audience if they provide revelations of the personal habits of public actors rather than merely an analysis of the implications of their public acts.)

If Sennett's interpretations are correct, then this orientation represents a highly self-centered definition of the values of freedom and equality. It is perhaps no accident that there is now considerable interest in new religions and quasi-religious movements which attempt to help the individual to cope more effectively with a complicated world. These movements are, to use Gouldner's terms, "person constituting," designed to placate feelings of inadequacy by bridging the gap between the behavioral restrictions of rationalized authority systems and the personalized promises of the values of freedom and equality.

I have dwelt primarily on the social limits to individual competition and the role of rational authority systems in perpetuating this competition, even while the costs imposed upon the public good are increased. More dramatic and more frequently cited consequences are the effects upon the physical environment—also a public good. However, these issues have been given an exhaustive treatment by others: hence, there is little to be added here. But they further reinforce and amplify the problem.[18]

To return to an economic expression of these problems, one may note that if the Canadian economy cannot expand at a sufficient rate, given the self-oriented nature of competition, conflict will likely intensify. Such conflict will increasingly take on political overtones as different groups maneuver for greater control. In the past, we have been able to avoid confronting the issues of poverty, of the rampant power of large corporations, of unemployment, and of inflation by arguing that economic growth will minimize these problems. But when the rate of growth declines, these problems stand out in bold relief; the older modes of expressing the values of freedom and equality are no longer appropriate. The utilitarian approach advocating the greatest good for the greatest number is no longer adequate when this is expressed as a summing up of individual goods. The public costs must also be taken into account. In the long run, the continued association of increasing material wealth with social welfare is not likely to be sustained. This does not mean that economic growth must be stopped. It does suggest, however, that the larger social consequences must be taken into account, especially as these pertain to the unequal distribution of "positional" wealth, whether in Canadian society or in the economy of the world.

If, in fact, there are limits to growth, then there must be a changed expression of values toward social responsibility and the creation and preservation of the public good. This might suggest, for example, an ethic that would argue that the aspirations of those in better positions are justified only if they are part of a scheme which improves the position of the least advantaged.[19] Such a formulation allows for the incentives of those with more talents or abilities to achieve demanding positions, but the extrinsic rewards provided by these positions are held in check by the effects upon those less advantaged. The problem of course, is that where there are large numbers of persons who are not subject to the social constraints of perhaps a typical community, there is no compelling reason why *each* person should adhere to this principle. In most cases, one person's action will not have much effect on the multitude. Further, even where there are effects, segmented rules serve to obscure knowledge of them. It becomes obvious that if the public good is to be served, the systems of authority will have to be changed, and the interpretations of the values of freedom and equality will have to be modified.

It would of course be inappropriate to argue for a return to authority systems based on arbitrary personal rule. These are even more potentially destructive than rational, formal systems of authority. But one can hope for increased participation in decision-making. Such involvement may lengthen the time required for making decisions but this delay is justified, for the *process* of making decisions is every bit as much a part of personal and public welfare as are the consequences of the decisions.

In the introduction to this book, I noted that the image of the world as a source of unlimited wealth may have to be revised. It is possible that the free-floating competitive style of western industrial man will be just an interlude in history. He may once again have to come to terms with the fact that wealth is at some point limited, that its implications are not restricted to merely the production and consumption of commodities, and that in any event it is a mistake to assume that the mere pursuit of *more* personal wealth will automatically contribute to the public good. When social positions are implicated, the problems of inequity can no longer be tolerated if the values of freedom and equality, contradictory though they may be, are to serve the public good while contributing to the welfare of the individual.

Notes

1. Albert O. Hirschman, *The Passions and the Interests* (Princeton: Princeton University Press, 1977), pp. 80–85.
2. Ibid., p. 41.
3. Ibid., p. 10.
4. From Adam Smith, *Theory of Moral Sentiments*, cited in Fred Hirsch, *Social Limits to Growth* (Cambridge: Harvard University Press, 1976), p. 137.
5. Harold L. Wilensky and Charles N. Lebeaux, *Industrial Society and Social Welfare* (New York: The Free Press, 1965), p. 44.
6. Fred Hirsch, *Social Limits to Growth* (Cambridge, Mass.: Twentieth Century Fund, 1976), pp. 124–125.
7. Rosabeth Moss Kanter, *Men and Women of the Corporation* (New York: Basic Books, 1977), p. 21.

8. See also Daniel Bell, *The Cultural Contradictions of Capitalism* (New York: Basic Books, 1976), p. 15. Bell argues that the "principles of the economic realm and those of the culture now lead people in contrary directions."

9. Hirsch, op. cit., p. 7.

10. Ibid., p. 27.

11. See Frank Parkin, *Class, Inequality and Political Order* (St. Albans: Paladin, 1973).

12. Hirsch, op. cit., pp. 84–94. See also Robert L. Heilbroner, *Business Civilization in Decline* (New York: W. W. Norton, 1976), p. 65.

13. This study, carried out by Gerald Newbould and George Luffman is reported in *The Economist*, May 27, 1978, p. 104.

14. Hirsch, op. cit., p. 131.

15. Ibid., p. 134.

16. Richard Sennett, *The Fall of Public Man* (New York: Vintage Books, 1978), pp. 19–24.

17. Ibid.

18. See for example Robert L. Heilbroner, *An Inquiry into the Human Prospect* (New York: W. W. Norton, 1974).

19. John Rawls, *A Theory of Justice* (Cambridge: Harvard University Press, 1976), p. 75.

Bibliography

I. THEORETICAL PERSPECTIVES: Societal Change

Althusser, Louis. *For Marx*, trans. B. Brewster. New York: Pantheon, 1969.

Aron, Raymond. *Main Currents in Sociological Thought*, 2 vols. New York: Basic Books, 1967.

Ash, Robert. *Social Movements in America*. Chicago: Markham Publishing Co., 1972.

Avineri, Shlomo. *The Social and Political Thought of Karl Marx*. London: Cambridge University Press, 1968.

Balinky, Alexander. *Marx's Economics: Origins and Development*. Lexington, Mass.: D. C. Heath, 1970.

Banks, J. A. *Marxist Sociology in Action*. London: Faber and Faber, 1970.

Bell, Daniel. *Marxian Socialism in the United States*. Princeton: Princeton University Press, 1967.

Bendix, Reinhard. *Max Weber. An Intellectual Portrait*. Garden City, N.Y.: Doubleday and Company, 1962.

Berger, Peter, and Thomas Luckmann. *The Social Construction of Reality*. Garden City, N.Y.: Doubleday, 1966.

Birnbaum, Norman. "Conflicting Interpretations of the Rise of Capitalism: Marx and Weber." *British Journal of Sociology*, Vol. 4, No. 2 (June, 1953) 125-141.

Bottomore, T. B., and M. Rubel, eds. *Karl Marx: Selected Writings in Sociology and Social Philosophy*. New York: McGraw-Hill, 1964.

Brinton, Crane. *The Anatomy of Revolution*. New York: Vintage Books, 1965.

Buckley, Walter. *Sociology and Modern Systems Theory*. Englewood Cliffs, N.J.: Prentice Hall, 1967.

Durkheim, Emile. *The Rules of Sociological Method*. New York: The Free Press, 1964.

Eisenstadt, S.N., ed. *The Protestant Ethnic and Modernization, A Comparative View*. New York: Basic Books, 1968.

Etzioni, Amitai, and Eva Etzioni, eds. *Social Change: Sources, Patterns and Consequences*. New York: Basic Books, 1964.

Etzioni, Amitai. *Studies in Social Change*. New York: Holt, Rinehart and Winston, 1966.

Gerth, H. H., and C. Wright Mills, eds. *From Max Weber: Essays in Sociology*. New York: Oxford University Press, 1958.

Giddens, Anthony. *Capitalism and Modern Social Theory*. Cambridge: University of Cambridge Press, 1971.

Giddens, Anthony. *New Rules of Sociological Method*. London: Hutchinson, 1976.

Glucksmann, Miriam. *Structuralist Analysis in Contemporary Social Thought: A Comparison of the Theories of Claude Lévi-Strauss and Louis Althusser*. London: Routledge and Kegan Paul, 1974.

Heilbroner, Robert. *The Worldly Philosophers*, 3rd ed. New York: Simon and Schuster, 1967.

Hirschman, Albert O. *The Passions and the Interests.* Princeton: Princeton University Press, 1977.

Joachim, Israel. *Alienation: From Marx to Modern Sociology.* Boston: Allyn and Bacon, 1971.

Johnson, Chalmers. *Revolutionary Change.* Boston: Little, Brown, 1966.

Kuhn, T.S. *The Structure of Scientific Revolutions.* Chicago: University of Chicago Press, 1968.

Marcuse, Herbert. *One Dimensional Man.* Boston: Beacon Press, 1964.

Marx, Karl. *Critique of Hegel's Philosophy of Right,* ed. Joseph O'Malley and trans. by Annette Jolin and Joseph O'Malley. London: Cambridge at the University Press, 1970.

Marx, Karl. *The Eighteenth Brumaire of Louis Bonaparte.* New York: International Publishers, 1963.

Marx, Karl. *Capital: A Critical Analysis of Capitalist Production,* 3 vols., trans. Samuel Moore and Edward Aveling. Moscow: Progress Publishers, n.d.

Marx, Karl. *A Contribution to the Critique of Political Economy.* Moscow: Progress Publishers, 1970.

Mark, Karl, and Frederick Engels. *The German Ideology.* New York: International Publishers, 1967.

Marx, Karl. *The Poverty of Philosophy.* New York: International Publishers, 1963.

Merton, Robert. *Social Theory and Social Structure,* rev. ed. Glencoe, Ill.: The Free Press, 1957.

Myrdal, Gunnar. "A Methodological Note on the Principle of Cumulation," *An American Dilemma.* New York: Harper and Row, 1944.

Nadel, S. F. *The Theory of Social Structure.* New York: Free Press, 1957.

Rawls, John. *A Theory of Justice.* Cambridge: Harvard University Press, 1976.

Runciman, W.G. "What is Structuralism?" *British Journal of Sociology,* Vol. 20, No. 2 (1969) 253-265.

Sennett, Richard. *The Fall of Public Man.* New York: Vintage Books, 1978.

Smelser, Neil. *Theory of Collective Behavior.* New York: Free Press of Glencoe, 1962.

Smelser, Neil. *Essays in Sociological Explanation.* Englewood Cliffs, N.J.: Prentice-Hall, 1968.

Timasheff, Nicholas. *Sociological Theory: Its Nature and Growth,* 3rd ed. New York: Random House, 1967.

Tucker, Robert C. *The Marxian Revolutionary Idea.* New York: W. W. Norton & Co., 1969.

Tucker, Robert, ed. *The Marx-Engels Reader.* New York: W. W. Norton Co., 1972.

Turner, Ralph H., and Lewis M. Killian. *Collective Behavior.* Englewood Cliffs, N.J.: Prentice-Hall, Inc., 1957.

Weber, Max. *Economy and Society,* ed. Guenther Roth and Claus Wittich. New York: Bedminster Press, 1968.

Weber, Max. *The Methodology of the Social Sciences,* trans. and ed. by Edward Shils and Henry A. Finch. New York: The Free Press, 1949.

Weber, Max. *The Protestant Ethic and the Spirit of Capitalism.* New York: Charles Scribners and Sons, 1958.

White, Morton. "The Decline and Fall of the Absolute," in *The Age of Analysis,* in *The Great Ages of Western Philosophy,* Vol. 2. Boston: Houghton Mifflin, 1962.

Zeitlin, Irving M. *Capitalism and Imperialism: An Introduction to Neo-Marxian Concepts.* Chicago: Markham, 1972.

II. THEORETICAL PERSPECTIVES: The Individual Actor

Bruner, Jerome S. *On Knowing: Essays for the Left Hand.* New York: Atheneum, 1973.

Faunce, William A. *Problems of an Industrial Society.* New York: McGraw-Hill, 1968.

Gruber, Howard E., and J. Jacques Vonèche, eds. *The Essential Piaget.* London: Routledge and Kegan Paul, 1977.

Piaget, Jean. *The Construction of Reality in the Child,* trans. Margaret Cook. New York: Basic Books, 1954.

Piaget, Jean. *Genetic Epistemology,* trans. Eleanor Duckworth. New York: Columbia University Press, 1970.

Piaget, Jean. *Structuralism,* trans. and ed. Chaninah Maschler. New York: Basic Books, 1970.

Remmling, Gunter W. *Road to Suspicion.* New York: Appleton-Century-Crofts, 1967.

Schutz, Alfred. "The Problem of Social Reality," in *Collected Papers,* Vol. 1, ed. Maurice Natanson. The Hague: Martinus Nijhoff, 1967.

Winch, Peter. *The Idea of a Social Science.* London: Routledge and Kegan Paul, 1958.

III. ECONOMIC DEVELOPMENT

Baran, Paul, and Paul Sewwzy. *Monopoly Capital.* New York: Monthly Review Press, 1966.

Bell, Daniel. *The Coming of the Post Industrial Society.* New York: Basic Books, 1973.

Bell, Daniel. *The Cultural Contradictions of Capitalism.* New York: Basic Books, 1976.

Bell, Daniel. *The End of Ideology.* New York: The Free Press of Glencoe, 1960.

Bendix, Reinhard. *Nation-Building and Citizenship,* Garden City, N.Y.: Doubleday/Anchor, 1969.

Bendix, Reinhard. *Embattled Reason.* New York: Oxford University Press, 1970.

Bertram, G. W. "Economic Growth in Canadian History, 1870-1915: The Staple Model and the Take-Off Hypothesis." *Canadian Journal of Economic and Political Science,* Vol. XXIX, No. 2 (May, 1963) 162-184.

Birnbaum, Norman. *The Crisis of Industrial Society.* Toronto: Oxford University Press, 1969.

Britton, John N. H., and James M. Gilmour. *The Weakest Link: A Technological Perspective on Canadian Industrial Underdevelopment.* Ottawa: Science Council of Canada, 1978.

Buckley, Kenneth. "The Role of Staple Industries in Canada's Economic Development." *Journal of Economic History,* Vol. XVIII (December, 1958) 439-450.

Caves, Richard, and Richard Holton. *The Canadian Economy: Prospect and Retrospect.* Cambridge: Harvard University Press, 1961.

Caves, Richard. *American Industry: Structure, Conduct, Performance,* 2nd ed. Englewood Cliffs, N.J.: Prentice-Hall, 1967.

Clough, Shepard B. *European Economic History: The Economic Development of Western Civilization.* Toronto: McGraw-Hill, 1968.

Creighton, Donald. *Towards the Discovery of Canada.* Toronto: Macmillan of Canada, 1972.

Dales, John. "Some Historical and Theoretical Comment on Canada's National Policy." *Queen's Quarterly*, Vol. 71, No. 3 (Autumn, 1964) 297-316.

Dobbs, Maurice. *Studies in the Development of Capitalism*. New York: New World, 1968.

Dobbs, Maurice. *Capitalism, Development and Planning*. New York: New World, 1970.

Drummond, Ian. *The Canadian Economy: Structure and Development*, rev. ed. Georgetown, Ontario: Irwin-Dorsey, 1972.

Easterbrooke, W. T., and Hugh C. J. Aitken. *Canadian Economic History*. Toronto: Macmillan, 1956.

Easterbrooke, W. T., and M. H. Watkins. *Approaches to Canadian Economic History*. Toronto: McClelland and Stewart Limited, 1967.

Eisenstadt, S. N., ed. *Readings in Social Evolution and Development*. Toronto: Pergamon Press, 1970.

Etzioni, Amitai, and Eva Etzioni, eds. *Social Change: Sources, Patterns and Consequences*. New York: Basic Books, 1964.

Fayerweather, John. *Foreign Investment in Canada: Prospects for National Policy*. Toronto: Oxford University Press, 1974.

Firestone, O. J. *Canada's Economic Development: 1867-1953*. London: Bowes and Bowes, 1958.

Firestone, O. J. *Industry and Education: A Century of Canadian Development*. Ottawa: University of Ottawa Press, 1969.

Fournier, Pierre. *The Quebec Establishment*. Montreal: Black Rose Books, 1976.

Gerschenkron, Alexander. *Economic Backwardness in Historical Perspective: A Book of Essays*. Cambridge: Belknap-Harvard, 1962.

Glenday, D., H. Guindon, and A. Turowetz, eds. *Modernization and the Canadian State*. Toronto: Macmillan, 1978.

Grant, George. *Technology and Empire*. Toronto: Anansi, 1969.

Guindon, Hubert. "The Modernization of Quebec and the Legitimacy of the Federal State," in *Modernization and the Canadian State*, eds. D. Glenday, H. Guindon and A. Turowetz. Toronto: Macmillan, 1978.

Habakkuk, H. J. *American and British Technology in the Nineteeth Century*. London: Cambridge University Press, 1967.

Heilbroner, Robert L. *An Inquiry into the Human Prospect*. New York: W. W. Norton, 1974.

Heilbroner, Robert L. *Business Civilization in Decline*. New York: W. W. Norton, 1976.

Heilbroner, Robert L. *The Limits of American Capitalism*. New York: Harper and Row, 1965.

Hobsbawm, Eric. *The Age of Capital, 1848-1875*, London: Weidenfeld and Nicolson, 1975.

Innis, H. A. *Essays in Canadian Economic History*. Toronto: University of Toronto Press, 1956.

Innis, Harold A. *The Cod Fisheries: The History of an International Economy*. Toronto: Ryerson Press, 1946.

Innis, Harold A. *The Fur Trade in Canada*. Toronto, University of Toronto Press, 1970.

Johnson, Harry. *The Canadian Quandary: Economic Problems and Policies*. Toronto: McGraw-Hill, 1963.

Jones, Richard. *Community in Crisis*. Toronto: McClelland and Stewart, 1972.

Kerr, Clark, John T. Dunlop, Frederick H. Harbison, and Charles A. Myers. *Industrialism and Industrial Man*. Cambridge, Mass.: Harvard University Press, 1960.

Kuznets, Simon. *Modern Economic Growth*. New Haven: Yale University Press, 1966.

Kuznets, Simon. *Six Lectures on Economic Growth*. Glencoe, Ill.: Free Press, 1959.

Landes, David S. *The Unbound Prometheus*. Cambridge: Cambridge University Press, 1969.

Mackintosh, W. A. "Economic Factors in Canadian History." *Canadian Historical Review* (March, 1923) 12–25.

Mackintosh, W. A. "Some Aspects of a Pioneer Economy." *Canadian Journal of Economics and Political Science* (November, 1936) 457–463.

MacMillan, David S., ed. *Canadian Business History: Selected Studies 1497–1971*. Toronto: McClelland and Stewart, 1972.

Mantoux, Paul. *The Industrial Revolution in the Eighteenth Century*. New York: Harper Torchbooks, 1961.

Manufacturing Industries of Canada: Type of Organization and Size of Establishment. Ottawa: Statistics Canada, May, 1970.

McNaught, Kenneth. *The Pelican History of Canada*. Harmondsworth: Penguin Books, 1969.

McRoberts, K. H. "Contrasts in French-Canadian Nationalism: The Impact of Industrialization upon the Electoral Role of French-Canadian Nationalism 1934–44." M. A. Thesis, University of Chicago, 1966.

Milner, Sheilagh, and Henry Milner. *The Decolonization of Quebec*. Toronto: McClelland and Stewart, Carleton Contemporaries, 1973.

Moore, Barrington, Jr. *Social Origins of Dictatorship and Democracy*. Boston: Beacon Press, 1966.

Myers, Gustavus. *A History of Canadian Wealth*. Toronto: James Lewis and Samuel, 1972.

Naylor, Tom. *The History of Canadian Business: 1867–1914*, 2 vols. Toronto: James Lorimer, 1975.

Pal, I. D., ed. *Canadian Economic Issues*. Toronto: Macmillan, 1971.

Panitch, Leo, ed. *The Canadian State*. Toronto: University of Toronto Press, 1978.

Pentland, H. C. "The Development of a Capitalist Labour Market in Canada." *Canadian Journal of Economics and Political Science*, Vol. 25, No. 4 (November, 1959) 450–461.

Perry, L. *Galt, U.S.A.* Toronto: Maclean-Hunter, 1971.

Polanyi, Karl. *The Great Transformation*. New York: Farrar and Rinehart, 1944.

Porter, G., and R. Cuff, eds. *Enterprise and National Development*. Toronto: Hakkert, 1973.

Porter, John. *The Vertical Mosaic*. Toronto: University of Toronto Press, 1965.

Postgate, Dale, and Kenneth McRoberts. *Quebec: Social Change and Political Crisis*. Toronto: McClelland and Stewart, 1976.

"Preliminary Bulletin," *1975 Annual Census of Manufacturers*. Ottawa: Statistics Canada, 1977.

Raynauld, André. *The Canadian Economy*. Toronto: Macmillan, 1967.

Rioux, Marcel. *Quebec in Question*, trans. James Boake. Toronto: James Lewis and Samuel, 1971.

Rioux, M., and Y. Martin. *French-Canadian Society*. Toronto: McClelland and Stewart, 1964.

Robinson, Joan. *An Essay on Marxian Economics*, 2nd ed. London: Macmillan, 1966.

Rostow, W. W., ed. *The Economics of Take-Off into Sustained Growth*. New York: St. Martin's Press, 1965.

Rostow, W. W. *The Stages of Economic Growth: A Non-Communist Manifesto.* Cambridge: Cambridge University Press, 1960.

Royal Commission on Canada's Economic Prospect. *Final Report.* Ottawa: Queen's Printer, 1957.

Ryan, William F., S. J. *The Clergy and Economic Growth in Quebec 1896–1914.* Quebec: Les Presses de l'Université Laval, 1966.

Ryerson, Stanley B. *Unequal Union.* Toronto: Progress Books, 1973.

Schumpeter, Joseph A. *Capitalism, Socialism and Democracy,* 3rd ed. New York: Harper Torchbooks, 1962.

Science Council Committee on Industrial Policies. "Uncertain Prospects: Canadian Manufacturing Industry 1971–1977." Ottawa: Minister of Supply and Services, 1977.

Skeoch, Lawrence A., ed. *Restrictive Trade Practices in Canada: Selected Readings.* Toronto: McClelland and Stewart, 1966.

Sweezy, Paul M. *The Theory of Capitalist Development.* New York: Monthly Review Press, 1942.

Teeple, Gary, ed. *Capitalism and the National Question in Canada.* Toronto: University of Toronto Press, 1972.

Touraine, Alain. *The Post-Industrial Society.* London: Wildwood House, 1971.

Tucker, Gilbert N. *The Canadian Commercial Revolution: 1845–1851.* New Haven: Yale University Press, 1936 (Republished by McClelland and Stewart, Carleton Library Series, 1964).

Wade, Mason. *The French Canadians: 1760–1967,* 2 vols. Toronto: Macmillan, 1968.

Watkins, M. W. "A Staple Theory of Economic Growth." *Canadian Journal of Economics and Political Science,* Vol. XXIX, No. 2 (May, 1963) 141–158.

Wilensky, Harold L., and Charles N. Lebeaux. *Industrial Society and Social Welfare.* New York: The Free Press, 1965.

IV. AUTHORITY STRUCTURES, THEORIES OF MANAGEMENT, AND THE INDUSTRIAL ENTERPRISE

Abrahamsson, Bengt. *Bureaucracy or Participation: The Logic of Organization.* Beverly Hills, Calif.: Sage Publications, 1977.

Albrow, Martin. *Bureaucracy.* London: Macmillan, 1970.

Argyris, Chris. *Intervention Theory and Method: A Behavioral View.* Reading, Mass.: Addison-Wesley, 1970.

Argyris, Chris. "Personality and Organization Theory Revisited." *Administrative Science Quarterly* (June, 1973) 141–167.

Ashley, C. A., and R. G. H. Smails. *Canadian Crown Corporations.* Toronto: Macmillan of Canada, 1965.

Avineri, Shlomo. *Hegel's Theory of the Modern State.* Cambridge: Cambridge University Press, 1972.

Bain, Joe S. *Barriers to New Competition: Their Character and Consequence in Manufacturing Industries,* 5th ed. Cambridge, Mass.: Harvard University Press, 1971.

Bain, Joe S. *International Differences in Industrial Structure: Eight Nations in the 1950's.* New Haven: Yale University Press, 1966.

Barnard, Chester. *The Functions of the Executive.* Cambridge: Harvard University Press, 1938.

Blake, Robert, and Jane Mouton. *The Managerial Grid*. Houston: Gulf Publishing Company, 1964.

Blau, Peter. *The Dynamics of Bureaucracy*, 2nd ed. Chicago: University of Chicago Press, 1963.

Blumberg, Paul. *Industrial Democracy: The Sociology of Participation*. London: Constable, 1968.

Bourgault, Pierre L. *Innovation and the Structure of Canadian Industry*, Background Study for the Science Council of Canada, Special Study No. 23. Ottawa: Information Canada, 1972.

Braverman, Harry. *Labor and Monopoly Capital*. New York: Monthly Review Press, 1974.

Burns, Tom, and G. N. Stalker. *The Management of Innovation*. London: Tavistock Publications, 1959.

Carey, Alex. "The Hawthorne Studies: A Radical Criticism." *The American Sociological Review*, Vol. 32, No. 2 (June, 1967) 403–416.

Caves, Richard. *American Industry: Structure, Conduct, Performance*, 2nd ed. Englewood Cliffs, N.J.: Prentice-Hall, 1967.

Chandler, Alfred D., Jr. *Strategy and Structure: Chapters in the History of the Industrial Enterprise*. Cambridge, Mass.: The MIT Press, 1962.

Chandler, Alfred D., Jr., and Fritz Redlich. "Recent Developments in American Business Administration and their Conceptulization." *Business History Review*, Vol. 35, No. 1 (Spring, 1961) 1–27.

A Citizen's Guide to the Gray Report. Toronto: Canadian Forum, 1977.

Clark, S. D. *The Canadian Manufacturers' Association*. Toronto: University of Toronto Press, 1939.

Clement, Wallace. *The Canadian Corporate Elite: An Analysis of Economic Power*. Toronto: McClelland and Stewart/Carleton Library, 1975.

Clement, Wallace. *Continental Corporate Power; Economic Linkages between Canada and the United States*. Toronto: McClelland and Stewart, 1971.

Cordell, Arthur J. *The Multinational Firm, Foreign Direct Investment, and Canadian Science Policy*. Ottawa: Information Canada, 1971.

Crozier, Michel. *The Bureaucratic Phemonenon*. Chicago: University of Chicago Press, 1964.

Cyert, Richard, and James March. "A Behavioral Theory of Organizational Objectives," *Organizations: Structure and Behavior*, ed. J. Litterer. New York: Wiley, 1969.

Department of Consumer and Corporate Affairs. *Concentration in the Manufacturing Industries of Canada*. Ottawa, 1971.

Deverell, John, and the Latin American Working Group. *Falconbridge: Portrait of a Canadian Mining Multinational*. Toronto: James Lorimer, 1975.

Dill, William R. "Business Organizations," *Handbook of Organizations*, ed. James G. March. Chicago: Rand McNally, 1965.

Foreign Owned Subsidiaries in Canada: A Report on Operations and Financing by the Larger Subsidiary Companies for the Period 1964–67. Ottawa: Queen's Printer, 1970.

Foreign Ownership and the Structure of Canadian Industry. Task Force on the Structure of Canadian Industry. *Report*. Ottawa: Queen's Printer, 1968.

Gaspel, Howard. "An Approach to a Theory of the Firm in Industrial Relations." *British Journal of Industrial Relations*, Vol. XI, No. 2 (July, 1973) 211–228.

Gulick, Luther. "Notes on the Theory of Organization," *Papers on the Science of Administration*, ed. Luther Gulick and L. Urwick. New York: Institute of Public Administration, 1937.

Hacker, Andrew, ed. *The Corporation Take-Over*. New York: Harper and Row, 1964.

Hymer, Stephen. "The Multinational Corporation and the Law of Uneven Development," *Economics and World Order: From 1970's–1990's* ed. J. N. Bhagwati. New York: Macmillan, 1972.

Kanter, Rosabeth Moss. *Men and Women of the Corporation*. New York. Basic Books, 1977.

Levitt, Kari. *Silent Surrender: The Multinational Corporation in Canada*. Toronto: Macmillan of Canada, 1970.

Lickert, R. *New Patterns of Management*. New York: McGraw-Hill, 1961.

Litvak, I. A., and C. J. Maule. "The Multinational Corporation: Some Economic and Political-Legal Implications." *Journal of World Trade Law*, Vol. 5, No. 6 (November-December, 1971) 631–643.

Lucas, Rex. *Minetown, Milltown, Railtown*. Toronto: University of Toronto Press, 1971.

March, James G., and Herbert Simon. *Organizations*. New York: John Wiley, 1958.

Marchak, Patricia. *In Whose Interests: An Essay on Multinational Corporations in a Canadian Context*. Toronto: McClelland and Stewart, 1979.

Maslow, Abraham. *Motivation and Personality*. New York: Harper, 1954.

Mathias, Philip. *Forced Growth: 5 Studies of Government Involvement in the Development of Canada*. Toronto: James Lewis & Samuel, 1971.

McGregor, Douglas. *The Human Side of Enterprise*. New York: McGraw-Hill, 1960.

Mouzelis, Nicos P. *Organization and Bureaucracy*. Chicago: Aldine, 1967.

Neufeld, E. P. *A Global Corporation: A History of the International Development of Massey-Ferguson Ltd*. Toronto: University of Toronto Press, 1969.

Oakeshott, Robert. *The Case for Workers' Co-Ops*. London: Routledge and Kegan Paul, 1978.

Pattison, J. C. *Financial Markets and Foreign Ownership*. Toronto: Ontario Economic Council, 1978.

Pratt, Larry. *The Tar Sands, Syncrude and the Politics of Oil*. Edmonton, Hurtig, 1976.

Reynolds, Lloyd G. *The Control of Competition in Canada*. Cambridge: Harvard University Press, 1940.

Roethlisberger, F. J., and William J. Dickson. *Management and the Worker*. Cambridge: Harvard University Press, 1939.

Rosenbluth, Gideon. *Concentration in Canadian Manufacturing Industries*: Princeton: Princeton University Press, 1957.

Rosenbluth, Gideon. "Concentration and Monopoly in the Canadian Economy," *Social Purpose for Canada*, ed. Michael Oliver. Toronto: University of Toronto Press, 1961.

Rosenbluth, Gideon, and H. G. Thorburn. "Canadian Anti-Combines Administration, 1952-1960." *Canadian Journal of Economics and Political Science*, Vol. XXVII, No. 4 (November, 1961) 498–508.

Safarian, A. E. *Foreign Ownership of Canadian Industry*. Toronto: McGraw-Hill Ryerson 1966.

Serrin, William. *The Company and the Union*. New York: Alfred Knopf, 1973.

Servan-Schreiber, Jean-Jacques. *The American Challenge*. Harmondsworth, England: Penguin Books Ltd., 1978.

Sheriff, Peta. "Sociology of Public Bureaucracies, 1965-1975." *Current Sociology*, Vol. 24, No. 2 (1976).

Silverman, David. *The Theory of Organisations*. London: Heinemann, 1970.

Simon, Herbert A. *Administrative Behavior*. New York: Macmillan, 1958.

Taylor, Frederick. *The Principles of Scientific Management*. New York: Harper and Brothers, 1911.

Tugendhat, Christopher. *The Multinationals*. Middlesex, Eng.: Penguin Books, 1973.

Vernon, Raymond. "Storm over the Multinationals: Problems and Prospects." *Foreign Affairs*, Vol. 55, No. 2 (January, 1977) 243-262.

White, Terrence H. "Worker Attitudes About Industrial Democracy." *The Canadian Personnel and Industrial Relations Journal*, Vol. 19, No. 4 (September, 1972) 39-42.

Wilkins, Mira. *The Emergence of Multinational Enterprise: American Business Abroad from the Colonial Era to 1914*. Cambridge, Mass.: Harvard University Press, 1970.

Wilkins, Mira. *The Maturing of Multinational Enterprise: American Business Abroad from 1914 to 1970*. Cambridge, Mass.: Harvard University Press, 1974.

Woodward, Joan. *Industrial Organization: Theory and Practice*. London: Oxford University Press, 1964.

V. THE ROLE OF IDEOLOGY

Anthony, P. D. *The Ideology of Work*. London: Tavistock Publications, 1977.

Apter, David, ed. *Ideology and Discontent*. New York: Free Press of Glencoe, 1964.

Ashford, Douglas E. *Ideology and Participation*. Beverly Hills: Sage Publications, 1972.

Bendix, Reinhard. *Work and Authority in Industry*. New York: Harper and Row, 1956.

Burke, Kenneth. *The Philosophy of Literary Form*. Baton Rouge: Louisiana State University Press, 1941.

Cohen, Anthony P. *The Management of Myths: The Politics of Legitimiation in a Newfoundland Community*. Manchester: Manchester University Press, 1975.

Drucker, H. M. *The Political Uses of Ideology*. London: Macmillan, 1974.

Gaudreau, Marie. *The Social Thought of French-Canada as Reflected in the Semaines Sociales de Canada*. Washington, D.C.: The Catholic University of America Press, 1946.

Geertz, Clifford. "Ideology as a Cultural System," *The Interpretation of Cultures*, ed. C. Geertz. New York: Basic Books, 1973; and *Ideology and Discontent*, ed. D. Apter. New York: Free Press of Glencoe, 1964.

Gouldner, Alvin. *The Dialectic of Ideology and Technology*. New York: Seabury Press, 1976.

Hargrove, Erwin C. "On Canadian and American Political Culture." *The Canadian Journal of Economics and Political Science*, Vol. XXXIII, No. 1 (February, 1967) 107-111.

Harris, Nigel. *Beliefs in Society: The Problem of Ideology*. London: C. A. Watts & Co., 1968.

Hoare, Quintin, and Geoffrey N. Smith, eds. and trans. *Selections from the Prison Notebooks of Antonio Gramsci*. London: Lawrence and Wishart, 1971.

Krupp, Sherman. *Pattern in Organization Analysis*. New York: Holt, Rinehart and Winston, 1961.

Lipset, S. M. *Agrarian Socialism*. Berkeley: University of California Press, 1950.

Mannheim, Karl. *Ideology and Utopia*. New York: Harcourt Brace/Harvest Books, 1936.

Marchak, Patricia M. *Ideological Perspectives on Canada*. Toronto: McGraw-Hill Ryerson, 1975.

Masters, Jane. "Canadian Labour Press Opinion, 1890-1914: A Study in Theoretical Radicalism and Practical Conservatism." M. A. Thesis, University of Western Ontario, 1969.

Penner, Norman. *The Canadian Left: A Critical Analysis*. Scarborough, Ont.: Prentice-Hall of Canada, 1977.

Percy, W. "Symbol, Consciousness and Intersubjectivity." *Journal of Philosophy*, Vol. 15 (1958) 631-641.

Rawin, John S. "The Polish Intelligentsia and the Socialist Order: Elements of Ideological Compatibility." *Political Science Quarterly*, Vol. LXXXII, No. 3 (September, 1968) 353-376.

Sapir, David J. "The Anatomy of Metaphor," *The Social Use of Metaphor*, ed. J. David Sapir and J. Christopher Crocker. Philadelphia: University of Pennsylvania Press, 1977.

Seider, Maynard S. "American Big Business Ideology: A Content Analysis of Executive Speeches." *American Sociological Review*, Vol. 39 (1974) 802-815.

Sennett, Richard. "The Boss's New Clothes." *The New York Review of Books*, Vol. XXVI, No. 2 (February 22, 1979) 34-36.

Simon, Herbert A. *Administrative Behavior*. New York: Macmillan, 1958.

Smucker, Joseph. "Ideology and Authority." *Canadian Journal of Sociology*, Vol. 2, No. 3 (1977) 263-282.

Smucker, Joseph. "Reformist Themes in the Canadian Labour Congress." *Sociological Focus*, Vol. 9, No. 2 (April, 1976) 158-173.

Sutton, Francis X., et al. *The American Business Creed*. New York: Shocken Books, 1962.

Taylor, Frederick W. *The Principles of Scientific Management*. New York: Harper and Brothers, 1911.

VI. CLASS CONSCIOUSNESS

Bendix, Reinhard, and Seymour M. Lipset. "Karl Marx Theory of Social Classes," *"Class Status and Power*, ed. Reinhard Bendix and Seymour M. Lipset. Glencoe: The Free Press, 1953.

Bulmer, Martin, ed. *Working Class Image of Society*. London and Boston: Routledge and Kegan Paul, 1975.

Chodas, Robert, and Nick Auf der Maur, eds. *Quebec: A Chronicle, 1968-1972*. Toronto: James Lewis and Samuel, 1972.

Cole, Robert. *Japanese Blue Collar: The Changing Tradition*. Berkeley: University of California Press, 1971.

Drache, Daniel, ed. *Quebec—Only the Beginning*. Toronto: New Press, 1972.

Egbert, Donald D., and S. Persons, eds. *Socialism and American Life*, Vol. 1. Princeton: Princeton University Press, 1952.

Giddens, Anthony. *The Class Structure of the Advanced Societies*. London: Hutchinson University Library, 1973.

Guindon, Hubert. "Social Unrest, Social Class and Quebec's Bureaucratic Revolution." *Queen's Quarterly*, Vol. 71, No. 2 (1964) 150-162.

Harrington, Michael. *Socialism*. New York: Bantam Books, 1973.

Leggett, J. C. *Class, Race, and Labor: Working Class Consciousness in Detroit.* New York: Oxford University Press, 1968.

Levitan, Sar, ed. *Blue Collar Workers: A Symposium on Middle America.* New York: McGraw-Hill, 1977.

Lockwood, David. "In Search of the Traditional Worker," *Working Class Images of Society,* ed. Martin Bulmer. London and Boston: Routledge and Kegan Paul, 1975.

Lukacs, Georg. *History and Class Consciousness.* London: Merlin Press, 1968.

Mann, Michael. *Consciousness and Action Among the Western Working Class.* London: Macmillan, 1973.

Mann, Michael. "The Social Cohesion of Liberal Democracy." *American Sociological Review,* Vol. 35, No. 3 (June, 1970) 423–439.

Marcus, Steven. *Engels, Manchester and the Working Class.* New York: Random House, 1974.

Marcuse, Herbert. "Repressive Tolerance," *A Critique of Pure Tolerance,* ed. Robert Wolff, Barrington Moore, Jr., and Herbert Marcuse. Boston: Beacon Press, 1968.

Parkin, Frank. *Class, Inequality and Political Order.* St. Albans: Paladin, 1973.

Pinard, Maurice. *The Rise of a Third Party: A Study in Crisis Politics.* Englewood Cliffs, N.J.: Prentice-Hall, 1971.

Quinn, Hubert. *The Union Nationale.* Toronto: University of Toronto Press, 1963.

Rinehart, James. "Affluence and the Embourgeoisement of the Working Class." *Social Problems,* Vol. 19, No. 2 (Fall, 1971) 149–162.

Sennett, Richard, and Jonathan Cobb. *The Hidden Injuries of Class.* New York: Alfred Knopf, 1972.

Stewart, Alexander, and Robert M. Blackburn. "The Stability of Structural Inequality." *The Sociological Review,* Vol. 23, No. 3 (August, 1975) 481–508.

Sullivan, Michael. "Sources and Varieties of Working Class Conservatism: The Working Class Conservative Debate Re-examined." M. A. Thesis, McGill University, 1978.

Westergaard, J. H. "Radical Class Consciousness: A Comment," *Working Class Image of Society,* ed. Martin Bulmer. London and Boston: Routledge and Kegan Paul, 1975.

VII. THE LABOR MOVEMENT

Abella, Irving M. *Nationalism, Communism and Canadian Labour: The CIO, The Communist Party, and the Canadian Congress of Labour 1935–1956.* Toronto: University of Toronto Press, 1973.

Allen, V. L. *Power in Trade Unions.* London: Longmans and Green, 1954.

Aronowitz, Stanley. *False Promises.* New York: McGraw-Hill, 1973.

Auf der Maur, Nick. "October 1971: Labour Comes to the Fore," *Quebec: A Chronicle, 1968–1972,* ed. Robert Chodas and Nick Auf der Maur. Toronto: James Lewis and Samuel, 1972.

Babcock, Robert. *Gompers in Canada: A Study in American Continentalism Before the First World War.* Toronto: University of Toronto Press, 1974.

Barnes, Samuel H. "The Evolution of Christian Trade Unionism in Quebec." *Industrial and Labor Relations Review,* Vol. 12, No. 4 (July, 1959) 568–581.

Beaucage, André. *An Outline of the Canadian Labour Relations System.* Ottawa: Labour Canada, 1976.

Bernard, Paul. *Structures et Pouvoirs de la Fédération des Travailleurs du Québec.* Ottawa: Queen's Printer, 1970.

Biljouw, Will van. "Industrial Diversity, Patterns of Organization and Strikes: An International Comparison." M. A. Thesis, Concordia University, 1978.

Brecher, Jeremy. *Strikes!* San Francisco: Straight Arrow Books, 1972.

Canada Department of Labour. *Union Growth in Canada, 1921–1967.* Ottawa: Information Canada, 1970.

Carrothers, A. W. R. *Collective Bargaining Law in Canada.* Toronto: Butterworths, 1965.

Corporations and Labour Unions Returns Act, Report for 1974 Part II—Labour Unions. Ottawa: Statistics Canada, 1976.

Crispo, John H. G. *International Unionism: A Study of Canadian-American Relations.* Toronto: McGraw-Hill, 1967.

Crispo, John H. G. *The Role of International Unionism in Canada.* Montreal: Private Planning Association of Canada, 1967.

Dion, Gérard. "The Trade Union in Quebec." *University of Toronto Quarterly,* Vol. 27, No. 3 (April, 1958) 369–385.

Estey, Martin. *The Unions: Structure, Development, and Management.* New York: Harcourt, Brace and World, 1967.

Flanders, A. *Trade Unions.* London: Hutchinson, 1968.

Finn, Ed. "The Struggle for Canadian Labour Autonomy." *The Labour Gazette* (November, 1970) 767–774.

Galenson, Walter, and S. M. Lipset. *Labour and Trade Unionism.* New York: John Wiley, 1960.

Hamilton, Richard. *Affluence and the French Worker in the Fourth Republic.* Princeton: Princeton University Press, 1967.

Hobsbawm, E. J. *Labouring Men: Studies in the History of Labour.* London: Weidenfeld & Nicolson, 1964.

Horowitz, Gad. *Canadian Labour in Politics.* Toronto: University of Toronto Press, 1968.

Hyman, Richard. *Strikes.* Glasgow: Fontana/Collins, 1972.

Ingham, Geoffrey K. *Strikes and Industrial Conflict: Britain and Scandinavia.* London: Macmillan, 1974.

Isbester, Fraser. "Quebec Labour in Perspective, 1949-1969," *Canadian Labour in Transition,* ed. Richard Ulric Miller and Fraser Isbester. Scarborough, Ontario: Prentice-Hall of Canada, 1971.

Jamieson, Stuart. *Industrial Relations in Canada,* 2nd ed. Toronto: Macmillan of Canada, 1973.

Jamieson, Stuart M. *Times of Trouble: Labour and Industrial Conflict in Canada, 1900–66.* Study No. 22. Ottawa: Task Force on Labour Relations, Information Canada, 1968.

Kinsley, Brian. "Strike Activity and the Industrial Relations System in Canada." Ph. D. Thesis, Carleton University, 1978.

Kovacs, Aranka E. *Readings in Canadian Labour Economics.* Toronto: McGraw-Hill, 1961.

Kwavnick, David. *Organized Labour and Pressure Politics.* Montreal: McGill-Queen's University Press, 1972.

Laxer, Robert. *Canada's Unions.* Toronto: James Lorimer, 1976.

Lester, Richard A. *Economics of Labor*, 2nd ed. New York: Macmillan, 1964.

Levison, Andrew. *Working Class Majority*. New York: Penguin Books, 1975.

Lipton, Charles. *The Trade Union Movement of Canada, 1827–1959*, 2nd ed. Montreal: Canadian Social Publications, Ltd., 1968.

Logan, H. A. *Trade Unions in Canada: Their Development and Functioning*. Toronto: Macmillan Co. of Canada, 1948.

McKenzie, Robert, and Alan Silver. *Angels in Marble*. London: Heinemann, 1968.

Miller, Ulric, and Fraser Isbester, eds. *Canadian Labour in Transition*. Scarborough, Ontario: Prentice-Hall of Canada, 1971.

Mitchell, Broadus. *Depression Decade: From the New Era to the New Deal, 1929–1941*. New York and Toronto: Rinehart and Co., 1948.

Nordlinger, Eric. *The Working Class Tories*. Berkeley: University of California Press, 1967.

Peitchinis, Stephen. *The Canadian Labour Market*. Toronto: Oxford University Press, 1975.

Perlman, Selig. *A Theory of the Labor Movement*. New York: Kelley, 1968.

Penner, Norman, ed. *Winnipeg 1919: The Strikers' Own History of the Winnipeg General Strike*. Toronto: James Lewis & Samuel, 1973.

Ritcher, Irving. *Political Purpose in Trade Unions*. London: George Allen and Unwin, 1973.

Robin, Martin. *Radical Politics and Canadian Labour, 1880–1930*. Kingston: Industrial Relations Centre, Queen's University, 1968.

Selznick, Philip. *Law, Society and Industrial Justice*. New York: Russell Sage, 1969.

Thompson. E. P. *The Making of the English Working Class*. London: Victor Gollancz Ltd., 1964.

Ware, Norman J. "The History of Labor Interaction," *Labor in Canadian-American Relations*, ed. H. A. Innis. Toronto: Ryerson Press, 1937.

Williams, Charles. "Canadian-American Trade Union Relations: A Study of the Development of Bi-national Unions." Ph.D. Thesis, Cornell University, 1964.

Woods, H. D., and Sylvia Ostry. *Labour Policy and Labour Economics in Canada*. Toronto: Macmillan, 1962.

VIII. THE EXPERIENCE OF WORKING

Berg, Ivar. "They Won't Work: The End of the Protestant Ethic and All That," *Work and Quality of Life*, ed. James O'Toole. Cambridge, Mass.: MIT Press, 1974.

Berger, Bennett. "The Sociology of Leisure," *Work and Leisure*, ed. Erwin O. Smigel. New Haven, Conn.: College and University Press, 1963.

Beynon, Huw. *Working for Ford*. London: Allen Lane/Penguin Books, 1973.

Blauner, Robert. *Alienation and Freedom*. Chicago and London: University of Chicago Press, 1964.

Blauner, Robert. "Work Satisfaction and Industrial Trends in Modern Society," *Labor and Trade Unionism*, ed. Walter Galenson and S. M. Lipset. New York: John Wiley, 1960.

Burstien, M., et al. *Canadian Work Values: Findings of a Work Ethic Survey and a Job Satisfaction Survey*. Ottawa: Department of Manpower and Immigration, 1975.

Caplow, Theodore. *The Sociology of Work*. New York: McGraw-Hill, 1954.

Chinoy, Eli. *Automobile Workers and the American Dream.* Garden City, New York: Doubleday, 1955.

Crozier, Michel. *The World of the Office Worker.* Chicago: University of Chicago Press, 1965.

de Grazia, Sebastian. *Of Time, Work, and Leisure.* Garden City, N.Y.: Doubleday, 1964.

Fraser, Ronald. *Work: Twenty Personal Accounts.* Harmondsworth: Penguin, 1968.

Friedmann, Georges. *The Anatomy of Work.* New York: Free Press of Glencoe, 1964.

Goldthorpe, John J., et al. *The Affluent Worker: Industrial Attitudes and Behaviour,* 3 vols. Cambridge: Cambridge University Press, 1969.

Goodman, Leonard. *Do the Poor Want to Work?* Washington, D.C.: Brookings Institute, 1972.

Haug, Marie, and Jacques Dofny, eds. *Work and Technology.* Beverly Hills, Calif.: Sage Publications, 1977.

Herzberg, Frederick, et al. *Job Attitudes: Review of Research and Opinion.* Pittsburgh, Pa.: Psychological Service of Pittsburgh, 1957.

Herzberg, Frederick. *Work and the Nature of Man.* Cleveland: World Publishing Co., 1966.

Kornhauser, Arthur. *Mental Health of the Industrial Worker.* New York: John Wiley, 1965.

Margolis, Bruce, and William H. Kroes. "Work and the Health of Man," *Work and Quality of Life: Resource Papers for "Work in America,"* ed. James O'Toole. Cambridge, Mass.: MIT Press, 1974.

Meissner, Martin. "The Long Arm of the Job." *Industrial Relations,* Vol. 10, No. 3 (October, 1971) 239–260.

Milton, Brian. "Styles of Alienation: A Theoretical-Empirical Examination of the Marxian Theory in a Study of a Group of Canadian Factory Workers." Ph.D. Thesis, University of Waterloo, Forthcoming.

Morse, Nancy, and Robert Weiss. "The Function and Meaning of Work and the Job." *American Sociological Review,* Vol. 20, No. 2 (April, 1955) 191–198.

O'Toole, James. *Work and Quality of Life: Resource Papers for "Work in America."* Cambridge, Mass.: MIT Press, 1974.

Parker, Stanley. *The Future of Work and Leisure.* London: Granada, 1972.

Rinehart, James W. *The Tyranny of Work.* Don Mills, Ont.: Longman Canada, 1975.

Smigel, Erwin O. *Work and Leisure.* New Haven, Conn.: College and University Press, 1963.

Terkel, Studs. *Working.* New York: Avon Books, 1972.

Tilgher, Adriano. *Homo Faber: Work Through the Ages.* Chicago: Regnery, 1958.

Westley, William A., and Margaret W. Westley. *The Emerging Worker.* Montreal and London: McGill-Queen's University Press, 1971.

White, Terrence H. "Production Workers and Perceptions of Intra-Organization Mobility." *Sociological Inquiry,* Vol. 44, No. 2 (1974) 121–129.

Wilensky, Harold. "The Uneven Distribution of Leisure: The Impact of Economic Growth on 'Free Time,' " in *Work and Leisure,* ed. Erwin O. Smigel. New Haven Conn.: College and University Press, 1963.

Wilensky, Harold. "Work, Careers, and Social Integration." *International Social Science Journal,* Vol. 12 (Fall, 1960) 543–560.

Index

Name Index

A

Abella, I.M., 200, 216n
Abrahamsson, B., 293, 300
Aitken, H.C.J., 68, 97n
Albrow, M., 146n
Alger, H.Jr., 2
Allen, V.L., 275n
Althusser, L., 56n, 267, 274n
Anthony, P.D., 292, 300n
Argyris, C., 142–143, 148n
Aron, R., 33, 40, 42n, 43n
Aronowitz, S., 274n, 275n
Ash, R., 214n
Ashford, D.E., 167n
Ashley, C.A., 99n
Auf der Maur, N., 238n, 239n
Aveling, E., 29n
Avineri, S., 29n, 300n

B

Babcock, R., 215n
Balinsky, A., 29n
Banks, J.A., 300n
Barnard, C., 147n
Barnes, S.H., 237n, 238n
Beaucage, A., 254n
Beausoleil, G., 238n
Bell, D., 98n, 209–210, 215n, 216n, 275n, 300n, 314n
Bendix, R., 17, 29n, 34, 42n, 98n, 124n, 157–159, 161–163 166, 168n
Bentham, J., 12
Berger, B., 281, 291, 298n, 300n
Berger, P., 56n
Bernard, P., 238n
Bertram, G.W., 97n
Beynon, H., 289, 299n
Bhagwati, J.N., 124n
Bird, F., 29n
Birnbaum, N., 56n
Blackburn, R.M., 298n
Blake, R., 143, 148n
Blau, P., 147n
Blauner, R., 285, 299n

Blumberg, P., 286, 294, 299n, 300n
Bock, B., 99n
Bonaparte, L., 24–25
Borden, Sir R., 94
Bottomore, T.B., 23, 29n
Bourgault, P.L., 125n
Braverman, H., 147n, 167n
Brecher, J., 267, 270, 274n, 275n
Brown, G., 181
Bruner, J.S., 8
Buckley, K., 97n
Buckley, W., 47
Burke, K., 168n
Burstein, M., 298n, 299n
Butler, D., 275n

C

Calvin, J., 35, 39, 280n
Caplow, T., 299n
Cardinal Villeneuve, 238n
Carey, A., 147n
Carey, D., 215n
Carrothers, A.W.R., 254n
Catlin, G., 57n
Caves, R., 96n, 97n, 98n
Centers, R., 282
Chamberlain, J., 110
Chandler, A.D.Jr., 109, 124n
Charbonneau, Y., 234–235
Chinoy, E., 291, 300n
Chodas, R., 238n
Clark, S.D., 161, 168n
Clegg, H., 300n
Clement, W., 57n, 96n, 111, 124n, 125n
Clough, S.B., 96n, 124n
Cobb, J., 270, 275n
Cole, G.D.H., 269
Cole, R., 275n
Conroy, P., 199–200
Cordell, A.J., 125n
Creighton, D., 67, 96n, 97n
Crispo, J.H.G., 204, 216n
Crocker, J.C., 168n
Crozier, M., 147n
Cuff, R., 98n, 125n
Cyert, R., 124n

330

Subject Index